SOCIAL & BEHAVIORAL SCIENCES Sociology

42-6193   HV1447   2003-23137 CIP
Williams, Rhonda Y. **The politics of public housing: black women's struggles against urban inequality.** Oxford, 2004. 306p bibl index afp ISBN 0195158903, $29.95 paper due 11/05

Williams (Case Western Reserve Univ.) depicts the ongoing struggles and poverty-related problems of poor black women in Baltimore public housing projects from the 1940s to the 1970s. The 50 women interviewed fought repeated battles to improve their lives, including obtaining apartments during segregation, battling the housing authority to adequately maintain units and complexes, and surviving under conditions hostile to black women. In the early 1960s, black women worked largely as domestics. Defying stereotypes, Williams shows the resilience these women possessed, conditions necessary for their efforts to succeed, and when public housing works. She interweaves examples of women acquiring the confidence to fight city hall within the larger social context of WW II defense housing, FHA loans facilitating white flight, different municipal administrations, growing racial and gender awareness, and deteriorating urban conditions. Williams is particularly effective in placing the women's growing political efforts in conjunction with Great Society programs, welfare rights organizations, and black power. The last chapter updates the residents and projects; expanding this chapter would have made this well-researched, well-written book even better. **Summing Up:** Highly recommended. Collections in inequality, housing, and public policy, all levels.—S. D. Borchert, Lake Erie College

THE POLITICS OF PUBLIC HOUSING

TRANSGRESSING BOUNDARIES

Studies in Black Politics and Black Communities

Cathy Cohen and Fredrick Harris, Series Editors

Rhonda Y. Williams

THE POLITICS OF PUBLIC HOUSING

Black Women's Struggles Against Urban Inequality

OXFORD
UNIVERSITY PRESS

2004

OXFORD
UNIVERSITY PRESS

Oxford   New York
Auckland   Bangkok   Buenos Aires   Cape Town   Chennai
Dar es Salaam   Delhi   Hong Kong   Istanbul   Karachi   Kolkata
Kuala Lumpur   Madrid   Melbourne   Mexico City   Mumbai   Nairobi
São Paulo   Shanghai   Taipei   Tokyo   Toronto

Copyright © 2004 by Oxford University Press, Inc.

Published by Oxford University Press, Inc.
198 Madison Avenue, New York, New York 10016

www.oup.com

Oxford is a registered trademark of Oxford University Press

Library of Congress Cataloging-in-Publication Data
Williams, Rhonda Y.
The politics of public housing : Black women's struggles against urban inequality /
by Rhonda Y. Williams.
     p. cm. — (Transgressing boundaries)
Includes bibliographical references.
ISBN 0-19-515890-3
1. Poor women—Maryland—Baltimore. 2. Poor women—Maryland—
Baltimore—Political activity. 3. African American women—Maryland—
Baltimore. 4. Welfare recipients—Maryland—Baltimore. 5. Women heads
of households—Maryland—Baltimore. 6. Low-income housing—Maryland—
Baltimore. 7. Public welfare—Maryland—Baltimore.   I. Title.   II. Series.
HV1447.B25M55 2004
305.48'896073075271—dc22   2003023137

9 8 7 6 5 4 3 2 1

Printed in the United States of America
on acid-free paper

Acknowledgments

There are so many people to thank. I conducted more than fifty interviews for this book, most of them with low-income black women who lived in public housing and were (are) tenant activists. I regret that two of the women, Clara Perry Gordon and Elizabeth Wright, died before the book was published. I am indebted to all the interviewees for revealing the personal and political details of their lives. Their willingness to share their stories proved critical to the development of *The Politics of Public Housing*, and their words will enrich and complicate ongoing debates.

While researching and writing this book, I have had tremendous financial, intellectual, and moral support. The American Association of University Women's Educational Foundation research leave grant (2002–2003) allowed me to conduct follow-up research and complete this book. The W. P. Jones Faculty Award, given by the College of Arts and Sciences at Case Western Reserve University, helped to underwrite research, photographic reproductions, and reprint permissions costs.

The Politics of Public Housing also had great archival and technical support, particularly from the following people: Rebecca Gunby and Gerald "Tony" Roberts at the Baltimore City Archives; Ruby Johnson in the microfilm room at the Enoch Pratt Free Library; W. John Shepard at the Archives of The Catholic University of America and jarda k. hiatt-booker of the Catholic Campaign for Human Development; Charles Owens (by way of Matthew W. Dogan III) and Christina D. Cruse at the *Baltimore Afro-American*; Lindsay Kelley at Baltimore SunSource; Ann Hanlon of the University of Maryland College Park's Special Collections Division; and William "Toby" Mathieson, a Case undergraduate in the Office of Institutional Technology and Academic Computing.

I have had the benefit of an extremely supportive and sharp editorial and production team at OUP: Dedi Felman, Jennifer Rappaport, Molly Barton, Stacey Hamilton, Merryl Sloane, Tracy Baldwin, and Sharon Sweeney. I am told that engaged "hands-on" editors are hard to come by these days, so I must give special thanks to my Oxford University Press editor, Dedi Felman, and the *Transgressing Boundaries* series co-editor, Cathy J. Cohen. They both read my manuscript with extreme care and insight, and their diligence has resulted in a better book—and for this I am ever grateful.

I would be remiss if I did not acknowledge that I have been blessed by the support and expertise of women inside and outside the academy. Dr. Mary Frances Berry has been my mentor since I was a graduate history student at the University of Pennsylvania. She continues to share with me her wisdom and experience. Along with Dr. Berry, Carroll Smith-Rosenberg and Farah Jasmine Griffin guided me through the dissertation, which constitutes the foundation of this book. Annelise Orleck and Eileen Boris, too, have been tremendously supportive and extremely generous with their time. I have benefited from their keen observations and sisterly collegiality.

For over a decade, Rhonda D. Frederick (or "Rhonda #1") has been a wonderful sister, friend, and intellectual colleague. She has gathered research documents for me, read drafts of my work, and been a voice of reason. Karen Sotiropoulos has made finishing my book fun. Her apartment often was my office away from the office. We read each other's chapters, binged on caffeine and chocolate, and just kept each other hyped intellectually. Angeliki Tzanetou was my neighborhood bookstore coffee shop buddy; we often met there and worked for hours on our manuscripts. Without a doubt, I must thank Elizabeth "Liz" Malby, the extraordinary photographer who took the contemporary women's portraits for this book. A dear friend, she has shared her space with me in immeasurable ways. I owe a special thanks to Peniel E. Joseph and Charles M. Payne; Cathy J. Cohen, Fred Harris, and the participants of the University of Rochester Works-in-Progress Workshop (2001); Christina Greene and Timothy B. Tyson for being great hosts when I conducted research at the Wisconsin Historical Society in Madison; and innumerable others who, over the years, were invaluable sounding boards and critics.

I cannot close without expressing my gratitude for the support of all my history department colleagues at Case Western Reserve University. Upon request, Angela Woollacott, Renée Sentilles, Theodore Steinberg, and David Hammack read and commented on drafts of my manuscript. Angela Woollacott deserves special mention. Acting as my mentor at CASE, she offered consistently good advice, practically on demand. I also would like to thank Poonam Bala, Rachel Chapman, Nancy Kryz, and Marissa Ross.

Finally, my family has been a constant source of inspiration to me: my mother, Virginia L. Williams, my father, Nathaniel McAlister Williams, Sr., and my brother, Nathaniel McAlister Williams, Jr. My uncle Oliver Frazier contributed advice, housing contacts, and a picture to this book. Grandmother Martha Bookman shared her memories. And finally, thanks to my partner and bassist extraordinaire, Craig A. Lee, who suggested the photo collage concept for my book cover and witnessed the last few years of this intense journey.

Contents

Abbreviations

ADC   Aid to Dependent Children
AFDC   Aid to Families with Dependent Children
BCHC   Baltimore Citizens' Housing Committee
BERC   Baltimore Emergency Relief Commission
BHA   Baltimore Housing Authority
BUL   Baltimore Urban League
BURHA   Baltimore Urban Renewal and Housing Agency
BWRO   Baltimore Welfare Rights Organization
CAA   Community Action Agency
CAC   Community Action Commission
CAP   Community Action Program
CCRO   Citizens Civil Rights Organization
CHC   Citizens Housing Council
CHCC   Cherry Hill Coordinating Committee
CIO   Congress of Industrial Organizations
CORE   Congress of Racial Equality

CP	Communist Party
CPHA	Citizens Planning and Housing Association
DHCD	Department of Housing and Community Development
DPW	Department of Public Welfare
DSS	Department of Social Services
ERAP	Economic Research and Action Project
FAP	Family Assistance Plan
FHA	Federal Housing Administration
FPHA	Federal Public Housing Authority
FWA	Family Welfare Association
HHFA	Housing and Home Finance Agency
HUD	Department of Housing and Urban Development
INCITE	Interested Citizens for Equality
MAC	Murphy Action Committee
MCSW	Maryland Conference of Social Welfare
NAACP	National Association for the Advancement of Colored People
NAHRO	National Association of Housing and Redevelopment Officials
NCC	National Coordinating Committee
NHA	National Housing Agency
NOI	Nation of Islam
NTO	National Tenants Organization
NWRO	National Welfare Rights Organization
OEO	Office of Economic Opportunity
OPA	Office of Price Administration
PTA	Parents-Teachers Association
PWA	Public Works Administration
RAB	Resident Advisory Board
RAC	Resident Action Committee
RIG	Resident Improvement Guild
SCLC	Southern Christian Leadership Conference
SDS	Students for a Democratic Society
SNCC	Student Non-Violent Coordinating Committee
TUG	Tenants' Union Group
U-JOIN	Union for Jobs or Income Now
USES	U.S. Employment Service
USHA	U.S. Housing Authority

VA	Veterans Administration
VISTA	Volunteers in Service to America
WCCL	Women's Cooperative Civic League
WCL	Women's Civic League
WRO	Welfare Rights Organization
YWCA	Young Women's Christian Association

THE POLITICS OF PUBLIC HOUSING

Introduction

In the early 1960s Rosetta Schofield was around thirty and raising one boy and two girls. She had left the father of her children for a fresh start. A black woman, Schofield worked off and on as a cook, making $25 a week and paying weekly rent of $18.50, leaving her little to buy food and necessities. She rented a cramped, two-bedroom apartment in a row house in west Baltimore. In an interview, she recalled the nice cabinets, the hardwood floors, the back porch, and the bay windows. But as the house deteriorated and became infested with rats that ate through the tin used to patch the holes, she was forced to look elsewhere for affordable housing. Schofield moved her family into the last family high-rise public housing complex built in the city; Murphy Homes opened in 1963. She "didn't have much thought of it. It was just a place for people to live. . . . It was gorgeous." In fact, it was one of the nicest apartments she had ever had.[1]

In the post-1930s New Deal era, Rosetta Schofield and many poor people like her struggled against formidable individual and social barriers to subsist and improve their life chances in urban America. Schofield's meager in-

Figure I.1 Displaced by the 1999 implosion of Murphy Homes, Rosetta Schofield now lives in McCulloh Homes. Courtesy Rosetta Schofield.

come limited her housing options. In her words, she "didn't have the education to get a job to make enough money and to put my children in a better neighborhood or better housing, understand?"[2] So she simply tried to provide daily bread, shelter, and clothing for her family, to make the best of—and stretch—the little she had.

The responses of impoverished black women, like Rosetta Schofield, to their own marginalization and urban inequality drive this study. How did these black women survive? How did they provide for their families' social welfare in cities structured by racial discrimination and economic disparities? How did their status and daily circumstances shape their political identities? In what ways were they motivated to act, if at all? By examining women like Schofield as political actors, *The Politics of Public Housing* seeks to recast historical understanding of the relationship among cities, poverty policy, poor people, and activism.

Many low-income black women turned for help to the burgeoning welfare state and the social welfare programs initiated during the New Deal and Great Society eras. The government, however, offered African-American women and their families a mixed bag of opportunity and discrimination, possibilities and restrictions, freedoms and surveillance. For just as race and class circumscribed poor black women's lives in cities, they also shaped black women's relationships to the state. Black people received benefits from some

Figure I.2 Murphy Homes under construction in 1961. The last conventional high-rise public housing complex built in the city, Murphy opened for residency in 1963. Courtesy Baltimore News American Collection, Special Collections, University of Maryland Libraries.

government programs. For instance, public relief and public housing did help black families subsist by providing needed services—minimal income and affordable shelter. These social welfare programs also allowed black women to escape sometimes harrowing domestic situations and the destitution that usually accompanied single motherhood.

But black people also suffered discrimination and exclusion from government programs. Most African Americans did not benefit from the initial Social Security legislation because the state excluded agricultural and domestic workers. This left 90 percent of black women workers uncovered. In the realm of housing, while the federal government provided white people with home-ownership options through Federal Housing Administration (FHA) mortgage loans, for instance, it excluded African Americans by restricting these mortgages to white neighborhoods. In particular, local government officials limited the effects of poverty programs by administering them in racially discriminatory ways and using them for political patronage. Better-paying jobs were given to whites. Black women were often denied public works jobs, even more so than white women, and instead were encouraged to perform agricultural, laundry, or domestic work. Governments' unequal treatment alongside private market and societal discrimination hampered African Americans' attempts to advance and improve their lives in urban communities.

Race, gender, class, and politics combined in insidious ways to engender unequal citizenship status. A hierarchy of welfare and housing programs existed, and the ones that black women and their families relied upon were generally at the bottom. The government support that low-income black women secured often came in the form of restrictive means- and morals-tested public assistance—the lowest tier of programs that evoked the most hostility. While the government subsidized mortgages for white people, black people were more likely to benefit from government largesse in the form of conventional public housing.[3] This program, like ADC, linked eligibility to middle-class character judgments and state surveillance.

Although black women and poor people had to contend with onerous and intrusive regulations as public assistance recipients, numerous low-income black women did receive a political education through their engagement with the welfare system. The federal government's subsidy of low-rent housing implied a right to decent living conditions for U.S. citizens. From the beginning, this implied right highlighted poor people's low citizenship status and politicized groups of tenants. For poor women, in particular, subsidized housing created a sense that the previously private sphere of home had become public and political space. In providing living space and setting forth rules governing working-class people's tenancy, government not only intervened in citizens' personal lives and women's domestic spaces, but also set a standard for decent housing and government responsiveness to and responsibility for tenants as renters, citizens, and recipients of federal aid. The state became landlord, paternal authority, guarantor of decency, and provider of rights. Public housing created a bridge between the private sphere of daily living and the political sphere of government. It linked individual rights with social rights, daily budgets with state economies, and familial duties with community participation and political activism.

By focusing on poor black women's daily interactions with public housing, their politicization, and their activism, *The Politics of Public Housing* asks different questions than conventional narratives that have focused on welfare state programs, race and social protest, and black working women's experiences. Ground-breaking studies that have employed race and gender lenses to explore the discriminatory nature of social welfare provisions tend to focus on the roles that middle-class women reformers played in constructing the welfare state, how the welfare state has shaped women's political status, and women's limited access to government programs. Most studies focus on cash benefits to needy mothers, known popularly as "welfare," not public assistance in the form of housing. One notable example, Linda Gordon's ground-breaking book, *Pitied but Not Entitled*, examines the creation of the much-maligned Aid to Dependent Children (which became Aid to Families with Dependent Children in 1962) by exploring how gender and single motherhood shaped the welfare state and created an unequal, two-tiered, gendered notion of citizenship.[4] *The Politics of Public Housing* shifts the angle of vision to the people on the ground affected by New Deal and Great Society social welfare policies, expands the discussion of public assistance to programs like public housing, and unveils the unrecognized spaces and strains of activism in poor black communities.[5]

The biographies, stories, and struggles of low-income black women have remained invisible in the historical narratives of black liberation, women's, and working-class movements. Poor black women's marginalized status, which has shaped their circumstances in life, has obscured their history too. The literature on black liberation struggles has tended to focus on men, national organizations, and civil rights issues narrowly defined as equal access to public accommodations, voting rights, and integration. Increasingly, black women have been recognized as critical participants in and shapers of black freedom movements. These black women, however, usually had middle-class status, operated within the confines of traditional civil rights organizations, or, in the case of black workers, engaged in paid labor. In similar ways, scholarship on the women's movement has primarily focused on white middle-class women, black and white women's labor struggles, or black middle-class women's social reform efforts. And narratives on working-class struggles have concentrated on the shop floor or labor organizing and therefore, by definition, have excluded discussions of black women as public assistance recipients. However, public assistance recipients, whether as public housing residents or welfare recipients, did engage in low-wage work and uncompensated labor in the home and in their communities. These poor black women, however, have remained invisible, because their lives and struggles have remained outside the traditional, normative, formal narratives of African-American, women's, and working-class histories, mirroring how these women are themselves a marginalized segment within marginal groups.[6]

The Politics of Public Housing reveals the texture and changing nature of poor black women's activist experiences. It explores their engagement with and reshaping of public institutions and the impact of their activism on urban inequality. These women asked for neither pity nor handouts, but fought for decent lives and self-respect. Poor black women activists saw themselves as responsible citizens, not troublemakers. During the New Deal years and the 1960s, the government encouraged citizen engagement. Cohorts of women, who took seriously responsible citizenship, responded by participating in community activities and even forging protests to make the government live up to its ideals and promises. These protests were shaped and encouraged by structures built into public housing. Resident councils, intended to promote community involvement, became outlets for more oppositional forms of political engagement and politicized multiple generations of tenants.

The stories of the lives of low-income black women in Baltimore, Maryland, also help recast the prevailing view that public housing was an unmitigated failure. Public housing did increasingly become disreputable in the eyes of much of the American electorate. And, in many cases, it became simply unlivable for tenants. But it also provided a measure of subsistence and a political context in which some low-income black women educated themselves about their rights. As Lyndon Johnson's War on Poverty came under attack and public assistance became increasingly unpopular, media coverage emphasized what was wrong about public housing: crime, decay, overcrowding. The grim popular-culture images of public housing have obscured its instructive political legacy. *The Politics of Public Housing* unearths and analyzes that legacy.

In Baltimore in 2003, Clara Gordon, a first-generation public housing tenant then in her nineties, lived many miles away from the central city subsidized development where she spent more than thirty years of her life between 1940 and the 1970s. Poe Homes, the first public housing complex to open in the city, became the site of Gordon's first independent household as a married woman and mother of two. She moved in during a time when the New Deal political context was creating opportunities for groups to make claims on the government for adequate housing, subsistence, and political involvement. Those groups included black families and mothers, like Clara Gordon, who took full advantage of government social welfare programs as they strove for shelter and respectability. In the late 1930s, the U.S. Housing Authority (USHA) and local management encouraged civic activism, giving support and legitimacy to tenants' concerns and desires. In the 1940s, the first public housing residents' clubs and organizations formed in Baltimore, and black working-class tenants set out on a path to secure decent homes, build community, and achieve social advancement and respectability.

World War II complicated tenants' politics of progress. Alverta Parnell, a black woman, moved into Douglass Homes in 1942. An outspoken advocate for tenants and a union organizer, Parnell embodied the sensibilities of black workers in the migrant generation. Black people found themselves working for a government that criticized fascism and racial hostility abroad, but rarely at home. As war workers and citizens in the crucible of world democracy, black people, like their white counterparts, felt entitled to specific freedoms and rights. Decent housing was one of them. That took concerted protest because, like the U.S. military itself, many World War II defense plants were segregated at the start of the war. And few communities were prepared to house the flood of new black workers who traveled long distances for job opportunities.

In Baltimore, Jim Crow, economic conservatism, and government intransigence initially stood in their way. Many black workers, like Alverta Parnell, turned to the federal government, and they demanded greater equity in working and housing conditions. After concerted protest, the federal government provided black people with wartime housing and, by extension, the channels to secure better treatment within the housing provided. Alverta Parnell's activism illustrates the battles for equal treatment and economic stability waged by black workers and migrants during World War II, particularly in subsidized housing. Her activist career also illuminates the daily concerns of poor black and white families in subsidized housing built for war workers. The demands for defense housing, the emergence of tenant councils, and residents' struggles for decency and fairness not only occupied the time and energy of World War II–era black tenants, but also shaped the activities of future generations of black public housing residents, though many did not know who Parnell was or that she ever existed. Her life story highlights the links between activism in the 1940s and the civil rights and black power struggles that later engulfed Baltimore.

Suffering from the growing disrepute and disrepair of public housing in the postwar years, tenants in the 1960s confronted additional challenges, but also had access to new resources. With Johnson's War on Poverty, HUD's modernization program, urban rebellions, and black freedom protests, more democratic possibilities opened. During the civil rights and black power eras—as in the 1940s—activism remained linked to citizenship. Black freedom fighters demanded that the government fulfill its obligations to excluded and neglected citizens. Poor black women experienced neglect, exclusion, and hardship, and again some of them publicly challenged the government's unresponsiveness. The post-1950s generation of tenant activists—women like Shirley Wise, Goldie Baker, and Rudell Martin—like earlier generations, made claims on the state. But they asked not only for subsistence and decent housing. Affected by the political context, example, and rhetoric of the 1960s rights struggles, this new generation of activists also demanded respect and dignity as their human rights. They expanded as well as departed from earlier arguments for respectability, which linked citizenship to the enactment of bourgeois behaviors.

Public housing—as a place of residence and as a social welfare provision—then helped galvanize tenants' and women's struggles, which often were expressions of poor black women's personal and political identities. Like the black and white militant housewives, mothers, and poor women in the first half of the twentieth century who engaged in food riots, rent strikes, and consumer boycotts, the daily struggles and organized protests of poor black women over the forty years covered by this study reflect the politicization of their traditional roles as mothers, family caretakers, and community leaders.[7]

As a teenage mother living in public housing in the 1950s, Rudell Martin already knew what it felt like to be an outsider years before she joined tenants' and welfare rights battles in the late 1960s. At Dunbar, a black high school, she felt like an outsider because she became pregnant out of wedlock and because of her family's limited income. When she transferred to Southern, a white high school undergoing desegregation, she was called a "nigger" and told to go home. As a hospital employee, she was fired for pulling down "white-only" and "colored-only" signs from over water fountains. Aware of racial inequities, Rudell Martin harbored an intense dislike of exclusion. She grew up in public housing, and although she left for a time once she married, her family eventually had to move back into public housing, where she participated in tenant and community activities. After separating from her husband, Martin became involved in welfare rights issues as well. As a single mom raising three children, she had to apply for AFDC to support her family and experienced shame and anger at the hands of an insensitive social worker. Shortly thereafter she went to a community meeting where she encountered government antipoverty workers interested in grooming community leaders. By the early 1970s, a couple of years after receiving training and participating in local welfare rights protests, Martin became the first paid executive director of the Welfare Rights Organization (WRO) in Baltimore.[8] Her life story, like many others, illustrates how social welfare bureaucracies not only provided subsistence, but also fueled subsistence struggles and human rights battles among low-income women in cities.

Goldie Baker's activism was similarly inspired. Baker, who as recently as 2003 continued to mobilize around poor people's rights even after two heart attacks, turned to public housing in 1964 after separating from her husband, trying to support her seven children on a low income, and living in crowded conditions. As a public housing tenant, she had contentious interactions with welfare and housing officials. She also began meeting black activists in organizations like the Congress of Racial Equality (CORE), the Community Action Agency (CAA), and the local poverty-fighting Union for Jobs or Income Now (U-JOIN). U-JOIN formed the city's first welfare rights group, Mother Rescuers from Poverty, which preceded the WRO. Baker's personal dilemmas, her growing political, civil, and welfare rights connections, and her historical memory fueled by an activist grandmother and mother, who hailed from the Jim Crow South and became human rights advocates, invigorated her and led her into a lifelong battle for poor people's rights.[9] Baker's life embodies the links among black women's activism in the 1940s South, World War II migration, postwar civil rights, black urban nationalism, the

War on Poverty, and welfare rights. Too often, these have been treated by historians as separate and discrete struggles. But Baker's biography highlights how interconnected these movements were.

Black women's political engagement reflected a variety of activities and had many targets. In the early 1940s, the first tenant councils focused on building community and engaged in cooperative efforts with management. By the mid-1940s, during World War II, black women tenants also opposed housing management. They protested poor maintenance policies that threatened their families' well-being, fought against evictions, and demanded to be treated as respectable women. In the 1960s, black women focused on enhancing and stabilizing changing communities, pressured the government to address their concerns, and also demanded the right to contribute to the formulation and administration of policies that affected their lives.

Experiencing hardship and viewing public housing as a way to provide a decent life for her family, Rosetta Schofield participated in community life in Murphy Homes in various ways. As a hall captain in her high-rise building, she kept the outside common walkway and stairs clean. Schofield always had in mind keeping "the place as it was"—decent—in the midst of urban decline. For a short time, she even went to an occasional tenant council meeting where residents considered "how we should work . . . to make a change when we began to see that the place was going down." Her external responses to personal dilemmas reflect the different forms of community participation and political activism operating simultaneously.

While Schofield contested marginalization and dehumanization through individualized daily acts (she only attended a tenant meeting here or there), other poor black women led poor people's interest groups and protested, both as individuals and in collectivities, against state authority. A few women took paid jobs with Volunteers in Service to America (VISTA) and in Community Action Agencies (CAAs) established under the War on Poverty program, and as a result, they became federal workers who rallied on behalf of their communities.[10] War on Poverty legislation did have impact on the local level—but only to the degree that black communities and black women in particular forced responsiveness and used the agencies as a channel for organizing. Other poor black women formed and served in welfare rights groups and on resident boards.

Shirley Wise moved into Lafayette Courts with her paraplegic mother, brother, sister, and newborn son in 1955—the first year the complex opened.

She moved into rehab housing in Park Heights in 1980. As a Lafayette Courts tenant, she worked with the Mothers' Club and tenant council before becoming a delegate on the housing authority's citywide Resident Advisory Board (RAB) in the early 1970s. Within a couple of years, Wise became the RAB chairperson and eventually worked with the National Tenants Organization (NTO). She traveled to conferences nationwide and in the Virgin Islands and received an education that she argued could not be paid for. A staunch advocate of tenants' rights who "agitated people," Shirley Wise said some housing officials labeled her a "troublemaker." "But the same people utilizes their rights to deal with their beefs, you understand," insisted Wise. "I don't see no difference. . . . There's a set of rules for everybody to operate under. . . . If you follow those rules, wouldn't be no need for Shirley Wise, the Resident Advisory Board, tenant council, or none of that. But there's a need, because somebody is not following the rules."[11]

While women participated in civic, community-based activities and joined and started organizations, poor black women's activism was not always manifested through group activities like Wise's. Other tenants, like Frances Reives and Gladys Spell, both of whom worked with their complexes' tenant councils in the 1960s, became resident aides. As housing authority employees, they provided tenants with needed services even as they policed residents' behaviors in their efforts to maintain decent neighborhoods and improve living conditions. Still other tenants wrote letters to management, the mayor, and federal officials. Examples of how public housing residency politicized tenants, these letters reflected individual expressions of outrage, disgust, and discontent. Finally, some black women vocalized their refusal to accept society's negative views of them and, in so doing, challenged the stereotypes used by dominant society—other citizens, the media, and the state—to rationalize the marginalization of poor black women and poor people in general. Listen to Rosetta Schofield:

> At least I had a home. It was comfortable, and it was clean, and I could have extra money to do things with my children, that I enjoyed doing and that I wanted to do. And these people that was making these little statements wasn't offering me no helping hand, understand? So it really didn't matter to me, because my head was still high. 'Cause if I had to go clean out a sewer and live in a sewer I would still hold my head high when I walk up out [of] that sewer.

Because at least I'm not taking, I'm not trying to beat anybody for anything. . . . And then I thought, why am I trying to beat my brains out, worry myself to death, when I have someplace that I can be comfortable with and because nobody's giving me anything, and I have to work hard. And why should I move out . . . of public housing, move into a place that maybe I would only be able to pay the rent, can't pay gas and electric, can't buy food, can't buy clothes, can never have no extra money to do anything with my kids? Well, in public housing I could do this, and have a few dollars left over.[12]

Exploring activism at the point of consumption—that is, around housing, food, clothing, and daily life in community spaces—reveals the existence of these unacknowledged daily struggles and protests. Black freedom struggles were increasingly being fought in neighborhoods around consumption as well as political issues. In addition to struggles for voting rights, school desegregation, and the opportunity to eat, sleep, swim, and play tennis wherever one liked, activists in northern and southern cities began to tackle a range of issues equally central to the achievement of full citizenship: the right to adequate housing, income, medical care, food, and clothing. These efforts, led largely by black women in the 1960s, represented another phase of the black freedom struggle—one that has now begun to be chronicled. In their own way, poor black women, who increasingly relied on public assistance, placed pressure on the welfare state to make good on its promise of provision and social rights, especially for some of its most marginalized citizens. Low-income women's political engagement helps unveil the gender and class dimensions of protest as well as broader freedom issues specific to cities.

In addition, documenting the community-based battles of these women contests superficial popular narratives that recount the urban experiences of low-income black women but cast them as unconcerned, as bearers and carriers of tainted cultures, and as victims of their own negligent behaviors. Such behavioral depictions fail to tackle the complexity of people's lives and miss moments of daily struggle and social protest. As a result, historical transformations, the shaping power of the state, and the successes and failures of social protest and policies are overlooked.

By the 1970s, the confluence of public housing and welfare rights activism exposed the new ways that race, class, and gender shaped public discourses, public assistance programs, and poor people's lives. As the low-income population relying on the means- and morals-tested social provision of housing became even poorer and increasingly black and female, public housing—like ADC—became less palatable. Ironically, poor black women's—and black people's—vociferous demands across the nation in the 1960s and 1970s heightened existing white resentment and antiwelfare sentiments that ultimately delegitimized and discredited those demands. Their very public struggles for autonomy and state responsiveness provided the "evidence" that antiwelfare proponents used to cast them as racial bogeywomen—the antitheses of American traditions of independence and hard work in a political atmosphere growing more conservative in the 1970s. This has had lasting effects on poor black women's subsistence and rights struggles, public assistance programs and policies, and public perceptions of the poor. By the 1990s, public housing and welfare (as we have known it) had met their deaths at the hands of the federal government.

While this book ultimately explores the lives and activism of poor black women like Clara Gordon, Alverta Parnell, Rosetta Schofield, Frances Reives, Gladys Spell, Shirley Wise, Rudell Martin, Goldie Baker, and many others, I include black men, white women, and white men. They were a part of the landscape, and the tensions and friendships that existed also reveal the ways that gender, class, and race interacted in the forging of and interference with political struggles. Moreover, white people are a substantial part of public housing, welfare, and urban history in post-1940 America.

White people lived in public housing from its inception. In the first decades of Baltimore's housing program, whites occupied almost as many public housing units as did black people, but in segregated complexes. In the 1940s, white mothers also protested housing authority policies. And during the purge of over-income families during World War II and desegregation efforts in the 1950s and 1960s, white residents fought to maintain access to public housing. Some white people cooperated with black tenant activists. But others believed that black demands for desegregation threatened the stability of white working-class citizenship. White tenants who could not afford suburban homes or who wanted to stay in the city believed government had an obligation to them as well. They too were entitled. And if they did not want to live next door to black people, the government should still protect their rights as citizens to have subsidized housing in decent neighborhoods with people of their choosing. They felt that interracial living threatened white working-class citizenship, because black residency predicted the growth of indecent conditions. Black people, they believed, were harbingers of danger, crime, and social disruption. Unable to stem the tide of change that hinged on race and poverty, however, many white families simply ended up leaving public housing. Their flight and the arguments they used to express their displeasure fueled the burgeoning public animosity toward public housing and strengthened the popular belief that public housing had been a failure.[13]

Not all white tenants left. Some white tenants, like Anna Warren and Rosaline Lundsford, did stay for a while. Rosaline Lundsford stayed in O'Donnell Heights for twenty-five years. Anna Warren still lives in Claremont Homes. As public housing residents, both of these women struggled to raise their children alone and became resident activists. Warren, who once would not socialize with black people, eventually grew in friendship with black women like Shirley Wise and Goldie Baker and became a welfare rights activist. In 2003, Anna Warren, one of the few white people still living in Baltimore's public housing, served as RAB chair; she was the first white woman to hold that position.[14] White women's struggles for improved conditions and greater political voice point to another continuum of activism and another hidden dimension of urban political history. Throughout the twentieth century, poor mothers of all races politicized their familial roles and used the moral authority of motherhood to make claims for their rights as citizens. This book touches on that story too.

Baltimore, Maryland, is the stage upon which the lives and activism of low-income black women in *The Politics of Public Housing* unfold. A border city, Baltimore brings together southern racial traditions and northern urban-industrial economies.[15] It is also a relatively unexplored postindustrial city. Harboring the largest free black population on the eve of the Civil War, Baltimore has had a history of racial discrimination that manifested itself in public ways and eventually in residential space. Segregation along with white political traditions, citizens' actions, demographic changes, New Deal and Great Society social policies, and local politicians' implementation of them hardened the city's racial contours and shaped black people's lives, opportunities, and relationships to the state. The fact that Baltimore neighbors Washington, D.C., the nation's capital and the home of federal lawmaking, further shapes its importance in discussions of state relations and political protest. In post-1930s Baltimore, everyday people who lived near the nation's seat of power actually and symbolically accessed the capital as they struggled to build decent neighborhoods, secure citizenship rights, battle poverty and exclusion, obtain respect, and demand human dignity.

The Politics of Public Housing depicts the lived realities and political activities of low-income black women in urban America through more than fifty oral history interviews, which I gathered, and documentary evidence. I have examined newspaper articles; city, state, and federal records; organizations' papers; and census data. The oral histories play a critical role, because interviews allow for the possibility of uncovering the motivations and views of marginalized groups, the varieties of experiences, and the continuums of struggle. Interviews also have the potential to reveal what Robin D. G. Kelley calls the "behind-the-scenes political discourse" and to expose what Alessandro Portelli has argued is the most "unique and precious element" of oral histories—speakers' subjectivities.[16] Finally, and just as important, oral histories bring the voices of these women to life and vividly portray the complexity of their fights—from respectability to respect—as marginalized citizens of the welfare state.

Beginnings PART I

Creating "A Little Heaven for Poor People"

Decent Housing and Respectable Communities

1

In the small isolated farm town of Winfall, North Carolina, on Virginia's border, Clara Perry Gordon's parents, Bolson and the elder Clara Perry, planted cotton. The tenth of eleven children, the young Clara, along with her three remaining siblings (three sisters had already migrated and four did not make it to adulthood), helped pick the cotton and heap it on the family wagon for transport to market. When not plucking white puffs from thorny bolls or working in the family garden at her mother's side, little Clara hastened down the dirt road to the little wooden school or the one-room wooden church. Or she played baseball, a lot and hard. "I would go out and stay. [My parents] tell us to be home before it got dark, and I just kept my sisters and brothers [from arriving home on time]. I was playing ball with the boys!" The words tumbled into a chuckle as she recounted the inevitable punishment—a whipping. "I was used to it. Because I was mischievous, I'm telling you!"[1]

Around 1925, the playfully naughty little Clara experienced sadness, migration like thousands of black southerners, and then excitement. That summer, her father succumbed to tuberculosis. Shortly after little Clara had donned her favorite white dress at her father's funeral, she, her siblings, and her mother packed their traveling bags and left behind their farm, garden, two-story wood house, smokehouse, church, school, chickens, pigs, cow, and her baseball buddies. The elder Clara had not worked for pay. So when Bolson died, the family had no source of income. Heeding the call of three other daughters already living in the northernmost southern city of Baltimore, the elder Clara gathered her children and took a wagon from Winfall to Norfolk and a boat from Norfolk to Baltimore. It would be ten-year-old Clara's first time on a boat, on the water, and in "a big city."[2] As new arrivals to the city, the Perrys joined tens of thousands of black people—some middle-class, many working-class, some native Baltimoreans, others migrants. In Baltimore, a "promised land" just south of the Mason-Dixon line and a commercial city built around its downtown docks and harbor, little Clara's family debarked. And as her family settled in, they, like other black working-class people, worked hard to keep at bay economic marginalization, to obtain suitable housing, and to struggle for respectable communities. If they could just do that, they would be able to breathe lighter, sleep easier, and experience a measure of contentment and progress as they moved closer to successfully fulfilling the desire to better their lives.

But urban America would not prove so welcoming, generous, or fair. Establishing better lives in industrialized and commercial cities proved to be a challenging proposition and required perseverance and ultimately struggle. In southern and northern cities, discrimination reigned, structuring job and residential opportunities. Securing good housing, envisioned as a cornerstone of independence and American citizenship, was a potentially explosive matter for black people—both before and after the rise of the welfare state and government intervention in the housing market in the 1930s. That intervention would unarguably affect the lives and well-being of low-income black people like Clara Perry Gordon as well as shape the direction of the cities in which they resided.

Race and Residential Limits

The dilapidated, overcrowded, and racially constrained housing which helped spur the reform movement toward government subsidized housing had its roots in the early twentieth century. As people swelled cities' populations, securing decent housing became difficult. Many working-class people, including ethnic immigrants, experienced horrendous living conditions, but the politics of race and geography particularly limited black people's housing opportunities. The city's white residents and power brokers sought to contain black people's living space and to protect their white communities from infiltration. Enormous housing demands, however, resulted in black people spilling into white neighborhoods, especially since "no new streets or subdivisions were built for black residents" until public housing in the late 1930s.[3] In the wake of such hardships, public housing would offer a way out, a chance, and a plausible strategy for obtaining adequate, affordable, and sanitary housing and respectable neighborhoods.

In the early to mid-1900s, many working-class people lived in squalid housing. While not a city of large multistory tenements, Baltimore's single-family, two- and three-story row houses were subdivided into apartments and often housed more families than was reasonable. Ethnic immigrants, who arrived in Baltimore in the late nineteenth century, often crowded into poorly ventilated apartments in cramped row houses in Fells Point, a maritime and merchant community in east Baltimore. The city also had a hefty supply of alley houses, some of which were built in the colonial era. Following numerous waves of black migration from rural Maryland and other states below the Mason-Dixon line, southern African Americans joined Baltimore's black city dwellers, 90 percent of whom were free before the Civil War. Black people lived in clusters, often in the alley rowhouse neighborhoods throughout the city. In the 1920s, Clara's two single sisters, who supported a family of seven on cooks' wages, rented a two-story, three-bedroom brick row house on Conway Street in a southwest Baltimore black neighborhood not far from the waterfront, the Baltimore & Ohio Railroad, industries, pig slaughterhouses, and the city's first black ghetto—"Pigtown." The Perrys slept two in a bedroom—not the best, but not the worst of conditions the city had to offer to families of their class status. For that reason alone, they were lucky.[4]

While ethnic and black city dwellers may have experienced a tight market as renters and less than optimal housing conditions, race increasingly limited where African Americans could live. In the early twentieth century, African Americans who initially had settled in black Pigtown and other south Baltimore neighborhoods moved to west central Baltimore. The demolition of black residences in southwest Baltimore to expand the Baltimore

& Ohio Railroad's Camden Station triggered this exodus. By 1904 Old West Baltimore, bounded by North Avenue and Franklin Street on the north and south and Fulton and Madison streets on the west and east, housed half of Baltimore's black population.[5] Changeover was quick; in one ward, the black population increased from 8 percent to 60 percent between 1900 and 1910.[6] The nineteenth-century scattered geographical pattern was changing. Black people were also more likely to be renters than white or ethnic people. By 1910, only 933 of 85,000 black people—.01 percent—owned homes.[7] But within a couple of decades of their immigration, Russian Jews, Czechs, Ukrainians, and Poles had begun purchasing homes, even if they were in need of repairs. By 1929, for instance, 60 percent of Polish families owned homes.[8] Overall, black people occupied an inferior place in the housing market, but they would continue to seek better, and that often meant pushing the boundaries of racial segregation.

Black movement into previously all-white neighborhoods not surprisingly alarmed white city dwellers. In northwest Baltimore, white residents and power brokers reacted by establishing municipal segregation ordinances between 1910 and 1913. White proponents claimed that the ordinances, which outlawed African Americans' movement into racially mixed or predominantly white blocks, protected "the general welfare of the city by providing, so far as practicable, for the use of separate blocks by white and colored people for residences, churches and schools." The first of their kind, the ordinances provided model legislation for other cities until the National Association for the Advancement of Colored People (NAACP) challenged them, and the U.S. Supreme Court declared them unconstitutional in the Louisville, Kentucky, case of *Buchanan v. Warley*. The 1917 Supreme Court opinion held that segregation ordinances denied African Americans their right "to acquire and to use property without state legislation discriminating against them on the sole basis of color."[9] With or without racial residential ordinances, however, Baltimore became a racially segregated working-class city.

Unlike the white middle class and elite, who increasingly lived in economically exclusive urban and suburban enclaves, the black middle class lived in mixed-income communities primarily in the central city. For instance, a black property owner and caulker who raised $10,000 to start the black Chesapeake Marine Railway and Dry Dock Company in 1866, Isaac

Myers resided on South Wolfe Street in east Baltimore alongside laundresses, stevedores, undertakers, barbers, physicians, domestics, and politicians.[10] In west Baltimore, poor, working-class, and middle-class black folks shared an area where clip-clopping horses' hooves hit the streets and Arabbers' cries of "strawbuees" wafted into rowhouse windows. Black middle-class and political families like the Murphys and Mitchells owned fancy homes, not so far from rented hovels. One of the city's worst alley neighborhoods, Biddle Alley in west Baltimore, bordered black institutions and middle-class homes. Dubbed the "Lung Block," Biddle Alley had the city's highest rates of tuberculosis cases after World War I. Horse stables, junkyards, abandoned cars, highfalutin and spiritualist black churches, schools, alley homes, and spacious row houses abutted one another. And Pennsylvania Avenue, the primary shopping district in west Baltimore, boasted clubs, social halls, the Baltimore Urban League (BUL) office, and the Royal Theater. "The Avenue" was also a center for jazz, drawing black musicians like Duke Ellington and launching the careers of black Baltimoreans like Cab Calloway and Billie Holiday.[11]

Black people of different classes may have lived near each other, but class still shaped black communities' geographies and social relations. In west Baltimore, the black middle class tended to occupy houses on main streets like Druid Hill Avenue and McCulloh Street. Poor and working-class blacks lived in more modest row houses and alley dwellings. Black civic reformers, many of whom were middle-class residents, critiqued working-class places of leisure. For instance, the city's black sections boasted many pool and billiard parlors, which black reformers considered "questionable asset[s] in organized leisure time," even as they acknowledged that such places served a need as social meeting places. Even so, they were not socially ideal. According to black middle-class reformers, "Baltimore and other large cities [had] failed to provide something that would be equally as human but more conducive to social standards and more in keeping with social ideals."[12]

Struggling daily to secure jobs, get an education, help the sick, "keep body and soul together," and achieve social mobility, black people labored to establish fit communities. White real estate developers had consistently ignored the black community's need and demand for housing; ethnic building and loan associations catered to their own constituents; and white landlords virtually monopolized the black rental market. In fact, landlords viewed the black renter as an easy mark. An anonymous white landlord confessed "the sordid truth" in a 1924 *Baltimore Sun Magazine* exposé. Black tenants were "legitimate game, with an open season of 52 weeks in the year." He continued: "Whenever a white person complains . . . I feel tempted to congratulate him that he is lucky not to have been born black." For black people, renting was a costly venture, because their "black skin marks [them] as a source of profit." Black people paid 50 to 60 percent, sometimes 75 percent, higher than white tenants.[13]

Although many African Americans earned meager wages, even for those better off, race trumped economics by restricting housing mobility. In Baltimore and cities across the nation, making a respectable home presented a challenge for African Americans. It not only meant fashioning life in often overcrowded and unsanitary sections of central cities, but also required confronting white resistance and eventually restrictive covenants—racial pacts used by white landlords and home owners that prevented black people from purchasing homes and living in white areas. When black people broke racial boundaries, violence awaited them. In the 1930s, white mobs freely terrorized black people who sought to improve their living conditions by moving into better housing in white neighborhoods. White residents vandalized black property by breaking windows and throwing paint on the steps. Neither the police nor city laws offered black people much relief or protection from violence or restrictive covenants. While black people could vote in Baltimore, white people controlled city hall and made the legislation. Describing the racial hatred and belief in black inferiority that infused politics, Parren J. Mitchell, who became Baltimore's first black congressman, recalled seeing a restrictive covenant with the clause "No pigs, no chickens, no Negroes."[14] Clearly, black people confronted formidable social forces in their search for security, better homes, and respectability.

Black Life during the Depression

The Great Depression wreaked havoc disproportionately upon black people's lives. According to a national Urban League memo to President Franklin Roosevelt, nationwide 39.5 percent of black people in cities collected relief versus 14.6 percent of the white population.[15] The living conditions of many people worsened. In an eighty-year-old southwest Baltimore neighborhood, more than 3,000 people in 820 families lived on 4.5 acres, a density of 109 people per acre. Families were doubled and tripled up in row houses, babies were dying, and residents suffered from tuberculosis at rates twice that of the entire city. In 1933 Baltimore's largest private charity, the Family Welfare Association (FWA), served this area more than any other. Residents in southwest Baltimore and throughout the city knew too well the insides of charity offices during the harsh 1930s. Mirroring nationwide trends, black Baltimoreans disparately suffered. In 1934, nearly 50 percent of the African-American community lacked jobs, and African Americans represented 42.2 percent of all families receiving emergency relief.[16] Because of African Americans' greater reliance on relief, Maryland's Democratic senator, Millard Tydings, argued in a Federal Emergency Relief Administration meeting that something must be "wrong with colored people" and dismissed the arguments of senators who claimed that white people received job preferences. In response to Tydings, the South Carolina Democratic senator argued that black people were spendthrifts. They simply could not manage money.[17]

While both black and white people collected inadequate relief, African Americans received even less money for rent, utilities, and food. A black disabled longshoreman had worked as a messenger for the Baltimore Emergency Relief Commission (BERC), the quasi-public agency that preceded the municipal Department of Public Welfare (DPW) created in 1935. When the BERC combined two relief districts and replaced the black longshoreman with a white messenger, the fifty-three-year-old longshoreman became the agency's client. His family of six received $11.26 weekly with $1.86 for rent while a white family of five received $15.19 with $4.60 for rent. The federal government's premise that black people could survive on less did not help matters. While African Americans undoubtedly made do with less, they had to. For instance, instead of providing increased support, a white BERC social worker suggested that the longshoreman work odd jobs, put his fifteen-year-old daughter "out to service," or even "do without food" to pay his rent. For this black man, losing his livelihood, resorting to relief, and then being advised to sell his daughter's labor signified a loss of respect and independence.[18]

While Clara as a child and teenager paid little attention to the constraints impeding her and other families' life choices, she became aware of existing hardships during the Depression years. She was starting a family then. In the mid-1930s, she met fellow parishioner Harvey Gordon, Sr., in Leadenhall Baptist Church, which was founded about a half mile from her southwest Baltimore home in 1873. They married, and the now-extended Perry-Gordon household moved to Old West Baltimore, following a familiar path of black migration within the city. Clara Perry Gordon birthed her daughter in 1933 and her son in 1934. She was a homemaker, and her husband, Harvey, worked for the family hauling and moving business. As a result of her husband's work, the Gordons fared better than other working-class people during the Depression: "I had two children, but we made it. Because the fellow that I married . . . was working for his father and that's how we survived. . . . The people were just on welfare, but luckily I didn't have to get on welfare."[19] Income from the family business paid rent and bought food. Surviving, however, was a far stretch from achieving financial stability. Her husband's job provided only a minimal level of security. The family's income remained so low that just a few years later they qualified for the city's newest hard-won local assistance program—public housing. Despite a level of self-sufficiency, the Gordons, as part of the black masses, still struggled against poverty. The difference was that they were the working poor, not the relief poor.

Figure 1.1 Clara Gordon. Courtesy Clara Parker.

During the Depression, continuous black migration into the city exacerbated the problem of overcrowding and made housing conditions increasingly intolerable for African Americans, especially with the decline in housing construction for the city's white residents. Black people depended on the secondhand housing market, and in 1934 only 119 new houses were built in Baltimore.[20] Black people went from 17.7 percent of the population in 1930 to over 21 percent in 1940.[21] In 1937 African Americans still paid exorbitant rents for "hand-me-down, deteriorated white residences," and 60 to 70 percent of black workers in Baltimore received wages that would "never permit them to live in adequate and decent homes" unless they were subsidized.[22]

The 1930s was a pivotal time. Many black people may have been in dire straits, but they also mobilized to challenge exclusion. Racial discrimination, the reality and fear of new housing exclusion, shrinking economic opportunities, and New Deal programs in the 1930s turned Baltimore into a cauldron of protests. African Americans fought on several fronts: for jobs, against lynching, against discrimination in public relief programs, and for the establishment of a public housing program.

Better Neighborhoods and Public Housing

Throughout the country, the daily living conditions of black people ignited a desire for social change. Obtaining better homes and neighborhoods became "a consuming passion" that symbolized black people's attempts to obtain better living conditions for various reasons: health, stability, social mobility, and respectability.[23] For black working-class and poor people, decent housing was a practical concern. Who wanted to live in drafty alley shacks with vermin and foul water seeping from outdoor privies? Who wanted to live in overcrowded row houses with weak floorboards, steps, and banisters and without private, indoor bathrooms? Who wanted to live next door, up the street, or around the corner from tuberculosis-ridden areas? Was this what native and migrant black people had to look forward to in urban promised lands?

Zealous black middle-class reformers viewed better housing as a practical issue as well as a strategic good. The mixture of black middle-class, working-class, and poorer residents, institutions, and businesses in black neighborhoods gave black reformers impetus to press for the elimination of poor conditions. Ultimately, disreputable neighborhoods tainted their social status and worked against their efforts to push for equal standing in white America. After all, the "niggero" was blamed for Baltimore being a "pesthole."[24] Cleanliness provided a way to counteract such perceptions. As far back as the early 1900s, Margaret Murray Washington, the president of the National Federation of Afro-American Women founded in 1895 and the third wife of Booker T. Washington, argued: "Where the homes of colored people are comfortable and clean, there is less disease, less sickness, less death, and less danger to others."[25]

African-American efforts to secure decent homes reveal a critical component of black cultural memory and political desire. Securing better homes had been a central citizenship goal of black struggle since Emancipation, when the federal government failed to fulfill its promise of giving newly freed slaves forty acres. Decades later in cities, the emergence of the "slums" gave new meaning and urgency to the desire for better homes. In the 1930s, black Americans regarded poor housing not only as a threat to their health and safety, but also as a denial of their democratic rights of citizenship, especially since the belief that "a good citizen" couldn't be "produced" in "slum areas" had public currency.[26] Black sociologist Ira De A. Reid wrote that because overcrowded houses were "in areas where street cleaning and lighting, paving, sewerage and police protection are sub-standard, the inhabitants do not have a fair chance for full citizenship."[27] In 1937 the *Baltimore Afro-American* newspaper dubbed the home and its environment "the mudsill of the democratic system of existence."[28]

Black middle-class reformers were part of a tradition of progressive housing reform. Progressive reformers believed that destroying corrupt environments led to the eradication of unworthy citizens. In the 1930s, Sarah Fernandis, a black social worker, club woman, and member of the local NAACP's executive committee in 1937, earnestly called attention to the decrepit houses occupied by black women and their families. Fernandis praised the courage of mothers who had managed to raise their children successfully, despite living in substandard alley homes and in communities where "immorality, vermin and diseases" prevailed.[29] In doing so, she disputed racial discourse that rendered African Americans and disease synonymous and recast the debate in terms of environment and opportunities. However, despite black mothers' success in salvaging their children, Fernandis, like her white and black contemporaries, believed black families deserved better communities.

With the emergence of the welfare state in the 1930s, black people turned to the federal government. While the New Deal provided numerous housing options, the politics of race created a discriminatory social welfare system. In the housing realm, federal guaranteed mortgage programs often excluded African Americans by refusing to insure loans in unstable areas— or racially mixed and black communities. Black people, therefore, often had to resort to means- and morals-tested public assistance programs to improve their living conditions and, by extension, social status. For African Americans, public housing, rather than private home purchases, provided the most unfettered government route to better housing opportunities. Black middle-class reformers believed public housing provided the chance to better black neighborhoods where trash-strewn alleys harbored "rats as big as cats," to check the spread of disease and immorality, and to build respectable neighborhoods.[30] Along with white reformist organizations, black civic activists vigorously lobbied for the creation of a housing authority. But social progressivism did not come easily to black Baltimore.

Black and white middle-class reformers knew that the federal Public Works Administration (PWA) had money for slum clearance and public housing construction. And reformers knew that the ring of "blight" around Baltimore's downtown made the inner city a perfect candidate for federal housing reform. In 1933 the Joint Committee on Housing of the Maryland State Advisory Board had conducted and published a survey, which underscored the city's need for affordable and sanitary housing. The six most blighted areas in east and west Baltimore, which included Pigtown, had substantial, if not majority, black populations, and almost all of them had high tuberculosis rates.[31] While this government report revealed the horrendous conditions of black people, who tended to live in the city's poorest housing, it also envisioned blight as a "problem of the Negro race." The blight and pestilence that were additional stigmas carried by black working-class people reveal the early tropes linking black urban life to pathology. In fact, the report portrayed poverty, substandard housing, and disease as the natural conditions and inevitable consequences of African-American residency.[32]

While acknowledging the disproportionate effect on black Baltimore, the state advisory board report seemed more concerned with providing jobs, removing blight and disease and, therefore, black nuisances, and preserving white neighborhoods—not attacking black people's poor living conditions. The recommendations reflected municipal and federal priorities, which included bailing out the construction industry, which suffered woefully during the Depression. The state advisory committee suggested redeveloping three predominantly black communities for white residency. The committee argued that one area "should be developed as a fairly good class white residential area. There is no reason except obsolescence of buildings for it to be inhabited by colored people."[33]

Black and white social reformers, however, emphasized the need for decent housing for working people, particularly African Americans for whom no new housing had been built for decades. Reformers demanded that local officials take advantage of federal money to provide low-rent housing. The Baltimore Urban League, a mainstream, interracial organization, became involved in housing issues early. Founded in Baltimore in 1924, the BUL aimed to improve the socioeconomic status and urban conditions of African Americans. The BUL relied on a board of volunteers, donations, and white philanthropic Community Chest funds, which paid two social workers. Carl Murphy and George Murphy, of the black activist and *Afro-American* newspaper family, served on the board.[34] Members of the black sorority Delta Sigma Theta, the black Druid Hill Young Women's Christian Association (YWCA), and the Colored Women's Club lobbied for "slum legislation" as well, and the North Carolina Mutual Insurance Company's Baltimore office, the National Negro Congress, and the Professional Chauffeurs' Association sponsored forums to support public housing construction. The Baltimore NAACP, led by Carl Murphy's friend Lillie M. Jackson, also sought to open up housing to African Americans, but primarily in the private market and through legal channels.[35] Just as he had exposed racism in the relief program, Carl Murphy highlighted black people's need and entitlement to public housing in the *Afro-American* newspaper. To ensure black people had a voice, Murphy established a committee to advise the federal government on potential PWA housing sites. Prominent black businesspeople and civic reformers comprised the black advisory board recognized by federal officials.[36] While the PWA Housing Division's director, A. R. Clas, encouraged state and municipal officials to work with it, Maryland Emergency Housing and Park Commission officials balked at the idea. The Maryland commission had already set up an official three-member "colored committee," which included Sarah

Fernandis. Unfortunately the commission's black members lacked power and were rarely consulted.[37]

Establishing a public housing authority was an uphill battle in this harbor city dominated by a probusiness, anti–New Deal, and fiscally and racially conservative administration. Baltimore's Democratic party operated as a ward-based political machine, which more often than not ignored black concerns and muted black people's political voice. The southern local party initially resisted the national Democratic party's New Deal programs even though the New Deal did not challenge urban machines, political foot-dragging, or local racial residential prerogatives.[38] Nor did Roosevelt markedly lend his presidential voice to racial democracy; he did not support antilynching legislation or the nondiscrimination clause in the Wagner Act of 1935, and he did not attempt to dismantle residential segregation. In fact, the federal administrators of the alphabet soup programs meted out small pieces of the economic pie to African Americans, and the New Deal, as a whole, facilitated localism. City officials could choose whether to participate in federal programs as well as administer the programs according to their own political and racial whims. Even so, federal intervention in local affairs troubled city officials.

In Baltimore the real estate lobby and Democratic mayor Howard Jackson proved indomitable adversaries for public housing advocates. Under the New Deal's PWA, federal officials had to purchase land from municipalities to construct low-rent housing. Local politicians, businessmen, and the real estate lobby had the leverage they needed. Cleveland R. Bealmear, of the real estate board, wrote Clas to protest subsidized housing: "We consider Government subsidized housing not only as unfair competition, but a means of establishing what we believe will develop into a permanent dole system for a large number of citizens."[39] Jackson and his supporters prevented the establishment of PWA subsidized housing in Baltimore by demanding exorbitant prices for undeveloped land. The mayor asked federal officials to pay an amount equal to the taxes assessed on developed land. Livid about local leaders' stalling tactics, Carl Murphy fired off a letter to Clas: "Our own group of people needs new low cost housing. If for any reason the real estate board or any white boards in town do not want government help, we do not feel this should disqualify us from receiving it."[40] Yet, disqualified they were. Since the federal agency lacked condemnation powers, PWA officials could not confiscate city property for redevelopment, and they refused to purchase the costly vacant land. Thus Baltimore built no public housing in 1935. Mayor Jackson rebutted citizens' criticism that he stymied the establishment of a local housing program: "The government simply wanted something for nothing. I could not permit myself to do an injustice to the real estate owners and to those who are now paying taxes on property by allowing the government to enter into competition with them."[41]

The struggle for public housing became reinvigorated in 1937 by a coordinated movement for agitation. The BUL helped organize the Baltimore Citizens' Housing Committee (BCHC), an interracial group of civic, religious, unemployed, workers', and women's organizations that pressured local officials to construct low-rent housing. The BCHC had among its founders the black BUL president, Edward S. Lewis, and Frances Morton, a white social worker and housing activist.[42] The Murphy family also continued to use the *Afro-American* as a mouthpiece for public housing. The editors believed that public housing alone could not offer a primary solution; black people also needed unfettered access to good jobs and private housing opportunities. Even so, the editors argued that Baltimore should take full advantage of the government program. In an editorial, the newspaper maintained that public housing "may offer a fine opportunity . . . to equalize opportunities in local communities like Baltimore, where inequalities are tolerated as a matter of policy." The editors, therefore, encouraged "colored citizens" to "stay in the position to get their share of whatever [New Deal] money is spent here" and to keep abreast of "whatever housing policies are being formulated."[43]

Increased local support for public assistance, citizenry pressure, and the creation of the U.S. Housing Authority (USHA) in 1937 heated up housing debates in the city and forced Mayor Jackson to respond. He appointed a commission of primarily realtors and builders to assess housing conditions and develop plans for local implementation. When the city council's sole Republican member, Daniel Ellison, introduced legislation to create a municipal housing authority, Jackson acted. Two days later, the mayor matched Ellison's move by introducing a similar bill; it passed in 1937.[44] Having achieved its goal to establish a municipal housing program and feeling weary, the BCHC disbanded. White social worker and BCHC member Frances Morton, however, decided to form the Citizens Housing Council (CHC), which advocated for public housing's speedy construction and had as its mission educating the housing authority, society, and even tenants about the power of better housing to improve people and neighborhoods.[45]

The increased pressure from civic, labor, religious, black, women's, unemployed, working-class, and middle-class groups, considerable federal resources for city governments, and the ability to strike "a deal that also served the demands of the local political culture" had made establishing a municipal housing authority politically and economically wise.[46] The USHA emphasized local control and autonomy in ways the PWA housing program had not. The federal government no longer owned and constructed low-rent housing, but funded municipalities that established housing programs. Federal regulations allowed city officials to secure money from the USHA without the fear of upsetting residential segregation. For instance, the federal neighborhood composition rule required that redeveloped areas adhere to demographic patterns. Racial liberals like Harold Ickes, the white former president of Chicago's NAACP and secretary of the Department of the Interior, and Robert Weaver, the department's black advisor, had mandated under the PWA that black workers receive a proportion of construction jobs and subsidized apartments. However, these federal nondiscrimination policies did not address residential integration. Federal officials' attempts to attack segregation or dictate cities' racial policies would have likely sounded the death knell for much New Deal legislation, including its public works, relief, and housing programs.

Jim Crow remained king and shaped the implementation of federal programs in local communities. In Baltimore, officials abided by the composition rule when it served their interests: to construct racially separate complexes in segregated neighborhoods. When the composition rule did not serve local officials' purposes, however, they deviated from it—usually to enhance Jim Crow. Local officials transformed racially mixed neighborhoods into racially homogeneous ones. For instance, Perkins Homes and Latrobe Homes exacerbated segregation and prevented black expansion or what James Edmunds contemptuously referred to as "the blight." According to Edmunds, the housing authority's first chair: "The Housing Authority felt it should take steps to prevent the blight from eating north" and enhance "the value of the white residential neighborhood north of Eager Street, one of the boundaries of the tract."[47] Housing officials encouraged black residents on the Latrobe site "to move east of the project boundary" so they could be included "in one of the colored projects."[48] Similarly, in west Baltimore, city officials targeted the McCulloh corridor to halt black encroachment into a white neighborhood.

In fact, the public housing program transformed neighborhoods by displacing not only black people, but also black institutions. In east Baltimore, the construction of Latrobe Homes resulted in the condemnation of a seventy-five-year-old, eight-room elementary school attended by 500 students and employing twelve teachers. The teachers and students were parceled out to three nearby elementary schools. Across town on the Poe Homes site in west Baltimore, the Baltimore Housing Authority (BHA) forced out the Watkins and Wells Printing Company, which had its shop for eighteen years at 816 Lexington Street, and the Mount Hebron Missionary Baptist Church on Fremont Street. On the McCulloh site, the housing authority displaced three secret fraternal orders, a pharmacy, a funeral parlor, a garage, a school, and two Baptist churches.[49]

The slum clearance and public housing program also decreased available housing in black neighborhoods while adding housing in white communities. Black Baltimoreans experienced the worst housing problems, but white working people benefited just as much from public housing in the program's early days. While black people represented two-thirds of the residents in blighted areas, the Maryland emergency housing committee's former director and the housing authority's first director, Clarence W. Perkins, developed a formula that designated 45 percent of the new units for white residents.[50] Nationwide, white residents received a significant proportion of public housing apartments. Between 1933 and 1937, under the PWA's Housing Division, a majority of the subsidized complexes housed white people. Between 1937 and 1940, 144 of 437 complexes, or 33 percent, were predominantly black.[51]

Building public housing often meant accepting and expanding urban segregation—even if reluctantly. Across the nation, public housing opened on a segregated basis under the PWA and the USHA. In the age of Jim Crow, pushing for "separate but equal" opportunities, which were rarely equal, was the least explosive path for social reformers and was more readily accepted by status quo politicians in municipalities. Even black civil rights activists, including Carl and George Murphy, believed segregated public housing was better than nothing. And some black people had not given much thought to segregation in government housing. For Clara Gordon, one of public housing's first tenants, the construction of blacks-only and whites-only complexes mirrored "the way we were living anyway." A black man and future public housing manager, Warren W. Weaver agreed that segregation "was part of the lifestyle. . . . At that time you couldn't afford to get upset about it because this was the pattern of life. . . . You didn't have any law on your side."[52] The legal assaults on Jim Crow public housing were still decades away.

Public Housing as an Entitlement

Because public assistance came to Baltimore for African Americans in the form of public jobs, public relief, and public housing, low-income black people's relationships to the state were structured in disparate ways. Public welfare and public housing programs were not like Social Security and the Federal Housing Administration (FHA) and eventual Veterans Administration (VA) programs. Cash relief, Aid to Dependent Children (ADC), and the "projects" were means- and morals-tested programs, part of the two-tiered social welfare system. In a racialized political economy, where the "slums" and "urban pathology" were considered "Negro problems" and black employment opportunities were limited, public assistance programs boded greater marginalization for African Americans even as they addressed relief and housing needs in the black community. Public housing was seen as a government "handout" in ways that federal mortgage loan guarantees were not. The federal government's public welfare and public housing programs, therefore, demarcated citizens along race, gender, and class lines. Even so, both black and white urban residents saw public housing as a right—the fulfillment of a federal government promise to protect and provide for its citizens.

Public housing, however, did not offer "a leg up" to all of the nation's ill-housed citizens. It was a right, but only for a select minority. Public housing primarily served the working poor or the self-sufficient—those who could "pay the rent minus the subsidy."[53] Families without a steady income did not qualify. Only the worthy, working poor benefited, reflecting another critical delimiting component of the welfare state. While those who resided in public housing could only make five to six times their rent, by design the tenants, black and white, still represented the ones white policymakers judged worthy of help. The housing authority ignored the needs of the poorest by limiting the number of unemployed and relief families. All but a minority of public housing families received income from employment, though their wages were meager with estimates ranging from $360 to $1,300 annually.[54] Housing authority interviewers accepted forty-seven original inhabitants of the Poe Homes slum clearance site; only three received public welfare. In December 1940, only 21 families out of the 298 that lived in Poe Homes received relief. In general, the poorest Baltimoreans, marked off within the working class, had to fend for themselves. Many black former residents paid higher rents for smaller, overcrowded, and dilapidated apartments. Some of the relocated families had to rely "on [their] food budget[s]" to meet the rent.[55] In its inaugural years, public housing rarely served people with little income; it was "a housing program, not a general relief program."[56]

Public housing as an assistance program raised the questions of not only financial eligibility and dependency, but also morality. In debates over the establishment of the 1937 federal housing program, Senator Robert Wagner of New York, the bill's original sponsor, assured other senators that only the most deserving and respectable would be moved into the subsidized apartments. Wagner argued that "of course, people of ill-repute will not be permitted to occupy the premises" and that "questions of character, of course, will always have consideration."[57] In addition, the institutionally embedded maternalist "moral-reform legacy" which held that "something more than the lack of money was wrong with the poor," shaped not only poor mothers' aid and ADC, but also public housing.[58] Middle-class reformers viewed public housing as a solution to the housing needs of the poor and "a social locus wherein the pathologies generated by poverty would dissipate."[59] A part of the Progressive generation of housing reformers, the CHC believed that public housing would build strong neighborhoods, endow "slum dwellers" with responsibility, and prepare them well for citizenship. Embodying federal sentiments regarding tenants' social character, housing advocates in major cities nationwide, like Philadelphia, Cincinnati, and Baltimore, also felt public housing residency would make "better citizens" out of tenants. Public housing became part of a tradition of poverty policy, including Progressive liberal reform strategies, that focused on using government aid and institutions as a lever to "improve" poor people.[60]

The selection criteria incorporated the reformist zeal of the CHC; housing officials had invited the group to participate in developing agency guidelines following its criticism of the agency's inept relocation practices. Applicants underwent rigorous and lengthy interviews. The microscopic investigations represented officials' intents to weed out those families perceived as "unstable" and "irredeemable"—those lacking jobs and "middle-class" aspirations. Personal worthiness and good housekeeping—in addition to low incomes, substandard housing, and traditional family forms—were indispensable attributes for securing residency.

Boarders were not welcome. That particular working-class strategy was objectionable in public housing communities. Not only did the practice challenge the two-parents-and-children family model, but it also conjured the images of ill-clad, filthy children and adults in overcrowded, poorly maintained tenement housing popularized by photographs like those of Jacob Riis. While defraying living expenses and generating income, boarding was seen as perilous, because unknown people entered the hallowed living space of families. According to W. E. B. Du Bois, who studied Philadelphia's black communities, boarding destroyed the "privacy and intimacy of home life" and admitted "the elements of danger and demoralization."[61] Given such adverse reactions by white and black reformers, forbidding the practice came as no surprise. Nancy Benjamin and her husband, who had a ten-month-old baby, did not even consider Poe Homes. They moved to a ten-room house on West Saratoga, where they could take in boarders and supplement their income.[62]

The exclusion of unwanted practices and "undesirable" tenants also tended to affect single mothers. Some female heads of households, like Rosaline Lundsford's white widowed mother, did receive public housing apartments. But many others did not. Former public housing resident and activist Shirley Wise claimed that the housing authority rejected her widowed mother's initial application in the 1940s because no man lived in the household. Shirley Wise's father, James Albert Foy, a truck driver, died of a massive heart attack when she was five years old. This left Shirley Wise's mother, Mary Savilla Blackwell Foy, to raise five children with the help of her mother-in-law. The large family lived in a substandard three-bedroom house in west Baltimore. The apartment had poorly installed indoor plumbing. Wise recalled: "We couldn't use the downstairs area in the winter because . . . the pipes would freeze and bust. I had vivid memories about that, because we had to move upstairs. In those days it wasn't no gas stoves. It was . . . not even a furnace. We had . . . potbelly coal and wood stoves." The floorboards were so weak that her mother fell through the kitchen floor, an accident that later created ill health and changed her life. After that incident, they moved twice more. When the housing authority began constructing Gilmor Homes, a low-rent complex, which would be temporarily turned over to defense industry workers during the war, her mother applied for residency.[63]

Shirley Wise insisted that her mother qualified: "Every house we lived in was substandard." Her mother received a minimal Social Security allotment and worked. Starting when the young Shirley was eight years old, her mother labored primarily as a domestic, except during the war years when she briefly worked at Edgewood Arsenal, a wartime industrial plant that should have further qualified the family for residency in Gilmor Homes. Wise conveyed her mother's disappointment and frustration: "She couldn't understand. They would give her the run-around. . . . She was persistent about it. See if you look at the 1937 preamble to the housing act, it says, . . . 'to replace substandard housing, and housing for people who are in need.'" Wise, who as a child sat on the curb and watched Gilmor Homes being built, vividly recalled her mother riding the streetcar down to the housing office. "I remember sitting down there with her, so I know she would go." She concluded the housing authority must have discarded her mother's application because her household did not meet the definition of "family" necessary for residency. Explaining the exclusive nature of the first black public housing complexes, Wise explained: "Poe Homes really was what the historians would say that it was: [an] ideal family situation, no single parents, mainly [two-parent] family structures. . . . McCulloh Homes too."[64] Two-parent families with a husband and a wife, at least one breadwinner and a diligent housekeeper, represented the model family thereby reflecting the power of middle-class standards to define propriety and public assistance programs.

So why did Rosaline Lundsford's mother gain access and not Shirley Wise's mother? Single black mothers with families, unlike single white mothers, may have experienced greater barriers, because they competed in a larger pool of prospective tenants. Given the hierarchy of selection and the plethora of two-parent black families applying, black single mothers simply may not have been the most attractive tenants. The objectification of black female-headed households in the 1940s could not have helped matters. Social workers and society increasingly regarded single black motherhood, particularly unwed mothers, as a sign of immorality and pathology.[65] Public housing was for upstanding, down-on-their-luck citizens, and maintaining that clientele was a critical priority.

The First Tenants

Clara Gordon, like many other members of poor and working-class black families, harbored a hope of better days. Those days arrived when relatives and friends told her about the subsidized apartments being built for black people in her west Baltimore neighborhood. Occasionally Gordon strolled by the construction site of the future Poe Homes to monitor its progress. In 1940, when her mother died of old age and her brother Oberlin married, Clara Gordon, her husband, and their two children left the Lexington Street row house for Poe Homes just blocks away. For the first time Gordon did not live with extended family and could afford a decent single-family apartment. "I knew when they built Poe Homes . . . that I wanted to be in the Poe Homes," she happily remembered. "I decided, oooh, take my children, we

Figure 1.2 Poe Homes was the first low-rent public housing complex, black or white, in Baltimore; it opened in 1940. Photograph by Elizabeth Malby.

going to public housing. . . . Because it was a good source. You have nice living conditions. . . . Rent was reasonable. . . . [It was] easier."[66]

In the nation's seventh largest city, which had the highest percentages of homes in the country with no flush toilets, no outside toilets, and no bath or shower and which were in need of major repairs, public housing provided a stark contrast and a step up.[67] The subsidized apartments had all of the technological conveniences lacking in many apartments occupied by the city's poor: indoor bath and toilet facilities, central heating, kitchen and dining areas, living rooms, and separate bedrooms. Compared to the city's substandard dwellings, the limited supply of subsidized housing offered exclusivity and affordable "luxury" living. Estelle Finks and her husband, Albert, an apartment house elevator operator, were evicted from their one-room apartment on Eutaw Street when the white landlord discovered they had applied for McCulloh Homes. Estelle Finks maintained it was the first new and comfortable housing in decades that "poor people" could claim as their own. Black people usually "don't get a chance to move into houses until they're pretty old or broken down. Here everything is perfectly clean and new."[68]

Interest in the first black complexes was widespread and competition fierce to obtain an apartment. In 1940 the *Baltimore Afro-American* published several advertisements asking the questions "Do You Want a Home in the Poe Project?" and in the McCulloh Homes?[69] The CHC sponsored a model apartment at Poe Homes. The model home lured some 25,000 black and white visitors, who filed in to see what the "projects" would look like. Black domestics, helpers, and laborers applied. Charles Dana Loomis, a white administrator for the housing authority, fielded telephone calls from employers who lobbied for their black workers: "We have been deluged with telephone calls from persons who wanted to know if their cook or somebody else couldn't get into one of our developments." Even black teachers, clerks, and office workers applied, but most of them failed to qualify because they earned too much money or their current apartments were not substandard. Black working people inundated the housing authority with applications— testaments to the dearth of affordable and adequate urban housing as well as the desire for better conditions. Warren W. Weaver remembered the first day that the housing authority started interviewing for Gilmor Homes; 150 people waited on line, and the first person stood patiently for eight hours. One of the first applicants accepted into Gilmor Homes was one of Weaver's classmates at Morgan College. "So it just indicates how hard and how much desire there was for public housing back then—and the need for it."[70] While a large number of whites applied for Latrobe Homes, 2,815 for 701 units, an even larger proportion of black tenants vied for the black public housing apartments. More than 1,500 people applied and at least 800 people were interviewed for 298 apartments in Poe Homes. More than 2,500 black people applied for 434 apartments in McCulloh Homes, and 2,300 for 393 apartments in Douglass Homes.[71]

The first tenants in Baltimore's public housing expressed necessity, gratitude, and exuberance. White Baltimoreans who moved into Latrobe Homes, the first whites-only complex, completed in August 1941, were pleased with their new quarters. Rosaline Lundsford, who became a tenant activist in the 1960s and 1970s, moved into Latrobe Homes with her mother and five siblings in 1941 when the sidewalks were not even down yet. She was eleven years old. The family survived off her father's pension. Lundsford described Latrobe as a fine place to grow up and fondly recalled that as a teenager she practically lived in the recreation center. A white elderly woman and her husband brought their son and granddaughter to see their future apartment in Latrobe Homes. When a newspaper reporter asked the elderly woman, who lived near Patterson Park, a white working-class community in southeast Baltimore, whether she liked her new home, she replied: "Why not?" Another Latrobe tenant who brought all new furniture with her was "perfectly thrilled" with her new home.[72] In August 1941, the first 200 families moved in.

White urbanites took advantage of segregated subsidized housing, but their public expression of enthusiasm paled in comparison to that of low-income black Baltimoreans, who confronted multiple barriers to sanitary and affordable housing. Viola Hardman was one of many who heard about Poe Homes. Excited, Hardman told her friends of her intent to apply. By the end of September, she had not only settled in her new apartment at 905 West Lexington Street, but she had entertained her former neighbors, who enviously exclaimed: "Well, Viola, I'm sure glad for you, but I'm sorry for myself."[73] Less than a block away at 802 West Lexington Street, the Spruills, who had trekked from North Carolina to Baltimore in 1929, admired their new apartment. Amaza Spruill and her husband, Charlie, a Baltimore Bottling Company employee, moved into Poe Homes with their five-year-old daughter. Amaza Spruill told a *Baltimore Sun* reporter that she had not been as "happy since my wedding day."[74] Two days after Mr. and Mrs. Augustus May moved into Douglass Homes in August 1941, they sang God's praise: "We are so happy that we want to tell the whole world what a blessing has been given us." The Finks similarly described public housing as a godsend. "It's a little heaven for poor people," asserted Estelle Finks.[75]

While the demand was high, housing officials and CHC members did have to thwart rumors, often propagated by real estate interests, which ignited working-class people's suspicions about public housing. Disapproving landlords maintained that public housing residency would be expensive and would require relinquishing freedoms: Tenants had to submit to daily inspections, abide by curfews, turn their lights and radios off by 10:00 P.M., and buy new furniture for their new apartments, and they were not allowed to have guests. The BHA and CHC mounted a campaign to combat negative publicity. The CHC helped dispel rumors about buying brand-new furniture by giving prospective black tenants tips on decorating with secondhand furniture in their Poe model home.[76] Housing officials assured prospective tenants, who heard rumors of imposed curfews, that "there will be no such restrictions on anyone, and the families will be allowed to conduct their personal lives, businesses, and associations with all liberties within good reason."[77] The "within good reason" phrase, however, did convey officials' intentions to scrutinize and control behavior and actions.

The layers of qualifications and rules, however, also meant that pioneer residents did not relinquish their status as deserving citizens upon residency as public housing residents would twenty years later. In fact, public housing residency tended to affirm tenants' worthiness on two levels: means and morals. Applying and qualifying for public housing may have served as an unavoidable reminder of tenants' low-income, working-class status and their former unsanitary living conditions, conditions some worked hard to keep at bay. But meeting specific economic and moral standards and successfully competing for the apartments allowed tenants to escape the stigma of the "slums" and endowed them with status and social currency. Monzella Cooper, who lived on the McCulloh Homes site, had hoped to move into the modern apartments. Cooper believed that "when the project is completed," the neighborhood would "get a nice class of people in the new homes."[78]

Who was a part of this "nice class of people"?—the up-and-coming members of the working class. Listen to Clara Gordon's recollections about Poe Homes: "It was the *first* public housing in Baltimore and it was elite. . . . You know, quiet, nice decent living. . . . the children would go to school to try to get an education. It was just an elite thing. . . . When they first had the

Poe Homes, they had nothing but the best families. Elite, because they could meet the level of what the rent was."[79] The *Baltimore Afro-American* lauded black public housing and its tenants as a "paying investment." In the first fourteen months of operation, BHA collected $75,000 in rentals with a loss of only $17. "That very excellent record doesn't surprise us," remarked *Afro-American* editors. "The families for the Poe project were carefully selected."[80]

Residency bolstered black working-class people's feelings of progress and respectability not just in Baltimore, but across the nation. Eligible and qualified, black public housing tenants received the honor of selection. In Illinois, residents of Chicago's Southside black community envied tenants in "the project" or the Ida B. Wells Homes.[81]

The complexes' openings received media attention and fanfare, further avouching the desirability of public housing communities and their residents. The *Baltimore Sun* newspaper interviewed pioneer black tenants in Poe, McCulloh, and Douglass homes. The *Baltimore Afro-American* dedicated almost two pages to Douglass Homes' opening. The newspaper printed pictures of neatly aligned trash cans and little Margaret Johnson sweeping dust from underneath her parents' bed in their new apartment—highlighting tenants' commitment to cleanliness and their respect for their new residences. The coverage depicted black public housing as pleasing and worthy. The articles discussed how "Douglass Homes Replaced a Community Eye-Sore" and relayed the jubilation of tenants like the Mays. The *Baltimore Afro-American* even printed the picture of the first black baby born in public housing: Leroy William Sydnor of McCulloh Homes. The new tenants, who had jobs and were handpicked by the housing authority, were attractive neighbors and they would engage in activities to maintain their pieces of heaven and to enhance their social status.[82]

Tenant Organizations and the Fight for Respectability

Black working-class tenants' exclusion from decent housing, the chance for respectability through public housing residency, and the view that public housing was an entitlement and a right of citizenship in an era replete with protest provide a backdrop for understanding the activities and battles of the first tenants. Together with USHA policies, these circumstances shaped black tenants' political culture and their social responses to their new homes.

Part of the federal government's New Deal, which encouraged citizen participation and organizational growth, the USHA considered smooth tenant-management relations to be a central aspect of a well-run housing authority and called for "resident participation" in local public housing communities.[83] In its 1941 manual, *Community Activities in Public Housing*, the USHA encouraged the creation of resident councils to initiate community activities, to establish groups in "accordance with American traditions," and to lessen "the likelihood of destructive activities based upon misunderstandings, bickerings, and personal and group antagonisms."[84] As early as 1933, across the nation, black and white tenants who lived in subsidized housing took advantage of participatory spaces opened by the government. Black and white tenants started resident councils, mutual benefit organizations, and resident newspapers, and they participated in programs ranging from preschool and parent education to health and safety, consumer services, and recreation. Encouraged and approved by the local and federal governments, these tenant organizations' aims reflected the goals of the reformist welfare state and arguably "company unions," which offered employees services and a sense of community by providing pathways for working-class engagement while still maintaining oversight and control.

The Baltimore Housing Authority's central office and most managers supported tenant activities as long as residents did not question agency policy. And the CHC, ever concerned about promoting better housing, saw tenants' organizations as a manifestation of the idea that better homes resulted in better citizens just as responsible activism produced responsible citizens. Housing officials, then, encouraged black and white tenants in low-income and eventually wartime defense housing to provide nonthreatening social and educational activities. During meetings that formally welcomed black tenants into Poe and McCulloh homes, the black manager, Avon B. Collins, outlined the "responsibilities, problems and difficulties" black tenants might face and "emphasized the importance of cooperation between the tenants, manager and community."[85] A former manager at Langston Terrace, the first black low-rent complex in Washington, D.C., and a Baltimore native, Collins helped black tenants start their resident councils.[86]

Black Baltimore already had a rich "web of organizational life," including self-help and recreational activities. By the 1930s, 400 civic and social clubs existed in the city.[87] While black activist groups in public housing were not unique in form, they became a significant base for future activism in the city's first planned, subsidized, working-class housing.

In public housing communities, not every tenant participated in community-building efforts, but those who did eagerly sought assistance to maintain their little pieces of heaven. The first public housing tenant groups in Baltimore emerged out of a cooperative ethic, not out of conflict, though the latter was only a few months away. Gordon remembered: "We worked closely allied with the management. And whatever suggestions that we would offer for the betterment of our children, they would push, introduce."[88] Tenants viewed public housing managers as facilitators of their goals to build decent communities and achieve social mobility, even though some housing officials, including managers, would soon become impediments.

Soon after settling into their low-rent apartments, a cohort of Edgar Allan Poe Homes tenants operated self-help civic clubs. Within the first year, Poe Homes tenants established a tenant council as well as five other organizations. The tenant council had fifty members, including its officers and building representatives. Led by Moses Knight, the council not only sponsored its own activities but also served as an umbrella organization that offered financial assistance to the complex's smaller clubs. Clara Gordon described the tenant council as an organization in which "we worked for the interest of the people."[89]

Women who had primary responsibility for domestic issues expressed concern about their families' living conditions. Black working-class women formed mothers' clubs, which had a tradition in the black community. As early as the 1890s, mothers' clubs promoted racial uplift by teaching the fundamentals of rearing children and homemaking and by raising money for schools and playgrounds. Black and white women social reformers believed that providing mothers with training in housekeeping and rearing children would improve the immediate state of the neighborhood and the future of the race by making good citizens of children. In Poe Homes, the Mothers' Club met twice monthly with the complex's nursery school teacher. The mothers learned techniques for rearing children and supervised the nursery, which had thirty-five children aged two to four years old from the community. Clara Gordon attended the mothering classes and any other activities that concentrated on the "welfare of the children and the family."[90] Given the focus on "deviant" working-class behavior, parenting classes may have reflected tenants' attempts to incorporate themselves "into conceptions of normal or dominant communities" by conforming to gender roles prevalent in white and black bourgeois society.[91] Many black working-class people, like Clara Gordon's and Shirley Wise's families, had relied on extended kin networks to survive. Parenting and child-rearing programs, which were concerned specifically with the responsibilities of the mother and father to their children, focused on enhancing the nuclear family and possibly reflected the way some marginalized people harnessed gender conformity in their search for acceptance.

Many members of the Poe Mothers' Club also participated in the Women's Club. However, unlike the Mothers' Club, which focused primarily on childcare issues, the Women's Club organized "to bring the women of the community together and promote social and civic endeavors."[92] Women's Club members, many of whom toured Poe's model home, helped to decorate and showcase a model apartment in McCulloh Homes for viewing. The fifty-eight-member Women's Club also sponsored the first annual tenant family outing in Druid Hill Park. In public housing where limited income defined occupancy, female residents developed services for families who fell on even harder times. They distributed Christmas baskets to less fortunate tenants and operated a fund to support neighbors who fell sick or had other emergencies. The Poe Homes women's groups were part of the legacy of national and local women's social and civic organizations and reflected broader maternalist reform efforts during the Progressive era. Women tenants' activities also revealed working-class people's recognition of the tenuous and exclusive nature of economic prosperity. As members of a striving class, one's style of life was as important as, if not at times more important than, wealth.

In public housing among the working poor, some mothers could not stay at home, as Clara Gordon did for her first five years of residency, and fulfill the bourgeois gender ideal of housewife. Some black and white women, along with their husbands, had to work to make ends meet. In Poe Homes, the tenant council "set as its first task the establishment of a nursery school for children of working parents."[93] Day nurseries also operated in whites-only complexes like Latrobe Homes. In the early 1940s, while working-class tenants viewed the day nurseries as practical and useful, housing officials and social reformers viewed them also as socially necessary, especially in public housing, which increasingly housed defense industry employees alongside low-income tenants. Assessing a need for childcare and parental education for working-class mothers, housing officials hoped that more day nursery programs might "develop in other projects, especially those dedicated to workers in war industries where many women may be in industry employment, and family routine is severely disorganized."[94] While women engaged in paid labor to aid the war machine or out of necessity, their gender identities as mothers and wives and their accompanying domestic duties still represented proper behavior. However, since wartime work was temporary and women's labor necessary, the government helped to provide services to ease women's burdens and curtail the "disorganization" that resulted from women's deviation from traditional duties. By the end of 1943, nine nursery schools or childcare centers and four public health or well-baby clinics operated in public housing, where one-third of the tenant population was under twelve years old.[95]

Parents worked with the city recreation department to provide structured programs. Black and white tenant councils sponsored activities like the girls' and boys' clubs. By ensuring that children had specific places for play within the public housing complex, parents could keep their children, as much as possible, away from the streets, often viewed as dangerous, disorganized, and crime-ridden. Helping to maintain external order by protecting the community, the Poe Homes Men's Club formed patrols to keep the area safe and quiet.[96] Although public housing complexes were new, the neighborhoods around them remained impoverished. In many cases, tenant activists acted as community stewards. Instead of cordoning themselves off from the surrounding communities, tenant activists reached out to their non–public housing neighbors. In the Poe Homes community, a local school's Parents-Teachers Association met in the assembly room to discuss school and community problems. By 1953 Poe Homes' Men's Club, already known for its work, was lauded throughout the neighborhood, according to the housing authority's 1952 *Annual Report* and was "frequently called on by families in distress residing outside the project." The Men's Club rendered "remarkably diverse" services, including administering first aid to a family whose home was badly damaged by fire.[97] In the white Perkins Homes, a debate ensued among tenants about whether to exclude neighborhood boys from the complex's new softball club. A white father, who was also the club leader, decided to include them. He argued that he knew firsthand the squalor, bitterness, and "festering misery bred in houses that had long since lost their right to be called home." Exclusion would breed ill will.[98]

Maintaining internal stability and neighborliness was also necessary, for in spite of the expressed goals of tenant activists, not every resident was amicable or cooperative. Like in any community, conflicts emerged between children and between their parents—whether they lived in public housing or its surrounding neighborhoods. In Poe Homes, Clara Gordon remembered one neighbor in particular—a woman who had a light-skinned husband and son. This neighbor's son constantly picked fights with the other children, and then told his mother they targeted him and maybe even were jealous because of his fair complexion. Such childhood skirmishes created dissension among mothers. In other words, public housing complexes were not places of unmitigated bliss. Discord was a part of life even in the black elite complexes.

Reminiscent of black reformers' call for sanitary and beautified neighborhoods, black tenant activists urged the maintenance of well-kept communities. They beautified otherwise drab brick buildings and bare green lawns and each year anticipated participation in the politically inspired *Afro Clean Block* beautification campaign. Sponsored by the Murphy-owned *Afro-American* newspaper, the campaign fought unsanitary conditions in black communities by holding a contest promoting cleanliness and improvement. The contest encouraged children, families, and neighbors to spruce up black neighborhoods citywide. The top winners received cash prizes. Poe, McCulloh, Somerset, Douglass, and Gilmor tenants planted flowers, scrubbed porches, manicured lawns, and put up small picket fences. The housing authority even praised Poe and McCulloh, which often won first place for public housing in the Clean Block campaign, as "the traditional beauty spots" of public housing, and Douglass and Gilmor usually followed close behind. Reflecting the spirit of black middle-class social reform, the *Afro-American* campaign merged with working-class desires for safe, decent, and healthy communities.[99]

Residents in white complexes had no similar citywide contest in which to zealously participate. But white tenants also cared about neighborhood upkeep. In the whites-only Westport Homes, children made trash pickers by affixing nails to old sticks and broom handles. In a 1946 housing brochure, *Birthright: A Decent Home*, after outlining black beautification efforts, housing officials described a "somewhat less lyrical note in clean-up activities." In Latrobe Homes, a four-year-old white lad beckoned the manager from his homemade tent pitched on the lawn; he squealed on another boy who was digging in the grass. When the manager responded that maybe the four-year-old should tell his friend to stop next time, the boy said, "No," maybe he would just "hit him over the head with a hammer."[100]

Tenants' activities were primarily civic and recreational, but they did not simply serve as a "safety valve" or a "'splendid medium of cooperation' for leisure activities" as progressive-minded managers and reformers had conceived them.[101] While residents did not possess decision-making authority in administrative matters, their programs conveyed black and white tenants' desire for clean comfortable homes. For black tenants, in particular, however, the panoply of activities seemed to unveil more: their visions of and drive for respectability. For instance, the ascription of status was key to conveying respectability among black workers who aspired to achieve greater social and economic heights and to contest public aspersions. Tenants' participation in the Clean Block campaign signified this. In Poe Homes, the tenant council held anniversary celebrations complete with speeches and entertainment and started a portrait collection to honor successful community stewards, primarily of their race. Tenants inducted George B. Murphy, Sr., and Avon B. Collins. Both Murphy and Collins were men who fought discrimination, and their success represented great possibilities. By venerating Murphy and Collins, tenants celebrated social advancement and equal rights as desirable and in return received accolades for embodying similar principles. When George Murphy accepted the honor, he thanked tenants for their "spirit of cooperation and good citizenship" and for proving that "despite public opinion to the contrary, . . . colored families could maintain decent homes if only given the chance."[102]

Reflecting a long-held belief in African-American society, education and its potential for upward mobility also were priorities among some tenants and community members. Clara Gordon wanted to give her children every advantage to succeed. After all, she liked public housing, not just because the rents were cheaper and the housing was safe and new, but because the money she saved on rent (and eventually from working) could go into a personal kitty for her children's education. "I wanted to educate my children in order that they might have a college education." And she did, as did others. Gordon's daughter and son graduated from elementary and high school. They even achieved advanced degrees. Her daughter became a registered nurse, finishing at the black Provident Hospital's School of Nursing, and her son graduated from Howard University and accepted a job as an engineer at

Westinghouse. Even Gordon went back to school, earning a degree in social work at Morgan State College. Numerous residents felt the same way about education, according to Gordon, who proudly recalled how some children from public housing became dentists, lawyers, and politicians.[103] While a community thrust, education was not a panacea. Many tenants remained trapped in public housing and poverty; some children had to leave high school to work; many could not afford higher education or find well-paid jobs to significantly improve their circumstances. And still others satisfied themselves with making ends meet.

Black working-class tenants also established clubs to teach etiquette—a marker of social status and hopefully preparation for upward social mobility. Poe, Douglass, Somerset, and numerous other black public housing complexes had Boy Scout troops, girls' debutante social clubs, and charm schools. Clara Gordon, who often sent her children to free activities sponsored by the recreation department, took pride in the compliments about their stellar behavior. Their deportment reflected her parenting skills, belied their poverty, and boded well for their possibility for achievement:

> They would give things for the children and . . . when they would go for these free activities, . . . the social worker, she said, "Are these children you sent me, they from the housing projects?" I said, "Yeah." "But they don't look like it. They dress well!" And [she] said they are so well behaved and they were greatly impressed. And so this is [also] why they called . . . Poe Homes, the elite projects.[104]

Black men tenants also worked with other black men to improve their position in society. In 1950 a group of twenty men, some of whom did not live in public housing, formed the Fathers Association of Baltimore under the leadership of Hansel Henry of Poe Homes. In addition to creating close relationships between fathers and sons, the association sought to stimulate fathers' interests in school and community activities and to provide educational programs in real estate, consumer buying, and insurance.

Participation in civic groups indicated black working-class people's desire for social status and elevation, revealing their middle-class aspirations even as they confronted their working-class status. Tenants' efforts to achieve better lives did not simply mimic white sensibilities; tenants responded to the very real hardships they confronted and the desires they possessed as black working-class city residents. Living in subsidized communities, black tenants developed a working-class sense of respectability that emerged as a result of racial exclusion and their eventual access to decent and sanitary physical spaces. By participating in neighborhood-based initiatives, black tenants continuously worked to build community, "make something good of marginality," and counter their exclusion. While they did not own their homes, they took ownership of them for the time they were there.[105]

No doubt the activities in which black public housing residents engaged defied common perceptions that characterized debates over whether the government should even build low-income subsidized apartments. Real estate interests argued that black people who lived in deteriorated neighborhoods— disparagingly referred to as "slum dwellers"—could not escape the slum because wherever black people moved they would recreate the same deteriorating conditions. Tenants' community efforts challenged the presumption that blight resulted simply from black residency instead of economic factors and city neglect. Residents' civic participation contested biological immutability and thereby undermined politicized arguments deployed to maintain black people as second-class citizens. At a Citizens Planning and Housing Association (CPHA) dinner in 1945, Thomas J. Waxter, the white director of Baltimore's welfare department, "declared that a visit to the Poe Homes is justification for the belief that decency to any group of people, regardless of color, begets decency in return."[106]

Through civic participation, working-class black people challenged an America that denied them access to the better things in life. These self-help civic organizations, however, represented only one side of tenant life and activism in the 1940s. Black and white resident councils were simultaneously a medium for political organizing and grievance resolution as early as 1941. City housing officials, however, maintained an ambivalent relationship with tenant organizations as residents became more politicized. That tenants were only laying claim to the ideal of participation espoused by the federal government and social reformers did not matter. During 1941, alongside community-building efforts, the exigencies of the war as well as the attendant housing and wartime emergency policies created hardship and dissatisfaction among black and white tenants, particularly those residing in subsidized housing for war workers. In an attempt to combat policies that threatened their lifestyles, expectations, and citizenship, tenants confronted the housing authority through councils that became bastions of opposition.

2 "A Woman Can Understand"

Dissidence in 1940s Public Housing

Within years of the first low-rent complexes' openings, war descended on the nation, bringing changes and new problems to working-class people and subsidized housing. In 1943 in Gilmor Homes, the outspoken tenant council leader, Lottie Hall, registered numerous complaints on behalf of 587 fellow resident families, many of them war workers. Hall argued among other things that the complex's heat level and hot water supply were insufficient. What were war workers to do when they came home late at night, their bodies drenched in the sweat of their jobs and their muscles aching? Didn't laborers deserve a hot bath without having to worry about heating pots of water on the stove? Weren't laborers entitled to a warm night's sleep in apartments without damp walls? What about keeping the apartments clean and healthy? How could women (some of whom also labored in war industries) do household chores in cold apartments lacking hot water? And why didn't the apartments have rear walkways? The absence of concrete paths made their neighborhood look "unsightly" and forced "tenants to track dust and mud into the apartments."[1] For women like Hall, the private and ordinary travails of daily living became political concerns. Contentious and insistent, these tenant voices provide another view of subsidized housing and working-class activism in cities mobilized by war.

During World War II, people crowded cities, housing was in short supply, and the rationing of steel, food, and oil was the norm. It was also a time when citizens' expectations for abundance, fair play, comfort, and government responsiveness rose—the combined effects of the New Deal, the international war against tyranny, and the centralization of bureaucratic power. The federal government did not take a back seat to municipalities as it had before the war. Federal officials were out front, making decisions and commandeering local spaces as best befitted the nation's wartime interests. And in the housing arena, this meant financing, building, and managing housing for war workers. The newest tenants—defense workers—gained access to subsidized housing as early as 1941. By March 1943, 1,826 low-income families and 4,357 war worker families resided in subsidized housing managed by Baltimore's municipal housing authority.[2]

And as Lottie Hall's complaints show, when it came to wartime housing and conditions, some tenants expressed feelings other than the exhilaration of the low-income black pioneers. The speedy construction of defense housing, wartime emergency policies like rationing services and goods, and municipal housing officials' attitudes and practices on the home front fueled a new wave of activism. Experiencing inadequate services, unhealthy homes, unaffordable living conditions, and managerial mistreatment, many black working-class women and their white counterparts became dissidents. And their dissidence elucidates the broader social and political dynamics in 1940s Baltimore. During these years, women tenants' demands fit within and exposed a continuum of women's battles. Waged in an era when war expanded women's job opportunities and encouraged political participation, women's varied home-front struggles—inside and outside public housing—politicized their roles as stewards and guardians of families and communities. Yet, the struggles of women tenants also broadly reveal workers' concerns about shelter, citizenship, mistreatment by the state, and, for African Americans, social mobility and inequality. As war workers and home-front citizens, public housing tenants exhibited a patriotic fervor. They planted Victory Gardens, sponsored military honor rolls, held flag-raising ceremonies, and were willing to sacrifice for the war effort—but not if it meant being denied a minimal standard of living or, for African Americans, experiencing second-class citizenship. Finally, women's activism also contributed to a successful organizational assault that resulted in the transformation of the city's housing agency. This chapter, then, is about the changes in housing and related policies, the battles those changes provoked, and specifically women's roles in them.

Wartime Housing Shortage

The United States' entry into the war against fascism forced the mobilization of troops abroad and of resources—industrial, natural, and human—at home. Responding to war necessity and desiring better lives and material abundance, black and white families left North Carolina, South Carolina, Virginia, and Maryland's Eastern Shore. They flooded into the Baltimore region to take advantage of war industries proliferating along a forty-mile stretch of the Chesapeake Bay. A mega–war center, the region had railroad terminals, accessible bays, docking ports, shipyards, military installations, weapons testing grounds, and booming industries like Glenn L. Martin Aircraft Company, Bethlehem Steel, and Bethlehem-Fairfield Shipbuilding Company. Migrants and city residents filled jobs manufacturing ships, B-10 bomber planes, gas masks, phosphorous bombs, rocket-launching bazookas, mine detonators, and poison gases.[3] Future Douglass Homes tenant Julia Matthews migrated to Baltimore from Elm City, North Carolina, during the war years to escape agricultural work. "I used to go back down there to visit, but not to stay. Because I didn't have no job, and I wasn't going to work nobody's farm."[4] In Baltimore, Matthews packed candy and tomatoes, delivered telegrams, and worked at Edgewood Arsenal and the Continental Can Company. Black laborers worked some skilled jobs, but overall tended to work the homefront grunt jobs like loading ships and cleaning up plants. Many black workers did not labor in defense industries at all. While by April 1943 about 25,000 black people (2,000–3,000 of them women) worked in Baltimore's war industries, African Americans only comprised about 11 percent of the workforce. Yet, they represented 20 percent of the city's population.[5]

As the United States hurtled toward war and urban and war center populations increased, housing became the "biggest headache" and a critical necessity for the war effort.[6] Armed with wartime powers, the federal government not only controlled food prices, rationed critical materials, and monitored rents, but also reentered the housing business. In 1940 the Lanham Act, a defense amendment to the 1937 housing act, redirected federal slum clearance money to defense housing. In 1942 President Franklin D. Roosevelt formed the National Housing Agency (NHA) to coordinate wartime housing policies. Under the Lanham Act, federal officials provided housing for war workers in cities across the nation by financing the construction of temporary and permanent housing or by buying or borrowing municipal low-income public housing complexes. The federal government turned 50 percent of 300 low-rent housing complexes into war housing and financed the construction of 100,000 apartments.[7] The Lanham Act, therefore, altered the dynamics of power by privileging federal wartime necessities over local autonomy. As a result, municipal-federal relations grew unsettled.

Despite the federal government's heightened involvement, few housing opportunities existed early on for black workers in cities across the country. In Chicago, the National Negro Council and the Chicago Citizens' Committee of 1,000 had condemned the NHA for its "failure to provide needed housing for colored war workers in many localities," including Detroit and Willow Run, Michigan; Chester, Pennsylvania; Buffalo, New York; and Lorain, Ohio. In some cities, like Philadelphia and Los Angeles, vacancies abounded in wartime subsidized housing, but the federal government refused to fill them "for fear of altering racial patterns." In Philadelphia, only 900 units out of 3,900 were allotted to African Americans.[8] In the Baltimore region, the NHA provided wartime housing, but primarily for white workers. The BHA sold the whites-only Armistead Gardens to the federal government for $2.2 million and diverted, for instance, whites-only Perkins Homes and Fairfield Homes, which was originally "programmed for Negroes," to "white war workers as part of the shift to war housing." Trailer camps and dormitories were set up, but these were all white as well.[9] By the end of 1942 the federal government had built seven war complexes for white workers, but offered no similar provisions for black workers.

The "war-inflated Negro population" strained black housing. Between 1940 and 1942 alone, 33,000 black people migrated to Baltimore with an average of 300 weekly; however, no new places existed to house them.[10] In 1941 Charles F. Nealy, who represented a delegation of black Bethlehem Steel workers, asked why no emergency housing existed "for colored citizens . . . similar to housing facilities for white workers near defense plants."[11] The BHA, serving as the NHA's local agent, did divert Gilmor Homes to black war workers, but only after significant debate. One of Gilmor Homes' street boundaries, Fulton Avenue, was a residential racial dividing line. "But it worked out all right, because the entrance to those properties that backed on Fulton . . . was inside the projects," recalled Warren W. Weaver. "So it wasn't a direct exposure to white" neighborhood residents.[12] The BHA also planned an extension to Douglass Homes—Somerset Courts—to temporarily house black wartime workers. Such actions were not simply an expression of patriotism, however; municipal officials reclassified low-rent complexes, like Gilmor, Somerset, and the whites-only Perkins, to secure the federal priority needed to obtain rationed building supplies necessary for their completion.

But even with these measures, Baltimore's civil rights advocates, like those in other cities, expressed concern about the dearth of housing and attacked federal officials and their municipal managing agents. The National Negro Council and the Chicago committee demanded NHA leader John Blandford's resignation, arguing that the federal government's inaction "repudiated the ideals [for] which 500,000 colored soldiers are fighting." Baltimore NAACP executive secretary Randall Tyus also pressured federal officials. He wrote Blandford, demanding "positive action on Housing for Negroes in the Baltimore area." Within a month of this letter, in February 1943, the federal government announced that it would construct 2,000 apartments for Baltimore's black war workers.[13] But even with this federal commitment, an inflammatory problem familiar to many cities arose—where to build that much housing for black people in a city already bursting at the seams of its racial residential boundaries?

The Controversy over Black Defense Housing

The provision and construction of black defense housing was a fault line for home-front disruptions nationwide. In 1942 in Detroit, where vacant housing was as "hard to find as hen teeth," white people tried to prevent black people from moving into the Sojourner Truth federal housing complex. There, racial violence spiraled out of control. In Baltimore, the construction of black war workers housing evoked heated protests from white residents, realtors, landlords, and politicians. On the brink of its own housing battles, the Baltimore NAACP and Urban League founded the Unity for Victory Committee in August 1943 to avert racial conflict, prevent the city from becoming another Detroit, and push for the actual construction of promised black defense housing.[14]

Despite the shift to federal wartime powers, municipal officials doggedly fought to preserve local autonomy and priorities. City government agencies like the housing authority continuously bowed to racial prejudice and business interests over site selection, especially concerning black defense housing on vacant land near white neighborhoods. For instance, in March 1943, the BHA inspected and opposed "construction of negro housing on [a] site because it was in a white area." Neighborhood groups also protested to federal authorities. A white Baltimore minister wrote to housing officials: "We cannot understand why the Federal Government insists upon putting negroes where white people are, except there be an ulterior purpose behind it all."[15]

Civic reformers, civil rights advocates, religious groups, union representatives, women and men, black and white—all housing advocates—also remonstrated. In particular, the NAACP's wary but relatively hopeful outlook turned into disgust between February and April. By March 1943, the housing problem was so bad that the Governor's Commission on Problems Affecting the Negro Population suggested the emergency construction of temporary dorms for black workers in empty buildings, churches, underutilized schools, and public parks.[16] In April 1943, the NAACP titled its housing report "Baltimore Housing Authority Rank with Prejudice." The civil rights group argued that the BHA's board chair, Cleveland R. Bealmear, who as a member of the real estate board had opposed municipal public housing, was "interested in perpetuating the separation of races, maintaining the status quo and preserving his own real estate interest." The NAACP wrote President Roosevelt and called for an immediate investigation of the "thieves and robbers of democracy" in the BHA.[17]

The civil rights group, however, did not criticize just municipal authorities, but also the federal government for not making judicious and speedy use of its wartime decision-making powers. In another letter to Roosevelt, Tyus lambasted federal officials for yielding "to the pressure of those . . . steeped in racial prejudice." He called for an investigation of federal housing agencies and the "elimination of 'those men who do not posses [sic] ability or intestinal fortitude to discharge their duties on behalf of the nation.'"[18] Waging a similar critique, the *Afro-American* newspaper ran an editorial cartoon with the headline "Stop Kicking that Football Around," indicting municipal and federal officials and the white citizenry for their prejudice. In the cartoon, a white man, who represents the Federal Housing Authority, has his leg anchored by a rope of "prejudice," holds the "plans," and scratches his head. The mayor, who served as a mediator, and the City Plan[ning] Commission kick around a football representing the promised defense homes, while two white men representing the "housing authority" and "biased whites" consort with one another over the game plan. On the sidelines, vital black war workers stand helplessly, barred from the field of play.[19]

A two-year controversy subsequently ensued in Baltimore. Every level of government—city, county, state, and federal—became involved, and "individuals and groups, mass meetings and special meetings, letters and resolutions, prayers, entreaties and threats of violence were employed to sway, determine or deter site selection."[20] In a 1944 report, the NHA used Baltimore as an example of how "in the case of projects programmed for Negroes," site selection carried "additional overtones." The NHA report

Figure 2.1 Editorial cartoon, Baltimore Afro-American, April 24, 1943. Reprinted with the permission of the AFRO-American Newspapers Archives and Research Center.

Stop Kicking that Football Around

reprinted portions of white citizens' letters. One white Baltimorean began his complaint with the introductory words to the Preamble to the U.S. Constitution. The mixture of patriotic anti-Nazism and antiblack racism to preserve segregation and white prerogative is only too evident: "We the people bought our homes out in this section to get away from negroes, and the slums and filth that follow them. Why are they forced upon us without our consent. We are fighting for freedom to live as we see fit but freedom doesn't, I hope, mean indiscriminate racial mixing."[21] Other white residents, businesspeople, landholders, and realtors argued that black people threatened property values, religious and ethnic cohesiveness, industrial progress, and neighborhood growth and stability.

In these neighborhood battles, white working-class women emerged as critical instigators. In Baltimore, alongside white and ethnic men, religious leaders, locally elected representatives, and housing officials, white working-class women attended protests, made statements, and disrupted city council meetings. In July 1943, 800 boisterous white protesters, three-quarters of them women, rallied downtown at the War Memorial Building near City Hall. The protesters argued that the proposed area not only lacked adequate water, sewage, and transportation, but also black schools, churches, and entertainment. The crowd booed and heckled Republican mayor Theodore R. McKeldin, who took office in the midst of controversy. Refusing to make a decision, McKeldin argued that the federal government had the right to choose where to build defense housing. A week later at a special session of the city council, 400 protesters, nine-tenths of them women, contested the construction of black defense housing in their backyards.[22] Like their counterparts in Detroit and Chicago, white women Baltimoreans, who were mothers, war workers, or wives of military men, labored to halt a black "invasion" and guard their domestic home fronts. The Ladies Harford Road Democratic Association president wrote McKeldin and asked him to "safeguard our community and our homes, by protecting them from invasion. If it is a social experiment that is being tried all over the country, please, preserve us from this trial."[23]

On the other side of the struggle, black and white women also tried to secure housing for black defense workers. These women were often founders, officers, and members of key reform and civil rights organizations, including the NAACP and the biracial Citizens Planning and Housing Association, an organization that brought together CHC members and planning constituencies in 1942. Half of CPHA's officers and numerous board members were women, and the Baltimore NAACP's president was Lillie Jackson. At the special city council session, the Women's Civic League and the League of Women Voters pressured the mayor to provide housing for black workers.[24] A white woman member of the League of Women Voters and assistant to CPHA's executive secretary, Mrs. Joseph Hirschmann[25] fought for black defense housing because, as she stated, the league was "interested in better citizens and better living conditions which make better citizens." Juanita Jackson Mitchell, an activist since the mid-1930s and daughter of Baltimore's NAACP president, pledged her support. Juanita Jackson Mitchell maintained that white opponents' rambunctious behavior was an "indictment of our educational and social agencies" and proved that the "real fight for democracy needs to be waged right here in Baltimore." Maud P. Bell, executive secretary of the Workers Alliance, contested opponents who attacked potential black tenants' characters. Foes argued that public housing apartments would not serve native black Baltimoreans, but "southern scum." While Bell did not challenge this demeaning label, she at least challenged the righteousness of withholding safe housing from black people by arguing that the denial of "equal rights and opportunities is what made the scum. It is our duty in a case such as this to help correct those conditions."[26]

Black women mailed support letters to the *Baltimore Afro-American*, which published regular columns advocating black defense housing. In a letter to the editor, Bell professed that white opposition to black wartime housing represented just one more example of Maryland's racist legacy. Bell wrote: "Maryland is running true to form by making it extremely difficult for its colored citizens whenever their comfort and well being are concerned."[27] Edith A. Graham, who lived on McCulloh Street in west Baltimore, expressed similar disgust and challenged arguments that black people's residency devalued property. She sarcastically referred to the state of elaborate three-story rowhouse mansions on a white residential street. Graham wrote: "Just look at what's left of the beautiful homes on Eutaw Place." Graham also questioned white protesters' loyalty to America and invoked a discourse of responsible patriotism, inquiring whether white people were "so afraid that we will have comfortable homes that they forget about Japs murdering American pilots? How can they find time to protest homes for honest war workers with the present war going on?"[28]

While protests delayed the construction and opening of 75 percent of black defense housing apartments for almost a year, eventually the standoff ended. Responding to intense organizational and citizenry protest, housing authority intransigence, and an initial belief that they had mayoral support, federal housing officials finally selected a site to build apartments for black defense workers and issued condemnation papers. The housing authority, city council, and even the mayor responded. In a municipal-federal compromise, officials agreed to build three black temporary defense complexes—Sollers, Holabird, and Turners Station—on small parcels of land bordering polluted streams, standing water, and a municipal airport. Cherry Hill Homes, the first permanent black complex for "a minority group on vacant land," also was built, but ironically over the vociferous protests of black leaders. Constructed on a site previously seen as a "damnable" selection by federal authorities, Cherry Hill Homes opened after VJ Day in 1945; a cemetery, a swamp, and a garbage reduction plant surrounded the complex.[29] Clamorous protests, white threats of racial violence, and the urgent need for black housing resulted in the construction of subsidized complexes in black neighborhoods or on marginal, often hazardous property. Municipal and federal housing officials abandoned the sites that had evoked white opposition; it seemed the only way to proceed. In wartime, racial privilege and segregation remained intact. The black complexes, however, were built. And once they were opened and occupied, protests spilled out of them. The first protests, however, emerged out of already existing white defense housing.

The First Wartime Tenant Protests

Racial hostility did not structure black and white tenants' relationships with each other inside subsidized housing. Since Jim Crow ruled, black and white tenants did not have to vie for the same apartments or complexes. But white residents, and eventually black tenants, would confront similar issues, like shoddy workmanship, inadequate services, and the managing agent, the BHA—an agency that was just as concerned with avoiding political controversy as it was with protecting racial privilege and maintaining municipal power among business and real estate interests.

Experiencing less than adequate living conditions, white tenants, especially women and men giving their labor and moral support to the war, protested housing conditions and practices. For instance, Armistead Gardens was built in three construction phases, the first by municipal officials and the second two by the federal government. The contractors built Armistead Gardens and its two annexes with hollow concrete blocks and failed to waterproof the buildings. White tenants railed against the housing authority, which avowed a commitment to slum improvement and promised war workers comfort and safety as the managing agent for the national defense housing program. Unlike home builders' groups, however, the supposed political and economic evils of subsidized housing did not concern residents. Instead, dissatisfied tenants expressed concern about unhealthy conditions, like cracks in walls and standing water that emitted musty smells and bred mosquitoes—problems that only worsened as the years passed.

Moved to action by inadequate services that affected their families' well-being, white mothers in Armistead Gardens confronted officials who had reneged on a promise to provide children free school bus transportation. Just one day before school started, mothers received housing circulars from the rental office announcing that there would be no bus service for 420 school-aged children. White mothers were furious, and they organized. Protests started locally—first against school and BHA officials. Leslie Ross, Mrs. William J. Proffitt, Ethel Fischer, and Mrs. Dale Ferguson staged a school boycott. The two-day strike drew support from three-fourths of the complex's 800 children who attended elementary and junior high school. The women declared: "When we rented these places, we were assured that our children would be taken care of as far as schools are concerned. We want the authorities to live up to their promise."[30] Ross argued it was "too far and too dangerous" to send children to school on public transit; the trip took an hour and forty-five minutes on two buses.[31]

When the local school board "pass[ed] the buck" to the BHA, which then blamed the federal government, which now owned Armistead Gardens, the four women collected 450 residents' signatures on a petition. The women sent that petition to John M. Carmody, Federal Works Agency administrator, who oversaw the implementation of war housing policy in 1941 before the NHA's formation. Ross, the petition committee chair who worked for the Social Security Administration in Baltimore, asserted: "Maybe we'll get some action there. Until then, the children are going to have to stay home." Ross had moved to Armistead Gardens from Kansas City, Missouri, with her husband and their two children, and by 1945 had developed a record of activism as a member and fundraiser with Armistead Gardens' Civic Club, a social reporter for the tenants' newsletter, and a nurse's volunteer for the Red Cross. Regarding school transportation, Ross declared: "Some [residents] say they will go back home rather than deprive their children of education." BHA's white executive director, Yewell W. Dillehunt, seemed little concerned about tenants' threats: "I don't think it will happen, but if it does, we will just have some empty buildings on our hands." Carmody did not respond directly to tenants. Instead municipal officials—as was their wartime job—mediated the conflict. Cleveland R. Bealmear, the BHA chair, conveyed to parents that the school board awaited federal money to build a school and furnish transportation for Armistead Gardens' students. In the meantime, school officials did order one bus.[32]

In a battle presaging a similar one in the blacks-only Gilmor Homes, white women tenants in Perkins Homes protested the housing authority's plan to ration heat and hot water. Just months after the passage of the Emergency Price Control Act in January 1942, the Office of Price Administration (OPA), which established rationing protocols, contemplated cutting the "normal consumption" of fuel oil by one-third. Baltimore housing officials decided not to wait for the OPA's report delineating the housing authority's fuel-oil allocations. Without federal mandate, local housing officials decided to implement rations early to protect the agency from future shortages. Hearing of the BHA's plan, Perkins Homes' women tenants acted, but unlike many white women during World War II, they did not assume the role of civic stewards who, for instance, monitored rent and price inflation, volunteered for local OPA offices, and encouraged sacrifice as part of citizens' wartime duties. They acted as their families' stewards, not against the war effort, but for a minimum standard of living as residents of defense housing and contributors to the home-front war effort.

White women tenants collected signatures from 500 of the 688 resident families and joined delegations to talk to city officials. Five women, along with their male tenant council president, met with Dillehunt before gathering for a planned mass meeting. One woman, Mrs. Paul Brogley, blamed the housing authority for her fourteen-month-old baby catching pneumonia.[33] White women argued that their husbands could not bathe properly after work. Perkins Homes tenants threatened a rent strike, saying they would not be cowed by a court summons: "No heat, no water, no rent and we'll all go to jail." They claimed that "Mr. Dillehunt has gone a little too far" and, employing rhetoric that conjured the gruesome specters of foreign tyranny, they argued that Perkins Homes "couldn't be much worse" than "a German concentration camp."[34]

While municipal officials wielded power in cities, perturbed tenants, aware that the federal government was in charge, turned to federal officials as final arbiters in local conflicts. Mr. and Mrs. Paul Brogley had planned to go to Washington with Perkins Homes' ten-person delegation. Just one day after tenants' complaints appeared in the *Baltimore Sun*, housing officials called a special meeting. The BHA's commissioners and executive director took seriously tenants' threats to trek to Washington. At the start of the board meeting, Bealmear argued that the housing authority may have acted prematurely—"we kind of went ahead of ourselves"—and suggested providing tenants heat and hot water as usual "until we get the report from the OPA." He continued: "And when we get that, we can bring [the tenant council] in and tell them what the OPA has allowed us to do. If they are not satisfied, let them go to the OPA and have their fight." Halfway through the meeting and after much debate, commissioners agreed that ultimately they did not "want these people running to Washington," nor did Washington "want them running there." Bealmear wanted to keep the authority's "sheets" clean with federal officials and feared that a tenant delegation might raise questions about more than just hot water: "Because when they get into oil they find a lot of trouble with everything else. That is the bad feature."[35]

The housing authority relented. Local commissioners decided to immediately go to the OPA and ask for instructions. They prepared a statement to calm tenant representatives and counter the effects of their hasty action. They strategically laid the blame on OPA and played to tenants' patriotism. The statement read in part: "The Housing Authority has presented this problem to the OPA and will continue to urge that the ration be made adequate to furnish a reasonable solution. We know that our tenants are as patriotic as any other citizens and will realize that we are all called upon to make sacrifices in these war times." In the meantime, the housing board rescinded the hot water rule, which limited hot water to two days a week, and assured tenants that their apartments would be heated to sixty-five degrees.[36]

Black Tenants' Wartime Activism

While black and white tenants had the same landlord and even contended with similar problems, including inadequate services, poor-quality wartime housing, and inflated wartime rents, black tenants experienced disparate treatment. Race influenced operations in defense and low-rent housing just as it did in other spheres of black life like employment and public accommodations. The war did not change the reality of discriminatory treatment. Black tenants and employees continuously confronted white men officials who reinforced the city's status quo. Nepotism and party politics ruled. The applications of potential employees who were Republican (African Americans tended to be Republican on the municipal level) were usually filed away, and the white executive director's family members and friends hired. Yewell Dillehunt hired his brother, William, as maintenance supervisor and paid him a hefty salary. Dillehunt also hired his sister-in-law, his brother's brother-in-law, and thirteen friends whom he gave managerial and supervisory jobs at white complexes.[37]

In a Jim Crow city and program, black people were hired to oversee black public housing, but this did not mean they were treated fairly. A black employee at Douglass Homes, Anthony Malone argued that "the day has come when the Housing Authority of Baltimore should be cleaned up so that it can do the task delegated to it. In order for [the housing authority] to do a good job for the community, it must free itself of race hatred and the petty prejudices."[38] Black manager and supervisor Avon B. Collins resigned twice, initially in 1941 and then again in 1943, arguing that machine politics and racial bias pervaded the agency.[39] Warren W. Weaver described Dillehunt as a politician who was "quite ignorant" without a "sociology background" and "ill-equipped for the job."[40] By 1945, according to the CPHA, tenant criticism surpassed "the stage of ordinary disgruntlement," and black tenants complained the most—about services, rents, repairs, rudeness, and managerial mistreatment.[41] The BHA seemed to lack the three "musts" of good housing management—impartiality, courtesy, and regard for tenants' well-being.[42]

Against this backdrop of racial political partiality, Lottie Hall and the Gilmor Homes Tenant Council was one of several tenant organizations that mobilized against the municipal housing authority. The council's campaign illustrates the existence of black women's activism, strained intraracial tenant-management relations, and wartime discontent. Between 1943 and 1944, during the same years as the struggle over constructing black defense housing, the black female–led tenant council engaged in an extensive battle inside Gilmor Homes. In addition to the debate over heat and hot water, another major concern expressed by the Gilmor council was "the attitude of management." Black tenants might have had black managers, but race did not automatically mute conflict, exposing political and economic diversity within the black community. Before turning to white central administrators, the tenant council had attempted to work with its black manager, J. Logan Jenkins, Jr. The tenant council took seriously its founding charge under the complex's former manager, Avon B. Collins, to "arbitrate and assist the manager in carrying out the desires and best interest of the residents."[43] Unlike Collins, who helped establish tenant councils and publicly criticized the agency, however, Jenkins was handpicked by Dillehunt, looked to the central office for orders, and evaded tenants for months. Jenkins snubbed female tenant leaders and ignored residents' demands. Angered by the manager's inaction and his refusal to dialogue with tenants, Lottie Hall called a complex-wide meeting in December 1943. She invited Jenkins, who repaid tenants by disrupting the "usually orderly manner" of the meeting. Lottie Hall and Hannah Taylor recounted the incident:

> He called us illiterate; said he was operating the project and that it would be run as he saw fit; said he was not interested in tenants' problems and did not need their cooperation; said that tenants should be glad they have somewhere to live at all; [and] said that he could dispose of any tenants' delegation that came to see him in less than five minutes.[44]

Following the condescending tirade, Jenkins accused black tenants of race disloyalty, saying: "You need a white man to tell you everything."[45]

While race governed the unfair treatment of black managers and tenants, status, party politics, and the pressure to succeed mediated tenant-management relations in individual complexes. Jenkins viewed the tenants as "illiterate" and rightly saw their activism as challenging his authority. That the top tenant leaders were working-class black women might have heightened Jenkins's sensitivity, especially in an agency where men possessed managerial control and wielded power.[46] Warren W. Weaver, a black manager at the time, remembered Jenkins as someone who "couldn't stand authority.

See some people get carried away and think that the tenants belong to them. You're servicing the tenants. And if you get confused like that then you're burying yourself."[47] Lottie Hall would have likely agreed with Weaver.

After Jenkins's protracted diatribe at the tenant council meeting, Lottie Hall still attempted to seek an audience with him—despite his threat that he could dispose of a tenant delegation in less than five minutes. But as she and other residents approached Jenkins's office, he retreated through another door and returned some thirty minutes later with two white housing authority officials: Dillehunt and the white manager of Perkins Homes, who had recently negotiated similar tenant demands. Jenkins's reliance upon white housing authority officials to legitimize his position was ironic since the black manager had tongue-lashed aggrieved tenants for supposedly needing white men to tell them everything. Gilmor tenants again departed empty-handed. After months of stonewalling, tenant-management relations reached crisis proportions. Attempted collaboration gave way to confrontation.

While the local housing authority's role as manager and the federal government's role as landlord resulted in greater surveillance of working-class people's daily lives, these relationships also provided tenants with the leverage necessary to resolve disputes. The Gilmor Homes Tenant Council bypassed Baltimore housing officials and sought action from the federal government. Hall and Taylor sent a letter, cosigned by 400 tenants, to Oliver C. Winston, the white director of Region III's federal housing office and the BHA's future executive director. Black women leaders argued that "the interest of the tenants generally in any constructive program of cooperation with management has waned to the point of collapse." In a protest letter dated January 12, 1944, tenant activists laid out their claims. The poor interior conditions have "been called to the attention of the manager and Executive Director over the past 12 months but to-date nothing has been done and neither have we been informed of any intent to correct the condition. This leaves us with the feeling that neither of these two officials are interested in our very real problems as tenants."[48] The battle lasted more than a year. By February 1944, however, tenant activists—Bealmear called them "a disgruntled faction at the project"—had won additional oil for more heat and hot water, although not twenty-four-hour service.[49]

Although relief came with federal intervention, black tenant activists experienced repression for exercising their rights in municipally managed housing—unmasking the contradiction between the wartime rhetoric of citizens' rights and social and political reality. Municipal officials challenged the right of citizen participation, especially when it threatened their status quo governance of public institutions. After Gilmor Homes' resident activists successfully appealed to federal officials and municipal officials were censured, Jenkins banned the politicized tenant council from holding meetings at Gilmor Homes, and central administration officials tried to replace the Hall-led council. The BHA called a tenant meeting in Gilmor Homes' assembly hall and mailed out notices maintaining that "representatives from the various buildings of the project" thought the council should be reorganized. These representatives remained anonymous. The letter instructed tenants to nominate a delegate from their buildings for the new group and to mail in their ballots for tallying. Unlike the Hall-led organization, this proposed committee, according to the BHA, would engage in acceptable organizing—formulating "plans for the pleasure and enjoyment of all tenants."[50] The wartime advocacy of black women residents and the tenant council apparently had transgressed cooperative self-help activities. And the women's brazenness, which reflected working-class pressure politics and citizen engagement during World War II, had obviously unsettled housing officials by threatening municipal control and political bossism.

Council leaders waged a successful countercampaign. They distributed their own letter with the heading "Gossip Is Cheap." Posing the question— "What is wrong with the present tenant council?"—tenant leaders answered it, writing: "Because the present tenant council is trying to make the project a comfortable and pleasant place to live." Hall listed a number of improvements—the hard-won results of tenant council struggles, including an outdoor public telephone and more heat. After listing the social affairs the BHA found acceptable—dances, fashion shows, and jamborees—tenant leaders concluded the letter by asking, "What are we paying rent for?" and urged, "Now! Let's cooperate!!!"[51] A month after the housing authority mailings, tenants had returned less than one-quarter of the ballots. At the housing commissioners' April 19 meeting, Dillehunt requested that Bealmear contact Gilmor residents again "for the vital action of setting up" the steering committee.[52] Apparently tenants had decided. A few years later, Lottie Hall still lobbied for Gilmor tenants at housing authority meetings.

Attempts to squelch black resident activism was not limited to Gilmor Homes. Leroy Parker, the black manager at Banneker, a temporary black defense complex, tried to prevent residents from organizing a tenant council in

1945. In response, seventy tenants appealed to the USHA's successor agency, the FPHA, "to determine their rights in this matter. They did not feel that the Housing Authority dealt fairly or frankly with them."[53] They petitioned to have Parker removed. Parker was transferred to Holabird. If white managers attempted to dismantle and suppress white tenant organizations in similar ways, the extant records remain silent.

Women and the Domestic Home Front

Just as women had marshaled forces in home-front battles against and for black defense housing, they also commandeered spaces inside public housing neighborhoods. Women tenants did not seek to change their ascribed roles as mothers and caretakers of the home. Like the black and white, poor and working-class urban housewives who engaged in food riots, rent strikes, and consumer campaigns in centuries-long traditions of female political participation, women tenants' activism during the war politicized their traditional roles as wives and mothers. As part of the New Deal citizenry and as working-class citizens committed to the home-front war effort, black and white women fulfilled their gender obligations to the family and accepted responsibility for the home. They spearheaded the call for government landlords to furnish comfortable, reasonably priced apartments and adequate services. As advocates for their children, extended families, and fellow tenants, they made demands that highlighted their conventional, "private" gender roles. Asserting their maternal authority, women played key roles in winning concessions from municipal and federal housing officials regarding basic household issues.

The mothers' protests also exposed black and white female tenants' overlapping concerns and the manner in which those concerns were expressed. Their confrontations with white-controlled, male-headed local housing agencies exposed how gender shaped women's protest arguments across race lines. Using their status as the families of war workers and highlighting their domestic duties and motherly roles, black and white women argued for expanding utilities necessary for personal cleanliness and health.

While black and white women's activism reflected the gendered nature of caretaking on the home front and in neighborhood spaces, their rationales were sometimes different. White women's arguments exposed a belief that they and their families provided valuable services to the government, and that meant the government owed them in return. More white women than black women actually worked in war-related industries. In Armistead, for instance, tenants criticized housing officials' seeming inability to provide adequate shopping services for war workers who "devoted their time and efforts to winning the war." The Armistead Civic Club's officers, the majority of whom were women, maintained that the men and women in Armistead Gardens "have learned to understand only methods of high speed production. It is therefore impossible to impress upon them that every possible effort is being made" by slow-moving government officials.[54]

Black tenants argued for a right to services and claimed their status as war workers as well, but they also inferred a broader right to better lives as citizens. Black women and men who took pride in neighborhoods also expressed concern that the BHA did not help them establish "healthy community living," which was considered a path for achieving social advancement. In this sense, black wartime workers and black low-rent tenant pioneers expressed familiar sentiments. Niles Kelley, the Douglass Homes tenant council president in 1946, argued: "My people want to know that their landlord will help them to help themselves. They want to turn away fear and set their minds to making useful citizens out of their children and to living happier lives themselves."[55] Another Douglass Homes tenant since 1942 professed this sentiment, not only as an individual tenant and worker, but also as a tenant activist and Congress of Industrial Organizations (CIO) housing advocate. "One of the long-suffering tenants" who knew "a great deal not only about conditions in the projects but about the feelings of the tenants who live there," Alverta Parnell viewed herself as a defender of low-income people. In black complexes, including Douglass, Gilmor, Somerset, and McCulloh, Parnell helped form a network of leaders to advocate against the housing authority. And like Lottie Hall, Parnell took confrontational stances. Her outspoken advocacy of tenants would make her a target of the white central administration and black managers.

Entering Peacetime

As wartime gave way to peacetime, layoffs, strikes, and changing family circumstances exacerbated tenants' problems. Paying market rent during the war was difficult; afterward, it became even more so. Wartime rent increases in defense housing went into effect as early as 1941. The BHA even raised rental rates in low-rent complexes like Poe, Douglass, and McCulloh homes. Although they could not exceed the private market rate, increased rents limited war workers' and low-income tenants' spending power and often strained household budgets. Citywide, rent increases elicited sharp criticism from renters in private and public housing; 75 percent of the complaints came from African Americans. Frances Morton, who worked for the federal Fair Rent Commission office in Baltimore, maintained that on some days whole blocks of city residents came in to complain. In protesting the high rental rates at Gilmor Homes in 1944, Hall and Taylor wrote: "The present levels are already as high as most family budgets can afford and [the] increasing cost of living generally is putting more strain on family budgets every day."[56]

Low-wage work, even in the industrial workforce, further hampered African Americans' chances to stay solvent, improve their economic positions, and increase their standard of living during and after the war. In their efforts to obtain skilled and better-paying work, black men and women workers were constantly embroiled in battles with white workers, industrialists, union rank and file, and even the U.S. Employment Service (USES).[57] Black workers did not accept their exclusion resignedly. They staged protests with the help of sympathetic union locals and filed Fair Employment Practices complaints. But these measures did not stymie discrimination. For instance, black men who had trained in the maritime service as firemen served as "Mess Attendants" on ships "sent out . . . from Baltimore Only," and in the major Baltimore industries, Bethlehem Shipyard and Martin Aircraft moguls refused to hire or were slow to promote black workers.[58] Some black women who attended training classes did find jobs in war industries. But by April 1943 black women only represented 3 percent of the total war industry workforce, compared to 20 percent for white women. Most black women still encountered tremendous hurdles; they were often steered toward work as charwomen and domestics or toward menial municipal jobs.[59] After the war, black men and women workers and veterans experienced similar treatment. They remained second-tier citizens; race still excluded them from educational institutions, public accommodations, and well-paying jobs. Black men and women earned less than their white counterparts, and this affected black workers' ability to provide food and shelter for themselves and their families.

By November 1945, three months after VJ Day, industrial employment in Baltimore had dropped to almost half of its wartime peak.[60] All workers suffered, but black workers filled the unemployment lines quicker. Many African-American men and women who had secured defense jobs lost them. Numerous black women, including Shirley Wise's mother and grandmother, who worked at Edgewood Arsenal and Bethlehem Steel in Sparrows Point, rejoined most black women in low-paying domestic and service jobs. On November 19, 1946, Douglass Homes residents Mrs. and Mr. Alvin A. Johnson wrote Mayor McKeldin about the "great difficulty" they encountered raising a family while paying wartime market rents in low-income public housing: "We feel that we are being imposed upon as law abiding citizens. The war is over and war rent should be over too."[61]

Alongside these new daily realities of demobilization after World War II, federal policies also shaped the lives of tenants, black and white. On February 26, 1946, the president ended the emergency use of subsidized homes for war workers, and the federal government began disposing of its temporary wartime trailers and housing complexes. Municipal authorities acquired some housing complexes from the federal government, operating them as low-income complexes, demolishing unwanted complexes, or selling them to tenant cooperatives, as in the case of Armistead Gardens. The USHA also ordered the return of subsidized apartments that were on loan to the federal government to their "original" purpose—housing low-income families. Responding to federal mandates, Baltimore housing officials began purging subsidized housing of over-income tenants, many of whom were war worker families. In cities across the nation, local governments, which had already become "giant landlords," became "mass evictors."[62] In May 1946, some 41 percent of Baltimore's public housing tenants received eviction notices.[63]

These government evictions did not occur without protest from black and white tenants. In Baltimore, mothers and wives begged Mayor McKeldin to intervene. Amelia Boyer, who lived in the whites-only O'Donnell Heights, wrote McKeldin without her husband's knowledge, because he would surely "laugh at me." Boyer told the mayor that she and her husband could not afford any higher than their $38 rent and that she worked intermittently to supplement her husband's income. Fulfilling the domestic ideal of female homemaker and male breadwinner was difficult enough. Eviction would only worsen their circumstances. "I have off and on all my married life had to go out and work so the children could be clothed not too good but decently. I or rather we have no savings as their [sic] is never any left to save. It's always sickness or some other thing."[64] Black women also asked for extensions on behalf of their families. The eviction notices fired up war workers and veterans as well. In June 1946, 185 white Latrobe residents, 122 of them veterans, protested. In the blacks-only Gilmor Homes, more than 200 tenants vowed to fight to keep their homes, and one tenant suggested that residents "get the CIO and NAACP behind us." The CIO and the NAACP had supported black defense workers' causes and argued that housing was a basic human need, a worker's right, and a civil right.[65]

The wartime contract that had provided defense housing to war workers and their families was being liquidated and replaced with expanded homeownership opportunities out of reach to some white families and most black families. This shift left many war workers, who had depended on subsidized housing, anxious and upset about their fate in postwar America. For African Americans, holding onto housing was particularly critical given their overall exclusion from the housing market. The establishment of FHA and VA mortgage insurance programs ultimately gave white citizens and veterans a real chance at independence through home ownership. But black people benefited little. The real estate and banking industries—the primary agencies that facilitated citizens' use of government programs—refused to sell houses to black people, guarantee loans, or provide reasonable interest rates. Even the federal government had built barriers into its mortgage programs that excluded black people. The practice of redlining (drawing a red line around a "high-risk" area on residential security maps used for assessing loans) labeled black or heterogeneous neighborhoods as bad investments, further dissuading banks and lending agencies from approving black applications. Given the housing and job market situations in postwar America, even some blacks who could afford to leave subsidized housing were reluctant to do so.

Tenant leaders like Parnell, a member of the CIO Housing Committee, and the CPHA rallied on behalf of tenants threatened by over-income evictions, as well as those who had dwindling resources and found themselves in debt to the housing authority. The BHA board, which had a new commissioner in the Reverend Dr. Don Frank Fenn (also a CPHA member) halted the immediate expulsion of over-income tenants. He cited a federal OPA regulation that held tenants could only be evicted if adequate shelter existed. The purging of tenants would not be complete until the early 1950s.[66]

In addition to fighting evictions, tenant, labor, and housing advocates gathered evidence of rent overcharges and slow readjustments. These activists publicized how black and white managers consistently filed eviction papers in People's Court. Florence Stanley, a black tenant who lived in Douglass Homes, was summoned to court for nonpayment of $32.15. The judge dismissed Stanley's case because she only owed $9.65 for April. The woman clerk, who closed her rent account books early, simply had assumed that Florence Stanley would not pay her May rent and charged her as delinquent—even before the rent was officially due. Between January 1942 and 1946, the BHA filed in People's Court more than 17,000 cases, 20 percent of all rent cases. Yet, public housing tenants represented only 4 percent of the city's renters. While the court dismissed over three-quarters of the cases, tenants nonetheless feared being put out. Losing a day's work as well as experiencing embarrassment, tenants summoned to court wove stories of desperation—of missing meals, selling furniture, and borrowing money just to pay their rent.[67]

In April 1946, white newspaper reporter and CPHA member Lois Felder publicized tenants' daily protests and hardship cases, many African American, in the *Baltimore Evening Sun*. For instance, Somerset Courts tenants since January 1944, Robert and Estella Gates had three children. In 1945, Robert Gates requested a rent decrease; his income had dropped to $1,800 annually. According to Felder: "Under the Housing Authority rent scale, his charge should have been $30 monthly, but it remained at $43 until January [1946]. By that time, Mr. Gates had a balance of $170.85."[68] Upon reexamination, the black manager, William Haynes, finally reduced their rent, but they still had to pay their overdue balance. By January 1947 Robert Gates's income dropped again to $1,560 annually at the Chemical and Pigment Company, where he earned about 75 cents for eight-hour workdays, five days a week. Estella Gates, who had previously held a job, fell and broke her arm and was no longer able to earn wages. Without two steady incomes, their overdue balance increased. Housing commissioners eventually evicted the Gates family.[69] Felder documented several similar cases of slow rent reductions among Somerset, Douglass, Gilmor, and Sollers residents.

With all the drama about rent reduction claims, black tenant leaders objected to the agency's "lack of encouragement to council heads attempting to aid tenants in their rent-paying problems."[70] The white director of housing management, James W. Rowe, denied tenant representatives access to tenants' information or to individual tenant-management meetings. At an April 1946 board meeting, the commissioners, including the two recent CPHA appointees, however, reversed this practice and affirmed tenant leaders' right to counsel and to represent tenants.[71] Less than a year later, Parnell's role in the investigation of a Gilmor Homes family's hardship case instigated conflict between officials and housing advocates again. In the process of investigating the case, a black employee discussed the investigation with Frances Morton, who had initially alerted housing officials of the family's difficulties. Apparently, Morton, without authorization, shared information with Parnell, who then shared it with the family. While available records do not discuss the substance of the comments, whatever Parnell conveyed caused a commotion, upsetting the family and housing officials.[72]

In an era of growing communist hysteria, tenant advocacy and anti-establishment community battles became suspect. Rowe cast doubt on Parnell's actions by questioning her patriotism. Citing the report of Douglass Homes' black manager, John Hazzard, Rowe claimed Parnell "may have communistic connections, which, under the circumstances, are not surprising, and have been suspected for some time." According to Hazzard, a tenant had claimed that Parnell, a CIO member, "tried to sell him some Communistic papers. He did not buy nor read the material, but did give her 10 [cents] as a contribution." Hazzard's memo also impugned Parnell's character and effectively questioned her status as an upstanding citizen and a respectable woman. Hazzard wrote that she helped a neighbor "devour a fifth of intoxicating liquors. While there she became so inebriated, she could barely walk home."[73]

Parnell's organizing efforts and affiliation with the CIO—and maybe even her desire for personal power and prestige—were represented as anti-democratic, anti-American behavior. But for Parnell, working with the CIO obviously made quite a bit of sense. During the 1930s and 1940s, the labor organization had expressed democratic, albeit limited, racial impulses. CIO officials supported employment opportunities, housing construction, and public housing reform for black workers—even sometimes against the wishes of the white rank and file. While the CIO stopped short of pressing for full racial equality in the workplace, the BUL executive director from 1931 to 1942, Edward S. Lewis, argued, "The C.I.O. has demonstrated its democratic philosophy of organization not only here in Baltimore, but all over the country."[74]

Parnell's link to the CIO, which had Communist party (CP) supporters, however, provided housing staff with a potent weapon to criticize her actions. As early as the 1930s, "Communist control haunted CIO organizers," and employers saw "a Red behind every CIO button."[75] In 1937, Baltimore

CIO activists held a conference, supported and publicized by the Communist party, to establish industrial union councils and "give labor a united voice." In the late 1940s, the CIO's connections with the Progressive party also raised the specter of communism since CP members unabashedly supported the Progressive party's presidential candidate, Henry Wallace. Baltimore's Progressive party was "the first official branch . . . on the Atlantic seaboard," and the majority of 630 delegates were young people and women. Fifteen percent were black.[76] Wallace, who was Roosevelt's former vice president and Harry Truman's secretary of commerce, campaigned for full democracy, peace, and freedom from want—the very things black working-class people sought. The CIO, however, to prevent its image from being further tarnished with business and elected officials, did subsequently purge its ranks of CP members and ended its support of the political party. Even so, Parnell's linkages to the CIO, the specter of communism, her protests of unfair treatment, and her demands that state officials be more attentive cast her and her actions as disloyal and troublesome.

Parnell confronted administrators about numerous issues that reflected black tenants' working-class status and exposed her compassion for tenants' health, family, and daily living conditions. In August 1946 Parnell wrote housing commissioner Furman Templeton, a black man and CPHA member, to complain about the unresponsive and nonchalant attitude of Charles A. Coles, a central management administrator, and John Hazzard. She questioned why tenants, who had been promised new window shades in January, had not received them as of August. She advocated for Douglass Homes tenants Ben Melbon and his paralyzed wife, who received relief, lived in a roach-infested apartment, and had to pay $1.65 for an exterminator. Parnell argued that the Melbons were "not able to pay this amount as it comes out of their food allowance." Parnell also inquired why Hazzard refused to allow John C. Mabe's sister to move in. Mabe's sister quit her job to care for her elderly, "feeble" mother. Mabe earned only $22 a week and could not pay his and his sister's rent. In yet another case, in McCulloh Homes, Parnell wondered why, after five years, Betty Davis and her husband, who had regularly paid their rent in twenty-five-cent pieces (because Mr. Davis was paid for his church work in quarters) could no longer do so.[77]

Housing managers and central office staff considered Parnell a nuisance. When Parnell called Coles about the window shades, he treated it as a "joke." When Parnell talked to Coles about the infestation of the Melbons' apartment, he told Parnell "that they should not have vermin in their apartment and then spraying would not be necessary." No matter that tenants at Banneker, Gilmor, Somerset, Douglass, and the whites-only Latrobe complained about bedbug, roach, rat, and mice infestations.[78] When Parnell received such responses, she merely bypassed uncooperative managers and staff and contacted the newly appointed housing commissioners, Fenn and Templeton. In doing so she strategically took advantage of the internal shifts of power in the BHA. In her letter to Templeton, Parnell relayed her disgust: "Isn't that a nice answer for Mr. Coles to give me about these poor, unfortunate people?" In her letter regarding the Mabe family's eldercare case, Parnell wrote: "The daughter is not living with the brother now but she is there every day and some nights except Saturday night until Monday morning. . . . Will you please see if there is anything you can do to get permission for this man's sister to stay and look after the mother[?]"[79]

White central office administrators and black managers of the complexes where Parnell agitated sought to curtail her influence. In particular, Rowe claimed that Parnell sponsored a "campaign to discredit the decisions and activities of a number of our Negro managers." Rowe sent Dillehunt a memo and letters from three black managers. Again exposing intraracial conflict, these letters argued that Parnell overstepped her proper role as a Douglass tenant council representative. Otho P. Pinkett, the black manager of the year-old Cherry Hill Homes, grumbled about Parnell's impetuousness and unwarranted intrusions in affairs not of her concern. Pinkett discussed the Robert Chase case. A prospective Cherry Hill Homes tenant, Chase looked at a five-room apartment and found the floors and stove satisfactory, but the walls dingy. Saying maintenance could not paint the apartment for several days, Pinkett offered Chase the paint to do it himself. Chase, who accepted the offer, told his uncle, who worked at Douglass Homes. His uncle asked Parnell to intervene. Parnell then called Pinkett and demanded that maintenance men, not the tenant, paint the apartment. Pinkett stated that Parnell "threatened to expose me to the Mayor of the City, or to any other people necessary if I refused to comply with her request." He accused Parnell of trying to build up a following at Cherry Hill Homes.[80] Hazzard recognized Parnell's "good work," but also maintained that she often operated on faulty assumptions and methods and was "a person who craves power."[81]

The Role of Tenant Councils in the 1940s

Lottie Hall's and Alverta Parnell's activism signifies more than the actions of individuals. Their involvement and battles reveal the roles of tenant councils as advocates for residents and as forces of contention. Tenant councils had become clearinghouses for tenants' concerns in addition to spaces of community building. In fact, tenant council leaders publicly objected "to authority officials, known as project services supervisors, guiding programs too closely" while "discouraging" tenants' political work, like seeking rent adjustments, repairs, and better treatment.[82] Tenant councils also complained about being stifled, as in Gilmor and Banneker homes.

In Cherry Hill, Douglass, Banneker, and Gilmor, black tenants consulted and relied on tenant councils and their leaders. Warren W. Weaver, then Sollers' manager, acknowledged tenant leaders' influence, saying they often persuaded residents to rely on the tenant councils to solve disputes. Weaver, who said that his most "unpleasant responsibility was evicting families with children," expressed concern about distressed tenants who were "disposed to recognize" Parnell and Mae Gould, Sollers' tenant council president. Both women had successfully convinced "a segment of the population that they are the authorized tenant representatives for this Authority." Weaver asserted that because tenants believed "outside interest and/or tenant council representation is necessary before approaching the management office with personal hardship problems," tenants caused themselves "inconveniences by loss of time in properly reporting their circumstances."[83] Unlike Los Angeles's housing authority, which "initiated a collective bargaining procedure through which tenants can deal with management" and which viewed the resident councils as an "official" voice, Baltimore's black and white housing officials met organized tenant activity with arguments resembling anti-union rhetoric.[84] Weaver characterized Parnell's and Gould's advocacy as "unnecessary interference from disinterested persons," which put the manager at a "disadvantage." He concluded his memo: "No individual, especially another tenant, should enjoy the license of representing tenants in their personal affairs."[85]

While white residents also had tenants' groups, which mobilized in individual complexes and criticized housing policies and practices, Parnell's brand of activism in the black community seemed to cause particular consternation. Rowe had lamented that Parnell had "able assistants in what might be called a local representative, who distorts every possible circumstance to the detriment of the Manager and of the Authority, according to Mrs. Parnell's own pattern."[86] Parnell's activism on behalf of black tenants citywide once again forced BHA staff to reconsider its policy on third-party advocates. At a February 26, 1947, board meeting, commissioners reviewed the "interference" memos regarding Parnell. McKeldin-appointed commissioners were more likely to support Parnell's activism, but they did express ambivalence. Furman Templeton, who talked with Parnell often, argued that "many times she was right and many times wrong in her statement." Mrs. Henry Corner, a new board member and also a CPHA member, supported Parnell's advocacy role; Corner argued that in several cases regarding rent reduction because of children, "Mrs. Parnell helped." The commission reaffirmed tenants' rights to have third-party representation. But to protect tenants' privacy, the board stipulated that families had to accompany representatives when they reviewed personal files. While this stipulation did not prevent continued advocacy, it limited representatives' ability to gather information independently.[87]

Women's Networks and the Assault on the BHA

The municipal housing agency always had its critics among social reformers and civil rights advocates. Wartime conditions, however, brought the problems to a head. During the mid-1940s, activists, who worked to depose the housing authority of its inept and intransigent leadership, took advantage of the federal government's wartime and even immediate postwar role as landlord.

Witnessing the daily travails of public housing tenants and the bad management practices, the CPHA's executive director, Frances Morton, spearheaded a campaign to attack the paternalistic, real estate–controlled, nepotistic housing authority. Meanwhile, Parnell emerged as an advocate for black tenants in Baltimore's public and defense housing and also as part of an interracial and cross-class network of women who served as watchdogs over the BHA during and after the war. In this domestic home-front battle, Morton strategically planted and relied on key white women in CPHA and labor circles to expose and eventually facilitate the BHA's takeover. Morton asked Marion Gutman, who edited a housing journal, to take a BHA public relations job, solicited the help of Lois Felder, and orchestrated the appointment of friend and CPHA vice president Mrs. Henry Corner to the BHA board of commissioners. Morton also garnered support from Sylvia Boethe, also a CPHA member and secretary of the Baltimore Industrial Union Council–CIO—and Alverta Parnell. In fact, Parnell played a critical role in this network's first publicized action against the housing authority. Parnell provided statements signed by tenants for the CIO Housing Committee's December 1945 report, which charged the BHA with "rent violations, discrimination against Negroes, failure to answer complaints, and growing mistrust and fear of the Housing Authority among tenants."[88] No wonder municipal housing officials were wary of Parnell. Not only was she mobilizing in black complexes, forming tenant networks, and a CIO member, she was working with white social reformers citywide to mount a public assault against the agency.

Armed with complaints, initiative, evidence, and broad support, the CPHA captured the attention of federal officials, who as the ultimate landlord during wartime, investigated the housing authority. The BHA had already garnered the attention of federal officials because of the tumultuous political battles over constructing black defense housing and black and white tenants' complaints to federal officials between 1942 and 1944. The NHA's regional director, John Kervick, who led an investigation of the housing authority in 1944, maintained that 90 percent of the property managed by the housing authority was in poor shape due to lack of maintenance. Under maintenance supervisor and Yewell Dillehunt's brother William Dillehunt, the BHA spent an average of 67 cents per unit each month on maintenance versus the national average of $4 per unit monthly. Kervick described the BHA as "more troublesome than any other in the area." A year later, Kervick maintained that the BHA was only 50 percent effective and still suffered "mismanagement and bad public relations."[89]

As the activism of black and white women showed, general disarray existed throughout the city's program, and many felt it was time to uproot the problem. Throughout the 1940s, black and white tenants were up in arms. When housing staff called a meeting in 1946, black and white tenant council representatives showed up, believing that maybe, just maybe, they would finally make headway on their demands. But when the staff began jabbering about the distribution of office publications and an essay contest for children, some twenty tenant leaders "grabbed" the meeting and insisted the housing authority address their grievances. They then formed a short-lived, biracial citywide tenant committee. The CPHA also verified the mismanagement and corruption of the BHA by conducting a study that pooled evidence from eleven tenant councils—eight in black complexes and three in white ones. Alongside the testimonies of Parnell, the CIO Housing Committee, and tenant leaders like Lottie Hall, the CPHA encouraged the BHA's board of commissioners, with its two recently appointed CPHA members, to ask for an independent FPHA investigation of the municipal agency.

While ultimately successful, the investigation was not accepted joyfully or with open minds by incumbent board members who were Jackson-appointed holdovers. Real estate lawyer, financier, and BHA vice president Samuel H. Hoffberger expressed resentment. He "objected most emphatically to anyone making a study of himself or the Authority, and further he did not consider himself on trial by anyone." Bealmear, the board chair, argued that the housing authority's critics "will never be satisfied" and "doubted very much if a study conducted by anyone would prevent them from continuing their criticisms at intervals." Bealmear instead urged the board of commissioners to discuss and remedy the situations by meeting with managers and staff. Fenn and Templeton, the only two CPHA members at the time, however, encouraged a "study," not an "investigation" of the BHA to improve future operations. Templeton even tried to assure Hoffberger that the study would be a "review of the policies and operating procedures—without reference to personalities." After more debate, the board resolved to ask FPHA officials to conduct the study, especially since they were "stockholders" and the board was merely the "director." They also decided to meet with public housing managers in an attempt to solve current and to offset future problems.[90]

Activists called for the resignation of the Mayor Jackson–appointed board members and Dillehunt and his cronies. Parnell consistently criticized Jackson's appointees and their hard-nosed, unsympathetic, and dismissive policies. In November 1946 Parnell congratulated Mayor McKeldin for responding to CPHA and tenant protests, which had provided a preponderance of critical evidence for Baltimore's "most prolonged, and controversial reform efforts"—the transformation of the housing authority from a nepotistic business to a technocratic social welfare agency.[91] McKeldin had already appointed Fenn and Templeton. Parnell maintained, however, that good works continued to be "held back because of the hold-over Jackson appointees," and "it will be a happy day for tenants" when McKeldin replaced Hoffberger, Bealmear, and Dillehunt as well.[92]

Unapologetic in her belief in women's superior administrative power and nurturing character, Parnell also publicly supported Morton's call and McKeldin's plan "to appoint a woman as commissioner." Parnell argued that women possessed empathy and therefore "can understand the difficulties and needs of poor people in a way that men can never do." Mr. and Mrs. Alvin Johnson of Douglass Homes also encouraged Mayor McKeldin to appoint more compassionate people. The Johnsons requested a woman, because "a woman can understand the family struggle and hardships from the high cost of living at a point where men are unable to do so."[93] Women were most familiar with the home, children, budgets, and bills—and balancing all those needs.

The woman whom McKeldin nominated as commissioner was Mrs. Henry Corner. Corner had a history of social welfare activism as a YWCA president, and her husband served as president of Goodwill Industries. Several city council members attacked her as un-American. Like Parnell's critics, Corner's detractors labeled her a "socialist and maybe communist. If she gets in, we shall be in danger of the socialization of the whole real estate business!" Her attorney, H. Warren Buckler, Jr., who also was CPHA's counsel and later was elected to the city council as an independent, defended Corner. Buckler argued that the all-male city council resented Corner because she was a "woman and because a non-machine 'people's organization' backed her."[94] After an intense battle, McKeldin named Corner to the BHA board in 1947. No woman had ever been appointed to the housing board; when it came to positions of power, the BHA was primarily a male and racially segregated preserve. With the appointment of Corner and Walter I. Seif, CPHA members controlled the entire board, and the male preserve of BHA was broken up.

A couple of months after Yewell Dillehunt resigned in May 1947, Oliver C. Winston, director of FPHA's Region III, became executive director of Baltimore's housing authority. Armed with twenty years of housing experience, Winston, along with the board of commissioners and new staff, began the task of reorganizing the housing authority, assessing the effectiveness of managers, and responding to 167 recommendations made by the FPHA in its study. By 1948, 534 jobs were reclassified, 113 employees had resigned and another 134 were fired, and 367 new employees were hired, including Ellis Ash, the new director of management. And in the process of assessing whether to retain, dismiss, or place on probation BHA managers, Ash fired Jenkins, after concluding that Jenkins had poor relations with his staff, maintenance crews, and tenants. According to Ash, Jenkins's "personnel attitudes [were] dictatorial and uncompromising"; he was "prone to heckle" and "openly display[ed] his temper before the public"; and his "tenant relations [were] very unsatisfactory." Ash determined: "The best interests of the Authority would be served by separation."[95] In 1949, Parker, about whom Banneker Homes tenants had complained, was charged with embezzlement and fired.[96] Jackson's Democratic boss system finally had given way to an administration that privileged expertise in social and management relations.

Conclusion

As citizens of a burgeoning welfare state and participants in the war against fascism, working-class people resisted autocratic rule and clamored for freedom from want in neighborhoods—and cohorts of women helped to lead the way. As early as 1941, home-front "soldiers"—black and white women tenants—contested unhealthy conditions and clamored for services. While their activism may have been a hidden story, it is not a surprising fact. Women have a historical record of politicizing their roles as mothers and wives and acting on behalf of their homes, their families, and the community, especially during wartime. Women tenants' wartime activism reflected the concerns of black and white working people. White working-class women in Armistead Gardens and Perkins Homes struggled to make the housing authority more responsive. And black working-class women like Hall and Taylor and Parnell alongside outspoken white middle-class women reformers dared to question the competency of BHA's central administration and managers. As political activists fighting for working-class people's rights in the public realm, they departed from the constraining effect of traditional gender norms. Instead, they used their domestic roles to carve out space as civic activists and entered the public and political realm on behalf of families and communities.

While black women took a publicly aggressive, arguably "unrespectable" stance in their battles against housing officials, the quest for respectability did not simply disappear. Alongside better services and fair rents, black tenants still desired social respectability and, increasingly, respectful treatment. These black women's aggressive stances, in particular against subservience and exclusion in urban America, portended another not-so-distant era of black women's activism—just about two decades away.

Shifting Landscapes PART II

Shifting Landscapes in Postwar Baltimore 3

Poe Homes' pioneer resident, Clara Gordon, had made a fairly comfortable home in public housing. But within a few years, that began to change. The happy times of courtship, marital bliss, and homemaking had waned. Her husband wanted to be boss in the household and was a philanderer in the streets. "I tell the truth," Gordon stated. "A spade is a spade is a spade." Furthermore, claimed Gordon, her husband did not possess the zeal for or faith in education that she did. And this was no small point. Gordon believed that through education "you could move. And he didn't feel that way." Deciding "to be who I am" and maintaining that she could do just as well alone, the homemaker took a job as an interviewer for the housing authority in 1945, and her husband moved out. At times, she had to work two or three jobs— not just to make ends meet, but with the hope of saving money for her children's post–high school education. By the time her children finished high school, the couple had divorced. For Clara Gordon, staying in Poe Homes made her rocky road easier.[1]

In 1948, the Edges family moved into Somerset Courts, a subsidized housing complex built during the war years near Douglass Homes in east Baltimore. A thirty-something female head of household, Mary Edges had eight children. Her husband, who had worked at Sparrows Point and supported the family, had died five years earlier of congestive heart failure when their newborn twins were just nine months old. Residents of a rundown row house, Mary Edges and her children had to find somewhere else to stay when the city condemned the property. A four-bedroom apartment on Young Court in Somerset became their home. Recalled Jean Edges Sherrod: "She felt that the project was the . . . safest place for her being a single parent to bring [us] up, you know." Mary Edges received money from her husband's Social Security and from the welfare department. Around 1950, with her youngest children now in school, Mary Edges went to nursing school and began working night shifts at different hospitals to make ends meet.[2]

Mothers with children were not the only black families entering public housing in the postwar decades. Mary and William Hynes, who had three children, moved into Murphy Homes when it opened in 1963, because they "couldn't afford no other place." William Hynes only earned about $50 a week from a maintenance job at a church near the housing complex. From 1948 to 1961, he had operated a crane in a plant, but he "put it down" because the plant's acidic fumes "wasn't good for you." Mary Hynes also worked; she packed bottles at a glass company and repaired and sewed army fatigues in the early war years. After the war, however, she raised her children and performed domestic work two or three days a week.[3]

These snippets of the Gordons', Edgeses', and Hyneses' lives illustrate how marital discord, death, job loss, low-wage work, medical problems, and other life-changing situations threatened families' economic security and made paying for basic necessities, including shelter, a challenging and stressful proposition. For mothers without husbands, public housing provided affordable shelter. For black families who lived in dilapidated housing or in urban renewal zones, public complexes served as replacement housing. For financially distressed black and white Baltimoreans, public housing remained a tool in their survival arsenal. Public housing therefore became home to blacks, whites, single mothers, husbands and wives, children, the elderly, and the disabled—all of whom, in their struggle to survive, resorted to the government for help.

It was help that some city officials, including the overhauled municipal housing authority's new board and new executive director, were committed to providing. Believing that "former slum dwellers" responded "to the stimulus of good housing," the BHA board's chair, the Reverend Don Frank Fenn, expressed an "urgent need for decent dwellings."[4] He proposed a postwar housing program that was part of a coordinated municipal redevelopment effort and called for the construction of 10,000 apartments over six years.

But while the housing authority rallied around low-rent housing, the changes accompanying postwar migration, redevelopment, and urban transformation spurred new concerns. BHA staff increasingly became distressed by the entrenched poverty of its newest tenants. The new BHA executive director, Oliver C. Winston, originally had a vision—to see public and private housing, low-rent and middle-income communities developed together to prevent economic ghettos. For Winston believed that "an association based solely on income is unhealthy and unnatural, and is a menace to community spirit."[5] Not only did the mixed-income communities that Winston had envisioned not come to pass, but tenants' declining economic status, which accompanied other changes, like the rising percentage of single-mother families and racial turnover, troubled officials. By 1964 in public housing, single mothers represented the largest subgroup of families (though still not a numerical majority), and 79 percent of all tenants were African Americans.[6] These racial and economic changes unveil the shifting landscapes as well as the complicated challenges that working-class women and men confronted in postwar Baltimore.

Postwar Poverty and Subsidized Housing

The changing demographics of public housing in the postwar era reflected not only an expanding black population and racial isolation, but also growing poverty in cities. After World War II, many working-class black people migrating to and remaining in central cities suffered disproportionately from financial difficulties. Layoffs and plant closures in Baltimore trimmed the number of available jobs for working-class people. Between 1947 and 1958, industrial employment dropped 7.6 percent. Between 1947 and 1963, "the city lost 123 industries and more than 17,000 manufacturing jobs."[7] And with the return of white veterans home, black workers began losing blue-collar jobs and had to resort to service and seasonal work or unemployment lines. By 1950, the median income of black tenants was $1,054 below whites; by 1953, that differential had grown to $1,500.[8]

Low-wage, low-skilled employment kept black workers impoverished. In 1951, 75 percent of black tenant families and 52 percent of applicants had at least one person working, yet they still qualified for low-rent housing.[9] According to a 1951 study of occupational distribution in Gilmor, McCulloh, and Cherry Hill homes, black workers held similar jobs as "Negroes in the community as a whole. This would not be true of the occupational distribution of workers in the low-rent white project. A much greater proportion of the total Negro population is concentrated in the low-income group of which the project residents are a segment." In Gilmor Homes, 25 percent of the primary workers in 1950 held operative jobs as truck drivers, machine operators, and chauffeurs. Nineteen percent were laborers, 13 percent worked as barbers, porters, and charwomen, and 8 percent were building service workers. Seventy-one percent of the primary workers in Cherry Hill and 67 percent of those in McCulloh were similarly distributed.[10]

Numerous black tenants' increasing inability to pay their rents—as illustrated by Alverta Parnell's and CPHA's advocacy—divulged their dire circumstances. So did their demand for public housing. In 1947 black people submitted 70 percent of the public housing applications and renewed their leases more often than did white tenants. In white complexes the residency turnover rate was almost ten percentage points higher. Since white people moved out of public housing more frequently, white applicants had a shorter wait. They could receive an apartment in a year, maybe even in a few months or less, especially since the housing authority still had whites-only complexes even after official desegregation in 1954. In 1959 Anna Warren, her husband, and their five children moved into Claremont Homes, which housed only white families until 1967. Before relocating to Claremont, the Warrens had rented a three- or four-room house with no indoor toilet, which meant they lived in substandard conditions. A few weeks after applying for public housing, the Warrens received an apartment.[11]

White tenants not only had a "greater choice of housing accommodations," but also a "greater opportunity to improve their wage earning prospects quickly." The federal government facilitated the growth of white suburban communities while doing very little to combat inequality and discrimination in cities.[12] The FHA insured mortgages in stable, racially homogeneous, white neighborhoods and even supported restrictive covenants to promote that stability through 1950—two years after the U.S. Supreme Court declared such covenants illegal in *Shelley v. Kraemer*.[13] In Baltimore, "the suburban migration of the late 1940s and 1950s was so exclusively white that few developers imagined it could be otherwise."[14] And while industrial production in Baltimore had decreased, the surrounding counties saw expansion, and their burgeoning white populations experienced prosperity.

The decrease in the city's white population—175,000 between 1950 and 1960 alone—was accompanied by a continuous rise in the number of black people residing in Baltimore, the result of natural increase and migration from the South. The black population increased by 60,000 between 1940 and 1950 and by 40,000 (another 45 percent) between 1950 and 1960.

Black migration to cities, the demand for more black housing, and middle-class and working-class whites fleeing cities forced open neighborhoods once off-limits to African Americans, transforming the urban geography of race and class. Middle-class African Americans, who sought newer, better residences, forced the expansion of racial residential boundaries. For instance, the racial divide along west Baltimore's Fulton Avenue corridor, which had been threatened but preserved in the early 1940s, had collapsed by the mid-1940s. As black people inherited hand-me-down urban housing and eventually secondhand suburbs through the fear mongering of real estate speculation, they moved farther away from the central city. This movement of financially better-off black people enhanced economic isolation in inner cities even as new housing opportunities opened up. Working-class black families, who could not muster the resources to pay inflated rents or mortgages outside the central city, remained in overcrowded, decaying neighborhoods increasingly devoid of blue-collar industries. A similar trend occurred in public housing. As the local housing authority began removing over-income tenants and disposing of war housing, subsidized housing lost its better-off residents just as a larger percentage of poorer black and white people applied. This trend, alongside the rise in single-mother families and public assistance recipients, became a topic of ongoing debate among housing officials beginning in the early 1950s.

Gender and Economic Crises

The number of welfare clients/tenants in public housing grew, partially the result of an increase in the number of the unemployed, the elderly, and single mothers raising children—exposing the feminization of poverty in postwar cities. In particular, fewer resources and altered families landed plenty of women on ADC, in public housing, or both. Rudell Martin's and Shirley Wise's life stories, in particular, help illustrate the economic struggles of single mothers and why they needed government assistance. Rudell Martin was born in 1938 in Norfolk. Martin's father worked at the Norfolk naval yard. When her parents separated in the 1950s, Rudell Martin, her two sisters, brother, and mother, Rudell Hinton, moved to Baltimore where her mother earned little money as a hospital food handler. Her mother tried to apply for ADC, but an existing court order for child support in Virginia thwarted her attempt. For even though Rudell Martin's father did not fulfill his obligations, the Baltimore welfare department included his potential contribution as part of her mother's income. Once the family had lived in Baltimore a year, Rudell Martin's mother applied for public housing.[15]

Widowhood, disability, and teenage pregnancy affected Shirley Wise's family. Around 1950, Shirley Wise's mother, Mary Savilla Blackwell Foy, who years earlier had fallen through a substandard kitchen floor, started having back and leg problems. Her mother went in for surgery and came out paralyzed. For the next four years, her mother was an inpatient at Baltimore City Hospital. In the meantime, the twelve- or thirteen-year-old Shirley Wise, the oldest child next to her half brother, took care of her siblings with the help of her paternal grandmother and women neighbors, especially Lucille "Celie" White. Fondly remembered as Wise's "second mom," the married housewife with ten children often "fed the whole neighborhood." Only after three and a half years, when the state intervened, did the teenage Shirley's family break up: "This is when we were placed in foster homes. I was sixteen then." Wise's mother slowly recovered, but never regained the use of her legs. A decade after she first applied for public housing, Wise's mother, an unemployed paraplegic who now depended on welfare, was finally accepted. She moved into Poe Homes. Within a year of her mother coming home, Shirley Wise became pregnant and dropped out of the eleventh grade. In 1955, when the city's first high-rise public housing complex opened, the family left west Baltimore for Lafayette Courts on the eastside: Wise, her newborn son, her mother, her sister, and her youngest brother were reunited as a family. Two years later, Wise married her son's father, who worked at Bethlehem Steel. He moved in with the family, just for a few years, during which time the couple had a daughter.[16]

White women also suffered family alterations that resulted in single motherhood. By 1952 about one-third of white tenants and applicants were single-parent families. In Latrobe Homes, divorce, separation, and death split about 40 percent of the families—a trend that concerned the manager. Rosaline Lundsford spent her teenage years in Latrobe Homes. After Lundsford met her husband, Jesse, they spent their four years of marriage in Perkins Homes. A serviceman, Jesse worked as a cook at Fort Meade in Maryland. But their marriage soured. Jesse, who had a drinking problem and disappeared for months at a time, left her with two young children and no money. She left public housing with an overdue account. Jesse returned, but left the family again. Lundsford, who had held jobs since she was fifteen years old and even worked between pregnancies as a telephone operator, had decided to get another job. Then she discovered she was pregnant with her third child. She applied for welfare, and the DPW agreed to allot her a grant if she moved into public housing. Lundsford went to see Father John Albert, whose church was already providing the family with food. He informed the housing authority of Lundsford's situation and assured housing officials that the church would continue to provide the Lundsford family with food so she could spend $10 of her welfare grant to update her overdue account. In case she could not pay, the St. Vincent de Paul conference underwrote her debt. Lundsford and her children moved into a two-bedroom apartment in O'Donnell Heights, which would serve as her home for the next twenty-five years.[17]

The experiences relayed by Rudell Martin, Shirley Wise, and Rosaline Lundsford exemplify how economically vulnerable working-class black and white women were. When families disintegrated, men were absent, or accidents happened, many women had relatively few alternatives in a society that presupposed men as the primary breadwinners and heads of household. Women had to financially support their children, either through work or welfare or both, while juggling familial and household responsibilities. They were often unable to secure jobs that provided an adequate income to feed, clothe, and shelter their children.

For these women and other working-class people experiencing hardship, old age, and disability, the government offered an available and immediate source of assistance through public housing. In 1951, nearly 48 percent of the black applicant families had no worker and relied on some form of public assistance, whether in the form of Probation Court, old-age pension payments, GI subsistence, or ADC.[18] The one program that touted the economic and social advancement of its recipients, the GI Bill of Rights, fell short of advancing black veterans. While veterans, as a result of the Servicemen's Readjustment Act of 1944, or the GI Bill, were supposedly guaranteed benefits like unemployment, tuition, subsistence allowances, and loans to purchase homes, black veterans had trouble securing good jobs, gaining entrance to educational institutions, and obtaining mortgage loans through the program. Racial prejudice by public and private institutions in postwar America stymied their efforts.[19] So some black vets turned to public housing. The number of subsidized housing tenants who were recipients of ADC tripled between 1949 and 1955. By 1955, 20.8 percent of public housing tenants received welfare in Baltimore, up from 12 percent during the war years.[20] Residents receiving public assistance and ADC, in particular, were still a minority of the public housing population, but this shift presaged their growing residency, especially as urban redevelopment displaced more and more poor families in the inner city.

Isolation and Housing Policies

Municipal and federal urban redevelopment policies spurred and reinforced geographical, racial, and economic isolation. Slum clearance, urban renewal, and public housing construction expanded racially impoverished neighborhoods not only in Baltimore, but also in major cities throughout the country. With the passage of the Wagner-Ellender-Taft Housing Act of 1949, housing authorities began remaking cities. Urban renewal, which displaced hundreds of thousands of black people stuck in substandard housing, encouraged the refurbishing "of central cities with office towers, hospitals, universities, and the facilities that service them."[21] Two-thirds of those removed from redevelopment and urban renewal zones were black people. Like in the late 1930s and early 1940s, postwar housing and renewal policies affected cities' residential and poverty patterns through the "long-standing uses of public power to shift and confine the black community to certain parts of the city."[22]

In postwar Baltimore, the housing authority and the Baltimore Redevelopment Commission, which was established in 1945, had the task of cleaning up the inner city and reviving its central business district. The housing authority built low-income housing, and the redevelopment agency cleared land for private redevelopment. The two agencies, which eventually merged as the Baltimore Urban Renewal and Housing Agency (BURHA), developed a coordinated program of slum clearance, public housing construction, and redevelopment.

After passage of the 1949 housing act, Baltimore's city council agreed to support the agency's efforts and approved a preliminary federal loan. But before more federal funding could be secured to clear land and build public housing, federal officials required that the municipal housing authority and city council have a formal cooperation agreement. The 1949 act also required that cities provide relocation housing, and public housing became the primary solution in Baltimore and other cities, including Chicago, Detroit, Norfolk, Philadelphia, and Atlanta.[23] Aware of the federal mandate regarding displaced persons, BHA officials wanted to construct the first 1,200 to 1,800 apartments—with 500 to 1,000 for black people—on vacant land to provide the necessary relocation housing. But vacant land development elicited concern and hardy protest from city council members, the private real estate industry, and white citizens—just as it had in the past and just as the cooperation agreement came up for consideration.

Housing officials' decision to provide additional black public housing by extending the blacks-only low-rent complex Cherry Hill Homes did not draw much criticism. Housing officials took the safest and quickest road—providing more black housing opportunities in black neighborhoods. But the housing authority proposal to build two white public housing complexes in white neighborhoods did provoke outrage. White communities did not want low-income white housing, nor did they want to contend with the possibility that black people might move into the apartments in the future. In early 1950, when the city council met to hear the terms of the cooperation agreement, some 250 white people who lived near the proposed sites crowded the city council chambers. Another 2,000 people jammed the corridors to express their extreme displeasure.[24] Eight patrolmen and a sergeant kept order. When Robert Merrick, a white housing commissioner and CPHA member who believed "public housing [is] the only effective way to correct

Baltimore's slums," rose as the first speaker, spectators chanted for several minutes.[25] The city council meeting, the longest in history, did not end until after midnight.

Confronted by citizens' protests, the city council used the cooperation agreement to control the municipal housing program. While city council members eventually approved the program, they also restricted the number of apartments the housing authority could build on vacant land, thereby limiting new public housing to already impoverished neighborhoods. The city council action pleased white citizens who sought to keep their neighborhoods racially, ethnically, and economically homogeneous and to protect their property values. The action also quieted opponents who feared the socialistic "evils" of public housing and preserved outer-edge and suburban development for the real estate industry, which experienced a building boom in the postwar era. Of the proposed public housing apartments, only 1,550 could be built on vacant land; the remainder had to be built in the inner city and replace, according to City Councilman William Muth, its "decadent neighborhoods."[26]

The results of these political machinations were costly and disruptive for the housing program: The two initial white locations were abandoned. Instead, white replacement housing, Westport Extension and Claremont Homes, was constructed near existing apartments housing low-income workers: Westport Homes, formerly defense housing now run as a low-rent complex, and Armistead Gardens. By the controversy's end, the original plan to build replacement low-income housing, which would have dispersed white poverty, helped create islands of subsidized and economically marginal communities. After just three years as BHA board chair, Fenn resigned in disgust, saying "political bargaining" was "contrary" to his "nature," and called the council's interference an "impossible burden."[27] G. Cheston Carey, another CPHA member, replaced him as chair of the housing authority's board.

These postwar debates expose the power of white citizenly pressure as well as class and political divisions within the white community. Overall, however, urban housing policies disproportionately affected black people's well-being. Contrary to popular understanding, redevelopment did not ease black people's housing plight, but made it worse by demolishing residences and shoving working-class black people into more geographically and architecturally confined areas of racial segregation and poverty. The housing

Table 3.1 Baltimore Subsidized Housing, 1951

	Units	Race
Existing Low-Rent Complexes		
1. Latrobe	701	White
2. McCulloh	434	Black
3. Poe	298	Black
4. Douglass	393	Black
5. Perkins	688	White
6. Gilmor	587	Black
7. O'Donnell Heights	900	White
8. Somerset	420	Black
9. Cherry Hill	600	Black
Developments under Construction		
10. Cherry Hill (Extension 1)	637	Black
11. Westport (Extension 1)	229	White
12. Claremont	292	White
13. Lafayette	805	Black
14. Flag House	490	White
15. Cherry Hill (Extension 2)	363	Black
War Housing Complexes		
16. Lyons	304	Black
17. Fairfield	300	White
18. Westport	200	White
19. Holabird (Temporary)	400	Black
20. Banneker (Temporary)	248	Black
21. Sollers (Temporary)	400	Black
22. Turner (Temporary)	200	Black
23. Armistead Gardens	1696	White
24. Brooklyn	500	White
Post-1951 Complexes (Not Shown on Map)		
Lexington Terrace (opens 1958, near #3)		Black
Murphy (opens 1963, near #2)		Black

Based on Baltimore Housing Authority publications: *Public Housing in Baltimore, 1943–44, Fourth Report;* and *Your Investment: Annual Report of the Housing Authority of Baltimore City, 1951.* Courtesy Baltimore City Archives, Baltimore, Maryland.

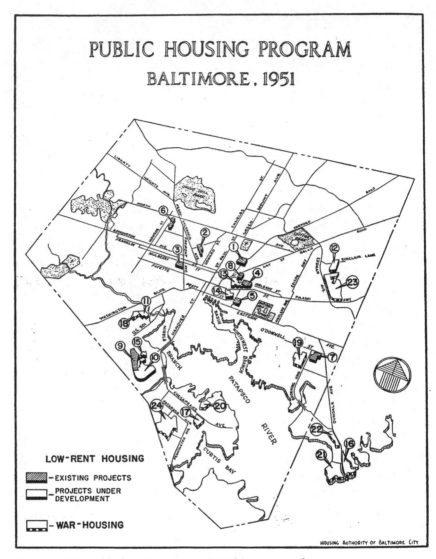

Figure 3.1 The public housing program in Baltimore, 1951, from
Your Investment: Annual Report of the Housing Authority of
Baltimore City, 1951. Courtesy Baltimore City Archives,
Baltimore, Maryland.

authority would build a second extension to Cherry Hill Homes. And in central Baltimore, where enclaves of black and white public housing already existed, the agency would construct high-rise public housing complexes—Flag House Courts for whites and Lafayette Courts for blacks on the eastside, and Lexington Terrace and Murphy Homes, both for blacks, on the westside. By the mid-1960s, black islands of subsidized housing, including the formerly whites-only Flag House, Latrobe, and Perkins, all of which experienced racial turnover, encircled downtown.

The central city, or Baltimore's "rotting core," was a primary locus not only of public housing development, but also of urban renewal—and, like in other cities, that meant displacing mostly working-class and poor black people. In east Baltimore the redevelopment commission under white director Richard L. Steiner demolished primarily black private housing, and private contractors redeveloped the areas for predominantly white or white-only residential or institutional use. In the Broadway-Hopkins area, which was close to existing and proposed public housing complexes, more than 1,000 families, 90 percent of them black, were displaced, and only 124 replacement homes were planned. Ralph Young, a physician who had a practice on Monument Street for thirty years, argued that while no one was against redevelopment, area residents wanted assurance that they would have some place to live. Argued Young: "There's no use kidding ourselves, colored people can't buy any place they would like, much less rent."[28] The Waverly project, which was one of the first urban renewal projects to be completed in the country, also set a bad precedent. In the Waverly area, which was 60 percent black, no new homes were planned for black residents at all. The situation was similar in west Baltimore. The clearance of twenty-seven acres near the Fifth Regiment Armory, adjacent to McCulloh Homes and bordering the predominantly white Bolton Hill, displaced 1,000 tenants—95 percent of them black. About 60 percent of that area became home to the Maryland state office complex.[29] Less than a decade later, *Baltimore Sun* reporter J. Anthony Lukas would write: "As the iron ball swings in an ever-widening arc, the fate of the displaced persons has become one of Baltimore's most complex social problems."[30]

When the redevelopment commission announced its plans for Broadway and Waverly in east Baltimore, black civic, religious, and civil rights leaders criticized the proposals. In 1951 Baltimore ministers and NAACP leaders contacted the NAACP's Washington bureau director, Clarence Mitchell, Jr., the son-in-law of Baltimore NAACP activist Lillie Jackson. In a letter to Nathaniel S. Keith, director of the federal Division of Slum Clearance and Urban Redevelopment, Mitchell argued that the Baltimore program "deprived colored people of living space and places the full strength of the Federal Government behind a policy of rigid residential segregation in that city." Mitchell called the Baltimore program a "backward step" because it cleared interracial neighborhoods, but required "racial segregation when the new dwellings [are] constructed." Mitchell also argued that the "well-known unwritten verbal agreement" that excluded black people from new apartments was no different from "a racial restrictive covenant in writing." He cited the 1948 *Shelley v. Kraemer* Supreme Court decision that outlawed racially restrictive covenants: "It is fundamental that no agency or government should participate in any action which will result in depriving any person of essential rights because of race or color or creed."[31] The NAACP demanded that the Housing and Home Finance Agency (HHFA) withdraw assistance from Baltimore's redevelopment and housing program. HHFA officials, however, argued that they did not "have the authority to compel any local public agency to establish requirements governing the racial characteristics of the families to be housed in redevelopment projects."[32]

Despite massive evidence of displacement and protests against municipal housing policies in the 1950s, the CPHA defended the agency's actions, more than likely an expression of loyalty to BURHA's commissioners who were CPHA members appointed by McKeldin in the late 1940s. The CPHA argued that "relocation is not the villain evicting families from their homes." Reaffirming its belief in the power of good housing, the CPHA argued that the agency alleviated "the hardship of families obliged to move (often paying moving expenses) and checks the spread of slums and blights by providing suitable shelter for those moved out of the substandard hovels."[33]

Displacement, however, often forced low-income black people to live in private deteriorating housing or in the city's limited supply of subsidized housing. Of the more than 1,000 black families displaced by the Broadway-Hopkins redevelopment project, 25 percent relocated to adjacent black public housing complexes. Half of those families moved into Somerset and Douglass homes; the rest had priority in the almost completed Lafayette Courts. According to Winston, the agency's executive director, the second extension to

Cherry Hill Homes "should help in the task of relocating families from the State Office Building site" on the westside.[34] The proposed Lexington Terrace was seen as relocation housing for the Harlem Park renewal project.[35] Between 1951 and 1971, 75,000 people were removed, 80–90 percent of them African American.[36]

Figure 3.2 A crowd lines up for Lexington Terrace's opening in west Baltimore in 1958. Courtesy Baltimore News American Collection, Special Collections, University of Maryland Libraries.

The "Ill Effects" of Poverty and Policies

Economic stresses and displacement led to a greater relaxation of tenant selection policies that had restricted public housing to primarily employed,
two-parent, low-income families. Black families who were displaced by
urban renewal but did not meet the "character" requirements established in
the 1940s gained greater access to public housing. According to a 1953 housing memo: "The necessity of giving priority to large numbers of welfare families living on slum clearance sites has resulted in a substantial rise of Negro
families receiving Public Assistance entering low-rent housing."[37]

As more black, impoverished, and welfare recipient families, particularly black women, turned to public housing, the program increasingly drew
criticism, exhibiting the interconnected dynamics of race, gender, class, and
disrepute in public assistance programs. The extension of ADC, especially to
unmarried black mothers, had already resulted in greater state surveillance,
including the establishment of DPW special units to investigate whether
women had men living with them or other income sources.[38] In 1956 Baltimore's DPW director, Esther Lazarus, outlined in her annual report the reasons for "frequent criticism" and "heavy censure" of the ADC program. They
were the "strong cultural reaction against continued public support of children belonging to deserting, absent or missing fathers," "the increasing preponderance . . . of assistance to a small part of the Negro minority group,"
and the "social 'outcasting' of children born out of wedlock."[39] While public
housing might have eased the economic burden that some of these women
confronted, subsidized living did not lighten the ideological burden wrought
by their double reliance on the government.

How to deal with families on public assistance also concerned housing
officials. The extremely low rents they paid fell below market rates and "sub-
stantially below the minimum average rent required to operate housing
projects."[40] Winston expressed particular concern about the rise of poor
black tenants and the decline of better-off, low-income white tenants. Increasing numbers of black and poor tenants boded disaster and threatened
the program's financial viability and social effectiveness. In a memo to Winston, housing officials wrote: "A danger sign showing the obsolescence of our
present [income] limits is that the trend is downward in the proportion of
white applicants eligible for low-rent housing." In 1951, 41 percent of white

applicants were eligible; in 1952, 39 percent. By May 1953, the percentage had shrunk to 27 percent.[41]

Housing officials argued that they needed to raise the income limits for admission and continued occupancy, which fell below the income maintenance level. Otherwise, the housing authority would be unable to accommodate those white tenants and applicants who still lived in substandard housing even as their wages steadily rose during the Korean War. Ever since 1950, the wage gap between white and black workers had increased. Yet "even with the increases . . . the lower paid workers in the community have faced greater problems in keeping up with the basic cost of living."[42] Based on a BHA wage survey of twenty-three leading Baltimore companies, the top 20 percent of the lowest-paid full-time employed male workers earned $3,218 in 1953 while a "modest but adequate" city worker's budget for a family of four was $4,348, and the basic "maintenance" budget was $3,283. During early 1953, the median income of white applicants was $3,051 and for black applicants $2,160. While white applicants' incomes were inadequate, black families made even less—on average about one-third below the "maintenance" line. Stated Winston: "So we have a dilemma—the law requires and conscience dictates that we should recognize the most urgent housing need and yet we must also operate a fiscally sound program."[43]

In an ironic twist, white people, who earned more money than black people, received special attention because they represented disappearing stability for officials. Officials argued that raising the ceiling on income levels would provide a social and financial balance in public housing by increasing the number of eligible white applicants by 50 percent, thereby offsetting "the larger proportion on welfare or receiving other sources of non-employment income" with "the higher rental ranges."[44] Morton Hoffman, the director of research and statistics, wrote: "In arriving at new income limits, special attention is always paid to white families, whose incomes are much higher than those of Negro families."[45] In September 1953, officials updated the agency's antiquated income eligibility limits and countered the "ill effects" of impoverished tenants. The growing percentage of poorer tenants and particularly the growth in the number of welfare recipients would remain an issue. More than a decade later, staff members still lamented the agency's inability to serve a cross section of poor people and expressed a continued desire: "to make public housing more attractive to non-welfare families."[46]

These programs and policy debates unveil several things. They provide even more evidence of the shifting demographics in public housing. Undeniably public housing complexes throughout the city had become home to more marginalized members of the working class as Baltimore changed. By 1964, single-parent families represented 40 percent of the households, "standard" families one-third, and elderly households one-fifth. Over 36 percent of all tenants—34 percent of white families and 38 percent of black families—received some form of public assistance. Over 60 percent of the single-mother households, a majority of them black, received public assistance.[47] The older low-rise black and white complexes tended to house a mixture of two-parent, single-parent, and elderly families while the newer slum-clearance, high-rise developments and extension complexes opened between 1952 and 1963 housed a disproportionate number of single-parent families. Alongside these familial, economic, and racial changes entered desegregation—a process that would further exacerbate racial divisions in urban communities.

The Role of Desegregation

For a short time in her early teens, Jean Booker lived with her mother and five siblings in the all-black complexes of Cherry Hill Homes and then Somerset Courts. When Jean Booker was a sixteen-year-old unmarried mother with a newborn baby, the family left Somerset and moved into her grandmother's old house. A few years later, around 1956 or 1957, Jean Booker married and took up residence in Latrobe Homes with her husband and now four children. When they moved in, she had no idea they were part of a "special" group—one of the first black families to integrate white public housing. "I just didn't know it was a white and a black thing. I found that out as I moved in," recalled Jean Booker. "I had no problem. All I did was speak and kept going. . . . The white people see you on the street, they ain't speak but that was all right. They ain't bother me." The Booker family stayed for a while and then moved out. The couple, both of whom worked, she as a nursing assistant and he primarily as a porter, grew tired of turning over their minimal raises to the housing authority in the form of rent increases. And Jean Booker was fed up with a white woman neighbor who incessantly complained about her children. Years later, when she and her husband separated, Jean Booker found herself back in Somerset Courts. By then, the late 1960s, all of the inner-city public housing complexes, even those formerly white, were predominantly black.[48]

In Baltimore, the desegregation of public housing began in 1954—the same year as the historic *Brown v. Board of Education* school desegregation decision. In fact, public housing and school desegregation efforts were part of a broad civil rights agenda led by the NAACP to provide black citizens with nondiscriminatory access to public institutions. While the NAACP contested Jim Crow schools, the civil rights organization also led successful actions to halt the construction of segregated subsidized housing in New Jersey, California, Indiana, and Michigan.[49] The *Banks v. San Francisco Housing Authority* case, in which the NAACP Legal Defense Fund contested municipal preservation of segregated neighborhood patterns, set a defining precedent. The California Court of Appeals ruled that such practices discriminated against African Americans and reaffirmed the illegality of residential segregation.[50] Baltimore housing officials became familiar with these court cases. On April 26, 1954, Ellis Ash asked the agency's counsel to outline the rationale for why "segregation in low-rent projects is unlawful."[51]

Given the ongoing debates and successful court challenges in other cities, Baltimore's housing commission altered its admission policy. On June 25, 1954, the BHA announced desegregation and dropped racial designations in housing placement. The BHA's decision prevented the potential of "a non-friendly, adversary lawsuit" by instituting change in an "orderly progressive fashion."[52] The BUL board chair, William M. Passano, wrote a letter hailing the housing authority's action. "You must know that the decision represents an objective in which this agency has been interested," he wrote to G. Cheston Carey, the housing commission's chair. As early as 1951, the BUL's Housing Committee had questioned the agency's racial policies. Continued Passano: "We regard it as a logical extension of the present trend toward truly democratic operation of public facilities. . . . Integrated living . . . undergirds a democratic society."[53]

The move to desegregate housing and schools reflected the liberal stances of local politicians like Republican governor Theodore McKeldin. An exhorter of tolerance, McKeldin believed in moderate change. As the state's governor from 1950 to 1959, McKeldin appointed African Americans, Jews, women, and independent liberals to government positions. As a friend of African Americans, McKeldin won his mayoral election in 1943 and his gubernatorial election in 1950 decisively with black votes. Succeeding McKeldin as mayor, Thomas D'Alesandro, Jr., a machine-aligned Democrat from Baltimore's southeast working-class Italian community, believed in postwar building, slum clearance, and redevelopment. In fact, two white public housing complexes, Perkins Homes and Flag House Courts, abutted Little Italy. The former city council president, D'Alesandro also believed in government authority and the law. D'Alesandro publicly avowed the *Brown* decision, pledged to follow the law, and supported gradual desegregation.[54]

For white citizens, however, desegregation represented a threat. Two public services and centers of community life—schools and housing—were in jeopardy. In May 1954 the Baltimore school board dropped race from its freedom-of-choice policy, which allowed students to "attend any school assigned to his or her race on a first-come, space available basis." The school board implemented its new policy in the fall of 1954—a year earlier than the Supreme Court issued its with "all deliberate speed" clause. While the school board action addressed segregation, members believed that manipulating "people to create an integrated situation" was "equally wrong."[55] While progressive, the school board's choice strategy (similar to the city's housing policy) still provided white citizens a loophole for salvaging segregation even with the racial designations abolished. Even so, three weeks after the desegregation announcement, white mothers and children began protesting integration of their neighborhood schools. One of the largest protests occurred at Southern High School. Cherry Hill Homes resident Rudell Martin remembers. She was pregnant, seventeen years old, single, and in eleventh grade. It was "a nightmare" having to suffer the anger, vitriol, and racist epithets hurled by white parents and students: "Every evening when you come out of school it was always a whole group of people, mothers. 'Go home, niggers.' And throwing eggs at you, and throwing stones at you. . . . I never got hit by anything, but it was just the devastation of seeing it happen and hearing it, being called these kinds of names." With the baby coming, Rudell Martin decided she could not handle the daily intimidation and potential personal violence. Martin told her counselor she was leaving school. The counselor convinced her to stay a little longer, but Martin eventually quit, secured a job, and took on the weighty responsibility of raising her child.[56]

Desegregation created contention and spurred racial violence throughout the country. And public housing was no exception. In Chicago's Trumbull Park, the housing authority's accidental leasing of a low-rent apartment to an African-American family (the wife was mistaken for white) triggered an explosive melee that lasted months. Avoiding similar racial fireworks that marred school and housing desegregation efforts in other cities, Baltimore housing officials closely managed the desegregation process.[57]

The BHA held a meeting for community groups on integration in July 1954. Participants avoided a press campaign, proceeded quietly, and readied themselves to answer questions if necessary. Those who attended the meeting included representatives from the CIO, Catholic Charities, the National Conference of Christians and Jews, the Baltimore Jewish Council, and Juanita Mitchell of the NAACP, Frances Morton of CPHA, and Furman Templeton, by then the BUL's executive director.[58] The housing agency sponsored a Human Relations Institute for staff. The institute featured race relations experts like black social psychologist Kenneth B. Clark, who served as an expert witness in the *Brown* case. In an August 18, 1954, letter, Edgar Ewing, a black staff member who organized the training programs, asked Clark to provide "concrete examples" of "the sociological and psychological implications of segregation" instead of "moral" imperatives.[59]

Using the model of federal housing literature on desegregation, BHA staff penned long memos detailing the perfect black family for integration. Officials selected families deemed "normal" and deserving and maintained that "no family whose behavior might be subject to criticism should be transferred." The BHA avoided families with "problems" like inadequate or irresponsible parent(s), poor housekeeping, poorly behaved children, poor morals, desertion, drinking, gambling, and difficulty getting along with neighbors, because they might be "a disturbing element in the project."[60] The perfect black family possessed social graces and led a "wholesome" family life. Preferably the family should be a young couple with or without children, but definitely not a "broken" family—a mother with children. Esther Frank Siegel, the supervisor of BHA's housing application office, suggested that military status was favorable because it "can carry with it additional dignity and respect generally associated with service for one's country." However, the father needed to be home, not missing as in "broken" families.[61] In a memo, Ellis Ash reaffirmed the agency's misgivings about single-mother families. Quoting exactly the federal housing agency's *Open Occupancy in Public Housing* manual, Ash wrote that the BHA should "avoid the selection of families of which young unattached women are the heads. . . . Such families quickly become the focus of attention and gossip, and any visiting male introduces an irritant through gossip that should be avoided."[62] These policies reflected officials' ongoing concerns regarding the proper social "balance" in public housing and portended social welfare policy beliefs that certain families, because of their character, were disruptive forces.

The BHA's decision to only consider the most "respectable" black families and, according to Warren W. Weaver, to avoid people not "sophisticated enough to adjust to integration" exhibited the agency's concern with disrepute and reflected a wariness similar to that of civil rights activists fighting for full American citizenship and its spoils. The NAACP sought "model" citizens as firsts or as plaintiffs in cases testing segregation, highlighting the organization's belief that black people who modeled middle-class behavior represented the race's best chances for achieving citizenship rights. The perceived deviance of poor women and single mothers raised flags and threatened this prospect. In the Montgomery bus boycott desegregation case, the local NAACP chapter held out for Rosa Parks over fifteen-year-old Claudette Colvin, who became pregnant after the incident, and Mary Louise Smith, a poor woman whose father had bouts with alcoholism.[63] Both Colvin and Smith had refused to give up their seats on city buses before Parks. The BHA and the Montgomery cases, as well as Rudell Martin's high school experience, raise the issue of worthiness and disrepute related to black citizenship claims during the 1950s.

A cautious and exclusive plan, the BHA's selectivity represented a strategic political move to initiate integration peacefully. If integration must occur, then calm and malleable black people—not those perceived to be fancy, outspoken, or socially driven—represented the least explosive candidates. While such choices did not preclude racial animosity, BHA officials wanted black working-class tenants to fit in, not cause tension with "uppity" behaviors. Improvement through education—a measure of respectability and a chance for black advancement—represented a danger for housing officials. If the first black tenants were more educated or expressed a desire to advance, they might anger white tenants. So, while black veterans were desirable, the BHA did not want those studying in professional schools under the GI Bill of Rights. Again echoing federal language, BHA officials argued: "Families with such educative background might well create hostility among the tenant families" rather than respect, because they may seem "snobbish" or "standoffish."[64] Moderate orderly change, not black advancement, had precedence, and if this meant subsuming black people's aspirations to avoid racial disturbances, then so be it. Black tenants had to walk a fine, cautious line and bear the physical and emotional brunt of desegregation. They had to be respectable, flexible, and not too openly aggressive or eager to improve their circumstances.

Despite attempts to circumvent potential hostility, some white people viewed desegregation as alarming no matter what. In these instances, housing officials simply avoided the problem. Between June and October 1954 some white residents in the Brooklyn Homes area protested integration. The former defense housing complex had become low-rent housing. White residents' concerns similarly extended to public schools and recreation facilities. On July 8, Brooklyn's recreation director informed Daniel Powell, the complex's manager, that the "children have been very talkative regarding the prospect of integration. They have said they plan to form gangs and attack any unit in which Negroes may be housed."[65] Volatile public disturbances did not emerge, because housing officials bypassed potentially explosive white communities. In a July 1954 letter to Harry Weiss, former maritime commissioner and now chief of BHA's tenant selection division, Samuel Warrence, of Newark's housing authority, wrote: "To date the only bombshell I have read about has been in Indo-China and not in Baltimore, so I trust that all goes well."[66]

Housing officials decided to desegregate white complexes in black and racially transitioning neighborhoods. The BHA had already slated the whites-only Fairfield for racial transition to help remedy the postwar black housing shortage. In December 1954, Fairfield operated on a desegregated basis; it was 60 percent white and 40 percent black—although it would not stay that way for long. The whites-only complexes Latrobe Homes and Perkins Homes in east Baltimore were next. To prevent the perception of a "Negro onslaught," the housing authority moved in both black and white families. On May 31, 1955, five white and nine black families moved into the formerly all-white Perkins Homes, and two white and seven black families moved into Latrobe on June 1, 1955.[67]

Even as housing officials implemented the nondiscrimination policy, they developed a freedom-of-choice policy that made integration voluntary. In Fairfield Homes and other complexes, officials relocated white families upon request. Given the chance, white tenants not surprisingly tended to choose white complexes. The freedom-of-choice policy also helped to forestall racial turnover—a consistent concern. As with their eligibility and continued occupancy policies, housing authority officials deliberated over whether "a trend toward a higher proportion of Negro tenancy" would be "good or bad."[68] Given black people's housing needs, Ellis Ash wrote to Oliver Winston: "If the applications are consolidated . . . what changes, if any, should be made to prevent our projects in time from becoming completely converted to a different racial group?"[69] By selecting the complexes to desegregate and allowing white tenants to pick where they wanted to live, housing authority officials averted racial wars like in Chicago and Detroit. And while they responded to the legal mandate of desegregation, their policy helped preserve white enclaves of public housing and promote racial changeover in the inner city.

In Perkins and Latrobe, the two white central city complexes targeted for desegregation, at least a portion of the tenants protested with their feet. Their actions reflected and contributed to a broader trend of white working-class families who deserted cities. In a survey, *Why Eligible Families Leave Public Housing*, more than half of the ninety-four white families who left Perkins and Latrobe between June 1956 and January 1957 admitted that they did not want black families in their complexes. They believed integration happened too fast, that the waiting list for white people was already "too long," and that soon blacks would "outnumber whites." The expressed feeling that black people threatened white workers' access to subsidized housing and government largesse exposes evidence of early resentment that fueled white working-class conservatism and critiques of social welfare programs by the late 1960s and early 1970s. Anti-integration white tenants also thought that black people's transgression of their "proper place" would only lead to undesired social interaction. Such white tenants expressed a fear of interracial mixing, because black men "get fresh with white women and the husbands fight," and "too much can happen like dating and perhaps even marrying." While only 18 percent of those surveyed offered integration as the reason for their move, when asked the question directly the proportion went up to one-third. The percentage was probably much higher than that since 59 percent of those surveyed disapproved of integration. Those who moved maintained that many of their neighbors "resented" integration and had told them that they "would move before they'd live next to Negroes."[70]

Throughout the pioneer days, World War II, and the 1950s, a significant percentage, some 45 percent, of public housing tenants were white working-class people. But by the 1960s, poorer black people became a significant majority of residents, and growing enclaves of black public housing emerged. In central Baltimore, black public housing stayed black, and white public housing complexes became black. Not one public housing complex that the BHA originally designated as blacks-only was ever truly integrated—unless one considers the residency of white families in the single digits to be exemplary. Flag House Courts and Lafayette Courts opened officially as "integrated." When Lafayette Courts opened in April 1955, 99 percent of its residents were black.[71] By December 1955, of 692 families living in Lafayette Courts, 9 were white. Dwight Warren, a pioneer tenant of Lafayette, recalled:

> It seemed as though public housing really provided an opportunity to segregate the black community. . . . I believe early on Flag [House] Courts was probably more heavily racially divided than Lafayette. But, eventually the white folks moved out. And it just got to the point where it's almost like when you in Rome and you can't speak like the Romans, you know. It's time to leave. I believe that's what happened to a lot of the white folk. They were just so overwhelmed at our numbers.[72]

Initially Flag House Courts did have a racially mixed population, but six years later, most of the complex's residents were black. Lexington and Murphy opened as all-black complexes and remained so. In the central city, more than 1,500 black people lived in formerly white housing complexes and 5,477 in complexes built exclusively for them. The three remaining white complexes, O'Donnell, Brooklyn, and Claremont, housed 70 percent of BURHA's white tenants.[73] By 1964, 7,910 of the 10,153 public housing families were African American. That was a far cry from the 1940s, when the racial composition was almost equal.[74]

The Last Bastions of Whiteness

In 1950s Baltimore, Anna Warren and Rosaline Lundsford lived in those untouched enclaves of working-class whiteness, but in 1966, civil rights activists broached the subject of integration. Across the nation, battles for fair housing proliferated. In Baltimore, double-digit vacancies in O'Donnell, Brooklyn, and Claremont raised eyebrows, especially with eight times more black applicants on the waiting list than white applicants.[75] Even an anonymous white tenant, who resided in an unidentified white public housing complex, wrote in January 1963:

> Coming home from church this morning I saw all the houses that are empty and badly damaged from ruffians. They are costing a lot of money to be fixed so why not rent them out to colored families, they aren't any worse or as bad as some of the families we have living here now. . . . There are colored families mixed in with the white people in other sections of town and [they] get along, so why not have them move in our project. . . . God put them on this earth the same as us white people so why not treat them equal. [I'm a] tenant who thinks it a disgrace the way all these homes are empty and being so badly damaged when someone could be living in them.[76]

Allowing vacancies to remain in white complexes with the waiting list so long for African Americans created a public relations fiasco, especially for an agency that voluntarily initiated its desegregation program in 1954. O'Donnell consistently had thirty to forty vacancies.[77]

In Baltimore, the integrated Activists for Fair Housing (Activists Inc.), cofounded by former CORE members, lambasted the housing agency. In 1966 Activists Inc. accused the housing authority of maintaining exclusively white public housing communities even as black people's needs for affordable housing increased. Activists Inc. charged that the housing agency privileged downtown revitalization over poor people's needs and questioned whether BURHA actually met the federal guideline of "contributing to a decent home for every American in a decent environment" because segregated housing was "ipso facto unequal and inferior." Activists Inc. publicly demanded that the federal government halt funding until the local agency responded to civil rights advocates' concerns.[78]

BURHA's chief responded. Richard Steiner wrote a letter to Warren Phelan, a regional administrator for the federal Department of Housing and Urban Development (HUD), countering Activists Inc.'s claims. Steiner argued that while BURHA engaged in projects that supported the revitalization of downtown, the "major thrust" of its activities were "toward improving housing conditions for low and moderate income Baltimoreans and removing blight from residential neighborhoods." He charged that Activists Inc. failed "to realize that BURHA must conduct a 'balanced' program of

Figure 3.3 A picture of the 1300 block of Gusryan Street in Brooklyn Homes, 1966. The public housing complex was all white before the Baltimore Housing Authority initiated its second wave of integration in 1967. Courtesy Baltimore News American Collection, Special Collections, University of Maryland Libraries.

housing and renewal and that the benefits must accrue to all citizens and be both social and economic." Steiner described BURHA as a "city agency that undeniably has the best record and the most progressive outlook wherever race relations are concerned (including support of fair housing legislation)."[79] But, he argued, the agency believed in a "positive program of integration . . . done within the framework of free choice." Some white people simply chose not to live with black people.[80]

Just months after the initiation of this debate, O'Donnell, Brooklyn, and Claremont became racially politicized battlegrounds. On December 20, 1966,

Steiner sent those 1,700 white tenants a notice. The agency reiterated its integration policy and referred to the Civil Rights Act of 1964, which prohibited racial discrimination in all federally subsidized undertakings. The agency steered clear—as it did in the 1950s—of espousing a moral claim, believing it would only create greater resentment and protest. Despite Steiner's hope that "all residents" would "understand the requirements of federal law" and "do everything possible to preserve harmonious neighborly relations," housing authority officials anticipated trouble. In Brooklyn Homes, O'Donnell Heights, and Claremont Homes, the housing authority installed telephone lines for black tenants, surveyed white tenants' attitudes, placed black tenants near each other and the complexes' offices, employed security guards, and requested that uniformed and plainclothes police officers patrol neighborhoods routinely.[81]

Numerous residents in and around O'Donnell, Brooklyn, and Claremont bristled at the thought of racial integration. Public housing tenants living in all-white complexes, even with the agency's desegregation policy in place, probably saw housing officials' actions as reneging on an unstated promise to maintain all-white complexes. White public housing tenants' low incomes placed them in a vulnerable position. Their fight against black residency reflected the confluence of their racial identity and class position. They not only wanted to protect racial exclusivity, which distinguished them from black public housing tenants, but also their own access to low-income housing and government programs. An unsigned letter to O'Donnell Heights' management expressed aversion to living with black people and fear that blacks were gaining all the benefits of government programs: "I just moved from Flag House Courts, because it all turn Negroes, and all the other project's all over the city, the same, no white's in them, and now just O'Donald [sic] Heights and [Claremont], are just white, and to think, you are going to fill them up now, with Negroes." The writer continued: "What's next. Where are we poor white people are going to live other words in the future, you are giving all the projects to the negroes you don't put the white with them, do you? How do you think this is fair? racial or no racial, we want to live in peace. A Family of 7."[82] Someone else returned to housing officials a defaced O'Donnell Heights desegregation notice. A swastika appeared on the body of the letter as did the words—"*We are Ready*."[83] O'Donnell became the first site of protests. In O'Donnell and Brooklyn Homes, local chapters of white supremacist groups like the United Klans of America and the National

States' Rights party played a central role in antiblack activities in public housing and throughout the city in the mid-1960s. In Brooklyn, the white supremacist groups rallied, burned crosses, and instigated physical confrontations. Disgruntled tenants, neighborhood youth, and these racist organizations tormented Brooklyn Homes' first black tenants, the Riverses and the Smiths, who moved to 820 and 822 Glade Court in April 1967. The United Klans of America handed out racist literature. One postcard stated: "The only reason you are WHITE today is because your ancestors believed and practiced SEGREGATION."[84]

Black families not only endured demonstrations, verbal obscenities, and leafleting campaigns, but youth intimidating their children. As in 1954, desegregation riled antiblack, anti-integration foes. Less than a week after they moved into Brooklyn Homes, Willie Esther Battle's children experienced harassment. Battle, who lived at 830 Glade Court, enrolled her four children in a school that only had one black student. On the first day of school, seven-year-old Steven Battle was called either a "black egg-head" or "nigger" by classmates—an incident reminiscent of Rudell Martin's Southern High School experience in the 1950s. Steven's teacher called the principal, who reprimanded the children, but Steven stayed home the next day. A housing memo maintained that once Steven returned to school, the children played "together fine."[85] The Rivers, who had preschool children, told their social service aide that shortly after the Klan's May visits, neighborhood children taunted their two-year-old son, saying that the Klan was going to "get him."[86] Racial intimidation remained prevalent throughout 1967.

Black tenants responded to the tirades in numerous ways. While some black families simply waited out or ignored campaigns of intimidation, others refused to passively accept such attacks. In a Malcolm X–style response to the Klan, twenty-five-year-old Marian Johnson posed in front of her window for a *Baltimore Afro-American* reporter. The young black mother wielded a shotgun. The May 2, 1967, front-page headline blared: "Mother of 4 with Shotgun Vows to Stand Up to KKK." According to the newspaper article, which differed from housing authority and Southern District Police accounts, fifty robed demonstrators (as opposed to ten to twelve robed and a number of onlookers) had paraded and made speeches. A single mother, former Lafayette Courts tenant, and Coppin State College student, Marian Johnson vowed to protect her home and her four children, ages three to nine, from KKK intimidation.[87] A few black families contacted civil rights

Losers . . . Again

Figure 3.4 Editorial cartoon, Baltimore Afro-American, May 6, 1967. In 1967 Marian Johnson and her four children were among those who desegregated the all-white Brooklyn Homes. Fearing white supremacists' reprisals, Johnson decided to protect her family by keeping a shotgun in the apartment. Reprinted with the permission of the AFRO-American Newspapers Archives and Research Center.

organizations. Clara Morant filed a complaint with the Baltimore NAACP, protesting the intimidation and mistreatment of her children. Juanita Jackson Mitchell of the NAACP alerted housing officials and visited Morant.[88]

Frank Rivers and Gordon Smith confronted the young white ruffians. Rivers slashed the back of a seventeen-year-old white man after three white male teenagers addressed him in "a provocative manner." When the police came, Rivers was promptly arrested and charged with attempted murder, disorderly conduct, and possession of a 7 1/2-inch knife; he was held on $3,600 bail. While Frank Rivers was in jail, CORE members became the protectors of Shirley Rivers and her children and secured legal representation for Frank Rivers. Led by black director Daniel Gant and white associate director Stuart Wechsler of the CORE Target City Program, CORE members stood guard outside the Rivers house and criticized the police for waiting so long before they arrested protesters who had been intimidating black tenants. Gant, also a national CORE field secretary, said: "It took the city fathers three days to decide black people's safety was in danger."[89] Frank Rivers was finally released two weeks later. Rivers's neighbor Gordon Smith, twenty-one, who tired of a fifteen-year-old white male teenager calling his wife a "nigger" and a "black ape," caught the boy and forced him to apologize. The boy's father swore out a warrant against Smith, and police investigated the incident. Marian Johnson, Clara Morant, the Riverses, and the Smiths refused to cower or be intimidated by angry whites. But other black residents could not cope with the racist intimidation. Fearful, three of the original eight black families in Brooklyn Homes moved.[90]

Racial hostility dissuaded many black people from seeking housing in white neighborhoods, that is, those inclined to move there in the first place. Some black people did not want to live with white people as much as obtain greater housing options. Still other African Americans preferred to live in black neighborhoods because they were safe and familiar. Shirley Wise believed black people had a right to live wherever they wanted. Although she applauded the efforts of the first black people to challenge public housing segregation, Wise argued that she preferred living in a black community instead of a community "not totally mixed," especially "with the problems during that time with integration" like "community fights, fires. And I knew I didn't want to be a party to that." Reflecting, Shirley Wise maintained: "I'm a pioneer in the sense that I like to be a pioneer for rights. I'm not a pioneer that I'm going to go into a racist community and attempt to raise my family or attempt to bring [white people] around to my way of thinking." She continued: "I'd rather be one of those people who sit with those racists and those people in power and cajole and do . . . whatever I have to [to] make them form some kind of legislation or policies that would effect change, rather than going on and moving into their neighborhood."[91]

Not all white tenants united against their new neighbors during the second wave of desegregation in the 1960s. In Brooklyn Homes during the welfare department's group meetings, a number of white mothers raised the issue of integration. Two mothers, one of whom lived next door to a black family, "were very vocal in their expression of resentment." A third mother, however, was "quite articulate in telling the group that she felt anyone of any race, creed or national origin had a right to live here if they had limited incomes." Some mothers criticized white extremist groups. Remarking on the police presence, these mothers mostly feared violence. One mother remarked that the "'fathead' Klansmen were going to keep going until they frightened all of the white tenants out of the area."[92]

White tenants' and community responses varied from fateful acceptance to neighborly cordiality. Claremont Homes tenant Anna Warren, who was against interracial dating and marriage, nevertheless felt that integration was inevitable: "This is the way it is. This is public housing. Don't have to intermingle, live, sleep with them. But you can say hi." Shortly after a black family, the Minors, moved in, Thelma Minor's husband died of a heart attack. Recalled Anna Warren: "Here she is in this neighborhood with all white folks, you know, right around her." Warren and tenant council president Warren Maxwell went to Minor's house and "asked her if there was anything we could do, and she gave us a key to her house."[93] Maxwell and Warren cleaned the apartment, stocked it with food, and went to the funeral. After that, Minor and Warren became friends. Minor even tried to teach Warren how to drive. Minor and her children moved about a year later, buying a house with her husband's life insurance money. Warren reasoned that meeting the "right" people challenged her racist viewpoints. "I told [Minor] I had a bad attitude. I was just like all white people. Then you start to get to know people. And then you realize somebody's wrong here!" An O'Donnell Heights tenant, Rosaline Lundsford recalled being labeled a "nigger lover." One of the first black families moved in next to her—Rose Mason and her four children. Lundsford recalled helping Rose Mason's daughter with reading, and Lundsford's son-in-law taught Mason how to play bingo. "Rose was a very nice person. When somebody used to come up and they would say, would yell, 'Rose,' outside, she'd open her door and say, 'White or black?'" Lundsford laughed at the recollection.[94]

Some communities and families remained divided over race. Even as Warren's attitude underwent change, her children and husband, who stayed with the family off and on, still had limited views on race relations. Her son, Nicholas, whom Warren claimed still had "that problem" in the 1990s, used to get involved in interracial fights with "his buddies" and call black youth "niggers." Anna Warren recounted: "He had more marks on him [from] me grabbing him, than he had from the fight." Anti-integration protests often played out among youth in the form of fights and over community resources. Anna Warren recalled a dance which resulted in white youth abandoning the recreation center while claiming black teenagers took it over. White youth wanted to have a band. Anna Warren, by then tenant council leader, told the youth, "no problem," but it would have to be open to everybody. She put flyers under everybody's door, but only black youth came. From then on, white youth "stayed away from everything. They didn't come down at all. And they couldn't understand why I was allowing the black kids to take it over. I said I didn't allow the black kids to take it over. You allowed the black kids to take it over."[95]

Liberalism and Extremism

The community-based racial battles around public housing revealed the broader anatomy of race relations and politics. In the wake of Nazism and the mass extermination of Jews based on "racial" difference, racial liberalism received new hope in the postwar United States. But while racial moderation and the desire for racial equality spurred change, Baltimore still exhibited its share of racial parochialism. Some white citizens and politicians recoiled; they still desired homogeneous neighborhoods and institutions, and this necessarily meant keeping black and white people separate. Walter Percival Carter, a Baltimore CORE member and a founder of Activists Inc., described Baltimore as "a complicated city": "It's not like New York. Here you can have the Ku Klux Klan in full regalia on one corner and the same guy [at a different time] on another corner in a gray flannel suit. You have to get the feel of this town." He continued that Bayard Rustin, who founded CORE in 1942 with James Farmer, "used to say when he came here, 'Take me back to the bus station.'"[96]

The anti-integration and antiblack protests, however, did not stave off desegregation in public housing. In a city where officials espoused racial moderation during the age of civil rights and law and order, white supremacist extremism worked against itself. The last bastions of whiteness in public housing did topple, although resegregation would occur. White liberal city officials, who operated in a framework of political moderation and loathed extremism, suppressed the actions of white supremacists. They legally banned rallies held by the white National States' Rights party.[97] Theodore McKeldin, who had regained the city's mayoralty in 1963, even presented to the city council an omnibus civil rights bill, which included fair housing legislation. City council president Thomas D'Alesandro III, who became mayor in 1967, publicly supported McKeldin's civil rights bill and the city council did pass it—but not before eliminating coverage of housing and limiting antidiscrimination clauses to public accommodations. The legislation excluded taverns, private clubs, parochial schools, tutoring, or faith-based hospitals. Within a year, McKeldin, displeased with the watering down of his omnibus civil rights bill, introduced a fair housing bill to the city council.[98]

As a Baltimore county executive between 1962 and 1966, Spiro T. Agnew, the soon-to-be governor of Maryland who became famous as Richard Nixon's vice president, also campaigned for an open accommodations ordinance, but with limitations. "Agnew was a 1930s liberal who believed in racial harmony, not a 1960s one who believed in black advances."[99] He did not like conflict whether it emerged from white or black communities. He denounced civil rights sit-ins to integrate Gwynn Oak Park *and* gubernatorial contender George P. Mahoney, who was supported by the Klan and whose campaign slogan was "Your Home Is Your Castle—Protect It!" Once governor, Agnew, true to form, supported a watered-down state Open Housing Act in 1967 that limited its reach to apartments and large developments. Activists Inc. criticized the state fair housing law, arguing that it was "near meaningless" and did not create "true open occupancy."[100] Agnew believed in the power of government, law and order, and gradual and limited change, especially regarding race relations. While Agnew had won 80 percent of the black vote in his 1967 election, his racially conservative stances and rabid critique of black discontent in 1968 estranged him from the black community and endeared him to white working-class people.[101]

Racial liberalism and moderation also infused Baltimore's housing agencies. In the 1960s, housing officials were prodded, and once encouraged, they proceeded—guardedly. Local officials tried to avoid litigation, disturbance, public protest, and extremism. In the 1950s this meant managing desegregation as well as giving white tenants enough leeway to maintain homogeneous white communities by choosing their neighbors even if the result was continued racial separation. In the 1960s, housing officials continued to manage desegregation efforts, meeting with school, church, recreation, police, and public welfare officials. For a short time, a few integrated public housing complexes existed, but just like their 1950s predecessors, O'Donnell and Claremont eventually became majority black.

Conclusion

The racial and economic contours of public housing mirrored similar divides throughout the city and between city and suburbs. In fact, racial segregation became a permanent feature of American cities in the years after World War II. In Baltimore, segregation hovered around 90 percent every decade between 1940 and 1970.[102] Islands of poverty also emerged. Personal circumstances, a shrinking industrial base, lack of economic opportunities, the legacy and ongoing practice of racial segregation, migration, local and federal policies, desegregation, and white flight conspired to create them. This changing racial and economic demography, however, did not just raise the question of poverty and what to do about it. The shifting population came to represent something much larger—a public, social, and cultural "problem" in the making.

4

"When Then Came the Change"

The Fight against Disrepute

In the 1950s, public housing still lured tenants like Frances Reives, who searched for an inexpensive yet "decent place" to "make a home." In 1955 when Lafayette Courts opened, she and her daughter, Mary, who had migrated years earlier from Greensboro, North Carolina, moved in. By 1957 Reives had married and birthed another daughter, and life was a little easier—just a little—for a short time. Her husband did not like public housing, but "he didn't try to buy us a house," and "I wasn't moving in no more shacks." Three more children and a rocky relationship later, Reives's husband left. A single mother yet again, Reives worked primarily as a domestic laborer and raised her children in Lafayette Courts. However, while Reives thought public housing "a nice place to live," she soon realized something. Over the course of a decade, the "projects"—and the people who lived there—were increasingly viewed as not so nice.[1]

As if providing food, shelter, and clothing for five children was not already an awesome task, Frances Reives also had to contend with disparagement of the poor and the public assistance programs that she relied on to

survive. She remembered the day when Mary startled her with a stark reve-
lation. Conveying how teachers and students perceived residents of public
housing, Mary warned her mother to send her siblings to other schools.
Reives recollected her daughter's words: "I believe because you live in public
housing they feel that they don't really want to educate you."

> [Children] from the projects was looked down on different from the
> kids from homes. And she said, they feel that you, how did Mary tell
> me, she said they feel that you on welfare, and you're not concerned
> about your children. And they feel you eat beans for breakfast and
> beans for dinner, and she said they feel as though . . . you were just
> nothing. Now how she came to that conclusion I don't know.

Frances Reives heeded Mary's caution; she sent her three youngest children
to different schools. Still disturbed, Reives reflected in the mid-1990s: "People
look down on you; 'til today people still look down on you."[2]

The painful words uttered by Mary Reives and her mother's immediate
response and lingering agitation more than thirty years later expose the daily

*Figure 4.1 Frances Reives lived in Lafayette Courts from 1955 to
1995, when the public housing complex was imploded. She now
lives in a town home in Pleasant View Gardens, which was built
on the site of Lafayette Courts. Photograph by Elizabeth Malby.*

baggage of poverty. Increased black residency and tenants' economic marginality not only signaled the "obsolescence" of a "balanced" public housing program, but also spurred an image of the residents of public housing as increasingly incorrigible and dangerous. In these decades, respectability steadily eroded, and stigma and disrepute took its place.

"Problem" Families and Communities

In the 1950s, when Frances Reives first applied for public housing, the media had praised Lafayette and Flag House courts as the cheapest places to get skyline views of the city's waterfront in east Baltimore. Some tenants also expressed excitement about living in subsidized penthouses. Seven years old when he moved into Lafayette Courts in 1955 with his mother, stepfather, and brother, Dwight Warren remembered feeling awe for the buildings reaching heavenward. Whenever he had visited his cousins in New York, he had wanted to ride the elevator to the top of the city's then (and now) tallest building—the Empire State Building. He never did, but in Lafayette Courts, "we had our own *elevators*."[3] A *Baltimore Sun* article also weighed in on these new elevator high-rises: While the "cliff-dwelling poor" might have lacked the amenities of rich cliff-dwellers and while "the effects of life in vertical honey-combs" was unforeseeable, "if the better-off can lead contented lives high in the air in their multi-story apartments, there is no apparent reason why the poor can't too."[4]

Yet, within a decade of opening, the novelty of high-rise buildings, in particular, began to fade, and in general public housing became the bane of cities. A 1962 *Baltimore News-Post* article described public housing as clusters of tall and short red-brick buildings "in a sea of deterioration and slum." The article also dubbed public housing "a blessing," "socialistic," and "a hotbed of disease and crime." No longer seen as simply the home of the unlucky, public housing became controversial, a problem, and home to "problem" families. The *News-Post* article did depict public housing as a community like any other with "good and bad housekeepers, destructive children, elderly people who complain of noise, substantial citizens and problem families." Yet, after discussing the diverse population in public housing, the article continued, "[F]amilies bred in slums possess other built-in problems, and often a radically different set of values."[5]

Social scientists and politicians increasingly described poor black people as participants in a culture of poverty and black single motherhood as a quintessential sign of cultural pathology. This postwar characterization did not represent the first time that urban black women were seen as a negative force or that the conflation of urban space, race, class, and gender resulted in power dynamics that focused on individuals versus the structures that shaped their lives. In the early twentieth century, white reformers concerned about vice, crime, and prostitution suggested policing the sexuality and bodies of black women migrants—as did black institutions and the black middle class.[6]

In the post–World War II era of the "nuclear family," however, discussions of pathology, while not devoid of the intimations of crime and disorganization, seemed to arise out of anxieties regarding "proper" families, acceptable gender roles, and male power in the family and state. By the 1960s "problem families" and "broken Negro families" became popular denigrating phrases describing female-headed households (whether the women were divorced, separated, or never married). Black female–headed households, poverty, deviance, and disorganization became inextricably intertwined—just as the battles to recoup black manhood and reinforce white male state power took center stage in the age of civil rights, the militaristic sounding War on Poverty, and black power. In *The Negro Family: The Case for National Action*, the assistant secretary of labor and director of the Office of Policy Planning and Research, Daniel Patrick Moynihan, faulted the black "matriarchal" family structure for black poverty. The cure: black men must be elevated to their rightful positions as primary providers and thereby free the government of its responsibility.[7]

For some black mothers, however, public housing and ADC had become a solution to the problems they confronted—problems undergirded by societal assumptions that maintained that men should support and run households—like women's inability to earn "breadwinner" wages and contentious domestic relationships that led to abuse. For them, reasserting male authority was not always desirable. A home owner with seven children, Goldie Baker left her second husband because of abuse. Alongside familial help, low-wage women's work, and fortitude, public housing and ADC provided Baker an opportunity to secure shelter and income. The programs, as demeaning as they had become to her, helped her work toward self-sufficiency and thrust her into political activism against insensitive social welfare institutions. Public housing aided Ann Thornton and Rosetta Schofield in similar ways. After three children, Ann Thornton left her first husband. Enlightened and disgusted by her mother's experiences with spousal abuse, Thornton vowed not to put up with physical or mental abuse from men. In her mother's day, she explained, "Parents stayed with their spouses, you know, so the children had a dad, you know. To me it was never worth it." Thornton moved back to her childhood home in Cherry Hill Homes with her mother, who had by that time separated from her husband. After about a year, Thornton moved to Perkins Homes: "That's how I got back into public housing." Rosetta Schofield similarly vowed "not to take no crap that my mom took." While she talked little about her children's fathers, Schofield said her mother's experiences shaped how she handled relationships. "Oh no, you not going to bust my eardrums, hit me in the head with no ax, kick me in my butt, and put me and my child that wasn't yours out in the street and say go on about your damn business. I was determined I wasn't going to take that." She continued:

> That's why, it's like public housing and welfare . . . they have done a lot. It has done a lot of good for the black woman. I'm saying from the black point of view [because] I'm black. . . . When I went on welfare and moved in public housing, I had a place for me and my children, a nice, decent, clean place for my children and I to call home. And that meant I didn't have to take no beatings and no type of abuse from no man out here in order to have a place . . . for me and my kids. Understand?[8]

Despite these complex realities, black women who sought low-income assistance became repositories of "deviance" as well as symbols "for all that could go wrong in American society."[9] White single women like Anna Warren and Rosaline Lundsford, who relied on social welfare programs, did not fit the rhetoric of cultural pathology, but households like those of Frances Reives, Rudell Martin, Shirley Wise, Goldie Baker, Rosetta Schofield, Ann Thornton, and many other black women did. And if poor black people, particularly single mothers, were deemed the problem, then it was not a far leap to cast their dire living conditions in public housing and inner cities as primarily their own fault.

By the late 1960s, high-rise communities, which housing officials also once considered a fine economical way to house large numbers of displaced, predominantly black poor people, had become scapegoats.[10] In Chicago,

St. Louis, Baltimore, and other major northeastern and midwestern cities, high-rise, high-density public housing complexes eclipsed the existence of other styles of subsidized housing, obscured residents' lives, and eventually were seen as the spawning grounds for social ills. In St. Louis the infamous Pruitt-Igoe, a conglomeration of thirty-three eleven-story buildings constructed in the 1950s, became the focus of public debates. In Pruitt-Igoe, tenants' travails were enormous. However, Pruitt-Igoe was not simply seen as a large poverty pocket, but came to represent violence, so much so that crimes committed in the vicinity became "Pruitt-Igoe" or "Negro" crime.[11] At a 1968 National Association of Housing and Redevelopment Officials (NAHRO) conference on the future of the American ghetto, Anthony Downs, a member of the National Commission on Urban Problems, maintained: "The image now is of high-rise buildings that are unsafe to be in and filled with broken Negro families. The term 'public housing' conjures up a vision of thousands of unstable people concentrated in huge buildings so that they swamp surrounding neighborhoods and schools."[12] This NAHRO member's assessment of public housing's "terrible public image" paralleled what Frances Reives's daughter had disturbingly relayed. Mary Reives had responded to a similar constellation of ideas and images about poor people and public housing tenants—ones that maintained she was a poor "project" youth living in the ghetto and, therefore, deemed insignificant and a potential problem.

Public housing's primary location in increasingly impoverished and dangerous black inner cities contributed to its disparagement. The crime rate did rise in cities, increasing 60 percent between 1960 and 1966, and 83 percent between 1966 and 1971.[13] Black people and their neighborhoods did suffer under the weight of overcrowding and housing deterioration. Increased poverty, job loss, inadequate city services, limited housing, and slum landlords all contributed to the undesirable conditions in cities. While people may have feared and criticized the central city and those who lived there, many black people who contended with these challenges daily also expressed fear, issued criticisms, and expressed a desire for better. Yet, black urbanites and their residency were reconstituted as the "blight" in new postwar clothes.

In O'Donnell Heights, the small group of white tenants who publicly protested desegregation in 1967 posted a flyer imploring white residents to beware the "perils" of black integration: crime and "Murder, Rape, Assault,

Robbery upon *You and Your Family.*" According to these tenants, who formed the O'Donnell Heights Ad Hoc Committee for Sound Government, black people, by their presence, by their very nature, brought turmoil and danger. These racist constructions contaminated and followed urban black residents, whether or not they were directly responsible. In addition to reacting to current urban travails, the Ad Hoc Committee led by Faith Gosnell also deployed time-honored white supremacist rhetoric or "technologies of power" by casting black men as oversexed rapists and murderers. The flyer's last lines highlighted the consequences and more specifically gendered implications of flouting the taboo of racial intermingling: "Warning: Once Your Child Is Raped It *Will* Be Too Late."[14]

Subsidized housing in troubled central cities no longer proffered public respectability to black working-class families. Burgeoning poverty, the increased absence of white families, and tenants' greater reliance on the government, not just for housing, but for their source of income, distinguished public housing communities of the 1960s from those of twenty years earlier. "Project people" had become "different," and black residents bore weighty stigmas. Society judged public housing tenants by the same narrow criteria. They were perceived as shirkers of hard work and uncaring or unconcerned parents who, in aberrant family forms and with questionable morality, would only reproduce children of the same ilk. That black—and white—two-parent families lived alongside black female heads of households in public housing and that all of them had to struggle daily to support their families seemed to matter little. When it came to race, working-class and poor tenants were tainted both by their public housing residency and by the increasing percentage of tenants receiving social services.

Responding to Stigma

These politics of race, poverty, residential geography, and social welfare programs shaped poor people's views of and responses to public housing: Hope and promise were accompanied by dismay, shame, anger, depression, and increasingly fear about public housing living. After thirty-two years in a west Baltimore apartment, Coleman and Rose Grant broke their necks to move into Cherry Hill Homes. They, like Frances Reives and thousands of others on the waiting list, were in need. With an impeccable wit, Coleman Grant explained: "Because where we lived was so cold, I had to buy Robitussin for the roaches." Their apartment had a big oil heater, "big enough to heat [the] Lord Baltimore [hotel]," but it "would just not work in that house." While happy, Coleman Grant remembered that one daughter did not want the family to move to Cherry Hill. But he told her, "Look I don't want no stuff out of you. . . . We got a chance to get a warm place here."[15] That was 1962.

Salima Marriott, born Louise Siler, who recalled that "moving to Cherry Hill [in 1946] was like the Jeffersons moving uptown," only ten years later slowly divorced herself from the Cherry Hill Homes community. As a teenager, she began hanging with friends who had either moved to or lived in west Baltimore, still a primary hub of the black middle class. She attended Douglass High School in west Baltimore where she reported in similar stead to Mary Reives and Rudell Martin that her public housing residency elicited negative reactions. Then a student in the business curriculum at Douglass High, Marriott remembers: "I always knew I was going to go to college, so when I got [to] the tenth grade I went to the guidance counselor, said I want to change and get in the academic program. She told me I needed to stay where I was, because I needed to get a job and I was from Cherry Hill." That incident opened her eyes: "Being from Cherry Hill was different." And over the years, even Salima Marriott increasingly regarded herself as different from the poorer working-class people in Cherry Hill Homes, so much so that she had left the community in her "mind, her head" before the family physically moved away.[16]

Sedonia Williamson, who lived in McCulloh Homes on the westside and also attended Douglass High School, began socializing outside the "projects" as well. She too felt increasingly disconnected from the home where she had grown up "very secure" and "very grounded." She claimed she was never ashamed of public housing; McCulloh Homes always had "fine families" and "good people." But she did begin to sense stigma by the time she entered high school in the early 1960s. When she formed a sorority with classmates, she was reluctant to bring them home. While clean and comfortable, her apartment lacked the flourish of luxury items. So she often entertained them at her godmother's house near the school. But something else bothered her. She also felt distant from public housing because some of her tenant peers called her "Miss Goody Two-Shoes" and "were taking a different direction, hooking school, doing drugs. I was always an honor student, loved school, did well. So I began to change my playground."[17]

Public housing increasingly evoked stigma—not a sense of privilege. Within the city and larger nonresident black community, public housing tenants would become "those people" who lived in "that housing." The experiences of youth like Mary Reives, Salima Marriott, and Sedonia Williamson testify to that. Like them, Jean Edges Sherrod, who grew up in the 1950s and 1960s, remembered her peers saying curtly, "Oh, they live in the projects," as if public housing tenants were "second-class people." But Jean Edges Sherrod thought residency a privilege, as did some of her friends in the old neighborhood. They often asked to come over. The teasing might have made her feel bad initially, but she eventually "overlooked" it. Even so, Sherrod never mentioned the taunts to her mother, Mary Edges, who eventually became a tenant leader and had a community daycare center named after her to honor her work with children. Sherrod did not want her mother to feel she was unappreciative.[18]

With the demographic changes in urban communities and ideological shifts in social welfare policy, tenants developed their own explanations for the changes they perceived in the social and political landscape of their communities. Among the pioneers—the first tenants in any complex—newcomers provided a visible and tangible explanation for, as well as a way to distance themselves from, disrepute. Loubertha Ward, her husband, the Reverend Horace Ward, and their four children had an apartment on the same floor as Frances Reives in Lafayette Courts from 1955 to 1965. Loubertha Ward distinguished between Lafayette Courts' first tenants and the next generation. "They called us mostly the cream of the crop that was getting first priority to the building, you know. Then there were others [*draws out word*]. People that moved in that weren't scrutinized; just anybody, you know." Rosetta Schofield, who lived in Murphy Homes, also marked change by focusing on the influx of new tenants: "I'd get up 5:30 in the morning, and I'd be leaving some time going to work. Had no fear. And the elevators worked better. The halls were clean and people . . . cooperated together. And then after years went by . . . they move[d] in new people. And so it just began to go down."[19]

Other tenants focused on single mothers, whom they acknowledged had rough times and specific challenges. But they offered an alternative view—one that did not simply conflate the problems with the women themselves. Women tenants, several of them single mothers themselves, maintained that young mothers, in particular, found themselves handling too much too fast. Rudell Martin and Frances Reives argued that some young mothers, whom they saw as immature and incapable of handling the responsibility of an entire household, lacked the support and guidance they needed. Frances Reives, whose community participation centered on showing young mothers how to "make the best of it," maintained that younger mothers "just didn't have the training to do right." Martin claimed that a Cherry Hill Homes policy that forbade two families from living together under the same lease forced young mothers, like her sister, out on their own prematurely. Salima Marriott, who became pregnant during her second year in college in 1961, confronted a similar dilemma as a Cherry Hill Homes tenant. In her case, the family decided to leave public housing instead of separating into two households. At the time, her father worked as a cook in a downtown cafeteria, and her mother was a private duty nurse. While making ends meet remained a challenge, leaving public housing and staying together at least meant paying only one set of bills. And Salima Marriott's mother, who was not working at the time, watched her baby girl while Marriott went to classes. Three years later, Salima Marriott had finished her bachelor's degree in physics and married her daughter's father; she eventually moved to New York for a few years and became a welfare caseworker. Young mothers without such supports did not tend to fare as well.[20]

The feeling of second-class status shaped the views of some poor black applicants and further elucidates the power and currency of negative images. Martha Benton felt shame. At twenty-three years old, the pregnant Benton moved into Somerset Courts in 1964 with her husband and two children. In 1966 she transferred to Douglass Homes for a bigger apartment; by then, she had five children and had put her husband out. Initially, Benton suffered profound contradiction when she had no alternative but to seek government assistance. Her mother, father, and husband "frowned" on public housing and welfare. Benton recalled: "They always thought the people there didn't want nothing, didn't care about nothing, wasn't trying to achieve anything, and that it would take away any incentive that I might have . . . to try to rise above the situation." However, her overwhelming desire to provide a stable home for her children instead of floating from house to house staying one foot ahead of eviction notices won out. Even though Benton felt that she and the kids "were blessed," as a resident, she remained aloof from other tenants. She went to work and came home. By the time she became "conscious of the community," a drunk driver had killed her deaf daughter, the wrong crowds had lured her youngest son to the streets, and she had become sick, had to quit her job as a clerk typist at the police department, and had to live on medical disability. At age thirty-six, Benton knew it would be tough to survive without subsidized housing and decided to participate in community affairs, especially regarding children and drugs. In the 1980s, under Goldie Baker's tutelage, Benton became a diehard tenant activist.[21]

Baker only turned to public housing out of desperation. She knew about public housing because her grandmother was one of Douglass Homes' first tenants. Goldie Baker, who attended Dunbar High School across the street from the Douglass housing complex, often stayed with her grandmother to avoid walking twelve blocks every morning to school, especially in harsh weather. She "didn't have an opinion" about public housing then: "I was in high school and I didn't know about much of the difficulties in public housing at that time." As an adult, after separating from her husband, Baker and her seven children initially lived with her mother, stepfather, and their eight children in a 2 1/2-bedroom row house. At the time, Goldie Baker worked at a state hospital, but she resigned to spend more time with her children, whom she saw only once or twice a week. Lack of support from and fear of her husband and overcrowded conditions forced Baker to apply for public housing. She waited two years, then she wrote to John F. Kennedy. Maybe the U.S. president could intervene on her behalf—a needy black working-class female citizen. "At that time looseleaf paper was 5 cents. I stayed up all night long [and] I wrote him a letter. And in that letter I put just about everything I'm telling you in here about my experience, about black people, colored people, white people and our livelihood," Baker recalled. "I don't know all what I didn't tell him. I told him if I was a white I would have been [accepted into] a . . . project."[22] The president's office referred her letter to Baltimore's housing agency.

When the housing authority offered her a high-rise apartment in Lafayette Courts, she "had a fit." Lafayette's high-rises looked "like a cage with link fences." She remembered thinking, "What do you think we are, a bunch of monkeys or something?" Baker refused the high-rise apartment. When housing officials refused her another apartment, she threatened to write the president again. "And so, they thought I was, I was one crazy nigger. They wasn't used to that [*laughs*]. Oh, believe me, they wasn't used to no nigger talking to them, talking to him like that." A few days later a housing

Figure 4.2 Goldie Baker (left) at her surprise seventieth-birthday party on July 23, 2002, in Baltimore. Goldie Baker lived in Lafayette Courts from 1964 to 1969 and in Oswego Mall from 1969 to 1971 before moving to her rehabbed house in east Baltimore, where she still resides. Jean Booker (right), a long-time friend, was one of the first African-American tenants to move into the all-white Latrobe Homes in the late 1950s. Photograph by Rhonda Y. Williams.

official offered Goldie Baker a low-rise apartment in Lafayette Courts. Baker took it; the scale of residence was more humane. But living in Lafayette Courts still depressed her: "I didn't want to live in public housing because I had already been familiar with the stigma and the label of people in public housing. Lazy, no-good, dumb, ignorant, don't want nothing, want somebody to give them something. . . . That was just in my mind." Goldie Baker admitted that she "didn't know anything about living in the project," except when she stayed with her grandmother. And then, she recalled, "It didn't seem like *they* were no good to me."[23] Baker's early experience with public housing as a decent place and the contemporary negative images of public housing collided, caused confusion, and swayed her assessment. However, personal revelations and clashes with housing officials would reveal public housing tenants' unseen challenges and ultimately hurl Goldie Baker into a lifelong struggle for poor people's rights—even after she left traditional public housing in 1971 and moved into a rehabbed row house, where she still lives.

Individually, these narratives do not fully explicate the changes in public housing or cities. However, taken collectively, they unveil a complicated picture of community change. These reminiscences reveal the existence of innumerable challenges. They expose how competing sensibilities and community conflict, housing policies and tenant-management relations, inadequate services and rising crime (alongside poverty, deindustrialization, and desegregation) contributed to the isolation, physical decay, and growing disrepute of public housing communities. Their reminiscences also help expose tenants' responses—those who went on the offensive, and those who did not.

The Politics of Policing Communities

Unlike the 1940s, when improving status and education and inculcating bourgeois values undergirded tenants' self-help efforts, in the 1960s self-policing also targeted the effects of postwar poverty. Rudell Martin discussed tenants organizing in Cherry Hill Homes "to police ourselves" and make management accountable. Gladys Spell and William Hynes recalled tenant groups' attempts to deal with other tenants and unkempt neighborhood spaces and to build community. A form of poor people and women's activism, self-policing reflected efforts to make life better and safer for tenants. A long-supported form of tenant organizing, self-help activities also accrued benefits for management. Resident maintenance, provisions of recreational activities, and community monitoring and services eased the housing authority's programmatic burdens.

The tenants who became active in community life and politics and who possessed an ingrained sense of respectability viewed public housing not simply as a temporary place, but as a home—at least while they lived there. Citizenship, decency, respectability, and community participation, then, became intertwined. Doing something served as a "calculus" of belonging and responsibility.[24] Aware of the negative feelings that nonresidents had for public housing and the range of tenants' concerns, Frances Reives argued: "A lot of people think when they move into public housing, oh, I'm going to be here for a couple of months and I'm leaving. It's not that easy. Unless you get a good job and you can pay that rent out there, you're not leaving. So why

Figure 4.3 Former tenant council leader and resident aide Gladys Spell moved into Murphy Homes when it first opened in 1963. She resided there until the complex's implosion in 1999. Photograph by Rhonda Y. Williams.

not make it as comfortable as you can while you're here." Gladys Spell maintained: "I tried to participate in [the community] because I said it's no use complaining about the neighborhood. Neighborhood supposed to be better because you are there. And if you're not doing anything to see that it gets any better, you don't have a right to complain. Just keep quiet about things."[25]

Striving for decency, a cadre of residents labored to rebuild respectable complexes and to contest disrepute in Baltimore's public housing. In a 1960 letter complaining about their manager's rudeness, Gilmor Homes residents on Spray Court demanded better treatment, arguing they were "human beaings [sic] and not scum."[26] Resistance included weaving alternative images. Gladys Spell dismissed the word "projects" to describe Murphy Homes. Divorced after sixteen years of marriage, Spell moved into Murphy Homes with her five sons in 1963. Her family's primary supporter, Spell, at different moments in her life, briefly collected ADC, labored as a domestic worker, and provided childcare for other tenants. A tenant leader in the 1960s who eventually became a resident aide for the housing authority, Gladys Spell said: "We wanted to call it a development of the Murphy Homes community, because if it were a project, it would still be on the drawing board. They would still be making plans." Drawing on the Murphy family heritage, Spell spun a positive narrative about Murphy Homes and residents' responsibilities: "Now, Mr. Murphy was an educator and we wanted to keep his name up with the things that he liked to do. That was to educate, rehabilitate, and work with people."[27]

Most tenants, however, went about simply fashioning their lives. Some could not foresee the possibility of change or feared losing affordable apartments. In the 1950s, tenant applicants had to sign loyalty oaths stating that they did not belong to "subversive" organizations listed by the U.S. attorney general.[28] While Baltimore housing officials maintained that no one "refused, or even hesitated, to sign," these oaths not only demanded conformity as a marker of good citizenship, but also carried the penalty of nonacceptance into or eviction from public housing. Other working-class and poor people did not have the time, or desire, to participate in community affairs or protest campaigns. The bureaucracy seemed so large and unshakable. Ultimately, many public housing tenants were like many U.S. citizens who quietly concentrated on their individual lives and families and left mobilizing efforts to those few willing to say or do something.

Competing Sensibilities and Community

Unusually dense and close living fueled disagreements among residents of public housing. Disharmony often erupted over how to use space, especially with large numbers of children. In the high-rises, many children used the tot lots or playgrounds in the air and the buildings' infrastructure to enjoy themselves. Screaming children bounced balls off walls. Some children, to their detriment, played on the elevators. In 1962 eleven-year-old Lafayette resident Larry Madison climbed through the elevator escape hatch and rode on top of the cab. He slipped and fell, crushing his skull.[29] Kids skated and rode their bikes in their apartments, in the complexes' hallways, or on their neighbors' lawns. Dwight Warren testified to the disturbances such activity caused: "Around Christmas time [roller-skating] would drive all the neighbors crazy. I mean for two months consecutively all you could hear was roller-skating. . . . that was probably one of the first things . . . banned from the high-rises . . . roller-skating on the floors."[30]

In public housing, where the elderly and families with children lived next to each other, conflict emerged. Listen to the letters written to the mayor and housing officials by one elderly woman tenant, Edith Wilson, in Murphy Homes. After hearing of the "comforts and convenienances [*sic*] for the elderly," she "felt I wanted to be there and being named for one of the best citizens of Balto. that meant much to me." In November 1963, she relocated to Murphy Homes, the first complex to designate 10 percent of its apartments for elderly people. A year later, she wrote her first of many letters complaining about noise and children. In December 1964, she wrote about "4 bad girls" who made an "awful racket" next door. In 1966, suffering arthritis, she wrote Edgar Ewing, a career black housing employee and by then an associate director: "There are five bad girls right next door. One is now a mother. Children galore [are] on this floor. I want a little peace and quiet some time." One time, she decided to escape to her sister's house for a few weeks "where there are children but you never see or hear them."[31] Murphy Homes was far from the peaceful and restful retreat she and others had expected.

Residents often called management about children and adults whom they felt misbehaved and disrespected individual and neighborhood space. In Cherry Hill Homes, the largest public housing complex after the two urban renewal extensions, the Resident Improvement Guild (RIG), which formed in 1964, expressed concern about unruly children. In 1969 RIG president Coleman D. Grant, who with his wife, Rose, raised two of nine children in Cherry Hill Homes, wrote a letter to tenants. Speaking for "law-abiding residents," the RIG expressed "embarrassment" about youth pulling false fire alarms and then verbally attacking firefighters. The RIG suggested that management cancel the leases of families whose actions threaten community safety.[32] According to Coleman Grant while "citizens did have problems" and "nobody to represent them," at "times when they [were] wrong you had to set 'em straight. . . . I can't stand up for you when you wrong." He remembered a woman whose five children littered their front lawn. He knocked on her door.

I said, here's a free copy of the *Cherry Hill News*. I'm president. We formed a tenant council, the Resident Improvement Guild. I said, there's no charge. I want to see you read that. How's your new home? [She said], oh it's nice. I never thought we'd have a nice place like this. [I said,] I don't think you're going to have it very long. "Why? I pay my rent." I said, look out here. Bones, that's garbage. . . . You don't throw them out on the ground, because if you do, you won't be here long.[33]

Public housing tenants also judged the behavior of other tenants, creating status hierarchies and cliques, or what Sedonia Williamson termed "class strata," within and among public housing complexes. Low-rise tenants categorized high-rise tenants. Clara Gordon argued that numerous Poe Homes tenants increasingly grew wary of Lexington Terrace, which sat right next door, because of high-rise complexes' tainted images and growing challenges. Gordon mentioned drugs and "different standards, and [we] was afraid of that." Williamson recalled many of her friends in McCulloh Homes were wary of Gilmor Homes' youth, whom they perceived as "tough" and "rough." In Lafayette Courts, Somerset, and Douglass, rival male youth groups, or small gangs, according to Dwight Warren, engaged in turf wars and even sometimes had fistfights after athletic league competitions. A neighborhood recreational center, the McKim Center, which sponsored sports programs for young men in the Lafayette Courts neighborhood, however, helped defuse pent-up energy. Taking advantage of its programs as a youth, Dwight Warren eventually became one of its directors. Competing sensibilities and territoriality were not unusual. Baltimore was a city of distinct neighborhoods, and residents claimed ownership of them. Sharing an impoverished status or residence in subsidized housing did not matter as much as claiming and protecting living space and establishing a persona of toughness in tough communities.[34]

In 1969, the housing authority started a demonstration Resident Aide Program based on an ethic of self-help and self-policing that already undergirded tenant participation. While mobilizing some tenants, this ethic also depoliticized the politics of race and inequality. The strategy of self-help, which reflected the tenor of government programs like the War on Poverty, focused on rehabilitating poor people's behavior without also examining the structural impediments that affected people's daily lives. In its first year, the Resident Aide Program employed four women tenants, Mary Bonner, Christine Jones, Frances Reives, and Gladys Spell, in the city's most troubled complexes, the high-rises encircling downtown. An odd combination of onsite managers, social workers, and advocates, resident aides carried on the housekeeping duties of government. Like teachers' aides, who helped educators, and social service aides, who facilitated service delivery in public housing, resident aides helped the housing staff establish "a good relationship with residents" and provide "the necessary services for residents to insure a cleaner, and safer building."[35] Resident aides had a long list of duties, including overseeing operation of the elevators and laundry room, arranging floor and building meetings, meeting with the managers and social service aides regarding tenant problems, making home visits, and encouraging good housekeeping. For all of this "housekeeping" work, resident aides earned a minimal salary of between $4,372 and $5,534. And if they moved out of public housing, they lost their jobs.[36]

The Resident Aide Program, however, allowed black women to combine their motherly duties with community work, earn a salary, and hopefully shape while regulating residential behavior and attitudes. For the black women who became resident aides, the job often dovetailed with their desires to work with young mothers, the elderly, and the disabled, as well as recapture their complexes from unclean and unsafe conditions. A resident aide motivated by a desire to once again make Lexington Terrace "a decent place to live in," Jones resided in the No. 700 high-rise building, which was reputed to be the "dirtiest and the worst building in the project." In her six-page report in November 1969, she wrote: "It was so bad until I was ashame[d] to tell anyone where I lived." She had contemplated moving but then was offered the resident aide job. "Then I decided if I could help make this building a better, cleaner, and nicer place to live in, then it wouldn't be fair not to except [sic] it when so many people felt that I was the right person. . . . I have put God before me and I ask him daily to protect me from any harm or danger."[37]

A manager fairly respected by tenants, Charles K. Anderson, who had left Gilmor Homes to manage Lafayette Courts, described Reives as possessing a similar desire to "a clean, peaceful environment for her family and for other families in the community. She works long hours trying to make her desires become a reality."[38]

Resident aides undoubtedly occupied a precarious position. Even as they provided services for tenants, they also were an official part of housing management staff and were directly supervised by managers. They met periodically with the social service aides, also women, who were assigned to their buildings to exchange ideas and to evaluate the program. Their job descriptions privileged policing while seeking to minimize tenant confrontation and protest. Resident aides were required to have not only a general knowledge of household management, but also an ability to relate to people and to work cooperatively with management. In fact, resident aides had to often rely on the support and power of management to enforce policies and contact "errant" tenants. Jones maintained in her report: "If I find trash with proof, I take it over to the manager's office, he takes it up from there by giving me his fullest cooperation. He get the proof date and time, he then get in touch with the tenant."[39] While resident aides reported harmonious relations with tenants in their buildings, many tenants probably saw them as pawns, interfering busybodies, or paid management collaborators. Occasionally, however, resident aides broached hot topics with housing management thereby reasserting their link to the larger tenant community and gaining not animosity, but empathy and support. For instance, Jones met with Van Story Branch, a black housing administrator, to complain about high electric bills, a hotly debated issue between organized resident groups and management.

Even if at times seen as suspect by tenants, resident aides themselves described gaining a sense of self-respect by looking out for their communities. They also said they tried to give respect as well. Jones's testimony speaks to the importance of "respect" as a concept and as a practical way of structuring community relations: "I love my job and I love what I am doing because it makes me feel as though I am needed, and I love doing things to help others. I get great respect from my tenants and I give them a great deal of respect in return."[40] Over the years, Spell claimed:

I never had any problems getting along with anybody, because . . . I know that everybody has rights that must be respected. And when you go into their homes, regardless of what you think they should be, you have to respect them and respect their rights as an individual, as a person. Because, you think, if it were you, you know, you wouldn't [want] nobody to come in your house trying to lord you around, you know.[41]

While some tenants complained about and policed the behavior of their neighbors, other tenants, including youth, engaged in community activities that catered to fellow residents through the recreation department, antipoverty programs, or their own initiatives. In July 1966, BURHA initiated a pilot program to train young mother welfare recipients as companions to elderly tenants. The program, funded by Work Experience Program antipoverty funds from the welfare department, paid young mothers $15 a month in addition to their regular monthly checks. Young mothers discussed the excitement and challenges of helping their elderly community members. They went shopping, gave them baths, made sure they took their medicine, introduced them to other elderly tenants and activities, and just talked with them. Men tenants started an inner city Boy Scout troop at Lexington Terrace and Poe Homes. In Murphy Homes, a group of tenant council youth members "concerned about the poor image of today's teenagers" formed the Traveling Stars of Murphy, which provided services for elderly tenants and sponsored youth recreational activities. According to Spell: "These kids were renowned wherever they went." Still other tenants offered aid on an individual basis by keeping an eye on neighbors' children and shut-ins, supplementing needy families' supplies, and even offering prayer and counseling.[42]

Residents and Management

Residents did not just target other residents. They also criticized housing management and other city agencies that stripped public housing of decency, residents of respectability, and neighborhoods of security. Their criticisms and complaints divulge the types of problems—not just internal, but also external—that made public housing and city living a challenging proposition. In 1966, a Lafayette Courts resident wrote a letter to Van Story Branch, the high-rise complex's former manager and then assistant director for housing management. She lamented days gone by and expressed current disgust: "When you were our manager at least we did not have to be ashamed to live in the projects, now the people who live here do nothing to keep it up and the maintenance do less yet. . . . We still have decent people that have to live in the projects and I wish everyone would understand this."[43]

For career black housing officials like Branch, civil service employment sometimes resulted in upward mobility. Warren W. Weaver joined the housing authority staff in the 1940s after being unable to get a permanent teacher's job in Baltimore's school system. The housing authority's third black manager, Weaver became the head of BURHA's relocation division and president of the Baltimore Urban League from 1966 to 1969. Like Branch and Weaver, Edgar Ewing also started out as a manager; he eventually became associate director of BURHA's renewal operations and then the director of the Model Cities Program. As the more privileged members of a racially marginal group, these black men gained opportunities for mobility by joining a municipal agency that initially required and allowed them only to regulate and manage working-class and poor black people's behavior. In the Jim Crow 1940s and 1950s, black managers only presided over black complexes. Long-term employment, however, did not automatically translate into advancement for black people. The housing authority had many black tenants and numerous black employees by the 1960s, but few occupied top offices. In 1963, Ewing was the only black staff person in a policymaking position. BURHA's director's office had no black people in supervisory positions, and the personnel office had no black employees. The majority of black BURHA workers—80 percent—were in maintenance and laboring jobs. And, still, by the early 1960s, no black manager had been assigned to public housing complexes that were more than 1 percent white.[44]

Some tenants believed that the housing authority had become primarily a path of career advancement for black administrators and staff versus a social welfare agency that expressed concern for tenants and their hardships. Rudell Martin argued that while some younger tenants had a "so-what" attitude, so did managers. Ann Thornton, a Perkins Homes resident activist, believed that by the mid-1970s some managers and staff were more "abusive" and that "they just stopped caring."[45] Once, in the 1940s, tenants had gained allies in the city's housing bureaucracy. But even then, new policies, which restructured the agency, also reified tenants' dependency on housing managers, who gained increased levels of decision-making authority and control from central administration. When the CPHA took over the housing board in 1947, the new administration not only set to work revamping policies, but also reassessed its relationship to tenants. Ellis Ash, the director of management, concluded that commissioners' intervention on tenants' behalf was "extremely unfortunate." He also believed that "many persons making the complaints were dignified with an over-amount of attention."[46] Managers, not the board or central staff, should address tenants' concerns. Underlying these adjustments lay an ethos that favored strict lines of authority—as well as paternalism. As the belief in bureaucratic order and the rehabilitative power of public housing infused managerial practices, the hallmark oppositional tenant voices of the 1940s eventually receded, and conciliation and more acceptable community activities like recreational programs followed.

But by the 1960s, a cohort of tenants became vocal once again, especially as public housing and urban landscapes changed. The rewards of upward mobility might have benefited career black employees and some tenants, but the majority of tenants still had much to bear. And some of them complained to and sought relief from city officials whom they believed viewed public housing residents "as a different breed of people," according to Elizabeth Wright, who moved into Westport in 1960.[47]

Poor maintenance and slow repairs of backed-up sinks and toilets, jammed trash chutes, and inoperable elevators were critical concerns. Substandard upkeep of high-rise buildings, which by their sheer height garnered greater visibility, was translated as moral human turpitude in the public eye. The high-rises, however, were not the only public housing complexes deteriorating prematurely. Tenants' protests during the war years and the 1960s proved otherwise. For instance, while some white tenants suggested that Claremont deteriorated after black people moved in, Anna Warren argued that the decline in housing officials' responsiveness and maintenance contributed to the complex's demise:

> Well when I first moved in it was a country club, okay. Because you had services. See everybody wants to say we became a prison or whatever you want to call it because black people moved in. But you see if they would have gave us the same services as I got when I first moved in here, this place would still be looking good, okay? But what happened was black people moved in and the services were gone.[48]

While tenants criticized management, they also worked with and even praised managers whom they considered allies. Black social service aide Hattie Turner and Jewish manager Walden K. Gorsuch helped Murphy Homes tenants control Elder's garage and his roaming dog. The tenant organization argued that Perry Elder cluttered their streets with old junky cars. Murphy Action Committee (MAC) members held a special meeting with city officials. As a result, Elder agreed to "remove his cars from the street and keep his dog from roaming the project by use of a leash and muzzle."[49] Apparently, however, the battle did not end there. Years later, Gladys Spell, as president of the Murphy Homes Improvement Association (the successor organization), still worked toward the removal of junk cars and an abandoned bus from the neighborhood. Spell argued that "often young girls were taken there by men, and it became a regular home for bums."[50] William Hynes, who similarly recalled nighttime sexual forays, labeled the garage a menace: "Well, it had a bunch of cars on both sides of the streets from in front of the garage near Fremont all the way down to in front of the schoolhouse. And at night, them young girls sit in there, and prostitutes. And going on."[51] After three years of tenants working with management, the police-community relations division, the traffic department, and the sanitation mobile division, the junk vehicles were finally removed.

In east Baltimore, Somerset Homes' management helped organize tenants and support their desire to confront Mayor McKeldin about the unsanitary conditions of the Maryland Chicken Company in 1966. Somerset tenants endured the putrid smell of chicken blood running down gutters. A tenant group wrote a petition and approached the mayor; they "felt that the entire community should be involved in the protest" and went to Parents-Teachers Association (PTA) meetings, neighborhood merchants, and civil rights organizations, as well as door to door, gathering signatures and support. The Reverend Melvin Swann, the pastor of Waters African Methodist Episcopal (AME) Church, which neighbored Somerset Homes, also complained to the city. In July a Bureau of Sewers representative assured Somerset Homes' manager of the installation of a storm drain from the Maryland Chicken Company to Low Street, a border of the complex. Shortly after that effort, tenants formed the Somerset Courts Improvement Association.[52]

In Cherry Hill, public and private housing tenants and home owners coalesced around environmental and health issues. Local residents had successfully prevented the placement of liquor stores in the area since 1946. They feared unwanted transient or "wino" traffic. Ann Thornton proudly remembers Cherry Hill Homes as a fairly alcohol-free neighborhood: "We didn't have a liquor store back then out there, so it was hard for people to get alcohol." Salima Marriott recalled parents' and tenants' efforts "to keep liquor stores out." In 1965 the Cherry Hill Homes manager, Bernard Mason, recommended in a memo to Van Story Branch that the housing authority "support strongly tenant opposition" to liquor stores. Community residents, however, lost that twenty-year battle.[53]

That same year, a coterie of Cherry Hill area residents banded together and formed Interested Citizens for Equality (INCITE). The cross-class, cross-gender coalition represented citizens' calls for environmental justice more than twenty years before a full-fledged movement against environmental racism, which united working-class and poor women across racial lines.[54] INCITE garnered the ears of city officials, including the mayor, city council president, health commissioner, sanitation director, and housing and urban renewal officials. An obsolete trash incinerator, a proposal to locate a new garbage disposal plant in the area, and the spraying of a poisonous and potentially lethal insecticide, chlordane, threatened the health and safety of Cherry Hill residents.[55] Leaders emerged from the well-known Murphy family of *Afro-American* and housing authority fame. Cherry Hill community organizer Madeline W. Murphy claimed that "vacant lots, the dump, [the] stench has grown to such magnitude that there are countless cases of respiratory infections and allergies out here." Cherry Hill community residents had been fighting against the Reedbird Avenue incinerator since 1948. Regarding the "new and modern" garbage disposal plant, Madeline Murphy argued: "We don't want it. Why don't they put [it] in [the rich white neighborhoods of] Guilford or Homewood?"[56]

Neighborhood Indefensibility and Inadequate Services

Public housing tenants, like other city residents, confronted the effects of deindustrialization and worried about rising crime and the lack of physical security. Of those in subsidized housing, elderly women and single mothers felt particularly vulnerable. In inner-city low-rise complexes like Perkins, Latrobe, and Gilmor homes, residents complained about break-ins through first-floor windows. A man raped an eighty-one-year-old Gilmor Homes woman after crawling through her bedroom window. Another Gilmor tenant, Eliza Herndon, suffered three burglaries, the last two of which were only three weeks apart. In a thank you letter to then Gilmor manager Charles K. Anderson, Herndon's niece, Dr. Mary Brooks, wrote that she heard her aunt say "that so many of the women who live alone were becoming concerned." In 1964, Latrobe management started assessing tenants' safety after numerous beatings and robberies of elderly black women tenants. In just under a month, the Douglass Homes management office and tenants' apartments experienced seven attempted or actual break-ins.[57]

Low-rise and high-rise public housing tenants also complained about nonresident traffic, gambling, and loitering in the buildings, in recreational spaces, and on abutting streets. Gladys Spell argued that "many times it is the people who don't belong, [who] come down from other neighborhoods. And they hang around, come in, or whatever they do, you know . . . and just go back to their neighborhoods and criticize us."[58] The desire to prevent outsiders from abusing public housing neighborhoods resounded in tenant lamentations. In 1965 at a Cherry Hill Homes community meeting, about 500 tenants met with police representatives. They wanted to stop the constant "crap" games, get rid of teenage gangs and "winos," and better understand the purpose of police-community meetings.[59]

Tenants in Murphy Homes, the Lexington Terrace–Poe Homes community, Lafayette Courts, and the majority-white Claremont Homes complained about the rising drug traffic—a problem that turned public housing and inner cities into open markets and would affect the children of tenants like Benton, Schofield, and Wise. In Lexington Terrace, Christine Jones, a resident since 1958, described her high-rise building as infested with dirt, rats, and heavy dope traffic. In 1968, Douglass Homes' manager, David Ramsey, maintained that drug addiction was steadily increasing, according to current crime figures. In the 1960s, the number of police-documented cases swelled from 1,084 to 2,338, and this did not include an additional 1,800 cases unveiled in a Maryland State Department of Mental Hygiene study. By the late 1960s, heroin had arrived on the scene alongside marijuana in Baltimore, and crimes like robbery and theft increased as this habit-forming, opium-based drug took hold.[60] Ramsey asserted in a housing memo:

> I have never been able, truthfully, to understand how Douglass Homes has had such a low level of crime for the whole time I have been here. East Baltimore as an area has probably the second highest level of crime in the city and yet Douglass Homes until recently has been an oasis of relative peace in a sea of crime. Unfortunately, of late, we have come of age.[61]

From the 1970s onward, crime and particularly the drug trade only worsened, not just in public housing, but throughout urban and suburban communities.

As early as the 1960s, residents criticized management and the police for not taking more proactive steps to maintain the safety of their neighborhoods. In Gilmor Homes in 1960 tenants asserted that police service was thin; eight years later they still complained about the dearth of police patrols and protection. In 1968 more than 360 Gilmor tenants signed a petition and sent it to housing officials and the mayor. The petition read in part:

> Our children have been molested, attacked, assaulted, forcibly abducted and raped. Our homes have been burglarized, broken into and damaged. Our possessions are in constant danger of being seized. Unknown and undesirable persons lurk in our hallways and court-yards, and are an ever-present danger to the safety, peace and happiness of the residents.

In the absence of police protection, some Gilmor Homes tenants demanded that the housing authority provide twenty-four-hour security, and Ella L. Strother, the tenant organization chair, wrote a letter to the police commissioner requesting protection.[62]

Public housing, which had acquired a reputation for being unpoliced, was becoming a sanctuary for unruly insiders and predatory outsiders. Public housing tenants throughout the city believed that the police and, to a degree, management left tenants open to the predations of outsiders. Many public housing communities, especially family high-rises, had indefensible space; unlike middle-class condominiums or neighborhoods, they initially lacked building security and municipal protection. Even Robert C. Embry, Jr., the new executive director and housing commissioner of Baltimore in 1968, was aware of how poorly public housing was policed and sympathized with tenants' concerns. A product of segregated Baltimore and a thirty-year-old Harvard-educated lawyer, Embry returned to his hometown in the 1960s invigorated by civil rights struggles. He joined the CPHA because the organization worked on poverty issues. Although he "wasn't thinking of" housing, he knew "there were people who were poorly housed . . . and paying an inordinate amount of money, and how did you get them in better housing paying less money? And that on the face of it seemed to be self-evident good." In 1969 at a meeting with police and tenants citywide, Embry stressed the need for transforming public housing's image by having visible and random police patrols to deter criminals. Embry stated that "the hoodlum element in the city regarded public housing as a sanctuary and as a route of escape when being pursued for their crimes and misdemeanors."[63] Embry called for an end to the construction of high-rise public housing because "they didn't work." The halls and the stairwells "were no-man's lands."[64] Eventually the housing authority did provide security, especially in high-rise complexes, through private agencies and a resident security program that trained women tenants as guards. But in the late 1960s those security programs, which had limited success, did not exist.

In the more open high-rise complexes, tenants had specific security concerns. For instance, they complained about mailbox protection and elevator safety. Tenants expressed their discontent to elected officials. A female Lexington Terrace tenant sent a letter to the mayor's office in December 1967 after her supplemental welfare check was stolen from her mailbox. A single mother employed at Londontown Manufacturing and raising a three-year-old son, she pleaded for help: "I really work hard to get ahead and to raise my son the proper way. Believe me it is not easy trying to make it alone and raise a boy." Her $36.14 check was for her rent, which she already received an extension to pay. She complained that maintenance had not repaired her mailbox and had even told her that fixing the mailbox would be useless because vandals would just break it again. After the mayor's community relations specialist forwarded the letter to Van Story Branch, the matter was resolved.[65]

A year later, Estelle Ratliff, a resident of the Lexington-Poe community, wrote Hyman Pressman, the city comptroller, regarding the same issue—the lack of response by the housing authority to mailbox vandalism. While BURHA memos did show that officials had expressed concern, Ratliff was not privy to these internal discussions. While a recurring complaint, Ratliff's preoccupation with mailbox vandalism surpassed the narrow issue of broken locks and stolen letters and checks. She protested the marginalization of poor people. Accompanied by a petition, her written complaint stated:

> It is claimed that the poor has no voice but I do hope that I am one of the poor that can be heard. In addition to broken mailboxes we have little or no protection for our homes, personal properties and our lives. Though we are considered as American poor we want the same things in life as every American does and that covers all aspects of American life.[66]

Ratliff's letter, the Gilmor Homes tenants' petition, and all of the concerned tenants' voices reflected their desires to inhabit respectable neighborhoods, take care of their children and households, and avow poor people's right to protection. Ratliff specifically countered depictions of public housing tenants, and poor people more broadly, as the producers of urban social ills and as undeserving of citizenship rights. Claiming voice, Ratliff not only demanded to be heard and safe, but also that the government respond—an increasingly familiar and insistent call of tenant activists in the 1960s.

Conclusion

In the midst of poverty and crime, tenants involved in community affairs held on to a vision of respectable living and a right to safety and security for poor people. In numerous instances, tenants attempted to address their neighborhoods' deterioration both in physical landscape and image. Given the travails of urban spaces and public housing, maintaining a "nice" place subverted societal stereotypes. Conscious of this, tenants—those who had memories of what public housing had offered, hopes of what it could still provide, the time to devote, or the will to care—labored as individuals and in groups against neighborhood decline and poverty.

Deteriorating economic means, negative perceptions, and declining neighborhoods dogged poor people, but they also laid the groundwork for a new activist consciousness. In the wake of the War on Poverty and black freedom fighters' convergence on inner cities, residents engaged in grassroots struggles in their communities to alter power relations and gain respect in these increasingly disreputable urban spaces. Women like Benton, who came of age as a community activist in the 1980s, benefited from the legacy of such struggles. According to Benton, who fondly recalled Goldie Baker and her community advocacy: "I am her creation." The postwar generation of black women public housing tenant activists like Goldie Baker asserted their rights as citizens, as did their 1940s predecessors. However, they struggled under significantly different circumstances: Low-income black women experienced greater scrutiny, government control, daily surveillance, and disrepute as recipients of postwar government aid. These challenges, alongside black freedom struggles in the 1960s and 1970s, unleashed low-income black women's social welfare activism and resulted in qualitatively different demands. In the civil rights and black power years, black women activists did not simply want housing officials to address their concerns, they now wanted a bigger, formal role in conducting housing affairs. Poor black women like Baker, Martin, Wise, and others sought to rally community forces against mismanagement and fight for tenants' voice, rights, and representation—all under the umbrella of respect, dignity, and survival.

Respect, Rights, and Power PART III

"An Awakening Giant" ⑤
The Search for Poor People's Political Power

Within a couple of decades of moving into Lafayette Courts on December 10, 1955, Shirley Wise had married and separated from her children's father, held several jobs, attended Cortez Peters Business School, and become a beautician. Possessing a sense of community belonging, she became active in the Parents-Teachers Association and Lafayette Courts Mothers' Club. But Shirley Wise avoided controversy and "leadership" roles. While she was happy to serve as vice president or treasurer, she did not want to be head honcho. "In those days . . . I did not want to be the leader" or the person "who had to do, to make sure everything happened."[1]

Between 1955 and 1970, Shirley Wise shed her timidity as she learned more about rights: her civil rights, legal rights, tenants' rights. By the early 1970s, the petite Wise had made an unpaid career of advocating for the poor in her housing complex and citywide. Before her political awakening, Shirley Wise often said, "[L]et somebody else take care of that. I was one of those people. Like I say, social commitments, that's me. Anything that was really rocking the boat, I wasn't into that until I found out I had the legal right to

Figure 5.1 Shirley Wise moved into Lafayette Courts in 1955. Around 1980, she moved into a rehabilitated house in the lower Park Heights community and continued on the Resident Advisory Board as a representative for tenants in scattered-site and rehabbed housing. Photograph by Elizabeth Malby.

do that—to rock the boat." Shirley Wise's transformation—her heightened consciousness of power relations, inequality, and rights—mirrored that of other poor black women living in cities. As black freedom movements and antipoverty programs grew in northern cities, rights, struggle, power, control, respect, and dignity became popular words—and goals. Referring to the local housing and political bureaucracy, Shirley Wise maintained: "[Public housing] provided a place for me to raise my children. It [also] provided me with a serious education that I couldn't have got in no school. I had good teachers—some of the best congressmen out there."[2]

Civil Rights in the Upper Urban South

In the 1960s, greater awareness of economic inequalities and poor people's rights ushered in intense disruptions and demands in cities. In Baltimore, militant black and white groups helped radicalize the urban terrain. To be sure, "traditional" civil rights protests occurred, like the boycotting of Jim

Crow restaurants, stores, hotels, and taverns in the city and along the fifty-mile stretch of Interstate 40. However, in the mid-1960s grassroots efforts also took another activist route—one seeking subsistence rights, empowerment, and economic equality. By the time black freedom activists and federal antipoverty workers converged on cities, concentrated black poverty had produced communities and situations ripe for organizing working-class people. Not coincidentally, public housing neighborhoods had lured civil rights, antipoverty, and black power activists, who invested their time in political education, agitation, and dispensation of services. This helped heat up the city.

A key organization was Baltimore's Union for Jobs or Income Now (U-JOIN). An interracial group of students from Morgan, Goucher, and Johns Hopkins formed the local Students for a Democratic Society's Economic Research and Action Project (SDS-ERAP). During the summer of 1964, SDS-ERAP opened ten offices, including Baltimore, Newark, and Cleveland, to expose the "clear failures of the liberal welfare state" and "fight for a bare standard of living in the most affluent society in the world."[3] Quite aware of Baltimore's segregationist politics, U-JOIN workers established an office on Gay Street for black people and another on East Baltimore Street for white people. Walter Lively directed the Gay Street office and unlike the ERAPs in Chicago, Newark, and Cleveland, he focused significantly on the poorest of the poor. This concerned ERAP organizers, who wrote: "Marxist warnings of the dangers of attempting to organize the lumpen proletariat were still occasionally heard from Baltimore."[4] Increasingly, U-JOIN aligned itself with local black freedom organizations. In 1968 a *Baltimore Sun* reporter described U-JOIN as espousing "responsible radicalism" under Lively. James Dilts continued: "U-JOIN is a potentially revolutionary group because it's committed to letting the people decide. It's a militant group because it's biased toward working, poor, black people. It's a radical group because it wants democratic control and basic social change."[5]

Baltimore CORE members also waged a war on urban "social evils" and moved "on what people want to move on."[6] In 1964 Baltimore CORE opened an office between a café and a fish shop on Gay Street and initiated its Eastside Project. Directed by William Bush, the Eastside Project attacked private slum housing in a twelve-block area, miles from the eastside's public housing complexes. Walter P. Carter, Baltimore CORE's chair from 1961 to 1963 and an executive board member, argued that defeating poverty remained crucial for black people's true liberation. Argued Carter: "We had broken the public accommodations aspect of civil rights down and we knew the real civil rights battles would be fought right there [in neighborhoods] where these people are whipped by everything—housing, unemployment, lack of opportunities, improper schooling."[7]

Two years later, in 1966, Baltimore became a gathering ground for activists who attended CORE's national convention. For instance, Martin Luther King, Jr.; Fannie Lou Hamer of the Mississippi Freedom Democratic Party; Richard Cloward, a sociologist at Columbia University and a future founder of the National Welfare Rights Organization (NWRO); Floyd McKissick, national CORE director; and Julian Bond, formerly of the Student Non-Violent Coordinating Committee (SNCC) and a Georgia state representative, converged on the city. Not all activists agreed with CORE's new exaltation of "black power," which came after SNCC's Stokely Carmichael popularized the slogan during a Greenwood, Mississippi, rally. Members of the "big three"— the Southern Christian Leadership Conference (SCLC), the NAACP, and the Urban League—boycotted several sessions in protest. CORE activists, however, firmly dedicated to black power, acted on the convention theme, "To Organize for Economic and Political Power," and agreed to focus on the inner city, which was dubbed "the awakening giant."[8] CORE conventioneers established six major goals: to better housing, improve employment, organize welfare recipients, upgrade and integrate public schools, establish freedom schools, and provide voter registration opportunities and political education. Baltimore's Mayor McKeldin greeted conventioneers and even welcomed CORE's Target City, saying, with a "bit of luck Baltimore could be the nation's safest big city during the long, hot summer." But like the "big three" civil rights organizations, McKeldin expressed reticence about CORE's black power declaration.[9] After the convention, CORE–Target City opened its first office on Gay Street, near U-JOIN and Baltimore CORE offices, and spoke of "'igniting' East Baltimore's vast, gritty Negro ghetto in 'one big push against a segregationist, racist backwater, the worst in the nation.'"[10]

As black freedom organizations expressed increased interest in the question of urban poverty in cities, so did the federal government, which incorporated citizens' participation as a public policy goal.[11] In 1964 President Lyndon B. Johnson established the Office of Economic Opportunity (OEO), out of which emerged the War on Poverty. The War on Poverty brought Community Action Program (CAP), Volunteers in Service to America (VISTA), and Legal Aid Services workers to cities. In 1965—a year after U-JOIN and CORE initiated programs to target poverty—CAP arrived in Baltimore. The city was one of the first to qualify for the federal funds based on a 207-page "Plan of Action on the Problems of Baltimore's Disadvantaged People" that focused on "human renewal" and targeted six square miles around the central business district. More than 200,000 residents (86 percent of them black) and 46,000 families (40 percent of which earned less than $3,000 a year) lived in the "action area," which included most of the city's oldest sections, public housing complexes, and urban renewal areas. OEO awarded Baltimore $4 million and required the city to match 10 percent of the grant.[12] That same year, one of the first neighborhood action centers opened in east Baltimore's Flag House Courts; 2,100 or 75 percent of the residents in that ten-block target neighborhood lived in public housing.[13] By 1967 Community Action Agency (CAA) offices operated in five public housing complexes (four in east Baltimore) and VISTA workers resided in O'Donnell Heights, Cherry Hill Homes, and the four high-rise complexes.[14] The vast, gritty ghettos of Baltimore—and its public housing communities—were becoming activist hot spots.

A Radical Presence

Out of east Baltimore's public housing complexes emerged black women like Shirley Wise whose activism ultimately altered poor people's relationship to government. Politicized by their living conditions and activist discontent after World War II, low-income black women grew more confrontational in the 1960s—in general a time when "people got to talking to people, [to] know more about their rights," according to Julia Matthews, a Douglass Homes tenant activist. Shirley Wise similarly argued that a "new generation of public housing residents came along who said, . . . we have rights too," and they worked to "effect some kind of change."[15] Viewed as "objects of charity" and policed by the state because they received government aid, poor black women mounted housing and social welfare campaigns. Joining generations of low-income, working-class activist women, these women mobilized in communities. Some drew on a familial historical legacy, and others built on the knowledge gained from their community participation efforts. They participated in parents' school groups, mothers' clubs, recreational activities, and other civic activities. They continued the age-old demand for safe neighborhoods and subsistence. But they also did something different: This new generation of activist women pushed for respect, a right to representation, and power as not only citizens, but as human beings deserving of basic rights.

Alongside family, historical, and community influences, the presence of militant grassroots activists and antipoverty workers helped politicize low-income black women in these new decades of struggle. Some public housing tenants met local officials, antipoverty workers, and black freedom fighters—or at least knew of their presence. Goldie Baker identified two of the city's most popular organizers, U-JOIN's Walter H. Lively and CORE's Walter P. Carter, as mentors alongside her grandmother and mother, who were activists for poor people's rights and Progressive party members during the McCarthy era. She recalled Lively's and Carter's diehard commitment to working-class black people's advancement: "They were really hard on white people, but they would keep black and white people accountable of the rights of poor people. . . . They were in the struggle and they were going to fight for their rights."[16]

These two men, who forthrightly confronted racism and inequality, hailed from circumstances similar to those confronted by poor black women like Goldie Baker. One of eight children, Lively grew up in Philadelphia's public housing and on welfare after his father deserted the family. As a University of Pennsylvania student, Lively participated in CORE's Maryland freedom rides in 1961, which brought him through Baltimore via Route 40. He also organized a CORE chapter in Philadelphia and served as the Philadelphia director for the March on Washington before settling in Baltimore in 1963.[17] Similarly, Walter P. Carter's war veteran and migration experiences spurred him to fight Jim Crow and economic inequality. Born in Monroe, North Carolina, in 1923, Carter migrated to Baltimore in 1948 and joined CORE in 1959. He protested hiring discrimination, participated in the freedom rides, and served as Maryland's coordinator for the March on Washington, mobilizing 12,000 people. Known as "Mr. Civil Rights," Carter helped found Activists for Fair Housing to push for better and integrated communities. In the late 1960s, Carter was briefly chief community organizer for Model Cities, and he supported the Baltimore Welfare Rights Organization (BWRO). Central city residents regarded Carter "as their spokesman in the political circles and bureaucracy that honeycomb the city's efforts to help the community's poor."[18]

Some poor black women activists not only met grassroots and anti-poverty activists, but also worked with them. For instance, a former military man, laborer, union activist, CORE member, Baltimore teacher, and employment discrimination investigator, Clyde Hatcher became a CAA neighborhood counselor at Lafayette Courts. Like Lively and Carter, Hatcher knew well racial discrimination, poverty, and welfare. When his father, a barber, died of a heart attack, his mother relied on welfare and surplus food to support him and his siblings. "I've been poor and I know how it is. You know [how] people talk about people on welfare. I take issue with that. If it hadn't been for, they called it relief then, if it hadn't been for that what would me and my sister and my brother . . . have done?" He left Latrobe, a small Pennsylvania coal-mining town, at fifteen years old and moved in with an uncle in Baltimore.[19]

The relationship among organizers and low-income black women was synergistic. Just as organizers inspired black women, black women inspired organizers. For instance, even though Goldie Baker labeled Lively and Carter mentors, she initially met them because they sought her out. They wanted her advice on how to deal with the welfare department and welfare rights issues. They learned from her even as she learned from them. Hatcher joined CORE and the civil rights movement partly at the insistence of "a lady I knew [who] lived around the corner." She urged him to attend CORE's 1966 national convention, where he heard an impassioned speech by Fannie Lou Hamer. "I mean she talked about how she had [been] picking cotton in the fields and she was trying to organize and how they came down and intimidated her. She was a dynamic person." Soon thereafter, Hatcher became a CORE member. As a neighborhood counselor, Hatcher interacted with many committed black women activists, who were sometimes more radical than he—like Goldie Baker, whom Hatcher described as a "legend" and "one of the most dynamic leaders I have ever seen."[20]

The Community Action Program

The War on Poverty and CAP also politicized cohorts of public housing residents and the cities they lived in. Men and women antipoverty workers, like Clyde Hatcher, came prepared to coordinate services and rally the poor to action, the most militant aim of a program that otherwise bought into the argument that poor people needed to be altered to succeed. That rhetorical mandate to rally the poor legitimized poor people's community action and provided them with an infrastructure to contest local city agencies. W. Lyndsai Pitts, Sr., a Perkins Homes CAA counselor, stated his mission as "enabling our clients to move in the direction of self-help and self-realization as it relates to our Great Society Programs."[21] Influenced by a 1964 *Yale Law Journal* article entitled "The War on Poverty: A Civilian Perspective," many Legal Services lawyers developed a consumer-oriented focus on maximizing feasible participation, which counteracted the "military approach" in which professionals exercised power on behalf of the poor. The "civilian perspective" required "that the promotion of neighborhood dissent and criticism be an avowed goal of the war on poverty, that its organizational structure make provision for the establishment of groups and institutions with the independence, power, and express purpose of articulating grievances."[22] Parren J. Mitchell, who became Baltimore's Community Action Commission's executive director in late 1965, stated a similar theory: "My theory is this: If you organize the poor people and you show them where they can get some services which were previously denied them, they'll begin thinking politically" and maybe then the status quo will change.[23] In fact, the status quo would prove quite resilient, but activists' heartfelt belief that local political culture and social welfare policies had to change fueled grassroots discontent.

Within the first couple of years of CAP in Baltimore and throughout the 1960s, power struggles emerged. U-JOIN criticized the Baltimore program for its lack of poor people on the CAC board and organized residents in private and public housing in east Baltimore to speak out at numerous city council judiciary committee hearings. Eventually the CAC expanded its eleven-member board, appointing four people from poverty areas.[24] Even then, neither poor people—nor the CAC board generally—had unhampered decision-making authority. Holding the purse strings and approval power for every CAC program, the city council exerted control and was so interventionist that even the OEO regional director, Sidney H. Woolner, expressed concern. While praising the work of Mitchell and his staff, Woolner urged the Baltimore CAC to become more independent by reining in the city council's power of appointment and program approval.[25]

Poor people and their advocates continuously charged that because the agency was top-heavy, it could not address their economic and social problems. In December 1966, poor people led by Murphy Homes tenant Mattie Parker held an Action Area Convention attended by sixty-three delegates—

two-thirds of them women—from twenty-one poverty centers in the city. Several Lafayette Courts and Douglass Homes tenants served on the steering committee, and other public housing tenants, like Daisy Snipes of Perkins Homes (also a welfare rights activist), attended as delegates. Overall the woman-led and majority-female delegation complained about "poor police protection and discourteous treatment, bad housing, rats, unemployment, money going to the Vietnam War instead of helping them, crime, low welfare payments, management of housing projects, and help for youth of today." This panoply of issues reflected the breadth of low-income women's concerns. Convention delegates also demanded the power to review the mayor's CAC appointments, an expansion of the CAC, and majority-poor representation on the board.[26] The CAC agreed to give poor people more seats, but not as many as they demanded. Commissioners argued that asking the city council for too much would result in the torpedoing or delay of programs. In January 1967, convention delegates and poor people's advocates attended a city council meeting where they threatened to "take to the streets." While convention delegates' demands were not fully met, the CAC did expand its board—the final tally was twenty-one members with ten poor representatives.

The city council held fast and refused to relinquish any authority. Years later, in 1968, the city council with William Donald Schaefer as its president rejected Mayor Thomas D'Alesandro III's appointment of Walter P. Carter as CAC director. CAA staff called the city council "callous" and accused the municipal body of waging a "secretive assault on the anti-poverty program and the people it serves."[27] Federal officials again questioned whether the council had "too much of a voice in the administration of the CAA."[28] Even a *Baltimore Evening Sun* editorial called the city council action a "conservative backlash slap" at the CAC and a "capricious and wrong rejection" that resembles a "calculated rebuff to Negroes and the poor."[29]

The neighborhood action offices, which had their own staffs, worked more closely with people. Although political tussling remained a consistent feature of the local program, and neighborhood action centers were not "fighting organizations," according to Goldie Baker, some antipoverty workers did really try to help poor people "organize the community." Goldie Baker recalled that public housing CAAs

> put enough literature and material out . . . to bring us together and let [the residents] know what it means to be united. . . . They didn't

get in the forefront of the fight, but they were educational. And as far as resources, you could find out different information on your rights, constitutions, you know, things you [were] entitled to. . . . And bringing people together . . . telling them how to stand up, be strong, and organize. I think that was their basic goal.[30]

Tenant activists made use of these resources as they struggled for economic stability and resident empowerment.

Some low-income black women nationwide took advantage of the federal government's urban community "organizational locations." The hiring of black women in CAAs and sometimes as VISTAs formalized their status "as central figures in the ongoing survival of their embattled communities."[31] Ann Thornton, who returned to public housing in 1967 with three children after a failed marriage, worked as a cashier until her doctor told her that her pregnancy required rest. When she was seven months' pregnant, Thornton quit her job, started collecting welfare, and volunteered in the Perkins Homes CAA office "where, you know, they would deal with community problems." She sent her children to a church daycare where she also volunteered. Eventually, she became a VISTA worker (as would a coterie of welfare rights activists in the late 1960s and 1970s). Thornton earned $50 a week and later became an advocate for tenants who registered housing complaints with Legal Services. Lafayette Courts' tenant leader, Bonnie Ellis, also worked with CAA. Julia Matthews, who already had a community participation record around health and school issues, took advantage of CAA and Legal Services by attending antipoverty and job-training meetings—as did Shirley Wise. Matthews proudly remembered: "At that time, when we were real active during the CAA, it was jobs out here for people they trained" both in the agency and elsewhere. These CAA jobs further validated poor black women's concerns and empowered them to speak; after all, they believed they had the federal government behind them.[32]

Rights, Respect, and Representation

While the housing authority welcomed federal agencies like CAA, Legal Services, and VISTA, the anti-establishment attitude of some employees and volunteers often made for harried relationships. The federal government and local officials did not desire a radical shift in power, competition, or even a critique of the way government operated; after all they did not believe the problem lay with the government or the economy, but with the people. The War on Poverty primarily sought to coordinate services, encourage behavioral alterations, and encourage self-help. If the Great Society programs had transforming impacts, it was because local black communities, poor black women, and poor people's advocates organized campaigns to alter systems and policies that affected their lives. An exchange of letters between CAA neighborhood counselor Lyndsai Pitts and Joel Newton, then Perkins Homes' manager, highlighted the sometimes contrary relationship between local welfare agencies and CAAs. Pitts described Newton as a tool of the "status quo" who was not dedicated to tenants' real concerns. Pitts argued that he and his assistants were "mandated by Law and Conscience to promote the ambitions and aspirations of the Residents" and that they would not oppose residents' actions "as they seek to obtain, by lawful means, a larger share of the American Promise."[33] In an era of increased rights and nationalist struggles, "self-help" and "self-realization" not only meant providing black working-class people with services, but also legitimizing their attempts to change and control the institutions affecting their lives and communities.

As public housing tenants talked and learned more about their rights, they targeted the housing authority, questioned management, and sought a participatory role in the decision-making process in their complexes and eventually agency-wide. Lafayette and Douglass tenants Bonnie Ellis and Mildred Lee led such a campaign. Mildred Lee moved into Douglass Homes in 1955. A widow, Lee worked as a domestic to make ends meet. She had a history of civic activism and leadership responsibilities. She was a member of the fraternal Elks and Reindeer Association, the Nazarites, and United Baptist Church.[34] Both Lee, who envisioned Douglass as her permanent home, and Ellis, who struggled to raise her family in Lafayette Courts, were invested in keeping Lafayette-Douglass (the two complexes were jointly administered) safe and that meant ensuring that management responded to tenants' needs. In the late 1960s Lafayette-Douglass tenants formed the Resident Action Committee (RAC) with help from CAA and Legal Aid volunteers. Ellis, RAC's chair, and Lee requested the administrative separation of the two complexes. This request represented tenants' attempt to secure official voice and input in the housing policymaking arena.

In public housing, residents' growing poverty had resulted in a concomitant decline in the operating budget, which depended on rent collections. In

Figure 5.2 Eugenia "Bonnie" Ellis Johnson Davis, a former Lafayette Courts tenant, helped found the Resident Action Committee in 1966 and served as a member of the first Resident Advisory Board in 1968. She moved out of public housing in 1969. Photograph by Elizabeth Malby.

1963 housing officials, who had hoped to realize "substantial financial savings," combined the staff of Douglass Homes and Lafayette Courts.[35] Within five years, however, the cost-cutting measure proved neither efficient nor desirable to tenants. Tenants argued that one staff could not efficiently manage and maintain more than 1,000 units nor address the entire tenant population's needs. Julia Matthews, who after twenty-five years of residency became Douglass Homes' tenant council president in 1971, argued that tenants felt Douglass was neglected: "This place was coming down. They was doing more for Lafayette. . . . Well, [we thought, if] we separate and have our own staff, it would be better."[36] RAC and tenant leaders also argued that Douglass's and Lafayette's residents had different needs. Over one-third of Douglass's households were elderly people, while in the newer high-rise complex of Lafayette Courts, 89 percent were families—34.5 percent were two-parent and 54.6 percent were single-parent households.[37] Ellis and Lee told officials that Douglass's elderly residents found it difficult to walk several blocks to Lafayette Courts to pay their rent, and they wanted their own community facilities for meetings and recreation. Tenant leaders maintained as well that

Lafayette needed a "seasoned manager" to deal with the problems of high-rise complexes like safety, elevator maintenance, and servicing families and children. In 1968, after six months of tenant-management meetings and negotiations, the administration of Lafayette-Douglass was separated.[38]

Challenging the housing agency's administrative purview, tenant leaders also fought for input in personnel decisions by demanding the right to choose their managers. In Douglass and Lafayette, tenant-management relations were so strained that even housing officials considered it "a matter of extreme concern to this Agency."[39] Managers' condescending attitudes spurred fear and discontent and stymied tenants' complaints. Goldie Baker of Lafayette and Ann Thornton of Perkins Homes (and, later, Rosetta Schofield of Murphy Homes) criticized Joel Newton, who served as a manager in all three complexes. Newton, Clyde Hatcher remembered, "was the man that [tenants] used to hate."[40] Never late with her rent, Ann Thornton recalled Newton's hostility when she requested a payment extension. At the time she was working, but her paycheck was short because she missed a week and did not have sick leave. She recalled: "Oh, he got to hollering at me. . . . I said, hey slow down. . . . Don't holler at me no more. Am I hollering at you? You treat me like you want to be treated and we going to get along fine." According to Thornton, that was when Newton uttered: "Well, just one of them welfare . . . " She cut him off, told him that she worked, and that, no matter, he had no "business classifying nobody. . . . You understand what I'm saying? See, people classify you and if you don't nip it in the bud and stop 'em, they'll continue."[41]

Managerial mistreatment exposed how some housing officials viewed tenants—"worse than, less than a dog." In one instance, Baker simply wanted housing maintenance to remove the ancient icebox in her apartment so she could make more space for a refrigerator—one of the few pieces of furniture she still possessed from her days as a home owner. The refrigerator sat in the middle of her floor and took up vital space in the small three-bedroom apartment. When she went over to maintenance to put in her request, she experienced unexpected condescension:

> I didn't know the residents, tenants had to go through all that kind of stuff they had been going through. . . . I had rights, you know. I was one of them . . . sassy niggers who had some right. They ain't

know where I come from. They ain't know who I was listening to all them years. So I said, you know, "I don't know who you think you talking to." . . . And then I went over to the manager's office to report them. . . . So anyway, Joel Newton, he talked to me and asked me was I crazy. Get out of his office. Honey, that's when I went to see the commissioner. And I told him, I don't know who he [Newton] think he's talking to. I am not nobody's slave. I *am not* nobody's *slave*, and he *ain't* talking to no slave. Slavery's over. . . . I said, he don't have no respect for me, he don't need to be over there.[42]

Given their experiences with the managers, a cadre of outspoken Lafayette and Douglass tenants sought the right to be treated decently in their homes and communities. Tenants asked for input in managerial selection because the manager represented, as RAC secretary and CAA tenant worker Margaret E. Johnson maintained, a "king in his kingdom." He set the "tone" of the complex. He controlled daily decisions like the flexibility of rent-payment procedures.[43] Echoing the laments of black tenant dissidents in the 1940s, Lafayette and Douglass tenants wanted to secure managers whom they thought would help them, "not talk down to them" because they were poor black people.

The RAC supplied officials with the names of candidates, but central administration told tenants that personnel decisions lay with housing administration. Dissatisfied RAC representatives, accompanied by CAA and VISTA workers, went to the February 6, 1968, housing commissioners' meeting. Margaret E. Johnson conveyed tenants' desire to select the new manager; she also told commissioners that Bonnie Ellis believed that management had retaliated against her after she ignored warnings to not hold organizing meetings. In what became a three-hour hearing, commissioners devised a compromise that incorporated tenants. Arguing that "the success of a housing project is a direct result of the tenant council," board members encouraged the establishment of a joint panel to develop criteria for the selection and evaluation of the manager. While commissioners incorporated tenants, the plan fell short of the RAC's demand to pick the manager. Tenant representatives, however, accepted the compromise even as they realized that management retained decision-making power. To this end, Johnson remarked that she hoped housing officials would not select managers whom tenants "violently opposed."[44]

The question of managerial mistreatment and retaliation, which partly had spurred the RAC's fight for inclusion in personnel decisions, remained unresolved in the Ellis case. Ellis claimed the staff reneged on a promise for a larger ground-level apartment because she helped to organize residents. In September 1967, Ellis, who had four girls and one boy, requested a larger apartment, maintaining that her eight-year-old son, who had numerous medical problems, needed his own bedroom. The housing authority asked Ellis for proof, and in January 1968, she gave them a doctor's letter confirming her claim. Ellis told officials that a four-bedroom apartment had been promised to her. Instead the apartment was assigned to an eleven-person family on the same day as an organizing meeting. Ellis understood giving the apartment to a larger family. She even stated that she "would have been content to let the matter drop" if the interim manager of Lafayette-Douglass before its separation had not "inferred that her position as chairman of the Resident Action Committee had some bearing on the matter."[45]

The *Evening Sun* published Ellis's claims, including what she considered a "subtle" suggestion that she should move to Cherry Hill Homes in south Baltimore.[46] The day the newspaper article appeared, Parren J. Mitchell, then CAC executive director, disturbed by Ellis's allegations, called for a probe. He stated: "We feel that it's unfair and unjust if residents organize to try to secure greater participation and retaliatory measures are taken by any public agency. . . . [T]he Community Action Agency has always encouraged poor residents to organize themselves and participate fully in community life."[47] The day after Mitchell's request, BURHA denied the charges. The facts in this case remain conflicted. Interestingly, however, six days after the publicizing of Ellis's claims, Ellis was given a four-bedroom apartment in Douglass Homes.[48]

The RAC's campaign marked Baltimore residents' entry into the policy-making arena. Their complaints and actions revealed their attempts to alter the institutions dispensing services, and that meant carving out a concrete, officially recognized space for tenant involvement. Tenants secured recognition and the power to negotiate policy. But local officials ultimately did not relinquish authority when acquiescing to residents' demands. The institutions, by incorporating tenants' voices, may have become more democratic—but the systems of inequality that kept poor women impoverished and reliant on public housing remained firmly in place. Even so, these women had achieved a primary goal—the right to affect the systems that structured their daily lives. And they also made clear, and public, tenants' expanding displeasure with public housing's living conditions.

Ellis, Lee, Johnson, and tenant groups like the RAC provided a representative voice for tenants, many of whom feared that speaking out would result in retaliation as Goldie Baker and others recounted. Baker recalled that tenants responded with extreme surprise when they found out she had spoken back to Joel Newton and even protested to the commissioner:

> Oooh, girl, how you talked to him like that?! Do you know you'll get put out! He had been putting people out. . . . people were scared of him. . . . And that's what got me concerned. 'Cause I said, oh, no, unh-unh, nobody is supposed to talk . . . down to you like [that], who they think they are? They work for you! You the tenant there. And you pay your rent. You pay his salary.

Shirley Wise similarly argued that fear prevented more tenants from acting in their own self-interest: "The fear structure . . . was attached to the units. You couldn't do this and you couldn't do the other. . . . I mean they had little spotters all over the community. . . . When they say public housing, they meant in the real true sense. Your life was public too."[49]

These stories illustrate the power that managers had, and some did wield, against tenants who protested a mite too forcefully about poor housing conditions. The repercussions could be detrimental, affecting the comfort and very survival of poor families who already found themselves relying on government subsidies to make ends meet. In 1967 in Durham, North Carolina, the housing authority evicted tenant leader Joyce Thorpe and her three children without a hearing and for no apparent reason except that she was organizing tenants. Her case went to the U.S. Supreme Court and would forever change housing policy: Retaliatory evictions were outlawed, and eviction and grievance procedures were established. While the fear of losing one's residence still endured, activist women like Julia Matthews remained resolute. Matthews argued that tenant participation, community responsibility, black empowerment, and advancement went hand in hand: "I have always been active in the community. What they say, charity starts at home. . . . This is my neighborhood. This is my tenant organization. All of us, get yourself together, have more say, input. . . . They've been too quiet. For how long we been slaves?"[50]

Modernizing Tenant-Management Relations

Politicized by their personal histories, daily circumstances, black freedom movements, and antipoverty workers, black women activists also benefited from federal housing officials' incorporation of the maximum feasible participation concept. In 1967 HUD staff members focused on addressing two urgent problems—deteriorating housing and residents' burgeoning discontent. Soon thereafter, HUD established the modernization program, which sought to upgrade the physical condition of public housing.[51] The program also aimed to improve tenant-management relations by requiring tenant involvement in developing local modernization plans, altering management policies, and expanding services. In a 1968 HUD circular, "Social Goals for Public Housing," the federal government suggested that municipal housing authorities "undertake a mutual commitment to cooperative action and trust with tenant organizations."[52] Essentially, in the words of *Journal of Housing* writer Jack Bryan, not only was "Public Housing Modernization . . . bringing not only modernized buildings but modernized tenant/management relations."[53]

This federal program, like CAP, provided residents, some of whom had confronted management already, with the necessary weapons to challenge municipal policies. The requirement of tenant participation and consultation in the modernization program helped transform the character of many tenant groups, which were clubs concerned with "activities and group interests of the tenants . . . not with management of the project."[54] In Minneapolis, the first city to receive modernization money, HUD delayed the program until the local housing agency satisfactorily showed that tenants had participated "in drawing the proposals." Shirley Wise, the self-described "Malcolm X of public housing" in Baltimore, maintained that the modernization program became a key residential "organizing tool." According to Wise: "I know people, now as they look back, they're sorry that HUD" required that "a resident group sign off on the modernization plan. . . . Because that gave [residents] their true rights to sit at the table with the decision-makers and effect some changes in their community."[55]

Federal dictates, however, did not necessarily translate into local agency cooperation with tenant activists. Some public housing authorities refused to share power with tenants and "told HUD to 'keep the money.'" Subterfuge also occurred. In 1970 in Nashville, according to Mattie Buchanan, president of the Nashville Tenants Organization, the housing authority disregarded tenants' participatory claims and still sought the grant—so local intransigence to federal mandates did occur. By 1971, 6 percent, or 169 housing authorities operating 306,000 apartments, three-fourths of them fifteen years old or more, established modernization programs. They included the largest cities with "the greatest needs." Baltimore was one of them.[56]

The new federal regulations gave black women public housing activists the authority to elevate their rights and power claims to include having a voice in central administration matters. Drawing on their organizing experiences with RAC and alliances with federal workers, activists in Baltimore mounted a campaign to push for decision-making power in agency matters and demanded citywide tenant representation. Led by Margaret E. Johnson of Lafayette, the nine-member delegation requested a meeting with Robert C. Embry, Jr.

Embry seemed responsive to change and to tenants. As a CPHA member, Embry had chaired a committee that issued a report urging the combining of public housing, urban renewal, and housing inspection into one agency. He ran for city council and won against John Pica, "who was seen as the personification of the anti-black faction of the city council, anti–open housing, [against] poverty programs." When Embry became a city council member, he pushed for implementation of the new combined housing department. In 1968 Mayor D'Alesandro III appointed Embry as head of the new Department of Housing and Community Development (DHCD). Embry also expressed concern about housing demolition and black displacement, which he felt were "destroying the neighborhood fabric of even poor communities" and "exacerbating racial tensions." On Saturdays, he often walked through public housing communities and talked to residents.[57] He also exhibited interest in getting tenants involved in the housing authority—in an advisory capacity. Embry recalled: "Nobody would think of asking the community what they wanted, particularly poor black people. . . . We had 40,000 people in public housing who had no voice really in how public housing was run, and they had a perspective. That wasn't the only perspective, but was an important one and needed to be heard." Embry maintained that residents were consumers and should be able to give advice and suggestions: "I mean now it seems self-evident. How could one think they shouldn't?"[58]

Shortly after Embry became executive director of the housing authority, residents from Lafayette, Flag House, and Perkins—accompanied by representatives from Legal Aid and CAA—met with him on August 16, 1968, and with the board of commissioners on August 17. The delegation demanded that housing officials withdraw the $3 million modernization budget for 1968–1969 since tenants were not consulted—a stipulation of the new program. Margaret E. Johnson also told Embry that the delegation wanted a "recognized channel for [citywide] representation." Although Embry acknowledged the validity of tenants' demands, he refused to withdraw the modernization budget, saying it was too close to approval and that Washington had expressed "no concern . . . that Baltimore was lagging in tenant participation." However, he did promise future participation—but only of tenants. Embry disapproved of the presence of Legal Aid lawyers and CAA workers. According to the meeting's minutes: "[Embry] wanted to let this group know of . . . his intentions to work with a tenant representative group to make public housing as pleasant as possible but he does not intend to be harassed by persons who are not tenants."[59] Tenants' demands and Embry's promise resulted in the formation of the citywide Resident Advisory Board (RAB).

Tenants' Rights and Urban Politics

Black female tenants' fight for tenant participation and power in Baltimore between 1967 and 1968 made them part of a vanguard of community activists in the civil rights and black power eras. Through the actions of many female tenant activists, Baltimore became one of the first cities to establish a formal citywide advisory board. Poor black women's early 1960s activism in east Baltimore had laid the groundwork for their citywide success. On October 3, 1968, Van Story Branch recognized the critical role of the RAC. Branch stated that the new RAB was "an opportunity to have total involvement for our residents." However, Branch added: "This did not begin today. It began about a year ago when Mrs. Ellis and Mrs. Lee from Lafayette and Douglass Homes requested the separation of Lafayette and Douglass and the right to help in the selection of their managers."[60] The extension of poor black women's traditional roles to the community garnered representation for all public housing tenants, black and white, women and men.

Baltimore's RAB was one of the first in the country. New York, while having representation in individual complexes, did not establish a citywide tenant council until 1970. That same year, Pittsburgh also formed a citywide group, and the Chicago Housing Tenants Organization, which sought "resident control," became embroiled in a fight with the Chicago Housing Authority to gain recognition as well as address its demands for participation in policymaking and management decisions. In 1971 a *Journal of Housing* article featured Baltimore, claiming the city was "one of a number of communities that report that greater tenant participation in management under the modernization program has also led to greater tenant responsibility for and understanding of the problems involved in operating public housing projects."[61] By 1972, Baltimore's RAB served as a liaison between the housing authority and 12,598 tenant families in twenty public housing complexes and 945 families in leased or renovated housing.[62]

Throughout the nation, poor black women emerged as leaders in public housing tenant struggles—some of which resulted in the establishment of similar representative groups—in their local communities in the 1960s and 1970s. In 1968, the same year that Baltimore tenants questioned their local agency's modernization budget, Philadelphia housing authority officials had refused to negotiate with their tenants. Represented by Legal Services lawyers

Figure 5.3 The Resident Advisory Board, December 27, 1972.
Photograph by SunStaff, Baltimore Sun.

and led by black resident activist Rose Wylie, Philadelphia public housing tenants successfully barred the agency's access to modernization money. In March 1969, Philadelphia housing officials finally entered into a "memorandum of understanding with the project organizations, recognizing the right of the tenant groups to help determine and to be regularly consulted on the modernization programs."[63] In Baltimore, Goldie Baker worked with a group of tenants who called themselves Residents in Action. Baker described the group, which had forty to fifty participants and pushed for improvements in Lafayette Courts and other complexes, as "an action group that was fighting." For instance, Residents in Action threatened a rent strike if the housing authority did not supply residents with new refrigerators. In 1969 in St. Louis, public housing tenants resorted to a citywide rent strike to address rent, repair, and maintenance issues. That action resulted in the withholding of more than $300,000 in rent. Led by tenant activists, including the "more militant strike leader" Jean King, the action had numerous results, including the selection of an entirely new board of commissioners and a new housing manager and the establishment of a tenant affairs board.[64] According to one private manager of middle-class and luxury apartments in Boston, women were the "big organizers," "the biggest complainers," and "some of them drive you nuts with their constant bitching."[65]

Black men also played a critical role in urban tenant politics. Jesse Gray led a series of successful rent strikes (500 buildings and 15,000 tenants) in Harlem in 1963, as did Anthony Henry in Chicago in 1966. Their efforts—alongside numerous others' nationwide—laid the groundwork for the development of a national coordinating body. In March 1969, Anthony Henry worked with the Nationwide Tenants Rights Program of the American Friends Service Committee, which provided the foundation for the National Tenants Organization (NTO). Already plugged into national housing rights networks, these men became the first leaders of national tenants' rights organizations. In 1969, Henry became NTO's first director, and Jesse Gray became its chair. Gray, originally from Louisiana, became involved in tenants' rights as early as 1953; he lived in private housing that had no heat or hot water in New York. He pushed for rent control legislation and helped establish a rent strike law in that city. In 1971, when Henry became the director of the National Tenants Information Service, Gray became NTO's director and Rose Wylie took over as chair. By then, Wylie had become a well-known tenants' rights advocate as the national media covered her confrontations with

Philadelphia and federal authorities.[66] Black men in Baltimore also organized around tenants' issues in public housing. Coleman D. Grant, George Milburn, Willie Winstead, Arthur Smith, and Melvin Smothers were common fixtures in public housing and familiar names in tenants' rights circles. White men, like Howard Watson and Gramley Buehler, were also known in their complexes and joined black women and black men on the interracial citywide resident board.

Tenants' rights had become commonplace in black community politics. The existence of actual movements and growing rights and self-determination rhetoric helped sharpen the critical consciousness of tenant activists, both outside and inside Baltimore. Demonstrations proliferated among private and public tenants. Low-income, middle-class, and public housing tenants in major eastern cities threatened rent strikes. In Baltimore in 1969, private renters formed the interracial Tenants' Union Group (TUG) in south Baltimore with the slogan "If you've got the GUT, go with TUG." The organization protested poor living conditions, confronted landlords, and worked with Legal Aid in filing rent escrow cases. U-JOIN also formed Tenants for Justice in Housing, which picketed landlords and politicians and pushed for rent escrow legislation in the city.[67] In 1972, five tenants' rights groups in Baltimore, including Fairfield, Lafayette Courts, Murphy Homes, RAB, and TUG, affiliated with the NTO, and Joyce Gray, a Lafayette Courts resident and tenant council president, served as NTO's at-large eastern regional representative.[68] By 1973 "tenant power," echoing the call for black power and reflecting poor people's contemporary grassroots fights for rights and voice, became a popular slogan.

Duly Authorized Representation

The creation of RAB, however, did not come without controversy. Debates ensued about representation and autonomy. Were the provisional delegates "duly authorized" by tenants and how long should they serve? Did RAB have autonomy? Did it serve the best interests of tenants? The result of tenants' political activism and their search for rights and power, RAB became a school for tenants' continued political education. Local housing and community development officials' decisions to incorporate residents within the housing bureaucracy provided structured, controllable outlets for dissent—a much more desirable alternative to attention-drawing direct action and confrontational protests. While RAB was a feat for tenants, the housing authority had incorporated tenants without relinquishing too much power. RAB had no veto power over budget decisions, and Embry chaired RAB meetings for the first two years. Recalled Embry: "I made it clear to them they were advisory, you know. That I was executive director. That I had the legal responsibility for making the decisions. That I wanted to hear what they had to say. That their interests were important, but they weren't the only interests. That there were taxpayers out there paying for these projects."[69]

The initial years of RAB provided tenant activists a lesson in how the creation of advisory organizations did not translate automatically into control, a necessary element for exercising power and spurring lasting change. When RAB first formed in 1968, the tenants in the individual complexes did not elect most of the initial RAB representatives. Tenant council executive committees, managers, or social service aides selected many of them. A few RAB members, like Bonnie Ellis and George Milburn of Lafayette, became representatives because they already served as tenant council leaders. About a month after the board's creation, RAB members formed an election committee and decided to hold elections every two years beginning in October 1970. Until then, provisional delegates would "continue their positions as representatives of their projects."[70] That report called into question the fairness of RAB's political process.[71] Formed to provide collective power, RAB had not only fallen victim to housing authority control, but also seemingly to a politics of prestige. Coleman Grant of Cherry Hill Homes argued that all "persons interested were present to vote. Others have to accept if they are not present." Murphy and Perkins homes representatives offered similar arguments. Sarah Singfield of Fairfield Homes, however, suggested that representatives raise the matter with "their own group and see if they are satisfied with their choice." In an interview, Embry maintained that some of the first representatives saw themselves as "unofficial mayors of their projects," and therefore were a "little dictatorial in gaining and keeping" seats.[72] It would not have taken much effort to hold elections again as a way to legitimize the process. As it were, select representatives successfully fought to maintain their board positions.

Embry's position as chair and the absence of full-fledged tenant elections raised questions among some residents and tenant activists about the degree of RAB's autonomy and whether, as an organization, RAB members really served as tenant advocates or as agency "lackeys." Catherine Monroe, an original member of RAB representing Fairfield Homes, resigned in August 1969. Monroe argued that the board was "manipulated by the staff." While Monroe returned to the board, her initial resignation "surprised" Embry, who wrote to her in a letter: "We do not pick the resident representatives. If a project does not think it is adequately represented then it can elect a new representative whenever it decides such a step is necessary."[73] While Embry was sympathetic to tenants' concerns, critics including RAB members believed that having the top administrative bureaucrat chair RAB meetings was an obvious conflict of interest and limited tenants' power. Shirley Wise described Embry as "fine," but argued, "[T]hat board had no business allowing a staff person who sets the policy for the agency . . . turn around and set the policy for the board."[74] The first tenant chair and commissioner, Lillian Jones, fifty-one years old and a resident of Gilmor Homes since 1942, was appointed in 1970.[75]

Confronted with a board that seemed increasingly based on exclusive, select membership, a group of unidentified tenants questioned RAB's operations. Without challenging "the existence of the RAB" and evoking solidarity as poor people, the group aimed to offer "constructive criticisms." In a letter recognizing a potential Achilles heel of marginalized communities, they wrote: "We recognize—and hope that you, too, recognize—that it is very important that we as poor people work together. We have too little power and influence when we work together—it is impossible when we are fighting among ourselves." The letter affirmed that some name-calling already had transpired: "There is nothing to be gained by you calling us 'troublemakers' and 'agitators' nor is there anything to be gained by us calling you 'lackeys.' We hope you agree." The letter writers critiqued the lack of "open meetings" and information regarding RAB's agenda. Residents had to seek permission to sit in on meetings. While permission was usually granted, the letter writers argued, "[A] lack of complete openness make[s] complete confidence and trust impossible." To popularize RAB, the group suggested a larger meeting area and outreach to tenants who did not normally attend their complexes' tenant council meetings. Acknowledging that the relationship between the commissioner and RAB was a "delicate one," they warned representatives to not be too friendly with Embry lest "they forget that their job is to represent the resident and that on some questions the interests of the residents and the interest of the Commissioner run counter to each other."[76] Goldie Baker expressed this discomfort, saying she believed then that RAB "rubber stamped" administrative policies. Baker recalled thinking: "You know good and well, y'all sit up there like the residents is like a bunch of children in school. . . . What kind of representation is that, you know?"[77]

Given all the criticisms of RAB, the group's election committee sought to develop election procedures that all viewed as fair. In a cross-class, cross-race gender alliance, RAB had help from the interracial Baltimore League of Women Voters and WomanPower, a black women's organization led by Victorine Q. Adams. Both organizations had worked with women tenants on several occasions at housing authority board meetings. A black woman and public housing's social services coordinator, Gordine Blount often facilitated the links between women tenants and middle-class women's organizations. In 1969, Blount took the resident aides to a WomanPower luncheon; it was an opportunity to link poor women to "energetic and ambitious women" and "enable them to help motivate our resident population into the mainstream of community life."[78] The two civic organizations' concerns with women's citizenship and empowerment through voting dovetailed with the concerns of poor black women tenants in public housing. In a letter to WomanPower, Gordine Blount thanked the group for agreeing to assist tenants and providing them with "a new experience as well as an educational one." Embry also praised the middle-class women. He hoped their actions would help "develop more awareness," "pride," and "commitment to the community" and that RAB elections would spark tenants' "interest and motivation to participate in all governmental elections."[79] In October 1970, when RAB had its first complex-wide, citywide elections, residents, many of them women, served as election judges in complexes other than their own, and members of the League of Women Voters and WomanPower served as poll watchers.

RAB and Tenants' Concerns

A newly elected RAB delegate in 1970, Shirley Wise quickly grew aware of the local debates surrounding the board's legitimacy. Her position on RAB not only represented her growing belief that poor people had rights, but also catalyzed her growing militancy with regard to tenants' issues. Before Shirley Wise's election to RAB, she said, "I was always wanting to be with the

Mothers' Club and the children and have activities." She helped organize benefits to raise money for children's uniforms, sponsored recreational activities for young adults, and cooked for gatherings sponsored by the tenant council. Shirley Wise eventually became involved in the Lafayette Courts tenants council, which was then led by Joyce Gray, and met Legal Aid workers, who offered leadership development classes. Even so, Wise said that she avoided any activities "that was really rocking the boat" until after she became a RAB delegate in 1970 and attended an NTO meeting that awakened her to the potential power of tenants.[80]

The NTO brought together poor people's, working-class, and civil rights concerns. In 1971 at NTO's national convention in San Francisco, speakers included Julian Bond and James Forman, a former SNCC leader who had socialist and pan-Africanist leanings and served as executive secretary of the Black Workers Congress. The group sponsored sessions on organizing around model lease and grievance procedures and the Brooke Amendment. Introduced as part of the 1969 federal housing act by Massachusetts senator Edward Brooke, the amendment mandated that families pay no more than 25 percent of their income in rent and offered federal subsidies to municipal housing authorities to pay the difference in operating costs. The national tenants' group also held workshops on organizing techniques, the philosophy of social change, and the farm workers movement.[81]

The NTO reflected another moment in consciousness raising for poor black women tenants and helped to reify their demands for rights and respect. Through the NTO, which had 140 affiliates in forty cities and twenty-five states by 1970, Wise discovered her legal rights as a tenant. Wise, who attended the conference with fellow tenants Hattie Graham, Coleman Grant, and Gramley Buehler, remembered: "Something happened . . . that made me know that things were not right here in Baltimore." Wise said the NTO conference raised her consciousness about activism, power, and inequality: "It was the first time I had ever seen that many residents together and that many resident groups who had won so many battles that we didn't even know anything about." Wise continued: "You go to your first [RAB] meeting, you say well this is what they do here, you know, and get up and go ahead about your business, and then I went to NTO and found that other resident advisory boards were not doing that. We were having like little tea parties." She criticized the old mentality: "They used to stand up every meeting and applaud the housing authority for allowing them" to participate. "That's the kind of mentality it was." According to Wise: "After the NTO conference, it suddenly woke up a lot of people's eyes and then . . . we kept on saying: It is really totally ignorant if you keep on continuing to do business as usual when all these other groups out there is doing something to make a difference in their communities, you know."[82]

Switching gears, however, still was not easy. When Wise came back from her NTO trip, she went to several meetings before she could summon the resolve to intervene: "I would go home from the meetings. I had gas pains. I would have palpitations." Then she mustered the courage to speak up: "I said to myself I cannot sit here and not say anything because the purpose for them paying for me to go to NTO . . . was to gather information" and to represent the interests of tenants. Shirley Wise recalled that when she first began challenging Embry, some "old school" senior RAB members maintained that she needed her "behind spanked." They told her, "[D]on't talk to Bob Embry like that. . . . That's the way people in that age group thought about authority figures." Residents were not the only ones who recognized the change in Shirley Wise's manner. "Mr. Embry said to me, 'Well, that's right, you went to that conference. . . . You trying to be another Rose [Wylie].'" At that time, between 1969 and 1971, Rose Wylie, the president of RAB in Philadelphia and a widowed mother of six, served as chair for the eastern region of the NTO.[83]

Once Shirley Wise exercised her voice, she had no problem complaining to the housing authority administration and pressing for more tenant control. She began challenging the agenda. "I said an organization that cannot . . . set its own agenda is an organization that's controlled." In 1971, Shirley Wise became RAB chair, replacing Lillian Jones, who had died of a heart attack. A year later, Wise complained about what she considered unfair administrative maneuverings and criticized officials for obfuscating issues. While tenants had gained a voice in housing authority operations and some decision-making power, Wise felt that "management comes in with its position pretty well determined, then they give the RAB members a lot of complicated explanations and legal papers, most of which the RAB delegates don't understand." Wise argued that, as a result, management usually "gets its way, because the delegates don't understand the issues. They just feel sort of overwhelmed."[84] Shirley Wise maintained that at that point she became the legal "go-to" person. The NTO conferences had prepared Shirley Wise well.

Like other tenants, she began to learn about different HUD regulations. Recalled Wise:

> Every regulation that come out of this federal government is tiny, because they know people don't like to read the fine print. But I would sit there and read the fine print, and draw circles around them and everything, and take it back. I say, while HUD is telling you to do this, it is also telling you to do that. They also is telling you to fund us. They is also telling you that we're entitled to some rights. They also telling you that we sit down at the table.[85]

By the early 1970s, Baltimore RAB, which affiliated with the NTO, was addressing tenant issues that were gaining national attention. Increased tenant activism against local agencies and the threat of retaliatory evictions brought eviction procedures to the forefront of public debates, especially in the wake of the 1967 Joyce Thorpe case. HUD responded by issuing a new rule: Housing officials must tell tenants why they are being evicted and give them an opportunity to reply.[86] In January 1969, the Supreme Court had ruled in the Thorpe case that tenants had the right to proper notification and to know the reason for their eviction. The development of model lease and grievance procedures followed closely behind. In Baltimore in May 1969, Bonnie Ellis suggested reviewing residents' leases, and RAB's Policy Committee consulted Legal Services lawyers and sought examples from other cities.[87] On the national level, following a publicized sit-in demonstration in December 1969 at HUD in Washington, D.C., the NTO, the National Housing Law Project, NTO's counsel, and the NAHRO entered into negotiations. On behalf of 2.5 million public housing tenants in 1,900 housing authorities nationwide, the NTO demanded a standard model lease to end "chronic complaints" of retaliatory evictions, evictions without hearings, unauthorized entry into tenants' apartments, unfair maintenance charges, and tenants' lack of voice in management. In March 1971, HUD adopted standard procedures, the first since the passage of the National Housing Act of 1937. Norman V. Watson, HUD's acting assistant secretary for renewal and housing management, said:

> Historically, the balance in landlord-tenant law has strongly favored the landlord, both in private and public housing. The time has come to make a fresh start to improve tenant-management re-

lations through the development of [a] credible and open communication process. The new policies offer real hope of ushering in a new era in the management of housing for low-income families.[88]

In concert with local wishes and national aims, the Baltimore RAB moved diligently ahead with its efforts to establish new model lease and grievance procedures. It solicited help from Legal Services and HUD to design a livable lease and entered into negotiations—and battles—with the housing authority. Conflict emerged between Van Story Branch and tenants who felt Branch never came to terms with the power that tenants had secured. "Needless to say we had some big arguments," recounted Shirley Wise:

> I don't know whether he respected me or not. I respected him for getting where he was. And I just simply told him and his boss, let me do the job people elected me to do and you do your job and wherever that leads us. . . . If it leads us to that table to sit down and try to iron out our differences . . . then that's where we end up. I will not get in your space, but don't you get in mine either.

Tenants and management often found themselves arguing over two small words—*may* and *shall*—that would make a major difference in the balance of power. Elizabeth Wright, a RAB representative from Westport Homes, remembered: "It took us forever to get [the lease] done." Wise argued that the housing authority wanted *shall* to be used when outlining tenant obligations, and *may* to be used when referring to management's responsibilities. Wise recalled: "He was not yielding on the *shall* and the *may be*." Recalled Wright, *may* meant "they didn't have to do it. So that's what took so long. He was determined and we was determined." Management did not want certain obligations listed at all. "Okay, say for instance we came up with seventy-two hours as a response time for certain maintenance items," recalled Wise. "[H]e didn't want that. He didn't want no time frame. And that's what we kept going back and forth on. . . . That's what the problem is now. My toilet and my water can be broke for six months and you don't come in." She claimed that tenants felt, "Oh yeah, this is our opportunity now to straighten out all the ills that was wrong with the program before we got these rights." Shirley Wise argued that during her mother's generation, "if they say that for whatever reason you had to leave, you left. You know, with no recourse. It was the housing authority's property and the managers said they don't want you there, so you're gone. But now it's not like that, and for that I'm glad I was a part of the system of change."[89] While a new lease could not hold water against declining resources and changing cities, tenant activists did attempt to stem the tide.

As poor black women struggled to democratize systems of social welfare and alter the housing service delivery system, they eased the pangs of daily living and garnered new rights for tenants in public housing. Just as important, poor black women, who occupied critical leadership roles in their communities, altered public poverty policy on the local and national levels. They no longer were simply clients who received services from housing and welfare bureaucracies and engaged in cooperative social service activities within their own communities. They also were consumers and constituents who fought successfully to influence the institutions that served them. And as active constituents, they engaged in social actions that earned poor people official voice in welfare institutions and resulted in concrete policy changes on the local and federal levels.[90]

RAB and Women's Political Inspiration

In addition to providing voice and representation for public housing tenants on city and federal housing issues, the Resident Advisory Board also further politicized, politically educated, and inspired women, black and white. Tenant activists' vocal stance, their questioning of the housing authority's administrative control of RAB, and their efforts to seek power on behalf of tenants in addition to official representation gained them respect. Other tenant activists described RAB representatives, like Shirley Wise, Laura Carrington of Perkins Homes, and Catherine Monroe of Fairfield, as strong black women passionate about securing tenants' rights. Goldie Baker, who met Catherine Monroe with Elizabeth Wright, remembered that Monroe would say in a minute if something were amiss: "We ain't taking this shit."[91] Jean Booker and Martha Benton described Goldie Baker as a political educator. Ann Thornton described Laura Carrington, a friend and her son's godmother, and Shirley Wise as "an awesome twosome":

> Boy, she [Laura Carrington] was something. Man, she would, oh my goodness, she would go down to public housing, a lot of the

managers hated her with a passion . . . 'cause she would just tell them what was on her mind and that was it. And a lot of them loved her. And she would just speak up for the residents, you know, in Perkins and just go all the way out. And I mean not only Perkins. Her and Shirley, Shirley Wise and Laura Carrington was like this. [*She signaled closeness by crossing her fingers.*] And I tell you, boy, they were bad! That was an awesome crew, . . . humph, they just hated Shirley and Laura with a passion. . . . [Carrington] would just hang in there with them folks. And tell 'em, bless 'em. I mean bless 'em good too. Her and Shirley, my gracious.[92]

Anna Warren says that while Claremont Homes already had a tenant council in place, the formation of RAB and a citywide delegate seat made the organization stronger. Anna Warren claimed that RAB also became a place of political education for her. Her identity as a white single mother in public housing already had politicized her. Before RAB even existed, she was already active in the tenant council and recreation programs in the community because she "had kids" and "wanted to be a part of whatever they did." But her positions as tenant council president and RAB delegate in the early 1970s and, eventually, as a welfare rights activist, allowed her to meet black women like Shirley Wise and Catherine Monroe, who then taught her a few things about politics, people, and race. The president of an integrated community, Warren said that she took pains not to offend black or white tenants. She remembered Shirley Wise's good advice: "Shirley said, 'Anna, well, you just say what you have to say and say it from your heart. . . . You might get one or two out there that's going to make a big issue of something, but [it's okay] as long as you know how you said it.' . . . I said okay . . . and that's how I went about my meetings."[93]

Anna Warren claimed that her desegregation experiences at Claremont Homes and mingling with poor black women activists resulted in "the right people" teaching her. Warren gained tremendous respect and learned lessons in political confrontation from poor black women activists. She recalled that white people told her she even "acted crazy," like black people. When she asked them what they meant, she understood, despite their suspect terminology: "What they were saying really was I took stands on things. And if I took a stand on something and I believed in it, it was hard to change my mind. . . . I don't get out here and fight because I feel like being in the head-

Figure 5.4 Anna Warren moved into Claremont Homes in 1959 and still lives there. She currently serves as the Resident Advisory Board chairperson and continues to direct Boys' and Girls' Club activities in her complex. Photograph by Elizabeth Malby.

lines, I get out and fight because I'm fighting for a purpose."[94] Anna Warren became the cochair of RAB under Shirley Wise (and Wise's oldest grandson's godmother), traveled to national meetings, and in 1999 became the first white RAB chair, replacing Elizabeth Wright, who had passed away.

In the late 1960s and 1970s, the existence of RAB spurred further tenant organizing in individual black and white public housing communities. Federal regulations and programs had generated local organizing that had local impact. Lafayette's and Douglass' improvement associations, established before RAB's formation and the first councils to develop a structure with the help of Jessie Webster from the CAA-funded East Baltimore Citizens Center and Legal Services, provided a model for other councils in Baltimore. Complexes that did not have active resident councils formed them. In those communities that already operated tenant-run councils, residents formalized them as a way to garner official recognition from the housing agency and representation on RAB. In Westport Homes in the late 1960s, Elizabeth Wright claimed residents "sort of took over" mandatory meetings held by management and developed a constitution and bylaws in concert with the Mt. Winans community. Claremont Homes and O'Donnell Heights formalized their tenant councils.[95] By September 1968, Murphy Homes' tenants had met at least six times to transform MAC into a "viable tenant organization" by writing its constitution and bylaws.[96] Exhorted Gladys Spell, who became president: "Instead of the managers making the decision for you, you make your own decision and you decide what you want, you know. He still managed, but yet and still some of that power that he had was given to you."[97]

Black Power and Tenant Politics

Tenants across the city pushed for a greater voice in the operation of their communities and the policy decisions affecting them. Like Lafayette-Douglass's RAC, the Murphy council eventually sought to gain greater control of housing operations by choosing its manager. However, there was a difference. While Lafayette Courts' tenants complained that they were tired of managers treating them in nasty ways, Murphy tenants sought to replace their manager in part because he was white. The Murphy struggle illuminates a particular constellation of political empowerment in public housing. Not merely the result of "actual" oppressive treatment, Murphy tenants acted on the oppressive history linked to whiteness. The campaign in Murphy reflected much more overtly racial cultural politics, particularly as the rhetoric of black power began to envelop the nation and black nationalist groups moved into the Murphy Homes neighborhood.

These links among race, representation, and power became apparent in Murphy tenants' direct encounters with the grassroots black nationalist group Soul School. The Soul School on Fremont Avenue served as a meeting place and cultural center. Black junior and senior high school students gathered there to organize a citywide Black Student Union. And police kept surveillance on Soul School leaders, particularly Benjamin McMillan (also known as Olugbala), a former CORE member.[98] They exuded militancy. Gladys Spell recalled that the Soul School would teach young people about themselves, but "they got so they would teach the children to be so militant, you know, until some of the parents had to stop sending them over there. But Soul School was over there, and them brothers they had a tough look."[99]

On June 11, 1969, Spell and the youth committee of the Murphy improvement council invited Soul School members to a tenant council meeting as part of their two-day Black Seminar series. The tenant council wanted Soul School members to display and talk about their African carvings and paintings. The recreation room at the George Street School, where they held meetings, filled to the brim—and that included their white manager, Walden Gorsuch, who left Perkins Homes in 1965 to head the Murphy management team. Spell recounted the event:

> But instead of bringing it and talking about that, first they said when they went up . . . our office was integrated then. Honey, McMillan and them, they insulted everybody with a white face that was there that night. And told me, "I wouldn't even be here if I had known you were going to have the blue-eyed devils sitting in here. . . . I thought it was just going to be the tenant council members. I thought it was just going to be a black audience. I had no idea." [*Laughs*] Oh, they carried on. . . . the black people in the management were there. But he begged their pardon, said he wasn't after insulting nobody black, but he was after getting rid of them blue-eyed devils. "They don't mean you no good. You should kill them right now. . . ." We didn't have to kill them. They got up and walked.[100]

While Soul School members clearly wanted to oblige black tenants, white people had no space in their vision of black power politics. The white managers and staff represented the oppressors, and their presence conjured up a long history, as well as the contemporary practice, of black subjugation—not a glorious past of African rule and innovation. They were "blue-eyed devils"—a popular phrase evoked in Nation of Islam (NOI) parlance and often used by Malcolm X before his separation from the NOI in the early 1960s. Gladys Spell maintained that she felt so awful that she apologized to management the next day, "because I felt really bad over that because you know some whites lost their lives in the civil rights struggle because they believed in right. . . . But [Soul School members] didn't look at it that way."[101]

Gladys Spell presented this incident as a turning point for some residents in the Murphy Homes Improvement Council. Shortly thereafter, according to Spell, residents started circulating a petition requesting a black manager and excluded white management from the meetings. Black nationalism had influenced some tenants, who believed that racial solidarity and self-determination led to black power and community control. Rosetta Schofield recalled the campaign for black management: "One of the guys, I remember in particular . . . was coming around knocking on the door, because he was then working here. And he said we need a change, and we need all black management, because the whites don't understand the blacks." Schofield asked the petitioner: "Who will take the white people's place? 'We don't know, but we want black power. We want all black. We want black power. We want black power.' I said, well it doesn't matter to me. 'Cause all I want is to have a place to stay, pay my rent. And I respect them, and in return they respect me. There you go."[102]

The black nationalist critique of white supremacy, particularly white participation in black affairs, shaped not only some Murphy Homes tenants' responses, but broader political activities throughout Baltimore. Before the rebellions in Baltimore, in March 1968, black activists "covering all shades of beliefs," including Homer Favor of Morgan College's Institute of Urban Affairs, Walter Lively, and Olugbala of the Soul School, participated in a conference to consider forming a united black front.[103] Unlike her characterization of CAA, which experienced financial difficulties by the 1970s and closed down one-third of its neighborhood centers, Goldie Baker described the Black United Front as "a fighting group" in the forefront of the black struggle.[104]

Within a month of this March meeting, the rebellions exploded. This time the uprisings heightened tensions between the city's moderate black activist cadre and local officials. Agnew called a conference with moderate civil rights leaders on April 11 at the state office building in Baltimore. There, the governor distinguished between the "legitimate" black leader who "*worked* his way to the top" and others, whom he described as "the caterwauling, riot-inciting, burn-America-down type of leader." He praised civil rights leaders who condemned the likes of SNCC's Stokely Carmichael and H. Rap Brown, and he upbraided moderate black activists who met with these black "demagogues" and "black racists."[105]

Moderate black leaders stormed out of that meeting with Agnew and said that he was forcing "us all to become militants." They also criticized Agnew's intentional exclusion of "many black leaders who play important roles in our community," like Walter Lively, whom police actually arrested and accused of orchestrating the rebellions because they spotted him at several "arson scenes."[106] When police arrested Lively of U-JOIN, he was the executive director of Baltimore's newly formed Urban Coalition, an alliance of business, labor, religious, social, and government organizations formed "in recognition of the need for people to exercise control over their own destiny." Mayor Theodore McKeldin served on the Urban Coalition alongside Parren J. Mitchell, then CAC director, and Homer Favor.[107] Black civil rights leaders attending the Agnew meeting also expressed shock at the "gall of the governor suggesting that only he can define the nature of the leadership of the black community. Agnew's actions are more in keeping with the slave system of a bygone era." Lively later commented that Agnew refused to face "the fact that the problems existed before and helped ferment the energies that caused the disturbance."[108]

Murphy Homes represented a microcosm of these larger political debates on the black political scene. Just as all tenants did not connect with the black power insurgency, some black political and religious leaders disagreed with the militant separatist wings. While Baker worked with black power advocates, she labeled herself a human being interested in liberation: "If you fighting for my rights and all the poor people's rights, I'll join you."[109] Maxine Stephenson, who worked with the Murphy Homes council, argued that equality and freedom did not mean separatism. Stephenson, who also had spoken out against the urban rebellions, stated that Dr. Martin Luther King, Jr., "wanted equal rights for everybody. He didn't say kick the whites over that side and we jump on this side."[110] Municipal judge Robert Watts argued that the Black United Front should tackle prejudice without engaging in polarizing politics. Yet while the exchanges between Watts and "militant groups on the matter of whites in black affairs" were "particularly vehement," even Watts acknowledged that the legacy of white supremacy and racial oppression probably had resulted in "every Negro, regardless of his background" having "some hatred toward whites in his heart."[111]

In Murphy Homes, cultural and political nationalism won. Activists' efforts exposed a simplistic belief—that a black manager would look out for their best interests. The knowledge of troubled black tenant-management relations in the 1940s, or even in the 1960s across town, seemed lost to those who decided that "black" was automatically better and unproblematic. The tenant campaign was successful, according to Gladys Spell. Murphy Homes received its first black manager in the early 1970s. Ironically it was Joel Newton, about whom black tenants and activists had complained in the late

1960s. Unfortunately, having a black manager did not enhance tenants' positions nor counter the demise of Murphy Homes, which just as its low-rise and high-rise counterparts across the city, ultimately worsened in the wake of budget and security issues and a neglected urban landscape.

Conclusion

Public housing residents did not operate in a vacuum. Black female tenants engaged in struggle in "customized wars" within their communities.[112] They took advantage of the spaces open to them whether through the Community Action Program, Legal Services, VISTA, HUD, or grassroots civil rights and black power organizations—all in an attempt to improve their lives, fulfill their roles as caretakers of their homes and communities, and achieve the rights of citizenship. They infused their activism with the empowering messages of equality, rights, and self-determination, which undergirded the more general black struggles for freedom. And they demanded a form of tenant power to address quality-of-life issues, like poor maintenance and increasing vandalism.

Tenants' search for rights—whether through the RAC, RAB, or tenant councils—not only encompassed a sense of what residents believed were their government entitlements, but also revealed a more expansive notion of community participation. The fight for resident empowerment through participation in the policymaking process reflected poor people's demand for justice in an activism-rich decade. Tenant organizers felt that living in subsidized housing did not mean they had to be quietly satisfied or forfeit their voice, even though many tenants clearly still feared that contesting management might result in retaliation. Nor did public housing residency mean they had to accept inadequate or unsafe living conditions without question.

6 "Sunlight at Early Dawn"

Economic Struggles, Public Housing, and Welfare Rights

On a rainy day in 1966, Daisy Snipes and thirty-four other women rode a bus and cars to Annapolis, Maryland. Outside the Maryland State House, these members of Baltimore's first welfare rights group assembled and sang civil rights songs. Inside the capitol, representatives of Mother Rescuers from Poverty, whom Maryland's legislative council had refused a hearing, walked unannounced into the council's meeting, demanded higher grants, and charged that the welfare system "keeps us down" and that welfare mothers are "treated like dirt." Snipes, a black mother raising her children in Perkins Homes in east Baltimore and Mother Rescuers' vice chair, critiqued the welfare system. She opened her statement: "We as welfare recipients, as American citizens and as Baltimore City residents and voters appeal to you to support our demands for a better life for ourselves and our families. We deserve the respect due to us as full citizens with equal rights under the United States Constitution." She continued:

> One of the things that we need is more money. Welfare is a right and we have the right to adequate welfare. We have a right to [a] de-

cent standard of living including enough money for adequate food, housing and clothing for our families. We have a right to be treated with dignity. We have a right to opportunities for good jobs, training and education. We have a right to fair hearings with legal help if we believe we have not been treated fairly.[1]

That day on Maryland's Capitol Hill, Daisy Snipes and others exposed the municipal and state governments' inequitable treatment of AFDC recipients. Her poignant comments also brought to light the demands and concerns of low-income black women—like Margaret "Peggy" McCarty. The Mother Rescuers' feisty first chair, who led the protest, McCarty had much in common with her public housing sisters. McCarty also raised her children in the central city, but in private housing. In fact, just months before the September 1966 protest, McCarty had issued an equally passionate statement—the echoes of which reverberated not only in Snipes's demands, but in poor women's grassroots efforts throughout the 1960s and 1970s. A determined and proud "woman who [wouldn't] let anybody tell her that being on wel-

Figure 6.1 Editorial cartoon, *Baltimore Afro-American, April 18, 1964. Reprinted with the permission of the AFRO-American Newspapers Archives and Research Center.*

fare meant that she can't speak out and hold her head up high," McCarty asserted: "I'm a citizen who has a job to do, instead of a poor forgotten colored woman, like some of our people feel."[2]

Their statements and activism symbolized what the *Baltimore Afro-American* described as "the new mood creeping slowly through the black ghetto of Baltimore like sunlight at early dawn—a mood that demands rights and respect and a chance for a decent life as the natural birthright of all."[3] Key to poor women's political movement ideology, the demand for respect and rights exemplified the shift in poor black women's social welfare activism. These poor black women did not harp on meeting bourgeois standards of respectability as a way to prove worthiness and achieve societal acceptance and equality. Instead, the very humanity of black women merited respect and rights. Every human being, regardless of race, class, or gender, deserved to be treated with dignity and to secure a life free from vilification and want.

The confluence of welfare and public housing recipients' economic identities and daily circumstances spurred activist links among poor black women and some white women as well. By 1968, more than half of Baltimore's public housing population, which was 81 percent black, received public assistance.[4] In 1971 the National Tenants Organization's national director, Jesse Gray, had even proposed merging the NTO and the National Welfare Rights Organization (NWRO). Gray argued that such a merger would create "a real people's movement": "We are both dealing with the same people. People on welfare are tenants too." Poor women not only shared common economic and social experiences, but also similar problems in the welfare state. Shirley Wise echoed that sentiment, arguing that welfare rights and public housing activists "had our own identity and our own mission, but the population we served were one and the same. That was our common bond."[5] And in this struggle against poverty and for respect, public housing became an organizational base for grassroots economic activism.

As they pushed for citizenship and economic self-sufficiency, low-income, urban black women expanded the vision of the black freedom and women's liberation struggles and contested state oppression. Their primary focus extended beyond the traditional civil rights issues of public accommodations, the vote, and legislative equality. Like civil rights activists Ella Baker, Fannie Lou Hamer, and Gloria Richardson, poor black women focused on questions of economics, survival, and dignity.[6] Poor black women's struggles also exposed the limitations of the women's liberation movements, which captured national attention. Poor black women were relatively unconcerned with some liberal feminists' and professional women's desires to exchange housewifery for careers. Such a goal did little to address bread-and-butter issues or poor black women's desires to choose their own paths, including the choice to be stay-at-home moms, and to secure adequate incomes. Instead, poor black women addressed issues that directly affected them, highlighting how race, class, and gender shaped people's positions and power relations. They formed food and economic cooperatives. They participated in welfare rights protests, formed welfare rights chapters in public housing, and became leaders in struggles for subsistence.

Cooperative Economics

Federal antipoverty and Legal Services volunteers, who served as tenants' advocates and provided services, facilitated black women's economic organizing in public housing. In Lafayette Courts and Douglass Homes, the interracial CAA staff provided resources to establish a food-buying club by securing the initial wholesaler and a housing authority truck to pick up and deliver the food. Women tenants provided the labor. Bonnie Ellis served as the club's treasurer, and Shirley Pryor and Louise Alston, who also organized around welfare rights, helped run the food cooperative, which was featured in the national *VISTA Volunteers* magazine in April 1967. Bonnie Ellis appeared on the magazine cover with Grafton Francis, a CAA counselor in the Lafayette community.[7]

Women's consumer cooperation has deep roots in black and white working-class communities. In the 1930s and 1940s, women formed consumer councils and participated in meat strikes to protest high food prices. They even lobbied the government, demanding regulation of food and housing costs. Middle-class black housewives' leagues focused on "directed spending" by boycotting businesses that did not employ African Americans. In a show of economic nationalism, these black housewives' leagues wanted to retain resources within the black community and to educate black people as consumers.[8] The Ladies' Auxiliary of the black union the Brotherhood of Sleeping Car Porters and Maids also politicized "wives['] spending habits."[9] The Ladies' Auxiliary established cooperatives to avoid high prices, milk shortages, and "low-quality goods sold by stores in racially segregated neighborhoods," provided consumer education, set up credit unions, and created wholesale food-buying clubs. Ladies' Auxiliary members sought economic power by controlling the resources and capital, rather than forcing white businesspeople, who still controlled the money, to act sympathetically.[10]

Economic cooperation, then, provided marginalized communities with a potential avenue for combating exploitation, securing life-sustaining daily services, and bringing self-sufficiency. Food-buying clubs formed across the nation, many times as the result of coalitions between antipoverty workers and poor people. The efforts of women in public housing to develop and sustain alternative stores exposed their consistent battle against exploitative shopkeepers in their communities. According to the April issue of *VISTA Volunteers*, poor people paid more for lower quality food than did middle-class families. The root of dissension was price gouging. When black mothers on limited budgets, including those who received welfare, ran out of food before their next check, they had to "buy on credit from a local grocery store where prices are fairly high, or go without." As a result, they engaged in a "monthly struggle [for] existence."[11]

In Baltimore, the Lafayette-Douglass food-buying club began with a $50 grocery order and grew to a thousand-dollar operation that involved some 125 women. A resident-run community mouthpiece, the *Lafayette-Douglass Newsletter*, encouraged tenants to join the food-buying club and enjoy the benefits of saving on their monthly bills. The Lafayette-Douglass food-buying club worked for a time, but tenants eventually decided that it was not very effective. Tenants had to purchase in bulk, and ended up with cases of food when they only needed cans. Smaller families benefited less, and transportation was costly.[12] Even so, by developing alternative stores with the help of black and white, men and women antipoverty workers and nonprofit organizations, a small cohort of mothers avoided inflated prices, stretched their dollars, put local grocers on notice, and illustrated their willingness to act in their own interest.

Economics and the Rebellion

In 1968 the urban rebellion exploded on Gay Street and Pennsylvania Avenue, the primary shopping thoroughfares in east and west Baltimore's poor black communities. Spurred by Dr. Martin Luther King, Jr.'s murder, the rebellion lasted from Saturday to Tuesday, with participants vandalizing, burning, and looting more than 1,000 businesses. The overwhelming majority was grocery stores followed by cut-rate drug and liquor stores, taverns, clothing and furniture stores, and cleaners and laundries.[13] At the time, Rosetta Schofield, who worked for a large laundry, "didn't go to work for three days." From her sixth-floor public housing apartment, Schofield looked on horrified: "I used to come out on the balcony and look and you would hear gun shots, you would hear glass smashing, you'd see fire and smoke, you'd see people ripping and running." The National Guard and police patrolled the streets. "It was like you were in a different world."[14]

Looters tried to sell different wares. Coleman Grant, who lived in Cherry Hill Homes, traveled from south Baltimore to west Baltimore to check on one of his daughters, who lived with her child in the Lexington Terrace public housing complex. He remembered: "On the corner of Lexington Street and the next street down, Vine Street, was a store on the corner, and people went in there and took everything, everything! Didn't burn the place." Welling up with laughter, he continued:

This Negro ran out of there . . . over top [of] the policeman almost. Had on his shoulder, guess what? A case of Kotex! Well, the street roared. It was about a hundred people out there watching. And I almost had a stroke. Even the cop had to laugh. Boy, that was one for the books! . . . They let him go. I guess the cop said, if you can use 'em, keep 'em.[15]

Maxine Stephenson, who lived in Murphy Homes with her husband, daughter, and granddaughter, Betty, recalled a man trying to sell her spareribs and pork chops. Without the hilarity of Grant's reminiscence, Maxine Stephenson soberly recounted her refusal to buy any meat; theft was wrong. But her granddaughter did take advantage of people hawking and sharing their goods. A man with a basket full of fifths of liquor ran by Stephenson's apartment door:

Betty reached in there and got her two. I said, "Betty you know you don't drink." . . . Girl come running with a bin down here . . . had just as many towels as she could get. . . . You know how they come in bulk. Had never been open[ed]. Betty got her a purple, aqua, and a white one. I said, "Betty you ain't bringing that stuff in here!" "Momma, I ain't stole nothing." And you couldn't get her out the door.[16]

The uprisings revealed poor people's frustration and fear and their desires to attack exploitation and obtain consumer goods. As in many poor and people of color communities, a market existed for durable goods and food, the basic necessities of life. While the man who swiped the Kotex may have grabbed the first big package he saw, women needed Kotex. And that man who had stolen the meat and tried to sell it to Maxine Stephenson knew he would have a market for it—even if Stephenson declined to buy any. In February, months before the uprising, Walter Lively had warned white decision makers that they had to "give colored citizens a stake in what America is before ghetto dwellers could see a chance to accomplish their goals without violence."[17] In the midst of the rebellions, Lively argued that the "completely spontaneous" urban uprisings indicated "that an overwhelming portion of the black community of this city do not want the white man to continue his economic colonization of our people."[18]

Empowering Consumers

After the uprising, economic exploitation remained a daily part of black people's lives in cities. Not much had changed in terms of quality of life for poor black Baltimoreans. Exploitation by shopkeepers, price gouging, and finding affordable, fresh food remained concerns. At the CAA–Lafayette Courts planning meeting to develop an annual program of action, CAA staff worker Ozella Richardson suggested to Clyde Hatcher that they expand the food-buying club into a store. A store could meet the needs of more tenants. The CAA provided set-up funds of $3,169. The Reverend Joseph Wenderoth, associate pastor of St. Vincent de Paul Church, nestled between Douglass Homes and Lafayette Courts, helped raise money from the Catholic archdiocese. The archdiocese offered $8,100 as long as tenants and CAA organizers raised matching funds. The matching funds came from money and in-kind donations, including the housing authority's donation of a rent-free space in Lafayette and help from the Council of Equal Business Opportunity.[19] On January 14, 1970, the store opened to fanfare and applause. Bonnie Ellis, a food store board member and a founder of the original food-buying club, recounted the store's history for those attending the grand opening.[20]

The food cooperatives in Lafayette-Douglass were the first in a wave of similar, although often short-lived, ventures. Between 1969 and 1970, Perkins Homes, Westport Homes, and Flag House Courts all explored establishing food-buying clubs. In 1975, six years after the start of the food-buying club in Flag House, the manager described the club as advantageous to tenants, who could purchase foodstuffs at wholesale or "supermarket sale levels." Tenant leaders clearly viewed the club as financially and socially valuable to residents. In Murphy Homes, black female tenants ran a food store well into the 1990s.[21]

In addition to establishing and maintaining community businesses, which required time, labor, subsidies, and loyal customers, black people also sought to force responsiveness from store owners. A small group, the Liberators for Black Consumers, which included public housing tenants, distributed a flyer criticizing the merchants on Gay Street, one of the shopping corridors targeted in the 1968 rebellion. "Everybody was talking about how they were being exploited on Gay Street," Hatcher recalled. "So what we did, we demonstrated all up and down there."[22] The Liberators had limited success. However, their demands echo low-income black women's demands in many cities. In a leaflet, the Liberators argued: "Because greedy Gay street merchants have been guilty of overcharging black people, they have taken from black people money needed for food, shelter and other necessities of life." The Liberators demanded that merchants charge comparable prices for major durable goods like appliances and furniture, extend $200 credit to welfare recipients, and stop the use of "'bait' misleading advertisements and high pressure tactics." However, just as important, they demanded that merchants treat "poor black people with respect and dignity."[23]

Together, such activist drives—examples of the continuous battles poor black people waged against market forces—represented black women's broader attempts to empower themselves as consumers. The *Lafayette-Douglass Newsletter* even encouraged tenants to participate in consumer education workshops: "People with little education and limited income should show quite a bit of interest in a program of this nature." The focus was on "deceptive prices," one of poor people's "main weaknesses, because of our desire for a bargain or special marked down items." The article continued: "Most of us having a limited income can't afford to waste a dollar but because of our lack of knowledge we become victims of the <u>Economic Block</u>. We can start to practice better management of our money, by learning <u>How</u>, <u>When</u>, and <u>Where</u> to spend our money, in and with reasonable merchants."[24] The newsletter also educated tenants about credit unions, describing them as "a cooperative organized by a group of people having a 'common bond' for the purpose of encouraging saving." In 1969, the newsletter implored tenants to join neighbors who already had joined: "The Credit Union is here to help you. *Borrow* where you *save* and *save* where you *borrow*—where it makes a dollar difference in your financial future."[25]

The struggles of public housing tenants and mothers raising families unveiled the explicit connections among gender, political power, and economic dependence. Black women who engaged in cooperative economics were among the many citizens concerned about their purchasing power in a consumer society and the many activists who contested poverty and exploitation. Consumer education and economic cooperatives, however, targeted a specific set of concerns: feeding families and saving money. Another struggle occurring simultaneously within the city among poor black women, whether residents of public housing or not, would attempt to attack the broader problems of economic inequality, unemployment, and the feminization of poverty.

The Emergence of Welfare Rights

In June 1966, three mothers receiving AFDC—one of whom lived in public housing—initiated efforts to organize welfare mothers into an interracial interest group. A twenty-year-old white New Yorker and former Goucher College student, Joan Berezin, joined them. Berezin ran a U-JOIN nursery school where she watched and tutored black children and took advantage of the opportunity to talk to the children's mothers about their problems.[26] On Monday, June 13, the four women stood in front of the welfare department in northeast Baltimore. Monday was a good day for organizers, because a larger than usual number of welfare recipients came to the welfare office with complaints. In fact, "the line of people who hadn't received checks extended down a stairway and almost out to the sidewalk on Oliver Street." The four women distributed flyers urging recipients to protest. The leaflet read: "It is time that mothers on welfare stop being treated like dogs. We must stand up together and fight for bigger welfare checks and the respect that every human being deserves."[27] The flyer outlined numerous problems—the welfare department's inability to meet mothers' emergency needs, the invasion of welfare recipients' privacy by investigators, and delays in receiving checks—and asked mothers to attend a meeting the next night.

On Tuesday at 7:30 PM, Peggy McCarty, Daisy Snipes, Zelma Storey, Joan Berezin, and some thirty other women who were also mothers and welfare recipients gathered at U-JOIN's office on Gay Street in east Baltimore. It was no surprise that they met there. U-JOIN led poor and working-class people's mobilizations and critiqued race, gender, and class inequality. U-JOIN also protested the exclusion of poor people from policymaking arenas, publicly critiqued municipal officials, and facilitated black women's assault against the state. In a 1965 pamphlet entitled *What Is U-JOIN?* the organization described twin battles: the elimination of slum housing and "organizing welfare mothers to pressure for more adequate services for their children and a more effective, human and democratic public welfare system."[28]

Radical groups like U-JOIN helped to politicize black welfare recipients who worked to achieve the goals of black freedom, prosperity, and the rights of citizenship. When McCarty first met U-JOIN organizers during the harsh winter of 1965, she was a married, separated mother, raising her children on a monthly welfare check of $237. Unable to buy fuel for her furnace, McCarty noticed a U-JOIN flyer advertising cheap coal on a CAA bulletin board. She went to the U-JOIN office for help. U-JOIN treated McCarty so well that eventually she became a member and began refining her "understanding of urban issues." Accompanying U-JOIN leaders to city council meetings, McCarty began to question a welfare system and a government that seemed to do very little to abolish poverty. Never involved in a movement before, McCarty stopped reading so many popular magazines and began reading political pamphlets. U-JOIN politicized McCarty not only as a welfare recipient, but also as a woman who felt that "every woman should know more about politics, more about welfare, more about what their rights are."[29]

That Tuesday night, the mostly black gathering of women spent hours discussing the formation of a group to fight the "welfare jungle."[30] McCarty was elected chair, Snipes vice chair, Storey alternate spokesperson, Betty

Figure 6.2 Margaret "Peggy" McCarty (standing), the first chair
of Mother Rescuers from Poverty, meets with Mayor Theodore R.
McKeldin (seated right), January 5, 1967. Mother Rescuers, the
city's first welfare rights organization, formed in 1966 with the
sponsorship of Union for Jobs or Income Now (U-JOIN). Courtesy Baltimore News American Collection, Special Collections,
University of Maryland Libraries.

Irvin treasurer, and Joan Berezin secretary of Mother Rescuers from Poverty,
"a civil rights organization." In just the first three months, the Rescuers had
75 active members and a mailing list of 200—the majority of whom, according to McCarty, were public housing tenants.[31]

While the group's goal was to change the local welfare system, the
Mother Rescuers also supported and drew strength from the nascent national interracial struggle of poor women welfare recipients. Poor mothers

receiving welfare had already staged protests or formed groups in cities like Memphis, Watts, Cleveland, Chicago, and New York. In June 1966 the Ohio Steering Committee for Adequate Welfare organized a march to the Ohio capital to protest cutbacks in the state's welfare budget and to demand increased benefits. Thousands of demonstrators showed up; forty of them had marched 155 miles from Cleveland to Columbus. In support of the Ohio organization and as part of a nationwide solidarity movement coordinated by George A. Wiley's Poverty Rights Action Center in Washington, D.C., the Rescuers and groups in twenty-five other cities staged local protests.[32] Following these actions, Wiley, a former associate national director of CORE, organized a convention in Chicago in August to discuss establishing a national welfare rights group. Peggy McCarty, Daisy Snipes, and Zelma Storey joined delegates from twenty other states at the convention, which resulted in the creation of the National Coordinating Committee (NCC) in 1966 to mobilize welfare mothers around economic issues like securing decent benefits. The first of many Baltimore representatives between 1966 and 1972, McCarty also served on the national body of the emergent NWRO.[33]

The Economics of Citizenship

Squarely focused on economics, poor and working-class mothers' demands for self-reliance, self-determination, control, dignity, and justice echoed the popular calls of black freedom struggles. Black women activists demanded their economic rights as citizens and voters and in so doing exposed the limitations of the recently passed Civil Rights Act of 1964 and the Voting Rights Act of 1965. While providing legal rights, neither act attacked economic inequality. In 1966 the NWRO penned a Bill of Welfare Rights, which was modeled on the U.S. Constitution's Bill of Rights, and drew on federal regulations and court decisions to make citizenship and antidiscrimination claims for poor women and mothers. They claimed their First Amendment right to freedom of association in forming welfare rights organizations, their Fourth Amendment protection against unlawful searches and the right to privacy, and their Fourteenth Amendment right to fair and equal treatment by the state. They also cited regulations from the federal handbook of the Public Assistance Administration, the Social Security Act, and Supreme Court decisions. At the end of the NWRO's Bill of Welfare Rights appeared bold exhortations that echoed low-income women's rights rhetoric, including that in public housing: "Know your rights, demand your rights, protect your rights, link up with Welfare Rights."[34]

Claiming their citizenship and voting rights, welfare recipients in Baltimore also threatened elected officials with the power of the ballot and demanded representation. Months before the 1966 gubernatorial election, McCarty told members of the Welfare Cost Committee of the Maryland Legislative Council that Mother Rescuers would urge their constituents to "vote for the group that supports us."[35] Mother Rescuers sent letters to the gubernatorial candidates, incumbent Millard Tawes and challenger Spiro T. Agnew, and asked for their positions on welfare.[36] Increasingly disgusted with the slow pace of change and unmet promises after the 1966 election, welfare rights activists even spoke of an organizational drive for independent political power. McCarty claimed that poor and working-class people would "run, vote, and elect our own people from our own neighborhood."[37] In July 1967 at a state public welfare department meeting, Mother Rescuers made clear to welfare bureaucrats their wish to be represented on the state's welfare advisory board—a demand reflecting black people's search for political participation. Maryland's welfare board chair, Edmund Dandridge, who "expressed a sympathetic awareness," told McCarty to contact Agnew. Agnew had beaten Tawes in the election and now as governor held the power of appointment. By February 1968 Barbara Stevenson had been appointed, but she had limited power. She could not vote on any policies related to the benefits she received. Even so, she became the first welfare recipient appointed to the board and remained the only one until the mid-1970s.[38]

Welfare rights groups used tactics similar to civil rights and black power activists. Following the strategy of U-JOIN, which according to the *Baltimore Afro-American* had the "reputation of getting in the Establishment's hair and pulling hard," Mother Rescuers confronted bureaucrats and commanded the public eye by frequently marching. They went door to door trying to recruit people, particularly in public housing communities because of the concentration of welfare recipients who were residents. Members also regularly protested outside the DPW office when welfare checks were issued. That way, activists could lure more women to their cause.[39]

Alongside direct action, the advocacy of liberal reformers engaged in Baltimore's social welfare causes facilitated poor women's struggles against the state. Organizations like the Maryland Conference of Social Welfare

(MCSW), led by M. Shakman Katz, as well as select state and local welfare officials supported increased welfare grants. As early as 1964, the MCSW, which aimed to educate the public, had published a sixteen-page pamphlet, *Public Welfare—Myth vs. Fact*, with the opening lines: "Public welfare plays a vital role in the lives of hundreds of thousands of children and families throughout this country. Yet rarely has a program of such importance been undermined by so many myths, misconceptions, and false charges."[40] At the state DPW meeting in Annapolis in July 1966, Katz, also a representative of Mayor McKeldin's Task Force Committee on Health and Welfare, read from a Baltimore City Community Relations Commission report that emphasized the disruptive potential of low welfare grants. They can "be a major causative of unrest and explosion because of its [*sic*] aligned ills of physical, psychological, social and cultural depression."[41] In the late 1960s, Raleigh Hobson, who was the state's public welfare director, Dandridge, and other board members expressed sympathy with welfare recipients' demands and lobbied the governor on their behalf. Baltimore welfare director Esther Lazarus and Maurice Harmon, who replaced her in 1969, also expressed public sympathy with recipients.[42]

Activist Mothers' Demands

Even with the support of some reformers, welfare rights activists did not have an easy road, nor were they always in agreement with social bureaucrats or reformers. While Mother Rescuers also argued the evil of insultingly low welfare grants, the activist mothers were concerned less with avoiding unrest. Instead they focused squarely on questions of survival. McCarty maintained that it was impossible to live on monthly welfare allotments of $119, $200, and $230 for families of two, five, and eight. She suggested raising them to $204, $303, and $456. For a family of four in Maryland, the average annual grant was $1,958.16, about one-third below the federal poverty line of $3,150.[43] According to Daisy Snipes, welfare grants were woefully inadequate because they did not cover the increasing costs of food, rent, and clothing.[44] In a statement to the governor, June Booth, a Mother Rescuer, wrote:

> I spend $80.00 for rent, gas and electricity a month which leave[s] me with $157.00 to be divided among eight people for food and clothes. Among eight people is $19.62 per child for a month. Can I

feed a child good meals on that amount; and to make it worse—you expect me to save money out of that to buy clothes. It is impossible.[45]

More than a few poor children had been sent or kept home from school "because they don't have proper clothing."[46] For working-class children, the lack of adequate and "proper" clothing affected not just their health and education. Their clothing also marked them as poor and as outsiders. Rudell Martin, a Cherry Hill Homes tenant and BWRO director in the early 1970s, recalled this debasing effect of poverty. Initially she had grown up "feeling very secure," even unaware that "we were poor," until she began attending Dunbar High School. "In Dunbar, it seemed to have been a class group there. . . . We didn't have fancy clothes, and so it always seemed like somebody was either making, or poking, fun at the way I talked or what I was wearing." As a young teenager, Rudell Martin took a $12 live-in weekend babysitting job in Pikesville, Maryland, to help with carfare to school and to purchase clothes for her siblings and herself—"so that I would fit in."[47]

Figure 6.3 A former tenant of Cherry Hill Homes, Rudell Martin served as the first paid director of the Baltimore Welfare Rights Organization in the early 1970s. She now lives in Windsor Mills. Courtesy Rudell Martin.

In a prepared statement to the governor and state legislators, Alease Coleman, a Mother Rescuer, echoed Martin's sentiments as well as those expressed by little Mary Reives years before. Wrote Coleman: "We demand clothing grants three times a year so our children can look like other children and so it won't cause any inferior feelings among them." Coleman maintained that the children of welfare recipients were teased incessantly and recited a common ditty as an example: "Welfare shoes on your feet—after a while you'll wish for meat." Coleman expressed her fear that children who felt excluded and ridiculed might resort to theft just so they did not stand out as different. "The things that they really need and can't get sometimes turns them into juvenile delinquents," Coleman argued. "We need help now. Our children are human-beings too and citizens of the U.S.A."[48] Moved by the testimony, the welfare board wrote the governor on activists' behalf.[49]

Minimal welfare grants, like substandard housing and insufficient food, prohibited poor families from achieving their natural birthright; they literally could not afford to live decently. Mother Rescuers not only suggested increasing grants, but also tried to convince elected officials and welfare bureaucrats of the importance of adult education. "You can't get anywhere without an education to back you up," maintained McCarty, who dropped out in the tenth grade. "People who pay taxes should want mothers to educate themselves. What is the sense of getting off welfare to work for $20 to $30 a week?" McCarty, however, acknowledged that not all welfare recipients felt as strongly as she did about education's saving grace. "Some may be satisfied with just more money, but I will constantly put my ideas before them. I want to act as a symbol for people who are struggling to help them to a better way of life."[50] Her statement reflected what some poor black women had believed for decades—education was crucial for not only upward mobility, but also economic stability.

Women like McCarty stressed employment, highlighting an often overlooked demand of the NWRO. In the NWRO's Bill of Welfare Rights, activist mothers echoed the philosophy of radical groups like U-JOIN: "Our goal is: jobs or income now! Decent jobs with adequate wages for those who can work; adequate income for those who can not work."[51] Mother Rescuers asked Maryland's welfare director, Hobson, to support economic stability and self-sufficiency by providing mothers with good jobs. McCarty suggested that the welfare department train and hire recipients as social workers. While McCarty believed most DPW caseworkers were "good," she described some as uncaring and unable to connect with clients. "What you need are people who have really lived in the slums, stayed up nights chasing rats, gone without bread and without shoes, listened to the wind whistling through the walls."[52] McCarty's statement—that poor mothers knew poverty better than anyone—revealed another key element of poor women's movement ideology alongside rights, subsistence, and respect.

The board voted to investigate the possibilities of hiring welfare recipients. Howard H. Murphy, a member of the state DPW board and *Afro-American* family, "heartily endorsed" the proposal, saying he wanted to break "down the cliché that these people are lazy and don't want to work." While two state welfare board members, including its chair, Dandridge, endorsed the proposal to train and hire welfare mothers, Hobson did not "hold out much hope." Hobson discussed federal requirements, specifically educational standards, and suggested that welfare mothers might use their skills in daycare centers. He told recipients that he thought more opportunities existed in poverty programs, referring specifically to Community Action Agencies or job training, like the young mothers' elderly companionship program, which operated in twenty public housing complexes in 1966.[53]

As citizens, Mother Rescuers also attacked the disparate treatment of welfare recipients with regard to state surveillance. Even though the DPW board prohibited welfare workers from surprising AFDC clients with investigative visits between 10:00 PM and 7:00 AM in 1964, welfare investigators could still show up unannounced during other times of the day and night.[54] Mother Rescuers claimed "the insurance of our Constitutional right of privacy" and maintained they had the "right to entertain anyone we want to." Activists argued that the welfare department invaded their privacy and harassed them because they were poor black women raising children alone. Snipes argued, "Investigators are trained to be nasty. They just come to your home whenever they feel like it, one at the back door while another rings the front bell. They look everywhere. 'Do you have a boyfriend? What's in the icebox?' is what they ask." In another statement, Snipes claimed: "Untrained appointed investigators visit welfare recipients to assure public funds are not misused. Recipients are not informed of their rights in this matter. Their entire investigative system should be abolished. . . . No other recipients of public funds are harassed in this manner."[55] Snipes and other welfare activists contested the idea that a woman's impoverishment or her reliance on welfare meant that she should be treated differently and suffer diminished citizenship status. After years of protest, in 1970 the Supreme Court barred states from reducing welfare payments because of a man in the house—unless he contributed directly to the family.[56]

While these specific battles reflected activist mothers' direct and intimate relationship with the state's social welfare system, their demands also resonated with the general concerns of working-class black women who organized around survival issues. Jobs, decent incomes, housing, and childcare were common concerns whether mothers worked as wage laborers, received welfare checks, or did both. While women and mothers on welfare demanded adequate grants, black women who found it difficult to survive on poorly paid laundry, retail, hospital, and nursing home jobs united with CORE–Target City workers and organized the Maryland Freedom Union in Baltimore. Baltimore served as the pilot city for the civil rights union idea, partially because it had a large black central city and one of the worst wage scales on the East Coast.[57] The union, which was 90 percent female and black and led by two black women, demanded higher wages. The civil rights union was the first to win a "major labor contract in a northern urban ghetto anywhere in the country."[58] Nationwide, similar struggles occurred. Just because black women held jobs did not mean they escaped poverty or the need for government assistance programs. Laboring (whether above board or under the table) in low-paid service and retail industries and private households, many working-class black women still had to rely on housing subsidies, food stamps, and AFDC even while working.

In 1967, the welfare rights struggle heated up, especially with increased coordination of poor mothers' pressure on the state and heightened critiques of poverty. Mother Rescuers clamored for legal representation for welfare recipients who were arrested in local government round-ups of suspected welfare cheaters and subsequently charged with welfare fraud. Mother Rescuers leafleted outside courthouses to inform defendants, most of them black women, of their guaranteed right to counsel.[59] That same year, the NWRO launched its basic needs campaign. In Baltimore, Mother Rescuers geared up for a battle to reinstate an increased budget for rent, food, and clothing, which the state DPW had submitted, but that Agnew's administration had cut. Forty activist mothers marched to Annapolis to protest a "'slap in the face' wholesale cutting of the State welfare budget."[60] Deploying the threatening image of a "long, hot, angry summer," McCarty and Mother Rescuers led a march on March 22. Dubbed Poor People's Independence Day by the organization, 300 adults and children rallied in Annapolis to protest the cuts.[61] That same year in August at the NWRO's national convention, a 1,000-member delegation, including Baltimore women, protested a federal government proposal to force welfare recipients to work or face losing their benefits. McCarty aroused the national delegation, drawing resounding applause when she bellowed that "lousy, dirty, conniving brutes" devised the welfare bill to "take us back to slavery. I'm black and I'm beautiful and they ain't going to take me back." She then stated that if protesters' voices did not motivate officials to change the laws and welfare system, maybe "force" would.[62]

The Broadening Activist Assault on Poverty

The assault on poverty, launched by working and poor people and radical organizations in urban communities, received increasingly broad support. In 1967 Martin Luther King, Jr., lent his mainstream civil rights voice to the fight against poverty. In his book *Where Do We Go from Here: Chaos or Community?* King spotlighted the travesty of poverty in a rich democratic nation. He suggested replacing the slogan of "black power" with "power for poor people." According to King: "The time has come for an all out world war against poverty."[63] In Baltimore, a cross-class and multiracial alliance manifested itself. Seventy-five welfare workers, who formed a union, supported welfare clients' struggles. Led by Bernard Miller, a graduate of Morgan State College in sociology, the social workers, who also protested poor salaries and too-large caseloads, demanded higher grants and rent and school allowances for welfare clients.[64] The MCSW and Dandridge also protested the low level of state welfare grants. In early 1968, Mrs. I. Hamburger, chairwoman of MCSW's Public Welfare Committee, read a statement to the Maryland Senate Finance Committee complaining about inhumane rent and food allowances. The organization argued, "Families living on this kind of allowance certainly provide a ready audience for those who urge civil disobedience" and said that the budget "prolongs the agony" of the poor.[65] Dandridge also wrote a letter to Agnew urging an adjustment in the present welfare allowances and even supported a tax increase if necessary. Otherwise, Dandridge wrote, "the result is slow starvation and misery for many." Melvin Cole, the governor's program executive, did respond to Dandridge. Cole argued that it was "not possible for us at this moment to make any real commitment to this worthwhile objective," because the governor was concentrating on the following year's budget.[66]

By 1968 poor people's issues, black women's activism, civil rights, and black militancy merged—creating tension and linking the multiple oppressions that working and unemployed black women confronted in cities. In Maryland, Governor Agnew increasingly clashed with welfare recipients, militant organizers like Lively, and social welfare advocates who contested governmental authority, power, and decisions. After the Baltimore uprisings, Agnew argued that "somewhere the objectives of the civil rights movement have been obscured in a surge of emotional oversimplification. Somewhere the goal of equal opportunity has been replaced by the goal of instantaneous economic equality."[67] Despite his critique of Baltimore's urban uprisings, Agnew correctly assessed that they symbolized a shift, one that actually occurred before April 1968: Black activists (including King) and black working-class people increasingly targeted poverty and pushed for economic equality as a basic citizenship right. The governor's comments also revealed white society's great fear of black militant and grassroots organizing against economic inequality and poor people's political exclusion, and it also exposed the limits of capitalism and American democracy.

Before his death, King cogently linked poverty and state complicity in his last SCLC presidential address: "The plantation and the ghetto were created by those who had power, both to confine those who had no power and to perpetuate their powerlessness."[68] Coretta Scott King also recognized the government's role in perpetuating violence against women, children, racial minorities, and the poor. At a May 12 Mother's Day march of welfare recipients, she declared to 5,000 people from twenty cities, who gathered at the Cardozo High School Stadium in a poor black D.C. neighborhood:

> [It is] not an easy way, particularly in this day when violence is almost fashionable, and in this society, where violence against poor people and minority groups is routine. I must remind you that starving a child is violence. Suppressing a culture is violence. Neglecting school children is violence. Punishing a mother and her family is violence. . . . Ignoring medical needs is violence. Contempt for poverty is violence. Even the lack of will power to help humanity is a sick and sinister form of violence.[69]

From the late 1960s through the 1970s, even as assaults on welfare rights and black militancy were under way, poor women continued to struggle nationwide. In Baltimore, protests were ongoing; the citywide Welfare Rights Organization was formed, opened an office, and received funding; and new community-based welfare rights groups were established. Poor women, particularly black women, upheld the battle cry issued by the NWRO. They stood firm and remained unwilling "to exchange our rights as American citizens, our rights to dignity, our rights to justice, our rights of democratic participation" or to give up their demands for the food, clothing, and shelter that they deserved but could not provide.[70]

Public Housing as an Organizational Base

From the beginning, public housing served as a base for organizing around subsistence and poor women's issues. In Baltimore and throughout the country, public housing tenants emerged as leaders, organizers, and participants in antipoverty efforts, including welfare rights groups. In Watts, Johnnie Tillmon of ANC (Aid to Needy Children) Mothers Anonymous, who lived in public housing and was active in a beautification program in her community, organized women tenants around welfare issues. A mother of six, she was also a laundry worker and a shop steward. In Memphis, thirteen women public housing tenants and welfare recipients started the Memphis Welfare Rights Organization (WRO) in 1967. In Las Vegas, welfare mothers in the Marble Manor public housing complex formed the Clark County WRO and galvanized a citywide struggle for better social services. They eventually established an independent social service nonprofit corporation, Operation Life.[71]

In the late 1960s in Baltimore, public housing tenants not only participated in Mother Rescuers, the city's first welfare rights organization. They formed and participated in welfare rights groups in public housing during the same moment that predominantly black women tenants fought for the establishment of the citywide RAB. Unlike the RAB, however, the welfare rights groups focused on economic issues. Women in Perkins Homes with the help of CAA had formed a welfare rights group to inform tenants of their legal rights and to recruit members for NWRO. Through her volunteer and eventually paid CAA work, Ann Thornton worked with welfare rights: "They had a big organization back then. And they did a lot of work for a lot of tenants' rights, as far as welfare." Thornton's tasks included talking with tenants about their concerns regarding welfare checks, food stamps, and treatment at the welfare department. The welfare rights group also held meetings at the CAA office.[72]

In February 1969, the resident association in predominantly white O'Donnell Heights sent a tenant delegation to Annapolis to participate in a Mother Rescuers protest. Mother Rescuers had charged that "the State of Maryland is trying to starve us to death," demanded that the state welfare board abolish maximum limits for emergency grants, contested the state board's sole decision-making authority, and suggested the establishment of a board and the appointment of "representatives of the community, and if at all possible, members of a welfare rights organization." Supporting the effort, O'Donnell Heights participants testified before state legislative committees. Within a month of that action, O'Donnell Heights women tenants decided to form their own welfare rights group, IMPACT.[73]

White women led the public housing chapter initially. Charlotte Minton, secretary of the O'Donnell Heights Community Council, and Barbara Jean Linkenhoker had become very active in welfare rights advocacy throughout the city in the late 1960s and early 1970s.[74] In 1970, Linkenhoker, who served as IMPACT's chair, joined the Advisory Committee on Child Welfare of Baltimore's Department of Social Services (DSS), the city's renamed welfare department.[75] In 1970, three years after the integration of O'Donnell Heights, black women like Fannie Hemphill, who succeeded Linkenhoker, took the reins of IMPACT and carried on the interracial battle on behalf of poor women in O'Donnell Heights.

In black complexes like Lafayette Courts in hot activist urban areas lived women like Goldie Baker. By the late 1960s, Baker was thoroughly engaged in struggles for poor people's rights—a far cry from those "depressed" days when she first moved into public housing. Her upbringing, personal dramas, and blossoming relationships with black activists thrust her into welfare rights organizing as those experiences had thrust her into advocacy for public housing tenants. As a preteen, Baker had marched with her grandmother and mother in interracial campaigns against the city's welfare department. In 1949, the unemployed and poor picketed city hall, asking the mayor, city council, and welfare department for more welfare funds.[76] Her mother could not afford a babysitter so when she went to meetings and protests she took

Goldie Baker with her: "I used to hate every minute of it; 'cause I didn't understand what it was about or why I had to go to all these meetings, you know. Sit in there, then walk up and down. I'd be cold [*chuckles*]." Once Goldie Baker became engrossed in poor people's struggles, she began to appreciate her mother and grandmother's aggressive activism: "I know that [my mother] and my grandmother were two strong black women. I can look back on it now and realize they were. I didn't understand at that time, but I do now."[77]

While not formally involved in Mother Rescuers, Baker argued that the welfare system similarly disgusted her and she spoke out. Like Peggy McCarty and others, Goldie Baker registered her objections to the meager AFDC grants given to needy families. Baker had seven children and could receive a maximum of only $250 a month. She detested the agency's policies that degraded recipients. Baker had to fight welfare caseworkers to keep her furniture and clothing, which they considered too luxurious. As with her refrigerator, Baker had held on to some of her belongings after she separated from her husband. "They told me I had to sell [my furniture] and then I could get a furniture grant and buy used furniture. . . . They said my clothes were too expensive. They were expensive [*laughs*], but I wasn't going to give them away." Embroiled in personal battles with the welfare system, as she had been with public housing staff, Goldie Baker readily entered the fray when activists like Walter Lively, "some other black men from CORE," and Salima Marriott, whom Goldie Baker had initially met through an educational action group, approached her for help. In 1967, Salima Marriott, who by then had two children, had left her husband and moved back to Baltimore where she became a welfare department caseworker. Knowing Goldie Baker "had a reputation for being real pushy," Marriott invited her to speak to a group of welfare mothers in her district in east Baltimore. When Marriott became a master's student in social work and an intern with the city Welfare Rights Organization, she and Baker worked together yet again.[78]

State oppression and the growing linkages between the battles for rights and against economic deprivation motivated women to act. Rudell Martin's encounter with discrimination and the public welfare system eventually led her into welfare rights organizing. After separating from her husband, Martin resorted to AFDC to support her children. Rudell Martin said she could not believe the way the black social worker, whose name she could not remember but whose face she still could see "just as good," talked to her: "'Well didn't you save any money?' I mean the things she was saying. . . . I don't have any money, no. If I had any money I wouldn't come here. Because you have to spend up everything, all your resources. They were the last resource you could go to."[79]

In the late 1960s, the degrading treatment that Baker and Martin recounted was not unusual. Many public housing tenants and AFDC recipients argued that their confrontations with social workers alongside their personal relationship with poverty pushed them toward welfare rights activism. Recalling the discussions at national organizing meetings, Johnnie Tillmon, NWRO president, witnessed: "We found out that all over the country the attitudes of the general public and the welfare departments were the same toward anybody on welfare. The people from New York got treated by the social workers and the other people the same as they did in Mississippi."[80] In Baltimore as elsewhere, it was a problem. While some welfare workers had pushed for increased benefits for welfare clients in 1967 and 1969, conflict and tension tended to mark personal encounters between workers and clients. Potential and actual recipients relayed unnerving and debasing run-ins with welfare department employees. White public housing tenant and welfare recipient Anna Warren stated: "[I]f you were white or black, they gave you a hard time. They made sure you felt small, going over there to ask for money."[81] Similarly, Bonnie Ellis remembered her one-time experience with the welfare department as harrowing and exasperating. She told her story:

I went to them once. That was a joke. . . . The lady told me, Miss Parks, I'll always remember that woman. My husband had left me. It was Memorial Day weekend, and that woman said to me, "Honey, it's not a thing I can do to help you." She said, "Because I'm getting ready to start my vacation. And I'm going to put it on my desk and when I come back in here on Tuesday, I'll see what I can do to help you out. Maybe I can get you some food . . . maybe I'll see if I can get you some food this afternoon." I said, "Thank you." Had five children. And she told me she would see what she could do.

Bonnie Ellis went to her mother's house, called a city councilman at home, and told him, "I was a registered voter, told him my situation. And that lady called me back I know in twenty minutes. . . . She told me to come up there, she would have a check for me." When Ellis went to pick up her check, she said the social worker told her "that she would give that check, but that I was going to have to reapply. . . . But I just didn't feel like I could go through any more of that hassle. That was the first and last check."[82]

The state, through one of its War on Poverty programs, served as a mechanism for Rudell Martin to mobilize, as it did for numerous other women in public housing who used the CAA to start tenant councils and to mount consumer campaigns and also used HUD to fight for citywide representation and voice. At a community meeting, Rudell Martin met some VISTA workers interested in the treatment of welfare recipients; they were also recruiting neighborhood people as potential leaders. Martin recalled: "I said, yeah that's what I want to do and the first place I want to hit is the welfare department."[83] After hearing her complaints, the antipoverty volunteers recruited her as a VISTA worker and put her in touch with veteran activist Peggy McCarty. Recalled Martin: "She told me, you know, what she did and what we could do and she would help us. And that's kind of how it got started." Shortly thereafter, Martin and some Cherry Hill Homes women who also received AFDC met and formed the Cherry Hill Homes WRO. When the group formed, only three other welfare rights groups in the city had affiliated with the NWRO: Mother Rescuers, IMPACT, and the Baltimore Welfare Recipients Protective Committee. By 1971 the Cherry Hill WRO was one of eleven Baltimore-based, NWRO-affiliated groups.[84]

Not long after Cherry Hill Homes' WRO's formation, Martin and its members, including Catherine Daniels, Claudia Williams, and Williams's daughters, Geraldine Randall and Betty Keaton, embarked on their first welfare rights campaigns. Betty Keaton remembers being "dragged to [community] meetings at age seven." Geraldine Randall, Keaton's older sister, received AFDC after separating from her husband in 1968. Supporting six children, she relied solely on AFDC for five years, and then she took a job driving a minibus and received partial benefits for five more years. Work did not exempt her from poverty. While her children went to school, she took classes at Sojourner-Douglass College to become a nurse's assistant. In her twenties when she began participating in welfare rights efforts, Randall "wanted to learn my rights."[85]

Cherry Hill Homes' welfare rights activists pointed out how the federal government gave higher priority to the Vietnam War than it did to its own citizens' daily well-being. In his 1967 Riverside speech, King argued that the "real promise of hope for the poor—both black and white—through the poverty program" was "eviscerated as if it were some plaything of a society gone mad on war."[86] The Cherry Hill welfare rights group officially opposed U.S. involvement in Vietnam, issuing a statement maintaining that the war assaulted black and poor people and misused American tax money. The group claimed that the federal government spent "80 billion dollars" on the "defense machine" each year, while only about "6 billion is used for public welfare and Medicare programs." Members maintained that big businesses like General Electric and AT&T, not the American people, benefited from the war: "The employees of these companies, the workers, are generally paid just enough to meet their immediate needs." Cherry Hill welfare rights activists also held that poor black women had to battle exploitation and, potentially, the loss of their sons. Their charges of economic exploitation echoed the concerns of many poor black women, including poverty-wage workers, tenants engaged in the creation of food-buying clubs, and welfare rights protesters. The Cherry Hill group maintained: "In addition, those of us who buy their products are charged outrageous prices for products, which are designed to fail with[in] a given length of time. Finally, the sons of these same hard working people are sent to Vietnam to fight the war."[87]

Cherry Hill Homes welfare rights activists joined with Mother Rescuers and IMPACT in the racially integrated Welfare Rights Coalition. The rights coalition, "a city-wide organization," aimed "to tell all welfare recipients of their rights to welfare and to work for a minimum standard of living with dignity."[88] In May 1969, these public housing tenants and welfare rights activists went to the city's welfare headquarters and requested an audience with the department's director, Esther Lazarus. Rudell Martin already had met with Irwin Brown of Legal Aid, who went over the welfare manual with her so she could make a convincing and airtight presentation to the welfare department. The thirty mothers (many of whom had children in tow) wanted action on a series of demands, including a quick turnaround on furniture grants. Martin told a *Baltimore Morning Sun* reporter: "Miss Lazarus told us last week to come back Monday for an answer. . . . Well when we got here today she told us she couldn't answer us till Thursday."[89] Lazarus told the newspaper reporter in a telephone interview that she had tried to tell the delegation, which was accompanied by four Legal Aid lawyers, that she was awaiting a ruling from Maryland welfare department authorities. A public proponent of improving services for and dispelling "popular but baseless misconceptions" of welfare clients, Lazarus had already approved five of their eight demands, including allowing coalition members to represent recipients upon request and to set up a "welfare rights advisory service" inside DSS headquarters. The three remaining demands—transportation for volunteer advisors, free use of telephones, and access to legal manuals—had required state approval, and the new state director, Nicholas Mueller, proved recalcitrant. Appointed by the new governor, Marvin Mandel, in 1969, Mueller retorted that he would not put up with "browbeating by WRO groups."[90] He was critical of recipients and even mandated that they itemize how they spent their checks.[91]

The mothers who had to scrape up carfare to come to DSS headquarters only to be met with inaction held vigil there all night, vowing to stay "until we get action." DSS officials let them stay.[92] Rudell Martin recalled that people gathered on the outside of the office once they saw that the mothers would camp out in the building. Supporters from a local church and other civil rights groups started bringing the protesters food, drinks, and blankets and kept in touch with them through walkie-talkies. Police confronted the demonstrators but made no arrests, apparently upon the request of Lazarus— a wise action given the fact that police mistreatment of welfare recipients and activists in other cities had escalated out of control. In Boston, the beating of welfare demonstrators by police led to three days of rebellion.[93] The day following the sleep-in, the Baltimore contingent, with Martin as a spokesperson, not only gained an audience with welfare officials and positive action on their remaining demands, but they also earned a reputation for speaking up for economically marginalized and stigmatized women.

Shortly after the sleep-in campaign, tenant welfare rights activists from numerous public housing complexes, including O'Donnell, met to discuss the formation of an organization that could concentrate on organizing public housing residents. Around that time, the BWRO opened an office on North Fulton Avenue in St. Martin's Catholic Church's rectory, ironically the same church at which, twenty years before, the white Fulton Improvement Association had held anti-integration meetings. With the help of two University of Maryland social work students, one of whom was Salima Marriott, welfare rights activists began raising money. Marriott had worked with Goldie Baker on education and welfare rights issues, and as a caseworker she facilitated the formation of a welfare rights group among her clients. "Committed" to welfare rights, Marriott decided to do her one-year social work field placement with the welfare rights group in 1970. She aided Rudell Martin and other activists in the grant-writing process.[94] Subsequently, Martin and the group submitted a grant proposal to the Catholic archdiocese's Campaign for Human Development and secured close to $15,000 in funding. Martin served as the organization's first paid executive director.[95] The Campaign for Human Development in the early 1970s funded numerous civil rights and welfare rights organizations throughout the country, including the Welfare Rights Organization in Allegheny County led by Frankie Mae Jeter and the Newark WRO led by Marian Kidd.[96]

The BWRO started organizing and working with chapters in public housing. For instance, the WRO organized a chapter in the still majority-white complex Brooklyn Homes. While public housing became an organizing base, welfare recipients living in the complexes did not simply flock to these rights groups. Cynthia Morgan, a Lafayette Courts tenant who served as BWRO chair and on NWRO's National Coordinating Committee in 1972, had a difficult time mobilizing large numbers of women to join the complex's welfare rights group in the early 1970s—and this in a complex with a history of tenant activism. Nevertheless, public housing tenants were both BWRO organizers and social services clientele. With the citywide WRO's support, the Perkins Homes welfare rights chapter held a demonstration at the First National Bank at Broadway and Eastern avenues on May 4, 1971, for "residents of Perkins and residents outside of Perkins who are on welfare, pension, and are of low-income." They protested the bank's fees on food stamp transactions and gas and electric bill payments. They also lambasted the bank for refusing to cash welfare checks. As BWRO chair, Rudell Martin demanded that the bank stop such "unfair practices."[97]

While WRO in Baltimore focused on recruiting public housing tenants as members, organizers did not confine their efforts to public housing. Aware of poverty's reach and the widespread discontent with the welfare system, the group helped any welfare recipients who had a problem or need, whether they lived in public or private housing. The BWRO established substations throughout the inner city for those who had trouble "getting welfare, filling out applications, collecting food stamps and anything else that comes up."[98] BWRO leaders sought to operate a welfare rights group that addressed the specific needs of AFDC recipients and other poor people. The citywide welfare rights group also mobilized around unemployment and health benefits. For instance, the group demanded that Provident Hospital staff provide welfare clients with "expedient" service despite the type of medical assistance they received. In later years, Rudell Martin joined Provident Hospital's board of trustees.[99]

Public housing tenants and welfare recipients often worked together through their organizations, the NTO and NWRO, as well. They attended the organizations' national conferences and rallied around issues of overlapping interests. Both NTO and NWRO members supported the Brooke Amendment and demanded that the legislation also cover welfare recipients/tenants. Initially in Maryland as in other states, the Brooke Amendment did not apply to welfare recipients who lived in public housing because if welfare recipients/tenants received a rent reduction, the social services department simultaneously decreased their checks. BWRO and public housing activists, with the support of housing and state DPW officials, pushed for special legislation that would extend coverage to recipients/tenants and prevent an income reduction.[100] At the 1971–1972 NWRO conference, "People Before Politics," welfare rights activists sponsored workshops on housing and tenants' rights. Recipients/tenants also closed ranks around President Richard Nixon's Family Assistance Plan (FAP), which sought to guarantee working-class people a $1,600 annual income. Activists argued that $1,600 was an abysmally low amount and that, in some cities, FAP would actually end up cutting welfare benefits. Employing the new NWRO battle cry, the BWRO held a "Zap FAP" hearing at St. Vincent de Paul Church. They labeled Representative Wilbur D. Mills (D-Ark.), the chair of the House Ways and Means Committee, "Public Enemy Number 1." Mills supported workfare and fiscal controls over welfare spending. Instead, organizers argued for a guaranteed adequate income of at least $6,500 per year.[101] The FAP died in Congress.

While the WRO was busy and solvent in the early 1970s, conflict and financial mismanagement taxed the local welfare rights group by the mid-1970s. Around the same time that the NWRO office closed, the BWRO began to splinter.[102] Rudell Martin claimed that the change in organizing style and strategic emphasis drew critics from within the ranks. She maintained that she sought to expand the group's organizing strategy by placing as much (if not more) emphasis on education and matching "wits" and "intelligence" as on demonstrations and protests: "We already had a reputation for being dumb and stupid. And all we knew how to do was make babies. So I felt like we needed to use a different approach and that was [to] match intelligence. . . . beat them at their own game."[103] Martin felt that demonstrations, which had their place, would not work 100 percent of the time—neither with bureaucrats nor with community people, who she felt were beginning to tire of the same old thing.

The BWRO experienced fiscal and organizational crises. Martin maintained that the organization in trying to generate its own money and become independent made a bad financial investment—in beauty, health, and household products. "That was not the best move," Martin recounted. The prices for the products were too high, and "we lost a lot." In January 1974, members made a plea to the community for $1,000 to pay office costs, but to no avail. By August, the BWRO had fallen behind on its telephone bill, and two weeks later the organization had to vacate its office on North Fulton Avenue. Rudell Martin blamed rising costs and unpaid back taxes. Martin also argued that "in-house fighting" and "tugging for power" alongside "grandstanding" were detrimental to the BWRO.[104] Feeling that the WRO had become "less effective" in representing poor and working-class people's needs, Goldie Baker and Geneva Clark, a former tenant of the Latrobe Homes public housing complex and BWRO board member, left the organization and formed the Citizens Civil Rights Organization (CCRO) in the mid-1970s.[105] Recalled Baker: "Rather than fight each other in the organization, we decided to have a spin-off." The CCRO had "the same goal, same purpose, same objective: to represent the mothers, and the rights of welfare clients, and the best interests of the children and families, and provide services for medical assistance, financial assistance, and different benefits and opportunities." The CCRO survived into the late 1970s and then dissolved when organizers "moved in other directions."[106]

The BWRO experienced turnover. Without funding, Martin lost her paid executive director position. Still a public housing tenant, she began to work with the housing authority to develop a resident security guard program. But before she left the welfare rights group, Martin contended that she asked Bobby Cheeks, a part-time activist and a former local semi-pro football star who went to Dunbar High School, to help revive the floundering organization. He had recently returned to Baltimore from traveling across the country working numerous social action jobs with youth gangs and the unemployed, supervising in health centers, and evaluating poverty programs. When Rudell Martin approached him, Cheeks was working in a CAA neighborhood center. Cheeks, who agreed to work with the BWRO, became the first man to head a welfare rights group in Baltimore.[107] Around the same time that Bobby Cheeks took over, Annie Rogers, a welfare recipient who would eventually have twenty-five biological children, became the citywide welfare rights group's board chair.[108] Annie Rogers had little schooling and few skills, except housekeeping. So when her husband left her, she relied on AFDC to help her support her large family. She eventually became active in welfare rights issues, serving as an advocate for welfare mothers inside DSS. Rogers described the impetus for, and importance of, welfare rights: "Even though we're fighting for civil rights, lots of people won't even have the money to buy that cup of coffee after we get them to that point."[109] In 1978, veteran civil rights, black nationalist, and welfare activists Rogers and Cheeks worked with the nine-year-old, now black-led IMPACT to help O'Donnell Heights tenants wage the city's first public housing rent strike.

The BWRO and the Public Housing Rent Strike of 1978

Rats, roaches, and mud, loose floorboards, sinking toilets, falling plaster, and live electrical wires—together these problems described a woefully substandard, if not condemned, house usually owned by a slum landlord. These conditions, however, also characterized many publicly owned residences. Between 1969 and 1977, O'Donnell Heights tenants complained to their resident association and management about the lack of repairs and maintenance and the upsurge in roaches and mice.[110] Echoing public housing tenants' complaints from as early as the 1940s, O'Donnell Heights tenants objected vociferously to their living conditions. A May 1969 resident council letter, in which tenant activists responded to housing officials' attempts to blame residents for maintenance, repair, and infestation problems, revealed the dilemma they encountered:

> *The Housing Authority Says It Is the Tenant's Fault. We Don't Think So!*
> Sure, some tenants do not take care of their homes and tear up the neighborhood. But, are they the ones who made the electric wiring and the plumbing bad? Are they the ones who kept our buildings from being painted and let our porches fall apart?
> The Housing Authority wants us to live in shacks, and they want O'Donnell to be a slum. We want homes in a community we can be proud of!!

We will pay $600,000 rent this year, and we want it spent to improve O'Donnell.[111]

Rosaline Lundsford, O'Donnell's tenant council president in 1969 and RAB delegate, remembered the intense problems with roaches. She recalled going to a RAB meeting, "and I said to Bob Embry I want to share with you what we have in O'Donnell Heights. And I dumped a whole jar of roaches on his desk [*laughs and smacks the table*]. I said, I think you should have the same thing we have in the Heights. I want to share. I dropped the roaches right on him."[112] By 1978, O'Donnell Heights tenants definitely had had enough. Led by IMPACT and the BWRO, tenants decided to publicize the travesties through collective action. They organized a rent strike.

The citywide welfare rights groups had a contentious relationship not only with local officials but also with the complex's tenant council. In February 1978 at a resident council meeting, Fannie Hemphill, the chair of IMPACT, read a letter from Bobby Cheeks asking to lease a one-bedroom unit in O'Donnell Heights for WRO. The tenant council president, RAB representative, and a long-time white male resident, Gramley Buehler, signed a letter objecting to the rental, saying the request did not follow authorized channels; the complex's resident council board had not seen the request before tenants voted. Buehler argued that one-bedroom units should be for the elderly. However, after Hemphill stressed to the forty-seven tenants in attendance that "there were no social workers available to help them like Mr. Cheeks could," forty-five of them approved leasing a unit to WRO.[113] This event presaged future discord between the resident association leadership and IMPACT during the rent strike. Even with tenant support for a BWRO office, however, Hemphill and Cheeks had a difficult time securing a home for the welfare rights group. In March, Cheeks and five residents, also welfare rights activists, met with the manager, Margaret Keen, and DSS counselor Thelma Millard. "After exhausting every possible area," the welfare rights group decided to request space on the second floor of the Urban Services Agency's neighborhood center. The Urban Services Agency was a reorganized CAP under the Nixon administration. Urban Services' temporary director, Steve Wilkie, provided office space to the welfare rights group. Three months later, however, when the center's white director, W. Edward Dorsett, returned from a two-year leave, he "ordered welfare rights to vacate the 2nd floor space." He also fired Wilkie.[114]

O'Donnell Heights resident welfare rights activists contested the agency's dictatorial stance. Dorsett's claim that he needed the extra space to develop programming elicited extreme protest from tenant welfare rights members, who argued that before the O'Donnell welfare rights office opened, very few people used the center. At the public housing meeting, which overflowed into two rooms and the hall, angry tenants shouted, "What programs are there? Nothing. There's nothing here." Dorsett found himself "pleading to the mostly female crowd, which was shouting insults." Tenants argued that they did not want Dorsett or Urban Services to dictate what kind of services they needed. Fannie Hemphill of IMPACT confronted Dorsett: "You're telling us what we're going to have, when we're the ones who ought to be telling you what we want." Annie Rogers, who attended the meeting with Dorsett, added: "Too often people come into our community and tell us what we're supposed to eat, where we're supposed to live. People think because we're low-income, we're damned flunkies, but we're tired of getting kicked. People are going to stand up." While Dorsett seemed bent on evicting the activist group, Lenwood Ivey, the city's director of Urban Services, expressed concern about the "tone of the confrontation." Ivey, who had earned a social work degree from Howard University and served as a caseworker for Baltimore DPW, joined Baltimore CAP as a neighborhood development supervisor in 1965, became CAA associate director in early 1969, and was executive director by the end of 1969. Ivey maintained: "If the Welfare Rights Organization needs the space and they can work out a way to get it, then it's fine by me. It's my position that if we can find a way to share space with any group, we're willing to do it."[115] The O'Donnell welfare rights group kept its office.

Public housing tenants who fought to maintain their welfare rights office in O'Donnell Heights used the organization to better their living conditions. The citywide welfare rights activists served as mediators and agitators. When housing officials asked tenants and welfare rights activists in meetings what they wanted, they answered, "safe and affordable housing." When housing officials asked them what that meant exactly, Annie Rogers recalled replying:

We don't want to step in a damn foot of mud when we wake up in the morning. We don't want roaches to bite our children all night and they crying. Roaches all in babies' ears, we don't want that. We don't want mice eating our food. We don't want to live with the roaches, the mice, and the mud. That became our battle cry—no mice, no roaches, no mud.[116]

Despite the obvious concerns of tenants regarding substandard conditions, Annie Rogers maintained that external and internal dissension existed: "We tried dealing with public housing. . . . We did everything we could, and we got a deaf ear. So we were sitting down at a meeting, and I remember[ed] rent strikes during the Depression. And I talked to them about doing a rent strike." Initially and throughout the campaign, the rent strike received mixed reviews. Annie Rogers argued that initially even Bobby Cheeks did not want to strike; he wanted to talk and negotiate with housing officials. "And I said, we have talked enough. Because we did at that date." WRO members began debating whether to hold the proposed rent strike. "We took six votes . . . because people would split up. Some people wouldn't vote at all." But when the final vote came, the rent strike strategy prevailed by one vote.[117]

Welfare rights activists not only experienced resistance to the strike from within their ranks and from housing officials, but also from RAB members. Annie Rogers recalled BWRO "approaching [RAB] for support, but we didn't get it." While RAB supported tenants' right to strike, Shirley Wise maintained that O'Donnell Heights' council leaders resisted the action because BWRO did not go through recognized tenant council channels to organize the rent strike; it was the same argument Buehler had made when the BWRO sought office space in O'Donnell. Continued Annie Rogers: "That's when housing really thought they would have the upper hand because they were the tenants' representatives, and the representatives were not going to support the rent strike." However, the strike moved forward; it included not only O'Donnell Heights' tenants, but also residents of Gilmor, Westport, and Fairfield homes. And by the end of 1978, O'Donnell tenants had elected to RAB Fannie Hemphill and another tenant, Valerie Wilmoth, who were sympathetic to welfare rights and the strike.[118]

The rent strike marked both a continuation and a break from previous protest activities. Poor black women continued to organize door to door around familiar issues of housing, rights, dignity, and empowerment. The rent strike, however, represented the first time that disgruntled public housing residents in Baltimore engaged in a court action as a group against the city agency. The rent strike also further exposed the coalitions and networks of low-income women in public housing and around welfare rights. O'Donnell residents, as tenants, used the local welfare branch to deal with public assistance more broadly conceived. Tenants addressed issues that affected the lives of women on welfare and poor people in general, including the state of housing and neighborhood safety.

In October, the *Baltimore Sun* newspaper published a series of articles highlighting tenants' despair and criticizing O'Donnell Heights' physical disrepair. Fannie Hemphill, black resident activist and IMPACT leader, argued that the housing authority placed Latina families in broken-down apartments and did not provide them with services. Two Latinas, who spoke sparse English, had trouble conveying their displeasure and, therefore, could be easily exploited and ignored, Hemphill maintained. The housing authority had no translators on staff although they knew that some of the Puerto Rican families that had been given apartments in O'Donnell Heights faced language barriers. Hemphill described the conditions that one Latina experienced: inoperable windows, a busted screen door, a nonworking stove, a leaking toilet, and a broken back door lock. She continued: "I raised hell. I asked them, 'How'd you like to be in the Dark Ages in Africa, speaking no African?' . . . What if she went over [to] the office and—in Spanish—she was shouting, 'My house is on fire, my baby's in the house'? No one would understand her."[119]

A week after the newspaper series, the former city council president who had become mayor, William Donald Schaefer, visited the complex and pledged his help. During his visit, Schaefer, whose administration focused on downtown growth and redevelopment projects, promised to investigate tenants' maintenance, service, and security complaints, but he talked to few residents. Frustrated, several women tenants yelled at him, echoing 1960s organizing slogans: "We're tired of being treated like dogs," "We need somebody to help us," and "God damned social workers, they don't do nothing for nobody."[120] After Schaefer's tour, M. Jay Brodie, the housing authority's executive director, who had replaced Robert C. Embry (President Jimmy Carter's choice for assistant secretary of HUD) in 1977, concluded that O'Donnell Heights "has not been neglected. . . . it has not been forgotten." After Brodie's public statement, the city sent out construction teams to survey plumbing and electricity systems in all 900 homes in O'Donnell Heights. With the advice and counsel of Legal Aid, tenant welfare rights activists decided to conduct their own inspection reports, which they subsequently mailed to the housing authority. The reports marked the first step in the five-month rent strike.[121]

While more than 200 tenants mailed complaints to the housing authority, at the start of the rent strike only a minority of them withheld their rent. According to John A. McCauley, a city housing official, only seventy-five public housing tenants had withheld their rent as of December 8, 1978.[122] A report issued in December 1978 by building inspectors showed that 849 homes out of 880 examined in O'Donnell Heights had defects. Baltimore housing authority crews labored day and night to remedy dangerous conditions by the court date—January 2, 1979.[123] By the time advocates filed the rent strike cases in People's Court, the number of unresolved cases had dwindled. Rushed repairs conducted by the housing authority and fear on the part of some tenants prevented further participation. According to Rogers, who went door to door with other activists trying to organize people for the rent strike: "We would go and knock on doors and talk to people. And you know, some people were afraid. . . . They didn't have nowhere else to go and they didn't know what would happen." Only when WRO legally secured the right to establish a rent escrow fund did the campaign "[pick] up more people, because people knew they wouldn't be evicted."[124]

Even so, the numbers participating still remained small. Paulette Pope, the first tenant to testify and one of thirty-eight plaintiffs from O'Donnell, detailed the twenty-six floods from seeping water, inadequate heat, exposed wires, mice, and leaky toilet that she and her four children had to deal with for seven years. Legal Aid lawyers presented evidence from experts regarding pests and vermin. Recalled Annie Rogers:

> I mean those lawyers were good though, because they brought in people we knew nothing about. People from control labs that could tell you about different types of roaches. And all roaches don't bite you, but Baltimore roaches bite. You know. And about how long mice can live in the ground. . . . They brought in those people that proved our case, helped us prove our case rather, and we won.[125]

Organizers won a majority of the cases in People's Court in February 1979 after the presiding district court judge and a participant in Baltimore's sit-in movement in 1960, Robert Mack Bell, saw the conditions for himself.[126]

The rent strike lasted only a few months and involved only a minority of households. While not as large as St. Louis's or Newark's public housing rent strikes in 1969 and 1970, in which tenants withheld hundreds of thousands of dollars, the Baltimore effort brought attention to the deteriorating conditions of O'Donnell Heights and public housing citywide. In a September 1979 inspection status report, Van Story Branch, by then director of the housing management division, suggested that the housing authority apply for federal housing rehabilitation money "rather than to continue with the current practice of 'band-aiding' the problems." In 1981, O'Donnell Heights received an $18.1 million federal grant, part of a $30.1 million grant from HUD to improve city public housing facilities. McCauley, who had characterized Cheeks's and tenants' complaints in 1978 as "wildly exaggerated," now agreed that such improvements were long overdue. A year before the final word on the grant, McCauley confessed: "[O'Donnell Heights] has been let go."[127]

Conclusion

Despite the national mood, poor people waged a battle that resulted in concessions from a seemingly all-powerful city bureaucracy. According to Cheeks: "This proves that you can fight City Hall and win. This gives hope and pride to the tenants. They can take pride in where they live, they are somebody. And it is this pride and hope that can also benefit the authorities." He continued: "What poor people lack in money and influence, they can make up in organized numbers and determination."[128] Engineered and organized largely by poor black women who confronted the power structure, the rent strike forced the housing authority to correct maintenance and management problems not only in O'Donnell, but also in other complexes that threatened to use the same tactic. According to Cheeks, the WRO through the initiation of the rent strike and creation of the housing coalition tried to spread "the idea that no matter what system a person is influenced by, they have certain rights and they can affect the way they are treated."[129]

Epilogue

The examination of low-income black women's politicization from 1940 through the 1970s has furnished invaluable insight into how this group negotiated life in postindustrial cities. Poor black women in Baltimore not only engaged in battles for daily subsistence, but also fought against societal marginalization and dehumanization. Confronting exclusion and vilification based on their race, class, and gender, cohorts of poor black women, black men, and children sought access to the democratic promises of society. Their efforts to obtain material needs like shelter and income, to preserve decent communities, and to secure a modicum of respect are all components of historic struggles for working-class social justice.

Twenty years later, in the 1990s, struggles over government-subsidized shelter and income continued to illuminate the embattled circumstances of poor black women and their families. In Baltimore, Lexington Terrace residents complained in 1993 about dangerous and unhealthy living conditions: water leakages and flooding, rat infestation, fungus infecting their children, exposed electrical wiring, vandalized vacant apartments, onsite drug dealing and shootings, and unaddressed maintenance requests.[1] A thirty-year-old mother, Sharon Wright, said that "her children have been horrified by three murders" in a year and that she did not "feel adequate as a mother trying to survive here. This is no way for children to grow up."[2] Lorraine Ledbetter, the Lexington-Poe Tenants Association president, argued that the housing agency's then executive director Robert W. Hearn's "history of unresponsiveness to our calls for a safe, clean, and most of all a healthy place to live forces me to conclude that the focus of his administration is elsewhere."[3] Fed up after begging for changes for two years, tenant leaders and residents threatened a rent strike. At a meeting of 100 tenants in Lexington Terrace Elementary School, the outspoken tenant activist Barbara "Bobby" McKinney, who grew up in the complex and was now raising her children there, invited officials to a sleepover so they could "wake up the same way we do." McKinney argued that housing officials needed "to hear the pipes clanging all night long," "to feel what it's like not to have hot water for three days and to come out and hear gunfire."[4]

Lexington Terrace's tenants' concerns, anger, desires, and tactics were quite familiar. They echoed residents' struggles over the decades. Lorraine Ledbetter's critique of Hearn in 1993 echoed Gilmor Homes' tenant council president Lottie Hall's critique of local housing officials in 1943, particularly Hall's feeling that officials were not "interested in our very real problems as tenants."[5] Lexington Terrace tenants' complaints about drugs resembled the concerns of that complex's first resident aide, Christine Jones, and other public housing residents citywide, in 1969. And Lexington Terrace residents' decisive threat to engage in a rent strike in 1993 conjures up the O'Donnell Heights rent strike spearheaded by tenant and welfare rights activists in 1978. Public housing complexes—and the cities of which they are a part—did not falter overnight. Their physical deterioration has a past. The similarities of the difficulties (for instance, questionable maintenance) and the differences (like increased drug dealing and murders) reveal the weight of historical legacies and ongoing challenges. And, like in the past, cohorts of poor black women responded. For just as social welfare programs, including public housing, have a history, so too does the activism that has arisen in response to their limitations and insufficiencies.

A few days after poor black women tenant leaders and residents threatened the rent strike in 1993, things began to finally happen. Newspaper articles further investigated the housing authority. One *Baltimore Evening Sun* news article reported allegations of housing mismanagement and discussed the debilitating effects of blight and crime on the complexes and neighborhoods—well-known realities. News reports discussed how Baltimore housing officials failed to use $42 million in federal community development block grants to maintain vacant public housing apartments in livable conditions, and documented the local housing agency's decision to give its 1,400 employees a $1,000 raise instead of using the $1.4 million to repair public housing apartments.[6] Federal government housing initiatives, scandals, and mismanagement under the Reagan and Bush administrations; the existence of appropriated but unspent HUD money; and inflexible HUD regulations could not have helped local matters.[7] After the publicizing of tenants' protests, administrative changes also occurred. Robert W. Hearn forced black deputy executive director, Juanita Harris, to resign and appointed new people. A month later, Baltimore's first black mayor, Kurt Schmoke, removed Hearn from his $89,600-a-year executive director position.[8]

Responding immediately to Lexington Terrace's mothers' invitation "to wake up the same way we do," Mary Pat Clarke agreed to sleep overnight in the housing complex on a "fact-finding mission." Schmoke did not accept tenants' offer, but he did express bafflement and surprise after a brief visit to Lexington Terrace that preceded Clarke's stay. He "couldn't believe what my eyes were seeing. No wonder you're angry. It looks like a place we forgot."[9] Schmoke apologized to tenants, vowed to take prompt action, and returned to Lexington Terrace after Clarke's stay. He spent eight hours talking with tenants and touring the complex, which had a 25 percent vacancy rate in its high rises. But, by then, maintenance crews had already carted away tons of garbage and made numerous superficial repairs—specifically to prepare for his visit.[10] The new HUD secretary under President Bill Clinton, Henry Cisneros, who was in Baltimore touring another recently rehabilitated community, made an unannounced visit to Lexington Terrace and stated: "Immediate things need to be done here."[11] Eleven months later, in December 1993, Schmoke and Cisneros announced Baltimore's receipt of a HOPE VI federal grant to implode the city's first high-rise public housing complex, Lafayette Courts. Eventually, local and federal officials would also wipe out Lexington Terrace's problems—through implosion. The buildings were demolished in 1996 with many tenants wishing them good riddance.

The year after the city demolished Lexington Terrace, tenant activist veterans Goldie Baker, Shirley Wise, and Elizabeth Wright, black women, and Anna Warren, a white woman, found themselves trying to help protect tenants' rights won in the 1960s and 1970s. In what must have been a moment of déjà vu, or at the very least an exasperating feeling of here-we-go-again, these black women asserted tenants' rights to do more than rubber-stamp housing policy—in this instance, a new lease then under consideration. Tenant representatives and residents who attended the board of commissioners meeting protested provisions of the proposed lease, which sought both to evict entire families for one family member's drug-related offenses and to mandate that tenants perform community service as a requirement of residency. Anna Warren, by then the Resident Advisory Board's vice chair under Elizabeth Wright, discussed the proposed drug policy: "We don't want drugs neither around the neighborhood. So we want them to go, but we want some family people protected. You can't help it if I got a son that does drugs and the other six don't do drugs. Why should everybody pay for what he does? You know, that's really unfair." Warren, who has run the Claremont Homes Boys' and Girls' Club for decades in addition to her RAB duties, then critiqued the proposed community service policy. "I do all kinds of community work. . . . I'm doing it every day, more than my share, and I would give a little piece to all the neighborhoods so they would have to get out there." But to say that "we have to [do community service] to live in public housing, oh come on now." To mandate community service for low-income citizens because they rely on subsidized housing to make ends meet casts them as societal transgressors who have to pay restitution to the state in the form of service. But for Warren and others, poverty is not a crime. As citizens who receive government subsidies, albeit as public housing not as home tax credits, they have a right to be treated equally and to have a roof over their heads: "Public housing was a right for me. I have a right to have a nice home, and be able to pay to live there. I say, my community work, I do it when I want to do it."[12]

At this 1997 commissioners meeting, the echoes of long-ago battles for rights, decency, dignity, and respect erupted in the room, exemplifying the seemingly never-ending struggle that low-income people, particularly black women, have waged. June Johnson, a black woman who lived in McCulloh Homes, stood up and told the board: "Snob hill is a little different from low hill. . . . I'm human and I want you to treat me as so. Treat all of us like you want to be treated." Goldie Baker reminded Daniel Henson III, the black executive director who replaced Hearn, that "slavery was over" and that in 1968 tenants received the right to sit at the table with the decision makers and make policy.[13]

While this volume has focused on the specific struggles of specific people residing in specific places, the strivings of Baltimore's low-income black women also illustrate broader social struggles. The fact that Wise, Baker, and others still had to safeguard public housing tenants' interests thirty years later and that RAB still operated serves as living testimony to low-income black women's—and poor people's—continued travails and their commitment to a humanistic agenda of social rights, progressive change, and fairness. Their ongoing struggle—and that of their activist descendants and protégés—speaks to how public housing and social welfare policy continues to politicize poor people. Low-income women and mothers still have to contend with economic marginalization and shoulder the responsibility of raising families in economically beleaguered and segregated black cities—some now controlled by black power brokers.

But even as the number of black people in key government positions, including mayors, has continued to grow since the late 1960s in cities, black low-income people continue to suffer. Between 1964 and 1975, the number of African-American elected officials increased from 100 to almost 3,000, 135 of them mayors. While Baltimore sent its first black congressman, Parren J. Mitchell, to Washington in 1971, the city did not elect its first black mayor, Kurt Schmoke, until 1987. Until then, the mayoral office and city council remained under white control, even though as early as 1972, about 44 percent of Baltimore's voters were African American. In some cases, black elected officials' urban reform agendas did not benefit low-income residents, but focused on maintaining and luring businesses and professionals to declining cities through tax breaks and other incentives. Just as important, however, many black municipal officials came to power in cities already beleaguered by structural and fiscal crises and during a time when the federal government grew increasingly insensitive to low-income people's and cities' needs.[14] As Anthony Downs, a white economist, member of the National Commission on Urban Problems, and consultant to the National Advisory Committee on Civil Disorders, presciently maintained in 1968:

Eventually, Negro mayors will rightfully take over many of our largest cities. But, by then, the fiscal conditions of these cities will be absolutely desperate. The new Negro mayors will have to appeal to Congress for aid even more strongly than present white mayors are doing. But Congress will then be dominated even more than now by the 98 percent white suburbs; it may refuse to vote such aid.[15]

For the most part, black elected officials have been excluded from "the dominant or governing coalition in Washington that exercises long-term control over policy issues of central concern to them."[16]

With or without constraints, however, the mere presence of black "representatives" has historically not always translated into policies beneficial to the poorest segments of the black community. According to political scientist Cathy J. Cohen, some black people experience secondary marginalization. They are marginalized twice over—by mainstream society and then by black power brokers, whose visions do not always dovetail with the needs and desires of the African-American community's more marginalized members.[17] In Baltimore's public housing and welfare programs, the presence of black managers and social workers did not necessarily translate into cross-class racial coalitions. In the 1990s, for instance, some resident activists described Daniel Henson III as condescending and as someone who had forgotten his roots. And tenants like June Johnson and activist veterans like Goldie Baker and Shirley Wise were not standing for it. As early as the 1970s, Wise had built an intolerance "for colored people who could not see the inequities, and just because of my address I was not equal to you. I didn't mind having to fight the other race, but I definitely didn't appreciate having [to fight] with people of my own color. I don't care how high they have made it, you know." She argued: "Nobody black, white, yellow, or green is going to take me back there. 'Cause I said, don't make a difference what color you are, you not going to put me [back] on that plantation. I have experienced the two worlds."[18]

The changing political economy also rendered cities vulnerable. In postwar America, migration, federal housing policies, and industrial jobs drew black people into cities just as white people and industries deserted them for the suburbs.[19] In Baltimore, racial and economic segregation's glaring expansion shaped black people's lived realities and opportunities as well as their relationship to the state. The American Civil Liberties Union (ACLU) believed the city's and housing authority's legacy of residential segregation to be so egregious that it readily filed a class-action lawsuit, *Carmen Thompson et al. v. U.S. Department of Housing and Urban Development et al.*, against the housing authority, the mayor, the city council, and HUD in 1995. Five of the six leading plaintiffs were black women public housing residents: Carmen Thompson of Lexington Terrace, Rhonda Harris of Lexington Terrace and McCulloh Extension, Joanne Boyd of Lafayette Courts, Doris Tinsley of scattered-site housing, and Lorraine Johnson of Murphy Homes; the sixth was Isaac J. Neal of Lafayette Courts. The ACLU filed the case in the wake of the major HOPE VI housing initiative to demolish and replace about 3,000 public housing units, including the four central-city high-rise complexes. In the relocation and rebuilding process, they wanted to "make sure that the mistakes of the past were not repeated."[20]

The ACLU, HUD, the Housing Authority of Baltimore City (HABC), and the city itself agreed to a court-mandated partial consent decree in 1996. The decree ordered HABC, HUD, and the city to replace the lost high-rise development units in a broad range of neighborhoods. Although not a final resolution to the case, the decree marked the beginning of the potential end of a sixty-year pattern of rebuilding public housing in solely impoverished, minority communities. The decree illuminates the broader shift in housing policy to constructing mixed-income urban communities and relocating low-income residents to urban neighborhoods and suburbs with low concentrations of poverty. According to Barbara Samuels, the ACLU's lead attorney on the case:

> Beginning December 1, 2003, the court will begin to consider whether the federal and local governments should be held liable for overt, purposeful, deliberate, and long-standing policies that maintained a racially segregated system of publicly assisted housing—and what the government must do to end segregation and expand fair housing opportunities.[21]

On December 23, the ACLU closed the liability phase of its case after presenting more than 600 exhibits and testimony from five expert witnesses and tenant representatives. In March 2004, the ACLU was still waiting for federal district court judge Marvin J. Garbis to finish reviewing the evidence and to issue a decision.[22]

Imploding Public Housing

Lafayette Courts, Lexington Terrace, Murphy Homes, Flag House Courts—
the implosion of each in 1995, 1996, 1999, and 2001, respectively, was marked
by glorious fanfare. Blocks away from the cordoned-off, gutted high-rise
towers, throngs of people climbed on top of cars and trucks, the roofs of
schools, or the closest accessible buildings. People gathered in the streets,
where they jostled for places to see, chatted, and laughed. Television news
cameras, radio broadcasters with tape recorders, and newspaper reporters
and photographers staked out positions and interviewed members of the
crowd. Young black girls from tots to teenagers swiveled hips as horn-
blowing, drum-rolling, quick-stepping black boys and girls in youth band
corps marched down the streets. At Lexington Terrace's implosion in 1996,
just three years after tenants threatened a rent strike, a sandy brown–
complexioned man sold loose bricks from a wheelbarrow; he claimed they
would soon be collectors' items. For Flag House Courts' implosion, people

Figure E.1 Murphy Homes' implosion celebration in 1999.
Photograph by Oliver Frazier, Jr.

Figure E.2 The Lexington Terrace high-rise development, which consisted of low-rise and high-rise towers, from behind a high-rise building's chain-link fence. The freeway divides Lexington Terrace from Murphy Homes, another high-rise development. The high-rise building with side stairways (far left corner) is part of Murphy Homes. Lexington Terrace was imploded in 1996, Murphy Homes in 1999. Photograph by Rhonda Y. Williams.

ceremoniously gathered on the twenty-seventh-floor observation deck of Baltimore's World Trade Center. At Lafayette, Lexington, and Murphy's implosions, VIPs sat on a dais. Local and federal housing officials, including Mayor Kurt Schmoke and HUD secretary Henry Cisneros, spoke of ruined lives, ravaged communities, and a new day on the horizon.

After hours of celebrating, it was time—almost noon. Quiet emerged. A countdown, 11:59:00, one, two, three, all the way to ten, then the pressing of the symbolic detonator button, followed by muffled booms, rumbles, oohs and ahs, cheers, and teary eyes. Then, towers of concrete and brick collapsed in domino effect—all within fifteen seconds. The high-rises that had characterized Lafayette, Lexington Terrace, Murphy, and Flag House and lorded over their companion low-rise apartments disintegrated. After each implosion, all that remained were piles of rubble amid white billowy smoke and an eerily unobstructed view of the neighborhood for blocks around. Public housing tenants relayed their dismay about the disappearance of communities that once served as home and their excitement at the prospect of new housing communities being born—like phoenixes from the ashes.

The 1995 implosion of Lafayette Courts, where tenants had spearheaded many of the 1960s public housing residents' rights campaigns, represented the beginning of the end of an era in public housing in Baltimore and around the nation. Raymond Rosen in Philadelphia, Christopher Columbus in Newark, Vaughn Apartments in St. Louis, Washington Park Extension in Chicago, and Techwood Homes in Atlanta also tumbled in 1995. The 2001 implosion of Flag House Courts gave Baltimore the particular honor of becoming the first city nationwide to "totally rid itself of what [former] Vice President Al Gore has called 'monuments of hopelessness.'"[23] But these family high-rises were not the only subsidized complexes literally reduced to dust and rubble. Fairfield Homes, Hollander Ridge, and Broadway-Orleans, two low-rise and an elderly high-rise complex in Baltimore, also met similar fates.

In the New Deal era, when housing authorities first began constructing subsidized housing, public housing embodied the tremendous hope of creating respectable communities of working-class people. Although high-rise complexes built between the 1950s and early 1960s offered altitude without frills, low-income people clamored for the apartments then. That excitement diminished as problems mounted. In 1983 Bob Cheeks, as WRO executive director, lambasted Mayor Schaefer and the city for ignoring the health and safety of low-income black mothers and their families, particularly in high-rise buildings. Cheeks argued that a six-month-old boy died because an inoperative elevator prevented him from receiving "proper medical services." Cheeks wrote to Schaefer: "In your arrogant, single-minded focus to build hotels, restaurants, shops, and housing for the rich while at the same time ignoring the concerns of the poor you have demonstrated an insensitivity equaled to that of your forefathers in their overt acts of human destruction." Cheeks continued: "As chief administrator for the affairs of this City, you have allowed despicable unsanitary, overcrowded and dangerous maintenance conditions to threaten and take the lives of innocent poor women and children." After this incident, low-income women residents formed M.O.M., a "Mothers Organization to Save Our Children from High Rise Housing." In 1992, about 85 percent of residents in high-rise buildings requested transfers.[24]

The demand for public housing remained high. In 1994, the Baltimore housing authority had a waiting list of 23,000 people, but many feared living in the high-rise complexes.[25] Despite the obvious deterioration of public housing, many tenants still struggled to make the best of what they had. A tenant since the 1960s, Rosetta Schofield eventually left her high-rise apartment, but she stayed in Murphy Homes in a low-rise unit. Around 1990, she moved to yet another Murphy Homes low-rise unit, No. 839, where amid the brick and concrete, she tended a prolific and robust vegetable garden of hot peppers, cucumbers, and tomatoes. In thirty years of residency, Schofield had witnessed the area's physical deterioration, vandalism, drug-related violence, growing fears (even her own), and negative depictions of public housing and its residents: "Public housing seem to have a bad name, you know. All the people, always say, oh, the projects. Oh, you live there. Oh, in the project. I said, yes I live in public housing. Oh, how can you live there? I said, very easily. I pay my rent and that's how I live there. You know. It isn't where you live. It's how you live."[26]

But negative images of the place and people have made a difference. Public housing not only had become unsafe, hellish, God-awful places, prisons and warehouses for the poor, but also monstrous steel, brick, and mortar symbols of black urban life in postindustrial America.[27] Even cultural depictions authenticating black city life in films like *Superfly*, *New Jack City*, and *Menace II Society* and television shows like *Good Times* and the *PJs* featured desolate and dangerous "projects," usually high-rises. These cultural narratives, shaped simultaneously by race, class, and gender, have worked to conflate black women and their children, public housing residency, danger, black urban experiences, and the city's ills. This is not to say that public housing and its neighborhoods had not become dangerous. Tenants' voices affirm that reality. But poor black women's voices also show a much more complex picture, one that unveils their attempts to combat unsafe and unhealthy conditions and exposes the changing political economy that has shaped postindustrial cities—and tenants' well-being.

Attacking Welfare

The federal government's reduction of already meager public housing and welfare budgets has undercut poor people's safety nets and negatively affected the public's assessment of subsidized shelter and income programs. The inaccurate and simplistic belief that these programs were dismal failures and that poor people's plight is incurable unless they are morally rehabilitated has guided social policy, led to welfare and public housing's demise as entitlements, and ultimately resulted in the dismantling of the New Deal and Great Society programs.

As federal officials dismantled AFDC, welfare recipients suffered verbal attacks. Depicting black women as a drain on public resources and as persons engaged in a socially destructive culture set the stage for welfare reform that imposed moral conformity, instead of addressing economic disadvan- . tage and protecting the social rights of the poor. The descriptors of black women welfare recipients as, for instance, "wolves" and "alligators" not only have clouded the complex structures, dynamics, and faces of poverty, but also have acquired a tremendous currency that has shaped welfare policy in egregious ways.[28] This process, however, which both dehumanized welfare recipients and delegitimized their concerns, started decades earlier.

The 1960s and 1970s spurred a political atmosphere ripe for the conservative assault on low-income black women and the AFDC program. With New Deal and Great Society programs in place and the Civil Rights and Voting Rights acts passed, white society began to tire of black people's ongoing equality demands and expressed disgust at the urban uprisings. White working-class citizens, in particular, felt that government programs excluded them, and they were angry. Feeding off this sentiment of white anger, white politicians who vowed to maintain law and order, quell black rebellions, and critique social welfare and government programs ascended to the nation's top positions. This increased hostility proved unfortunate for low-income black women, who began mobilizing in cities to demand economic equality.

Frontline activists during the age of civil rights and black power activism, low-income black women were the most vocal welfare rights advocates in Baltimore and nationwide. Goldie Baker argued that black freedom movements and a historical legacy of state repression translated into a greater sense of urgency for black women.[29] In Baltimore, Walter Lively of U-JOIN and CORE organizers committed themselves to organizing poor people and focusing on welfare rights. Former CORE member and national founder of NWRO George Wiley brought a commitment to black equality and poor people's rights to the welfare rights organization. In numerous ways, then, the welfare rights movement was "an expression of a large protest movement among black people in the United States."[30]

Others argued that many white women feared aligning themselves with a cause identified with the "pariah class of a success-ridden America."[31] Maintained Geraldine Randall, a Cherry Hill Homes resident and former welfare rights activist: "White status was supposed to be higher than black. . . . So, because of [the] situation they were in they didn't want you to know" that they received welfare. Rudell Martin echoed Randall, arguing, "[A]t that time white folk didn't want folk to know that they were on welfare, okay. . . . it was black women who decided that I've just had enough!"[32]

Martin, Baker, and Randall hit on critical points. As Martin and Baker intimated, white low-income women did not confront group oppression or have an analysis laid out by civil rights, black power, women's rights, and other grassroots activists. Nor were low-income white women as geographically restricted as poor black women, who were cordoned off in neighborhoods that became hotbeds of political activity. And as Randall's comment suggests, poverty had become racialized and feminized. For white women, then, poverty evoked a sense of failure and stigma. This was not true of all white women, of course. Baltimore did have white welfare rights activists like Charlotte Minton and Anna Warren, who acted despite the stigma. "I was poor," Anna Warren stated, "and I never worried about it because I was white. I just knew that I needed help and the only place that was going to give it was welfare rights."[33]

Even so, public, government, and media attention focused on black female welfare rights activists. Black visibility and white invisibility helped to further concretize the race and gender image of the dependent citizen. That poor black women often carried the banner of poor people's protests in cities during a time of heightened backlash against black people's demands created further hostility. The actual activism and visibility, therefore, of low-income black women activists, who as their heads of households were arguing for rights, supported society's value-laden concept of the "black matriarch." Taking on "male" responsibilities, poor black women became defeminized, emasculators of black men, and usurpers of male power. This undifferentiated black woman, who became the primary caretaker, was depicted as too strong and independent, as too weak and dependent on government, and as too aggressive and demanding of the state. Black women became the problem: not sexism which prevented women from earning equal wages or securing well-paying jobs, not racism, not poverty, and definitely not the state.

Depicted as lazy, shiftless, irresponsible, breeding welfare queens, poor black mothers essentially became the embodiment of a calamitous social welfare system and urban social ills. And once again, these representations of poor black mothers lacked the depth, complexity, and often painful drama of real women's lives—the Rosetta Schofields, Frances Reiveses, Rudell Martins, Goldie Bakers, and even Anna Warrens of the world—who suffered travails and depended on AFDC to provide subsistence.[34]

Ironically, poor black women's attempts to attain dignity and basic necessities and to improve their life circumstances by demanding that the New Deal and Great Society welfare state treat its citizens with justice bolstered demeaning caricatures. Poor black women's welfare rights activism, which had become a marker of poor people's newfound militancy, became anathema to the American ideals of independence, self-sufficiency, and hard work. It mattered little that poor black women's fights contested the wholesale image of passivity and idleness underpinning perceptions of the welfare mother (and public housing resident) or that their activism helped illuminate the limitations of American capitalism, democracy, and the welfare state. Poor black women's activism, in actuality, reflected desires to be free of dependency, to acquire safe and sanitary homes, and to gain greater independence from government control. Margaret "Peggy" McCarty, who now operates a daycare center and is a member of Baltimore's Victory Outreach Ministries, argued in 1969: "In the first place, welfare is not charity. It's a right. I worked and my husband worked for years before I had to apply for assistance, and I didn't think anything about any stigma or anything when I applied. But I found out."[35] What women like McCarty found out was that their demands for government support; their race, class, and gender; and their residence in central cities during a tumultuous social and political era "affirmed" federal and public images of black dependency and provided unmitigated evidence of the danger existent in the welfare way of life.[36] Therein lies the paradox of poor black women's political activism.

In the 1990s, as in the past, the debate over AFDC continued to exemplify "the racially divisive character of the American welfare state."[37] Under the watch of Democratic president Bill Clinton and the Republican Congress in 1996, AFDC met its demise as a federal program and was turned over to the states in the form of Block Grants for Temporary Aid to Needy Families. Ultimately, welfare reform reversed the limited gains of the 1960s and 1970s, tried to force "mothers to establish connections to men and the labor market" through wage work and marriage requirements, and assaulted poor mothers' rights and citizenship status.[38]

Shelter and Income—Continuing the Struggle

Despite the decline of urban communities, the existence of entrenched poverty, and the shift in social welfare policy, poor black women's past and contemporary struggles should not be minimized. Black women's public housing and welfare activism helps to unveil the inability of discourses of pathology to explain the complex forces that have shaped people's real lives. The activism of low-income black women—whatever their circumstances— has exposed the various social, economic, racial, and political forces structuring their lives and the experiences of poor people generally. Their activism also has revealed how the welfare state, in contrast to its claim of democracy, has not worked for all of its citizens, and, in fact, has worked against many—even with the limited pathways for activist opportunity. The federal government needs to remember its responsibility to and the rights of poor people and provide even broader opportunities for citizens' engagement and advancement. The state is not all-powerful, as these women's struggles reveal. Nor were their struggles in vain; for their resistance reaffirmed their humanity, and their protests show that vigilance and continued activism are crucial to securing democracy and justice. "The intent was to get dignity and respect and fairness for everybody," asserted Rudell Martin. "I'm glad I didn't sit on the sidelines."

Abbreviations in Notes and Bibliography

AAVF	African American Vertical Files
ACLU	American Civil Liberties Union, Baltimore, Maryland
ACUA	Archives of The Catholic University of America, Washington, D.C.
BAA	*Baltimore Afro-American*
BCA	Baltimore City Archives, Baltimore, Maryland
BCP	Baltimore City Department of Planning Collection
BES	*Baltimore Evening Sun*
BMS	*Baltimore Morning Sun*
BNA	*Baltimore News American*
BNHP	Baltimore Neighborhood Heritage Project
BN-P	*Baltimore News-Post*
BURHA Collection	Baltimore Urban Renewal and Housing Agency Collection
CASC	Community Activities and Service Correspondence
CGEE	Commission on Government Efficiency and Economy Collection

CORE Papers	Congress of Racial Equality Papers
CPHA Collection	Citizens Planning and Housing Association Collection
CR	*Congressional Record*
EPFL	Enoch Pratt Free Library, Main Branch, Baltimore, Maryland
ESL	Edward S. Lewis Papers
GWP	George Wiley Papers
HABC	Housing Authority of Baltimore City
JOH	*Journal of Housing*
KSL	Kelvin Smith Library, Case Western Reserve University, Cleveland, Ohio
LC	Manuscript Division, Library of Congress, Washington, D.C.
MDSA	Maryland State Archives, Annapolis, Maryland
MDVF	Maryland Vertical Files
MHS	Maryland Historical Society, Baltimore, Maryland
MSRC	Moorland-Spingarn Research Center, Howard University, Washington, D.C.
NA	National Archives and Records Service, College Park, Maryland
NARA	National Archives and Records Administration, Philadelphia, Pennsylvania
NWRO Papers	National Welfare Rights Organization Papers
NYT	*New York Times*
PI	*Philadelphia Inquirer*
PRAC	Poverty Rights Action Center
RG	Record Group
SCRBC	Schomburg Center for Research in Black Culture, New York Public Library
SDS Papers	Students for a Democratic Society Papers
SDSS	State Department of Social Services
Sun	*Baltimore Sun*
UBA	University of Baltimore Archives, Baltimore, Maryland
WEL	Welfare
WHS	Wisconsin Historical Society, Madison, Wisconsin

Notes

Introduction

1. Schofield interview.

2. Ibid.

3. Kivisto, "Historical Review," 4. On race and federal housing programs, see Hirsch, "'Containment' on the Home Front"; Radford, *Modern Housing for America.*

4. Gordon, *Pitied but Not Entitled.* Also Gordon, "Black and White Visions of Welfare"; Mink, "The Lady and the Tramp"; Mink, *Wages of Motherhood*; Muncy, *Creating a Female Dominion*; Quadagno, *Color of Welfare*; Skocpol, "African Americans in U.S. Social Policy."

5. Payne, *I've Got the Light of Freedom,* 5. In *Making Ends Meet,* Edin and Lein interview 379 low-income, welfare- and wage-reliant women about their daily struggles. The study, however, focuses on the contemporary period.

6. For a more detailed discussion of marginalization within marginal groups, see Cathy J. Cohen, *Boundaries of Blackness,* 1–77.

7. Abramovitz, "Fighting Back"; Lizabeth Cohen, *A Consumer's Republic*; Collins, *Black Feminist Thought*; Hine, "Housewives' League of Detroit," 223–241; Orleck, *Common Sense & a Little Fire*; Orleck, "'We Are That Mythical Thing

Called the Public." Also see Naples, *Grassroots Warriors*; Feldman, Stall, and Wright, "'The Community Needs to Be Built by Us.'"

8. Martin interviews.
9. Baker interviews.
10. Naples, *Grassroots Warriors*.
11. Wise interviews.
12. Schofield interview.
13. Kenneth Durr, *Behind the Backlash*; Meyer, *As Long as They Don't Move Next Door*; Sugrue, *Origins of the Urban Crisis*.
14. Lundsford and Anna Warren interviews.
15. Arnold, "Baltimore," 25–39; Sherry H. Olson, *Baltimore*.
16. Kelley, "The Black Poor and the Politics of Opposition," 295; Portelli, *Death of Luigi Trastulli*, 50.

Chapter 1

1. Gordon interviews.
2. Ibid.
3. Sherry Olson, *Baltimore*, 276.
4. Power, "Apartheid Baltimore Style"; Shopes, "Fells Point."
5. Karen Olson, "Old West Baltimore," 59–61.
6. Sherry Olson, *Baltimore*, 276.
7. Power, "Apartheid Baltimore Style," 290, 308.
8. Shopes, "Fells Point," 137.
9. On municipal segregation ordinances, see Power, "Apartheid Baltimore Style." Quotes appear on page 289 and page 313, respectively.
10. Myers's company failed after twenty years. See "East Baltimore," *The Road from Frederick to Thurgood: Black Baltimore in Transition, 1870–1920*. Online. Available: http://www.mdarchives.state.md.us; Shopes, "Fells Point," 126.
11. Freeman, *Arabbers of Baltimore*, 9; McDougall, *Black Baltimore*, 32, 39; Karen Olson, "Old West Baltimore," 61; Skotnes, "Black Freedom Movement," 134.
12. Ira De A. Reid, *Negro Community of Baltimore*, 29. Also see Power, "Apartheid Baltimore Style," 295–296.
13. "The Confession of a Baltimore Landlord," *Sun Magazine*, July 27, 1924, found in Envelope: Negroes—Baltimore—Housing, MDVF, EPFL.
14. Mitchell interview.
15. "League Tells F.D. [*sic*] Relief Is Unequal," *BAA*, January 16, 1937.
16. Argersinger, *Toward a New Deal in Baltimore*, 3–5, statistics on p. 8.
17. "What Are the Hidden Reasons Why So Many on Relief," *BAA*, March 16, 1935.
18. Carl Murphy, "Is There Race Discrimination in the Handling of Federal Relief Funds?" *BAA*, July 13, 1935.
19. Gordon interviews.

20. Power, "Apartheid Baltimore Style," 320.

21. "Growth of the Total White, and the Colored Populations of Baltimore City from 1790 to 1940," Reel 1316, Series 1, RG 48, BCA.

22. "The Mayor's Committee," *BAA*, May 15, 1937.

23. Drake and Cayton, *Black Metropolis*, 663. For discussions of the black community, uplift, and respectability, see Gaines, *Uplifting the Race*; Higginbotham, *Righteous Discontent*; Wolcott, *Remaking Respectability*.

24. Sherry Olson, *Baltimore*, 271.

25. Washington quoted in Gilmore, *Gender & Jim Crow*, 152.

26. See senatorial debates regarding low-cost housing in *CR*, August 5, 1937, 8256.

27. Reid, *Negro Community of Baltimore*, 17.

28. "The Mayor's Committee," *BAA*, May 15, 1937.

29. "Housing Group Organized for Northwest," *BAA*, July 16, 1938.

30. William Perkins, BNHP interview, July 12, 1979, Box 84, UBA.

31. "Report of the Joint Committee on Housing in Baltimore," *Baltimore Engineer*, January 1934, in Maryland Room, EPFL.

32. William Theodore Durr, "Conscience of a City," 206. On tropes of black inner cities, see Gregory, *Black Corona*, 5–10. For another example of the links among black women, urban housing, and disease, see Hunter, *To 'Joy My Freedom*, 187–218.

33. Reid, *Negro Community of Baltimore*, 15–17.

34. "Baltimore Urban League–1924–1974," Box 2: BUL, ESL, SCRBC.

35. Bascom and Mitchell interviews; NAACP Memo: "What the NAACP Has Done in Maryland, 1935–1940," II.C.76, Folder: Baltimore, Maryland, 1940, NAACP Branch Files, LC. The NAACP's 1937 lawsuit, *Edward Meade v. Mary Estelle Dennistone et al.*, was filed a decade before the Supreme Court ruled restrictive covenants to be unconstitutional in *Shelley v. Kraemer* (1948).

36. A list of Murphy advisory committee board members appears in Folder: H-2700.703, Box 208, RG 196, NA.

37. "Who Killed Baltimore's Housing Project?" *BAA*, October 19, 1935.

38. For a more detailed discussion, see Argersinger, *Toward a New Deal in Baltimore*, 1–113.

39. Letter to A. R. Clas from Cleveland R. Bealmear, June 11, 1935, Folder: 2700.09, Box 206, RG 196, NA.

40. Letter to A. R. Clas from Carl Murphy, September 6, 1935, Folder: 2700, Box 206, RG 196, NA.

41. "City Blames U.S. for Hold Up in Housing Project," *BAA*, October 19, 1935.

42. "To Push Housing Bills," *BAA*, February 27, 1937; Argersinger, *Toward a New Deal in Baltimore*, 97–98; Skotnes, "Black Freedom Movement," 57, 62–65, 264.

43. "Simplifying Housing," *BAA*, January 23, 1937.

44. Argersinger, *Toward a New Deal in Baltimore*, 98–99; William Durr, 84–86.

45. "Information Requested of the Citizens Planning and Housing Association

by Baltimore Council of Social Agencies," July 1947, Folder 10: CPHA, Histories, Box 1; Elmore McKee, "Crusade in Baltimore," July 13, 1953, Folder 10, Box 8, Series I, both in CPHA Collection, UBA.

46. Peter Henderson, "Local Deals and the New Deal State," 88.

47. "Plan Up Today in Removal of Negro School," *Sun*, August 1, 1939; "Third Housing Job Will Start Soon," *Sun*, February 4, 1940, both in Envelope: Housing—Baltimore—Latrobe Homes, MDVF, EPFL.

48. "First Actual Work in Slum Area H," *BAA*, April 1, 1939.

49. "Slum Clearance Displeases Many," *BAA*, June 11, 1938; "Housing to Move 3 Secret Orders," *BAA*, April 6, 1940; "Sound of Last Call for Poe Project Tenants," *BAA*, May 25, 1940; "School 129 Now in Project, Has No Students," *BAA*, September 13, 1941.

50. "Baltimore to Get Low-Cost Housing Unit," *BAA*, February 12, 1938; Peter Henderson, "Local Deals and the New Deal State," 52, 163. For a similar case in Boston, see Vale, *From the Puritans to the Projects*, 194.

51. "Planning Meeting Report, Conference Planning Committee of the Council on Negro Organizations," Folder: Planning Meeting Report, Conference Planning Committee of the Council on Negro Organizations, Box 2: BUL, ESL, SCRBC.

52. Gordon and Weaver interviews.

53. Senate Bill 1685, "Low-Cost Housing," *CR*, August 3, 1937, 8098.

54. Information on incomes from "Planning Meeting Report, Conference Planning Committee of the Council on Negro Organizations," Box 2: BUL, ESL, SCRBC.

55. Department of Public Welfare, *A Study of the Edgar Allan Poe Homes in Relation to Public Assistance Clients*, December 1940, in Envelope: Housing—Baltimore—Edgar Allan Poe Homes, MDVF, EPFL; Lee McCardell, "The Stories of the Families Who Got No Poe Homes," *BES*, October 11, 1940.

56. "Information regarding the Public Housing Program with Special Reference to Baltimore," February 1949, Folder 3: Information regarding the Public Housing Program with Special Reference to Baltimore, Box 22, Series I, CPHA Collection, UBA.

57. Senate Bill 1685, "Low-Cost Housing," *CR*, August 3, 1937, 8098.

58. Gordon, *Pitied but Not Entitled*, 304.

59. Kivisto, "Historical Review," 1.

60. Fairbanks, *Making Better Citizens*; Katz, *Improving Poor People*, 26–37; Wright, *Building the Dream*, 220–239.

61. W. E. B. Du Bois quoted in Hunter, "The 'Brotherly Love,'" 141. Also see Wolcott, *Remaking Respectability*, 53.

62. Lee McCardell, "The Stories of the Families Who Got No Poe Homes," *BES*, October 11, 1940.

63. Wise interviews.

64. Ibid.

65. For a more detailed discussion, see chapter 4. Also see Solinger's *Wake Up Little Susie*, which focuses on single mothers.

66. Gordon interviews.

67. HABC, *The Story of Public Housing*, part 4, July 11, 1945, Baltimore, Maryland, Bohn Collection, KSL, CWRU; "Information Requested of Citizens Planning and Housing Association by Baltimore Council of Social Agencies," July 1947, Folder 10: CPHA, Histories, Box 1, Series I, CPHA Collection, UBA.

68. "Cried and Prayed with Joy—Douglass Tenants," *BAA*, August 30, 1941; "Filling of Last Three McCulloh Units Slated," *BES*, October 29, 1941.

69. *BAA*, February 3 and 17, 1940, and March 2, 16, 23, and 30, 1940.

70. Loomis quote in Lee McCardell, "Rumors of Rent Raises Worry Neighbors of New Poe Homes," *BES*, October 9, 1940; Weaver interviews.

71. "Let's Look at Housing in Baltimore: The President's Report on the First Year's Activities of the Citizens' Housing Council of Baltimore," Baltimore, Maryland, May 1941, Envelope: Citizens' Housing Council of Baltimore, MDVF, EPFL; HABC, *Annual Report 1941*, Folder: G1–74(1), Box 243, Series 21, RG 9, BCA; "1,400 Families Place Bids on 298 Units in Area H," *BES*, March 28, 1940; "Housing to Move 3 Secret Orders," *BAA*, April 6, 1940; "800 Apply for 298 Poe Homes," *BAA*, June 22, 1940. Also see "Sixty Negro Families to Seek Poe Project Homes—29 Fail," *Sun*, June 20, 1940, Envelope: Housing—Baltimore—Edgar Allan Poe Homes, MDVF, EPFL; "Prospective Tenants to Get Lessons in Home Furnishing," *Sun*, August 31, 1940; "Negroes View First Poe Unit, Furnished in Hand-Me-Downs," *Sun*, September 7, 1940, Envelope 1: Housing—Baltimore, MDVF, EPFL; "Poe Homes Open to Public," *Sun*, September 17, 1940; McCardell, "Rumors of Rent," *BES*, October 9, 1940.

72. Lundsford interview; "A Slight Puzzle at Latrobe Homes," *Sun*, August 18, 1941; "Latrobe Unit Occupied; 200 Families Move Belongings into Low-Rent Apartments," *BES*, August 18, 1941, in Envelope: Housing—Baltimore—Latrobe Homes, MDVF, EPFL.

73. "First Tenants Move into Poe Project Homes," *BES*, September 30, 1940.

74. McCardell, "Rumors of Rent," *BES*, October 9, 1940.

75. "Cried and Prayed with Joy—Douglass Tenants," *BAA*, August 30, 1941; "Filling of Last Three McCulloh Units Slated," *BES*, October 29, 1941.

76. "Prospective Tenants to Get Lessons in Home Furnishings: Demonstration Apartment Planned for Families Moving into Poe Homes," *Sun*, August 31, 1940; and "Negroes View First Poe Unit, Furnished in Hand-Me-Downs," *Sun*, September 7, 1940, Envelope #1: Housing—Baltimore, MDVF, EPFL; CPHA, *You Ought to Care . . . You Live Here!* (1946), Bohn Collection, KSL.

77. "Opening of Poe Project Delayed by Bad Weather; Curfew Rumors Are Branded False by Housing Officials," *BAA*, March 2, 1940.

78. "No Relief Unit for Section H," *BAA*, February 18, 1939.

79. Gordon interviews.

80. "Colored Housing Is a Paying Investment," *BAA*, November 22, 1941.

81. Drake and Cayton, *Black Metropolis*.

82. "First Baby," *BAA*, August 30, 1941. Also see *BAA* issues August 23, 30, 1941, and September 14, 1941.

83. On the New Deal and citizen participation, see Argersinger, *Toward a New Deal in Baltimore*, 99–100, 106–108, 111–112.

84. U.S. Housing Authority, *Community Activities in Public Housing* (Washington, D.C.: Federal Works Agency, 1941), 14, found in Folder 2a: Housing—Management II, Box 18, Series I, CPHA Collection, UBA.

85. "BHA Approves 200 Families," *BAA*, August 17, 1940; "McCulloh Tenants' Meet Attracts 650," *BAA*, August 8, 1941.

86. "New Manager of Poe Homes Takes Over Job," *BAA*, July 20, 1940.

87. Skotnes, "Black Freedom Movement."

88. Gordon interviews.

89. Ibid. Also see "Form 6 Tenant Organizations at Poe Housing Project during First Year," *BAA*, October 4, 1941.

90. Gordon interviews; Drake and Cayton, *Black Metropolis*, 658–666; Higginbotham, *Righteous Discontent*.

91. Cathy Cohen, *Boundaries of Blackness*, 39.

92. "Form 6 Tenant Organizations at Poe Housing Project during First Year," *BAA*, October 4, 1941.

93. Argersinger, *Toward a New Deal in Baltimore*, 106.

94. HABC, *Annual Report 1941*.

95. HABC, *Third Report: A Summary of Two Years of Activity, 1941–1942*, Folder: G1–48(5), Box 253, Series 22, RG 9, BCA. Also see "List Nursery Schools in Baltimore," *CIO News* (Baltimore edition), December 20, 1943, Reel 7920, MDSA.

96. HABC, *Third Report*.

97. Memo from Bernard Mason to Ellis Ash, October 5, 1950, Folder: Lexington-Poe—CASC, 1948–66, Box 27, Series 14, RG 48, BCA; quote appears in HABC, *Annual Report 1952: Progress: 15 Years of Public Housing* (1953), MDSA.

98. HABC, *Birthright: A Decent Home* (1946), Bohn Collection, KSL.

99. Ibid.

100. Ibid.

101. Schwartz, "Tenant Unions in New York City's Low-Rent Housing," 418.

102. "Project Unveils BHA Official's Portrait," *BAA*, October 20, 1942.

103. Gordon interviews.

104. Ibid.

105. Halpern, *Rebuilding the Inner City*, 12.

106. "Sobeloff Lauds Residents' Care of Housing Projects," *BAA*, June 23, 1945.

Chapter 2

1. Letter from Lottie Hall to Oliver Winston, January 12, 1944, CPHA Report on the Baltimore Housing Authority, Exhibit A, Folder 9: Studies, 1940s, Box 8, Series I, CPHA Collection, UBA.

2. HABC, *Public Housing in Baltimore, 1941–1942* (1943), MDSA.

3. Callcott, *Maryland & America*, 36–43.

4. Matthews interview.

5. "Only One of 15 War Plant Employees in Baltimore Colored," *BAA*, February 13, 1943; "News from Baltimore Branch N.A.A.C.P., April 1943," Folder: Baltimore, Maryland, 1943, II.C.76, NAACP Branch Files, LC. Also see "13,600 Employed in Baltimore War Plants as Job Barriers Fall," *BAA*, May 15, 1943.

6. "OWI Reports War Problems Are Unsolved," *Sun*, May 9, 1943.

7. Margaret Crawford, "Daily Life on the Home Front," 92, 98; Meyer, *As Long as They Don't Move Next Door*, 67.

8. "Defense Housing Bars Us in Ohio," *BAA*, January 9, 1942.

9. "5 Defense Projects Bar Our Tenants," *BAA*, July 7, 1942; "Housing Failure Said to Impede War Effort," *BAA*, May 29, 1943.

10. Callcott, *Maryland & America*, 148.

11. Ted Waters, "Defense Housing Plans Overlook Our Workers," *BAA*, September 6, 1941.

12. Weaver interviews.

13. NHA, "Preliminary Draft of Problems of Site Selection during the War Housing Program," Oct.–Nov. 1944, Document #62, "Index to Plaintiff's First Request for Admissions," vol. 3, *Carmen Thompson et al. v. United States Department of Housing and Urban Development et al.*, ACLU. Also see "Report of the Executive Secretary for the February Meeting of the Executive Board N.A.A.C.P." and "Report of the Executive Secretary for the March Meeting," II.C.76, Folder: Baltimore, Maryland, 1943, NAACP Branch Files, LC; Peter Henderson, "Local Deals and the New Deal State," 242–243.

14. "Police Cautioned to Move to Avoid Rights; Atkinson Considers Naming of Additional Colored Officers," *BAA*, August 7, 1943. Quote on Detroit is in Capeci, *Race Relations in Wartime Detroit*, 33. Also on Detroit, see Sugrue, *Origins of the Urban Crisis*; Takaki, *Double Victory*, 50–55.

15. NHA, "Preliminary Draft of Problems of Site Selection."

16. "Park Barracks for Negroes Suggested," *BES*, October 2, 1942. The commission also considered the emergency regulation of migration, the voluntary evacuation of families not involved in the defense effort, and the development of a program so that industry could outline its employment needs. "Report of the Governor's Commission on Problems Affecting the Negro Population," March 1943, Box 448, RG 228, NA.

17. "News from the Baltimore Branch N.A.A.C.P.," April 1943, II.C.76, Folder: Baltimore, Maryland, 1943, NAACP Branch Files, LC.

18. "Baltimore NAACP Seeks Housing Talk with FDR," *BAA*, August 14, 1943.

19. "Stop Kicking That Football Around," *BAA*, April 24, 1943.

20. NHA, "Preliminary Draft of Problems of Site Selection."

21. Ibid.

22. "Clergy Foremost in Protest . . . Crowd of 800 Boos Mayor for Favoring Colored War Homes," *BAA*, July 17, 1943; "Housing Foes Tell Why They Oppose Homes," *BAA*, July 17, 1943; "Government by Mob," *BAA*, July 24, 1943.

23. Quoted in Peter Henderson, "Local Deals and the New Deal State," 249–250.

24. "State Officials Protests [*sic*] Site; 100 Asks [*sic*] Action," *BAA*, July 24, 1943;

CPHA flyer listing the spokespeople at the Hearing on Herring Run Site, July 21, 1943, Folder: G10–48(2), Box 253, Series 22, RG 9, BCA.

25. In the historical documents, many women are identified with "Mrs." and their husbands' names. This practice was widely used by women during this time period. When their first names are unknown, I use this convention throughout the book.

26. "State Officials Protests [*sic*] Site; 100 Asks [*sic*] Action," *BAA*, July 24, 1943.

27. Letter to the Editor, *BAA*, June 5, 1943.

28. "Bigotry Puzzling," *BAA*, May 1, 1943. On responsible patriotism, see Boris, "The Right to Work Is the Right to Live!" 121–141.

29. "McKeldin Seeks End to Housing Wrangle," *BAA*, June 12, 1943; "Site for 550 Homes Okeyed [*sic*]," *BAA*, June 19, 1943; "Mayor Eager to Solve Dilemma over Housing," *BAA*, July 3, 1943; "U.S. Housing Head Raps Mayor, City Council," *BAA*, August 28, 1943; "FPHA Picks Housing Site," *BAA*, September 18, 1943; "Housing Heads Confer on Retreat from Herring Run," *BAA*, October 9, 1943; "Herring Run Site Still Choice of FPHA for Housing Units," *BAA*, October 30, 1943; "4 War Homes Sites Dubbed Undesirable," *BAA*, November 6, 1943; "Ask for Abandonment of Permanent Housing," *BAA*, December 11, 1943.

30. "Irate Parents Keep Children from School," *BMS*, September 10, 1941, in Folder: Armistead Gardens Housing Disposition, Box 261, Series 23, RG 9, BCA.

31. "Talk of Quitting Housing Project," *BMS*, September 18, 1941, in Folder: Armistead Gardens Housing Disposition, Box 261, Series 23, RG 9, BCA.

32. Ibid.

33. "Turn Up the Heat Is Demand of U.S. Tenants," *BMS*, November 18, 1942; "Housing Board Gets Protest," *BES*, November 18, 1942; "Householders Win Hot Water," *BMS*, November 19, 1942, all found in Envelope: Housing—Baltimore—Clarence Perkins Homes, MDVF, EPFL. On women's civic activism and black consumer protests during World War II, see Lizabeth Cohen, *A Consumer's Republic*, 41–54, 75–100; Jacobs, "'How about Some Meat?'" 911–941.

34. "Turn Up the Heat Is Demand of U.S. Tenants," *BMS*, November 18, 1942.

35. Special Meeting of the Commissioners, Baltimore Housing Authority, November 18, 1942, Reel 1320, Series 1, RG 48, BCA.

36. Ibid.; "Householders Win Hot Water," *BMS*, November 19, 1942.

37. CPHA Report on the BHA, 1945; Peter Henderson, "Local Deals and the New Deal State," 274–275.

38. Letter written by Anthony Malone, October 1, 1946, and "Memorandum—Douglass Project," both in Folder: H1(2), Box 255, Series 22, RG 9, BCA.

39. "Charge 'Politics' in Baltimore Housing Authority," *BAA*, July 10, 1943.

40. Weaver interviews.

41. CPHA Report on the BHA.

42. Citizens Housing Council's Management Committee Report, "Public Housing Management," c. 1940–1941, Folder 9: Studies, 1940's, Box 8, Series I, CPHA Collection, UBA.

43. CPHA Report on the BHA, Exhibit A.

44. CPHA Report on the BHA, Exhibit A; William Durr, "Conscience of a City," 240.

45. Ibid.

46. Interestingly, Jenkins's wife worked as assistant district chief for the Civilian Mobilization Committee, which met in Gilmor Homes. It does not seem that he was totally against black women organizing, but the class of the women and issues of politics and authority may have played roles in his response.

47. Weaver interviews.

48. CPHA Report on the BHA, Exhibit A.

49. "Gilmor Homes Tenants to Get Improvements," BAA, February 1, 1944.

50. Letter, "To Tenant[s] of the Gilmor Homes" from the HABC, addendum to CPHA Report on the BHA. Also see Peter Henderson, "Local Deals and the New Deal State," 273–274.

51. Tenants' council letter signed by Lottie Hall and Hannah Taylor, addendum to CPHA Report on the BHA.

52. Special Meeting of the Commissioners, April 19, 1944, Defense, Reel 1316, Series 1, RG 48, BCA.

53. CPHA Report on the BHA.

54. *Armistead Gardens Civic News*, June 1945, Folder 5: CPHA Public Housing, 1946 & Older, Box 8, Series I, CPHA Collection, UBA.

55. Quoted in Lois Felder, "Housing Tenants Present Protests Almost Daily," BES, April 5, 1946, Folder 11: CPHA Literature, Box 1, Series 1, CPHA Collection, UBA.

56. "Rent Raises Complaints in City Increase Sharply," BES, October 30, 1941; "Tenants in Two Projects Face Higher Rents," BAA, May 12, 1942; CPHA Report on the BHA, Exhibit A.

57. On African Americans and employment discrimination, see "Fairfield Yard, Drydock Co. Violate F.D.'s [*sic*] Order, Giving Token Employment," BAA, June 27, 1942; "Md. Drydock Refuses Skill" and "Union Blames Workers for Bad Working Conditions," BAA, May 23, 1942; "Labor Board to Hear Drydock Workers," BAA, June 13, 1942; "225 Workers Discharged Last Week by Shipbuilding Company Get Jobs Back," BAA, July 11, 1942; Robert C. Weaver, "The Negro Come[s] of Age in Industry," *Occupational Reports and Abstracts*, No. 157, found in Envelope: Employment, AAVF, EPFL; "Office of War Information Report," May 1943, Folder: G1-S218, Box 244, Series 21, RG 9, BCA. Also see Exhibit B in "Report of the Governor's Commission on Problems Affecting the Negro Population," March 1943; "News from Baltimore Branch of the N.A.A.C.P.," April 1943; "13,600 Employed in Baltimore War Plants as Job Barriers Fall," BAA, May 15, 1943.

58. On Bethlehem and Glenn L. Martin, see "Report of the Executive Secretary for the February Meeting of the Executive Board of the N.A.A.C.P." and "Report of the Executive Secretary for the March Meeting."

59. "42 of 57 War School Grads Are Women," BAA, April 10 1943. On black women and job discrimination, see "Report on Paid Hospital Personnel—Maid[s],

Porters, Orderlies Made to the Civilian Mobilization Committee," Minutes of Meeting of the Baltimore Civilian Mobilization Committee, August 4, 1942, Folder: G1–5336, Box 244, Series 21, RG 9, BCA; W. A. Brower, "War Work Applicants Get Run-Around; US Employment Service, Key War Plants Turn Down Skills of Colored Women Despite Acute Labor Shortage," *BAA*, April 3, 1943; "3 Plants Fire 500 Women, Report," *BAA*, April 10, 1943; W. A. Brower, "Refused War Jobs, Women Clean Streets," *BAA*, April 17, 1943; "Office of War Information Report," May 1943. Black women faced similar barriers in other cities; see Anderson, "Last Hired, First Fired," 82–97; Milkman, *Gender at Work*, 55; Phillips, *Alabama North*, 232.

60. *Annual Report of the Department of Public Welfare* (Baltimore, Md.: 1945).

61. Letter to Mayor Theodore McKeldin from Mr. and Mrs. Alvin A. Johnson, November 19, 1946, Folder: H1(2), Box 255, Series 22, RG 9, BCA.

62. Schwartz, "Tenant Power in the Liberal City," 134.

63. HABC, Letter to Tenants from J. W. Rowe, May 1946, Folder: H1(1), Box 255, Series 22, RG 9, BCA.

64. Letter to Mayor Theodore McKeldin from Amelia Boyer, May 25, 1946, Folder: H1(1), Box 255, Series 22, RG 9, BCA.

65. "400 Families Must Leave Latrobe," *BNA*, June 2, 1946, and "Tenants Fight to Keep Homes; 200 Plan for Action at Gilmor Project" (n.d.), both in Folder 5: CPHA Public Housing—1946 & Older, Box 8, Series I, CPHA Collection, UBA. Thomas D'Alesandro, Jr., was mayor from 1947 to 1959; Callcott, *Maryland & America*, 81.

66. Peter Henderson, "Local Deals and the New Deal State," 257–258.

67. "Landlord Haste Blamed for Many Rent Actions," *BES*, May 13, 1946.

68. Felder, "Housing Tenants Present Protests Almost Daily," *BES*, April 5, 1946.

69. Minutes of a Regular Meeting and Meeting Notes, February 12, 1947, Reel 1321, Series 1, RG 48, BCA.

70. "Tenant Leaders Upset HAB Meeting," *BES*, April 11, 1946.

71. Minutes of the Board of Commissioners Meeting of the HABC, April 24, 1946, Reel 1319, Series 1, RG 48, BCA.

72. Memo to J. W. Rowe from R. Clarke Davis, January 31, 1947; Memo to Y. W. Dillehunt from J. W. Rowe, February 12, 1947, both in Reel 1321, Series 1, RG 48, BCA.

73. Memo to Y. W. Dillehunt from J. W. Rowe, February 12, 1947; memo to J. W. Rowe from John C. Hazzard, February 11, 1947, Reel 1321, Series 1, RG 48, BCA.

74. Ryon, "An Ambiguous Legacy," 29.

75. Ryon, 21.

76. Pedersen, *Communist Party in Maryland*, 101, 157–158.

77. Letter to Furman Templeton from Alverta Parnell, August 27, 1946, Folder: H1(2), Box 255, Series 22, RG 9, BCA.

78. CPHA Report on the BHA.

79. Letter to Furman Templeton from Alverta Parnell, August 27, 1946; letter to Templeton from Parnell, October 7, 1946; letter to Theodore McKeldin from Par-

nell, November 18, 1946, all in Folder: H1(2), Box 255, Series 22, RG 9, BCA; Peter Henderson, "Local Deals and the New Deal State," 263–280.

80. Memo to J. W. Rowe from O. P. Pinkett, February 10, 1947, Reel 1321, Series 1, RG 48, BCA.

81. Memo to J. W. Rowe from John C. Hazzard.

82. Felder, "Housing Tenants Present Protests Almost Daily," *BES*, April 5, 1946.

83. Memo to J. W. Rowe from W. W. Weaver, February 10, 1947, Reel 1321, Series 1, RG 48, BCA.

84. "Residents 'Bargain Collectively' with L.A. Authority," *JOH* 4, no. 4 (1947): 16.

85. Memo to J. W. Rowe from W. W. Weaver.

86. Memo to Y. W. Dillehunt from J. W. Rowe.

87. Minutes of the Board of Commissioners Meeting of the HABC, February 26, 1947.

88. Quoted in William Durr, "Conscience of a City," 251–253.

89. Lois Felder, "Housing Authority Critics Includes Friends, Foes," *BES*, April 4, 1946.

90. Minutes of the Commissioners, HABC, Defense, April 24, 1946, Reel 1317, Series 1, RG 48, BCA.

91. Peter Henderson, "Local Deals and the New Deal State," 280.

92. Letter to Mayor McKeldin from Parnell, November 18, 1946, Folder: H1(2), Box 255, Series 22, RG 9, BCA.

93. Letter to Mayor Theodore McKeldin from Mr. and Mrs. Alvin A. Johnson.

94. Quoted in Elmore McKee, "Crusade in Baltimore," July 13, 1953, Folder 10, Box 8, Series 1, CPHA Collection, UBA.

95. Memo to Oliver C. Winston from Ellis Ash, September 7, 1948, Folder: 1946–48, Organization: Directives, Box 10, Series 13, RG 48, BCA.

96. "Parker Guilty of Embezzlement," *BAA*, January 8, 1949.

Chapter 3

1. Gordon interviews.

2. Sherrod and Edges interviews; Harry B. Weiss Memorial Fund Award, Nomination of Project Resident Form, Mary Edges, May 27, 1968, Folder: 1968, Harry B. Weiss Award, Box 2, Series 8, RG 48, BCA.

3. Hyneses interview.

4. Virginia Paty, "Public Housing, on 10th Birthday Here, Takes Stock of Progress," *BES*, December 12, 1947; "Council O.K.'s Surveys for Housing Plan," *BMS*, August 19, 1949, CGEE, UBA.

5. Virginia Paty, "Public Housing, on 10th Birthday Here, Takes Stock of Progress," *BES*, December 12, 1947.

6. BURHA, *Types of Families Living in Baltimore's Low-Rent Projects, 1951–1964* (1965), Folder: 1964–69 Reports and Statistics, Box 13, Series 13, RG 48, BCA.

7. Kenneth Durr, *Behind the Backlash*, 58, 192.

8. Ibid., n. 31, p. 231.

9. HABC, *A Comparison of the Characteristics of Negro Applicant and Tenant Families, 1951* (1952), Maryland Room, EPFL.

10. HABC, "Occupations of Workers in Gilmor Homes," April 19, 1951, Folder: Gilmor Homes—CASC, 1948–70, Box 17, Series 14, RG 48, BCA.

11. Anna Warren interviews.

12. On race and suburbanization, see Bartelt, "Housing the 'Underclass'"; Kenneth Jackson, *Crabgrass Frontier*; Katz, *Improving Poor People*, 82–83; Orser, *Blockbusting in Baltimore*; Welfield, *Where We Live*.

13. Massey and Denton, *American Apartheid*, 54–55; Meyer, *As Long as They Don't Move Next Door*, 80; Sugrue, *Origins of the Urban Crisis*, 44–45, 62–63.

14. Callcott, *Maryland & America*, 70.

15. Martin interviews.

16. Wise interviews.

17. HABC, *The Characteristics of White Applicants for Public Housing, Baltimore, Maryland, 1951* (1952), Maryland Room, EPFL; Lundsford interview; Memo to Harry B. Weiss from F. C. Hochreiter, October 22, 1956, Folder: O'Donnell Heights Tenant Relations Cases, 1956–70, L–Z, Box 39, Series 14, RG 48, BCA. The percentage of single-parent households among whites declined in 1961 to 27.6 percent. See Peter Henderson, "Local Deals and the New Deal State," 406.

18. HABC, *A Comparison of the Characteristics of Negro Applicant and Tenant Families, 1951* (1952), Maryland Room, EPFL.

19. On the GI Bill and black veterans, see Lizabeth Cohen, *A Consumer's Republic*, 137–144, 166–173.

20. Letter to Esther Lazarus from Oliver C. Winston, November 1, 1955; Memo to Walter I. Seif from Oliver C. Winston, August 13, 1956, both in Folder: 1948–69, Rents—Tenants Receiving Welfare, Box 12, Series 13, RG 48, BCA.

21. Katz, ed., *The "Underclass" Debate*, 462.

22. Bayor, *Race & the Shaping of Twentieth-Century Atlanta*, 70.

23. Bauman, *Public Housing, Race, and Renewal*; Bartelt, "Housing the 'Underclass,'" 118–157; Bayor, *Race & the Shaping of Twentieth-Century Atlanta*; Hirsch, *Making the Second Ghetto*; Mollenkopf, *Contested City*; Sugrue, *Origins of the Urban Crisis*.

24. "Vacant Land Use by HAB Will Aid Slum Displaced," *BES*, August 18, 1949, Folder: 1949, Box 14, Series VI, CGEE, UBA; "Crowd Flocks to Hearing on Housing Bill: Police Called as 2,000 Jam Corridors, Shout to Hear Speakers," *Sun*, February 19, 1950.

25. "Merrick Asks Public Housing Program to Clean Up Slums," *Sun*, February 18, 1950.

26. "Vacant Land Use by HAB Will Aid Slum Clearance," *BES*, August 18, 1949.

27. "Dr. Fenn Quits H.A.B., Blames City Council," *BMS*, May 2, 1950.

28. "Slum Clearance Project Brings Confusion, Alarm," *BAA*, June 13, 1950; "Waverly Site Families Fight for Homes," *BAA*, July 18, 1950. For statistics, see "Group Complains Bitterly of Redevelopment Project," *BMS*, January 18, 1955, Box 14, Series VI, CGEE, UBA.

29. "The Waverly DP's," *BMS*, July 12, 1952; "City to Clear Slum Areas Near Armory," *BMS*, April 9, 1953; "New Housing Project to Start Soon," *BMS*, August 14, 1953; "Planner Hits Office Move," *BMS*, September 17, 1953, Box 14, Series VI, CGEE, UBA.

30. J. Anthony Lukas, "Baltimore's Displaced Persons: Before Renewal, Destruction," *Baltimore Sunday Sun*, January 1, 1961.

31. Letter to Nathaniel S. Keith from Clarence Mitchell, December 17, 1951, *Carmen Thompson et al.* (1995), ACLU Case Document 192.

32. Memo to Raymond Foley from Nathaniel S. Keith, April 19, 1952, *Carmen Thompson et al.* (1995), ACLU Case Document 195.

33. "Unit Defends Relocation of Broadway Families," *BES*, April 6, 1955, Box 14, Series VI, CGEE, UBA.

34. "New Housing Project to Start Soon," *BMS*, August 14, 1953, Box VI, CGEE, UBA.

35. "Housing Chiefs Open Fremont Razing Bids," *BMS*, June 17, 1955, Box 14, Series VI, CGEE, UBA.

36. Power, "Apartheid Baltimore Style," 320. Also see J. Anthony Lukas, "Baltimore's Displaced Persons," *Baltimore Sunday Sun*, January 1, 1961; Sheldon Smith, "Most Removed Families Find Better Homes," *BES*, July 7, 1961, Box 14, Series VI, CGEE, UBA.

37. BURHA Memo, June 3, 1953, Folder: 1949–68, Continued Occupancy Policy—Over-Income Families, Box 4, Series 13, RG 48, BCA.

38. Solinger, *Wake Up Little Susie*, 22; Bell, *Aid to Dependent Children*.

39. *Twenty-Second Annual Report of the Department of Welfare* (Baltimore, Md.: 1956).

40. Memo to Esther Lazarus from Oliver C. Winston, November 1, 1955, and January 18, 1956, both in Folder: 1948–69 Rents—Tenants Receiving Welfare, Box 12, Series 13, RG 48, BCA.

41. BURHA Memo to Oliver C. Winston from Morton Hoffman, June 3, 1953, Folder: 1949–68, Continued Occupancy Policy—Over-Income Families, Box 4, Series 13, RG 48, BCA.

42. BURHA Memo, July 14, 1953, Folder: 1949–68, Continued Occupancy Policy—Over-Income Families, Box 4, Series 13, RG 48, BCA.

43. BURHA Memo to Oliver C. Winston from Morton Hoffman, June 3, 1953; Winston quote found in BURHA Memo, July 14, 1953.

44. BURHA Memo to Oliver C. Winston from Morton Hoffman, June 3, 1953.

45. Ibid.

46. BURHA/HABC Summary of Commission-Staff Discussion, November 2, 1965, Folder 10, Box 1, Series I, BURHA Collection, UBA.

47. BURHA, *Types of Families Living in Baltimore's Low-Rent Projects, 1951–1964* (1965), Folder: 1964–69, Reports and Statistics, Box 13, Series 13, RG 48, BCA. For a similar demographic story in Philadelphia, see Bauman, Hummon, and Muller, "Public Housing, Isolation, and the Urban Underclass," 275–278.

48. Booker interview.

49. "Jim Crow Public Housing Outlawed," *BAA*, June 29, 1954; Hortense Label, "Housing Roundup," *BAA*, July 20, 1954.

50. Meyer, *As Long as They Don't Move Next Door*, 141–143.

51. Memo to E. M. Feinblatt from Ellis Ash, April 26, 1954; Memo to Ellis Ash from Eugene M. Feinblatt, June 7, 1954, both in Folder: 9/50–6/54, Desegregation, Box 5, Series 13, RG 48, BCA.

52. Memo to Commissioners of HABC from Eugene M. Feinblatt, Folder: 9/50–6/54, Desegregation, Box 5, Series 13, RG 48, BCA. Also see "Segregation Out for City Housing," *Baltimore Sunday Sun*, June 27, 1954, Box 14, 1934–55, Series VI, CGEE, UBA; "Report on Racial Occupancy Policies of the Housing Authority of Baltimore City," June 24, 1954, Folder: 9/50–6/54, Desegregation, Box 5, Series 13, RG 48, BCA.

53. Letter to G. Cheston Carey from William M. Passano, June 30, 1954, Folder: 7/54—Desegregation, Box 5, Series 13, RG 48, BCA.

54. Arnold, "Baltimore," 29; Callcott, *Maryland & America*, 152.

55. Between 1954 and 1964, Baltimore's freedom-of-choice school board policy became state policy. Callcott, *Maryland & America*, 244. Also see "Many Mixed Classes as Schools Open, Parent[s] and Pupils Hail Integration," and "600 Mixed Classes Here," both *BAA*, September 4, 1954; "School Board," "School Pickets Tip Brings Top Money," "Pickets Use NAAWP Technique," all in *BAA*, October 2, 1954; "The City Redeems Itself," "Ministers Deplore Picketing," and editorial picture entitled "Proof That They Were Ashamed," all in *BAA*, October 9, 1954. Also see Callcott, *Maryland & America*, 244–245; Kenneth Durr, "When Southern Politics Came North," 316.

56. Martin interviews.

57. Hirsch, "Massive Resistance in the Urban North."

58. "List of Persons Invited to First Meeting of Community Groups on Education" and "Notes on Desegregation Meeting, July 27, 1954," both in Folder: 7/54—Desegregation, Box 5, Series 13, RG 48, BCA.

59. Letter to Dr. Kenneth B. Clark from Edgar Ewing, August 18, 1954, Folder: 8–12/54, Desegregation, Box 5, Series 13, RG 48, BCA.

60. Memo to Ellis Ash from Esther Frank Siegel, July 21, 1954, Folder: Desegregation, 7/54; Memo to Ellis Ash from Morton Hoffman, September 21, 1954, Folder: Desegregation, 8–12/54, both in Box 5, Series 13, RG 48, BCA.

61. Memo to Ellis Ash from Esther Frank Siegel.

62. Memo to Oliver Winston from Ellis Ash, June 24, 1954, Folder: 9/50–6/54, Desegregation, Box 5, Series 13, RG 48, BCA; Public Housing Administration, Housing and Home Finance Agency, *Open Occupancy in Public Housing* (Washington, D.C.: 1953), Folder: Statistics/Studies Open Occupancy in Public Housing (1952–53), Box 3, Intergroup Relations Branch, RG 196, NA.

63. Lynne Olson, *Freedom's Daughters*, 92–94.

64. Memo to Ellis Ash from Esther Frank Siegel.

65. Memo to Edgar Ewing from Daniel Powell, October 22, 1954, Folder: 8/54–12/54, Desegregation, Box 5, Series 13, RG 48, BCA.

66. Letter to Harry Weiss from Samuel Warrence, July 19, 1954, Folder: 7/54—Desegregation, Box 5, Series 13, RG 48, BCA.

67. "Latrobe, Perkins Projects Integrate, 70 at Lafayette," *BAA*, June 4, 1955; Memo to Edgar M. Ewing from Esther Frank Siegel, April 22, 1955, Folder: 12/54–10/55—Desegregation, Box 5, Series 13, RG 48, BCA.

68. BURHA, *Report on Racial Occupancy Policies of the Housing Authority of Baltimore City*, June 24, 1954, Folder: 9/50–6/54—Desegregation, Box 5, Series 13, RG 48, BCA.

69. Memo to Oliver C. Winston from Ellis Ash, July 23, 1954, Folder: 7/54—Desegregation, Box 5, Series 13, RG 48, BCA.

70. BURHA, *Why Eligible Families Leave Public Housing* (Baltimore, Md.: 1957).

71. "Both Races Apply for New Housing," *BAA*, September 18, 1954; "Lafayette Cts. to Open in 10 Days," *BAA*, February 12, 1955; "First Tenants Move into Lafayette Courts," *BAA*, April 16, 1955.

72. Dwight Warren interview.

73. "Project Tenant Selection Policy," c. 1963, Folder: 6/62–9/67—Desegregation, Box 5, Series 13, RG 48, BCA.

74. "Project Occupancy at June 30, 1964," Folder: 6/62–9/67—Desegregation, Box 5, Series 13, RG 48, BCA.

75. Letter to Ralph Matthews from Richard L. Steiner, May 3, 1963, Folder: 6/62–9/67—Desegregation, Box 5, Series 13, RG 48, BCA.

76. Letter from anonymous tenant, January 14, 1963, Folder: 6/62–9/67—Desegregation, Box 5, Series 13, RG 48, BCA.

77. Memo to Saul M. Perdue from Richard L. Steiner, July 19, 1966, Folder: Claremont Homes—Open Occupancy, 1966–67, Box 11, Series 14, RG 48, BCA.

78. Letter to Warren Phelan from Richard L. Steiner, October 18, 1966, Folder: Correspondence and Memoranda, Oct.–Dec. 1966, Box 1, Series II, BURHA Collection, UBA. On President Kennedy's executive order, see *Highlights*, 1962, Box 1, Series VI, BURHA Collection, UBA.

79. *Highlights*, 1963, Box 1, Series VI, BURHA Collection, UBA; letter to Phelan from Steiner, October 18, 1966.

80. Quote appears in document dated July 1966, Folder 11, Box 1, Series I, BURHA Collection, UBA.

81. Letter to residents from Richard L. Steiner, December 20, 1966, Folder 7: Correspondence and Memoranda, January–March 1967, Box 1, Series II, BURHA Collection, UBA. Also see Memo to Ewing from Branch, September 20, 1967, Folder: Brooklyn Homes—Open Occupancy, 1966–67, Box 5, Series 14, RG 48, BCA.

82. Anonymous letter dated December 20, 1966, Folder: O'Donnell Heights—Tenant Relations Cases, 1967–70, A–K, Box 39, Series 14, RG 48, BCA.

83. Returned letter in Folder 7: Correspondence and Memoranda, January–March 1967, Box 1, Series II, BURHA Collection, UBA.

84. Pamphlet accompanying Southern District Police Report, April 28, 1967, Folder: Brooklyn Homes—Open Occupancy, 1966–67.

85. Memos to Van Story Branch from Patrick B. Kirwan, April 24 and 26, 1967, Folder: Brooklyn Homes—Integration, 1966–68, Box 4, Series 14, RG 48, BCA.

86. Memo to Van Story Branch from Lucille Bucklew, May 29, 1967, Folder: Brooklyn Homes—Open Occupancy, 1966–67.

87. "Mother of 4 with Shotgun Vows to Stand Up to KKK," *BAA*, May 2, 1967.

88. Southern District Police Report, submitted by Sgt. Calvin Lotz, May 31, 1967; Memo to Van Story Branch from George H. Miles, June 5, 1967, both in Folder: Brooklyn Homes—Open Occupancy, 1966–67; Memo to Richard L. Steiner from Van Story Branch, June 6, 1967, Folder: Brooklyn Homes—Integration.

89. Quoted in Roger Nissly, "Ku Klux Klan Terrorizes Mother; 14 Jailed," *BAA*, September 9, 1967.

90. "Note to the File—Incidents at Brooklyn Homes—9/2, 9/3, 9/4/67," Folder: Brooklyn Homes—Integration, 1966–68, Box 4, Series 14, RG 48, BCA; "Chronology—Filling Standing Vacancies—Brooklyn Homes," Memo to Edgar Ewing from Van Story Branch, September 20, 1967, Folder: Brooklyn Homes—Open Occupancy, 1966–67, Box 5, Series 14, RG 48, BCA; Memo to Van Story Branch from Patrick B. Kirwan, October 10, 1967, Folder: Brooklyn Homes—Monthly Reports, 1965–71, Box 5, Series 14, RG 48, BCA.

91. Wise interviews.

92. Memo to Van Story Branch from Lucille Bucklew.

93. Anna Warren interviews.

94. Lundsford interview.

95. Anna Warren interviews.

96. James D. Dilts, "The Warning Trumpet: CORE Is the Only Voice Black People Ever Had," *Baltimore Sun Magazine*, December 1, 1968, Folder: Congress of Racial Equality, MDVF, EPFL.

97. "City, State Seek Legal Ban on Racist Rallies," *BES*, July 29, 1966; "90-Day Injunction Bans Rallies Here by States['] Rights Party," *BES*, August 11, 1966.

98. Max Johnson, "Pass Civil Rights Bill, 12–9, after Housing Deleted," *BAA*, February 25, 1964; "Rights Groups Marching for Housing Law," *BAA*, April 27, 1965; "Mayor Speaks Wednesday at Housing Rally," *BAA*, May 11, 1965.

99. Callcott, *Maryland & America*, 214.

100. "Activists Say Housing Bill 'No Good,' Ask Agnew Action," *BAA*, June 10, 1967.

101. Callcott, *Maryland & America*, 215–218; Carson, 256; Marable, 112.

102. Massey and Denton, *American Apartheid*, 46–47.

Chapter 4

1. Reives interviews.

2. Ibid.

3. Dwight Warren interview.

4. "Cliff Dwellings for the Subsidized Poor," *Sun*, February 26, 1952, Folder: Housing—Baltimore, 1951–1959, MDVF, EPFL.

5. Barbara Koeppel, "Urban Renewal Can Add to the Total of Homeless," *BN-P*, February 4, 1962, Series VI, CGEE, UBA.

6. Carby, "Policing the Black Woman's Body," 738–755; Higginbotham, *Righteous Discontent*; Hunter, *To 'Joy My Freedom*; Wolcott, *Remaking Respectability*.

7. Feldstein, *Motherhood in Black and White*, 142–147; Katz, *Improving Poor People*, 69–71; Kelley, *Yo' Mama's Disfunktional!*; Kunzel, *Fallen Women, Problem Girls*, 144–170; Daniel Patrick Moynihan, *The Negro Family: The Case for National Action* (Washington, D.C.: Office of Policy Planning and Research, U.S. Department of Labor, 1965). For studies by black sociologists, see Frazier, *The Negro Family;* Clark, *Dark Ghetto.* For discussions of the mythic "nuclear family," see Berry, *Politics of Parenthood*; Coontz, *The Way We Never Were.*

8. Baker, Schofield, and Thornton interviews.

9. Feldstein, *Motherhood in Black and White*, 146. Also see Solinger, *Wake Up Little Susie*, 20–103.

10. A. Scott Henderson in "'Tarred with the Exceptional Image'" argues that public housing was viewed positively between the 1950s and early 1960s, but that by the mid-1960s, racialized negative images of public housing dominated.

11. James Bailey, "The Case History of a Failure," *Architectural Forum* 123 (December 1965): 18–25.

12. Anthony Downs, "The American Ghetto: What's the Future?" *JOH* 25, no. 11 (1968): 567.

13. Kenneth Durr, *Behind the Backlash*, 138; Jonnes, *Hep-Cats, Narcs, and Pipe Dreams*, 248–252.

14. Flyer, Folder 6: Correspondence, Memoranda: October–December 1966, Box 1, Series II, BURHA Collection, UBA.

15. Grant interview.

16. Marriott interviews.

17. Williamson interview.

18. Sherrod and Edges interviews.

19. Ward and Schofield interviews.

20. Reives, Martin, and Marriott interviews; Bauman, Hummon, and Muller, "Public Housing, Isolation, and the Urban Underclass," 265, 282–285; Peter Henderson, "'Local Deals and the New Deal State,'" 410–412.

21. Benton interview.

22. Baker interviews.

23. Ibid.

24. Cathy Cohen, *Boundaries of Blackness*, 74.

25. Reives and Spell interviews.

26. Letter, December 10, 1960, Folder: Gilmor Homes—General, 1951–70, Box 17, Series 14, RG 48, BCA.

27. Spell interviews.

28. "Tenants Signing Loyalty Oaths," *BES*, March 21, 1953; "Loyalty Oath for Tenants Discarded," *BMS*, August 10, 1956, CGEE, UBA.

29. "Police Probing Death of Boy on Elevator," *BES*, August 21, 1962.

30. Dwight Warren interview.

31. Letter from Edith Wilson to Thomas D'Alesandro III, December 23, 1964; letter from Edith Wilson to Edgar Ewing, June 24, 1966; letter from Edgar Ewing to Edith Wilson, July 11, 1966; letter from Edith Wilson to Van Story Branch, June 13, 1967; letter from Van Story Branch to Edith Wilson, June 22, 1967; letter from Edith Wilson to Van Story Branch, c. December 1968; letter from Van Story Branch to Edith Wilson, January 23, 1969, all in Folder: Murphy Homes (Tenant), Box 37, Series 14, RG 48, BCA.

32. Letter to residents from Coleman Grant, November 24, 1969, Folder: Cherry Hills—Tenants Notices, 1954–74, Box 9, Series 14, RG 48, BCA.

33. Grant interview.

34. Gordon, Dwight Warren, and Williamson interviews.

35. Department of Housing and Community Development, "Sample Announcement," Folder: Resident Aides, Box 13, Series 13, RG 48, BCA. Other cities also established similar programs. See "Public Housing Tenants Raise Their Sights," *JOH* 23, no. 9 (1966): 528; Edward White, Jr., "Tenant Participation in Public Housing Management," *JOH* 26, no. 8 (1969): 416–419.

36. "4 High-Rise Residents Named Tenant Aides," *BES*, October 16, 1969, Folder: 1969, October–December, Public Housing—Local Newspaper Clippings, Box 49, Series 75, RG 48, BCA; "DHCD Residents Earn $5534," *BAA*, October 25, 1969.

37. Christine Jones, Report, November 24, 1969, Folder: Resident Aides, Box 13, Series 13, RG 48, BCA.

38. Memos to Van Story Branch from Charles K. Anderson, May 12, 1972, and July 17, 1972, Folder: Lafayette Courts General, 1970–77, Box 21, Series 14, RG 48, BCA.

39. Christine Jones, Report, November 24, 1969.

40. Ibid.

41. Spell interviews.

42. On the Companion Aide to the Elderly Program, see David Filker, "Employing Young Mothers to Assist the Elderly," *JOH* 23, no. 11 (1966): 650–653. On other activities, see Spell, Ward, and Wise interviews; Harry B. Weiss Memorial Fund Award, Nomination of Project Resident Forms for James Brockington (May 24, 1968) and Stephen Arvinger, Jr. (May 27, 1968), Folder: 1968, Harry B. Weiss Award, Box 2, Series 8, RG 48, BCA.

43. Letter from Phyllis Patillo to Van Story Branch, February 12, 1966, Folder: Lafayette Courts—Monthly Reports, 1965–67, Box 22, Series 14, RG 48, BCA.

44. Ralph Matthews, Jr., "Racial Picture in Housing Agency—Many Clients, Few Top Jobs," *BAA*, May 11, 1963.

45. Martin and Thornton interviews.

46. Report on Management Division Activities, Ellis Ash, November 1949, Folder: 1949–51 Organization Directives, Box 10, Series 13, RG 48, BCA.

47. Wright interview.

48. Anna Warren interviews.

49. Memo to Van Story Branch from W. K. Gorsuch, May 15, 1967, Box 35, Series 14, RG 48, BCA.

50. "Association Gets Action on Blight of Junked Cars," *BAA*, February 15, 1969.

51. Hyneses interview.

52. Monthly Report Memos, June 6, 1966, June 30, 1966, and August 3, 1966, all in Folder: Somerset Courts—Monthly Reports, 1965–68, Box 45, Series 14, RG 48, BCA.

53. Marriott and Thornton interviews; Memo to Van Story Branch from Bernard E. Mason (housing manager), November 30, 1965, Folder: Cherry Hill Homes—CASC, 1965–70, Box 6, Series 14, RG 48, BCA; "Disturbed Pickets" (picture with caption), *BAA*, December 20, 1966.

54. On environmental racism, see Bullard, *Unequal Protection*; Bullard, ed., *Confronting Environmental Racism*; Camacho, ed., *Environmental Injustices*; and Medoff and Sklar, *Streets of Hope.*

55. "Cherry Hill Residents to Grill City Fathers," *BAA*, June 25, 1966; "Cherry Hill Residents Say Spray Is Poison," *BAA*, July 2, 1966; "Cherry Hill Council for Benton Plan," *BAA*, July 16, 1966; "Our Readers Say: Want Incinerator Out," *BAA*, August 20, 1966; "Cherry Hill Incinerator Is Attacked," *BAA*, August 23, 1966.

56. "Cherry Hill Residents to Grill City Fathers," *BAA*, June 25, 1966. Also see Madeline Murphy interview (1973) by Nick Kotz, Series III: Equality Series, Kotz Papers (unprocessed), WHS.

57. Memo from Richard H. Chrystie to Harry B. Weiss, January 17, 1964, Folder: Latrobe Homes, 1950–1970, CASC, Box 25, Series 14, RG 48, BCA; Memo to Van Story Branch from Charles K. Anderson, December 27, 1966; letter to Charles K. Anderson from Mary N. Brooks, May 15, 1967; Memo to Van Story Branch from Charles K. Anderson, May 16, 1967, all in Folder: Gilmor Homes—General, 1951–70, Box 17, Series 14, RG 48, BCA. For other examples of burglary incidents in Gilmor Homes, see Folder: Gilmor Homes—General, 1951–70, Box 17, Series 14, RG 48, BCA.

58. Spell interviews.

59. Memo to Gordon Leatherwood from Glenn Simmons, October 8, 1965, Folder: Cherry Hill Homes—CASC, 1965–70, Box 6, Series 14, RG 48, BCA.

60. Jonnes, *Hep-Cats, Narcs, and Pipe Dreams*, 249–251.

61. Memo to Van Story Branch from David L. Ramsey, November 3, 1971, Folder: Douglass Homes—CASC, 1968–77, Box 11, Series 14, RG 48, BCA.

62. "Petition for Adequate Police Protection," June 28, 1968; letter to Commissioner Donald D. Pomerleau from Mrs. Ella L. Strother, July 19, 1968, both in Folder: Gilmor Homes—General, 1951–70, Box 17, Series 14, RG 48, BCA.

63. Embry interviews; Minutes: Crime Prevention and Security Guard Committee Meeting, August 29, 1969, Folder: 1969—Resident Advisory Board, Box 13, Series 13, RG 48, BCA.

64. Embry interviews.

65. Letter to Mayor from Phyllis Scriber, December 11, 1967; letter to Marguerite Campbell from Van Story Branch, June 27, 1968, both in Folder: Cherry Hill Homes—General 1968–70, Box 7, Series 14, RG 48, BCA.

66. Letter to Hyman Pressman from Estelle Ratliff, December 30, 1968, Folder: Crime in Projects, Box 19, Series 13, RG 48, BCA.

Chapter 5

1. Wise interviews.

2. Ibid.

3. A leftist student organization, SDS grew out of the southern civil rights movement and was heavily influenced by the Student Non-Violent Coordinating Committee, a black student civil rights organization; see Frost, *An Interracial Movement of the Poor.* For quote, see Richard Rothstein, "A Short History of ERAP," and Students for a Democratic Society monthly bulletins, October 1964– January 1965. Both online. Available: http://sunsite.berkeley.edu:2020/dynawe.

4. Rothstein, "A Short History of ERAP."

5. James D. Dilts, "Organization Man from the Other America," *Sun,* June 16, 1968, Folder: Lively, Walter H., MDVF, EPFL.

6. Ralph Matthews, Jr., "CORE Team Digs in on Eastside to Help People with Their Problems," *BAA,* June 27, 1964. Also see "CORE Elects New Chairman, Plans Slum Action Program," *BAA,* June 6, 1964; "City Backs CORE Eastside Project," *BAA,* July 18, 1964; Ted Handy, "CORE Condemns Secret 'Summit,'" *BAA,* August 8, 1964.

7. Quoted in Ralph Matthews, Jr., "Captives Hurt by Rats, Trash, Horses," *BAA,* August 15, 1964.

8. James D. Dilts, "The Warning Trumpet: CORE Is the Only Voice Black People Ever Had," *Sun Magazine,* December 1, 1968, Envelope: Congress of Racial Equality, MDVF, EPFL.

9. "Mayor Says Target City Could Be Summer's Safest," *BAA,* July 5, 1966.

10. Ben A. Franklin, "CORE's 'Target City' Program in Baltimore Now Hailed for Its Moderation," *NYT,* April 16, 1967.

11. On the War on Poverty and freedom rhetoric, see Greenstone and Peterson, *Race and Authority in Urban Politics,* 5–6; Thomas Jackson, "The State, the Movement, and the Poor"; Naples, *Grassroots Warriors;* Quadagno, *Color of Welfare.*

12. "Poverty War in 2nd Year," *BAA,* June 18, 1966.

13. Letter to Richard Steiner from Morton Macht, October 7, 1965, Folder 9: October 19, 1965, Box 1, Series I, BURHA Collection, UBA.

14. Memo to Richard Steiner from Van Story Branch, July 21, 1967, Folder 2: July 25, 1967, Box 5, Series I, BURHA Collection, UBA.

15. Matthews and Wise interviews.

16. Baker interviews.

17. "Poverty War Critic May Soon Get Chance to Work with CAA Project," *BAA,* May 21, 1966; "Dead at 34, Walter H. Lively Was Activist," *BAA,* September 14, 1976; Rudolph Lewis, "Walter Hall Lively: A Christ among Us—Civil Rights Ac-

tivist & Black Liberationist," in *ChickenBones: A Journal for Literary and Artistic African-American Themes*, Special Issue on Walter Hall Lively (Spring 2002). Online. Available: http://www.nathanielturner.com/walterlively.html.

18. Walter P. Carter obituary, August 4, 1971, Folder: Carter, Walter P., 1923–71, MDVF, EPFL. Quote appears in "Activist Leaders Hit D'Alesandro," *BAA*, June 3, 1967.

19. Hatcher interview.

20. Ibid.

21. Letter to Joel Newton from W. Lyndsai Pitts, Sr., January 30, 1967, Folder: Perkins Homes—CASC, 1954–70, Box 41, Series 14, RG 48, BCA.

22. Charles H. Baron, "'Neighborhood Legal Services': Friend or Foe?" *JOH* 28, no. 3 (1971): 129.

23. Quoted in Ray Abrams, "Why Anti-Poverty Fight Lags," *BAA*, November 20, 1965.

24. "Poverty Plan Is Questioned," *BAA*, December 15, 1964. On U-JOIN protests, see *Jobs Now Newsletter* of U-JOIN, February 8 and 15, 1965; "We Call for a Real War on Poverty" (flyer, n.d.), all in Folder 12: Baltimore, Newsletters and Leaflets, 1964, Box 22, Series 2B, SDS Papers, WHS. Also see "Baltimore U-JOIN Report War on Poverty," n.d., submitted by David Harding and Kim Moody; CAP Report submitted by Bob Moore; ERAP Report, n.d., submitted to Rennie Davis, all in Folder 13: SDS Baltimore Reports and Prospectuses, 1964, 1965, SDS Papers, WHS.

25. "Why Anti-Poverty Fight Lags," *BAA*, November 20, 1965; George W. Collins, "OEO, CAA React Quickly to Critique," *BAA*, May 14, 1966; "How Council Holds Up Major Poverty Plans," *BAA*, July 23, 1966; "Uncle Sam Advises CAC to Be More Independent," *BAA*, July 23, 1966; "City Council 'Conservatives' Want Poverty Program Control," *BAA*, March 18, 1969. Also see Callcott, *Maryland & America*, 204–205.

26. "Poor Speak Out at First Convention; Firm Plans Due in Dec. 18 Meeting," *BAA*, December 13, 1966; A. W. Geiselman, Jr., "Battle Looms in Poverty Program," *BES*, January 19, 1967.

27. "Statement of the Staff of the CAA on the City Council Decision against Mr. Walter P. Carter as Executive Director," Folder 29: CAA, Box 2, Series III, BURHA Collection, UBA.

28. Peter J. Koper, "Council Control over CAA Here Now under Probe," *BAA*, February 1, 1969.

29. "A Slap at the Mayor," *BES*, October 1, 1968.

30. Baker interviews.

31. Naples, *Grassroots Warriors*, 3.

32. Eugenia Davis, Matthews, and Thornton interviews. Eugenia "Bonnie" Ellis's name has since changed to Eugenia Ellis Johnson Davis.

33. Letter to Newton from Pitts, January 30, 1967, Folder: Perkins Homes—CASC, 1954–70, Box 41, Series 14, RG 48, BCA.

34. James D. Dilts, "Housing Project Life in Baltimore," *Baltimore Sun Magazine*, September 24, 1967.

35. Douglass Homes was formerly part of another "combo" with Somerset Courts. Memo to Robert S. Moyer from Van Story Branch, January 30, 1968, Folder: Douglass Homes—General 1949–1970, Box 11, Series 14, RG 48, BCA.

36. Matthews interview.

37. BURHA, *Types of Families Living in Baltimore's Low-Rent Projects, 1951–1964* (1965), Folder: 1964–1969, Reports and Statistics, Box 13, Series 13, RG 48, BCA.

38. Eugenia Davis and Matthews interviews; Memo to Charles Knight from John Meehan, July 1, 1968, Folder: Douglass Homes—General, 1949–70, Box 11, Series 14, RG 48, BCA.

39. Memo to Moyer from Branch, January 30, 1968, Folder: Douglass Homes—General, 1949–1970, Box 11, Series 14, RG 48, BCA.

40. Hatcher interview.

41. Thornton interview.

42. Baker interviews. Also see Boris, "When Work Is Slavery."

43. Thomas B. Edsall, "Tenant Cites Retaliation," *BES*, February 10, 1968.

44. Minutes of the Commission Meeting of the HABC, February 6, 1968, Folder 13: February 6, 1968, Box 5, Series I, BURHA Collection, UBA. Also see Thomas B. Edsall, "Residents Help to Pick Project Manager," *BES*, March 25, 1968.

45. Eugenia Davis interviews; Memo to Robert S. Moyer from Van Story Branch, February 23, 1968, Folder: Douglass Homes—Tenant Relations 1961–78, Box 11, Series 14, RG 48, BCA.

46. Minutes of the Commission Meeting of the HABC, February 6, 1968; Edsall, "Tenant Cites Retaliation," *BES*, February 10, 1968; Edsall, "Reprisal-Case Probe Asked by Mitchell," *BES*, February 13, 1968.

47. Parren Mitchell became Maryland's first African-American congressperson. He represented the Seventh District in Baltimore and served five terms. See Edsall, "Reprisal-Case Probe Asked by Mitchell," *BES*, February 13, 1968.

48. Memo to Moyer from Branch, February 23, 1968.

49. Baker and Wise interviews.

50. Matthews interview. On the Joyce Thorpe case, see Greene, "'Our Separate Ways,'" especially chapter 4; "Supreme Court Decides to Rule on Eviction Case," *BAA*, April 18, 1967.

51. Jack Bryan, "Public Housing Modernization," *JOH* 28, no. 4 (1971): 169.

52. "Minneapolis Gets First Modernization OK," *JOH* 25, no. 3 (1968): 153; HUD circular quote in "Philadelphia Authority Contracts with Residents," *JOH* 27, no. 3 (1970): 144; "Tenant-Management Issues," *JOH* 27, no. 3 (1970): 540.

53. Bryan, "Public Housing Modernization," *JOH* 28, no. 4 (1971): 167. See Venkatesh's *American Project*, 57–62, on the HUD modernization program in Chicago. Chicago established a citywide board in 1969, a year after Baltimore.

54. Bryan, "Public Housing Modernization," *JOH* 28, no. 4 (1971): 170.

55. "Tenants Participate in Modernization Programs," *JOH* 26, no. 8 (1969): 419; Wise interviews.

56. Bryan, "Public Housing Modernization," *JOH* 28, no. 4 (1971): 170; "Tenant-Management Issues," *JOH* 27, no. 10 (1970): 540.

57. Embry interviews; "All to Live in Floating City—Housing Commissioner," *BAA*, July 26, 1969. Embry also criticized blockbusting and called for suburbs to accept public housing. See "Low-Income Housing," *BNA*, July 17, 1969, Folder: 1969, June–September, Public Housing—Local, Box 49, Series 75, RG 48, BCA.

58. Embry interviews; Paul D. Samuel, "Low-Income Groups More Active, Have Public Housing Issues, Voice," *BES*, December 27, 1972.

59. Minutes: Public Housing Tenant Representatives, August 16, 1968, Folder: 1968–69—RAB, Box 13, Series 13, RG 48, BCA.

60. Minutes of the First Meeting of the Resident Advisory Board, October 3, 1968, Folder: 1968–69—RAB, Box 13, Series 13, RG 48, BCA.

61. Bryan, "Public Housing Modernization," *JOH* 28, no. 4 (1971): 173. Also see Memo to Embry from Branch, September 16, 1968, and Minutes of the First Meeting of the Resident Advisory Board, October 3, 1968, both in Folder: 1968–69—RAB, Series 13, RG 48, BCA; "Tenant-Management Issues," *JOH* 27, no. 10 (1970): 536; Steven R. Weisman, "Tenants' Council Will Advise City," *NYT*, November 22, 1970; and John Herbers, "Tenants Win Policy Voice in Nation's Public Housing," *NYT*, November 27, 1970, Folder: 1970, November–December Clipping Files: Tenants' Rights, Box 58, Series 75, RG 48, BCA. On New Haven, Connecticut, community-based tenant organizations, see Edward White, Jr., "Tenant Participation in Public Housing Management," *JOH* 26, no. 8 (1969): 416–419.

62. "Low-Income Groups More Active," *BES*, December 27, 1972.

63. Bryan, "Public Housing Modernization," *JOH* 28, no. 4 (1971): 171–172.

64. Jean King was a leader at Darst-Webbe and Peabody complexes. See "Public Housing Tenants in St. Louis Have Been on Rent Strike for Six Months," *JOH* 26, no. 7 (1969): 351–352. Also in Newark, public housing residents led by a group called Poor and Dissatisfied Tenants initiated a rent strike, picketed up to four complexes, and demanded a reduction in the maximum rent of tenants receiving public welfare. Washington public housing tenants also withheld rents, protesting bad upkeep and slum conditions. "Tenant-Management Issues," *JOH* 27, no. 10 (1970): 534–543. On the St. Louis case, see Lipsitz, *A Life in the Struggle*, 145–171.

65. "Tenants Begin Newark Strike," *BES*, April 2, 1970, Folder: 1970, May–April Clipping Files: Tenants' Rights; Sanford J. Unger and Michael Hodge, "Consumers' New Weapon: Rent Strike," *Washington Post*, July 26, 1970, Folder: 1970, June–October Clipping Files: Tenants' Rights; "Newark Tenants Will Defy Court Order," *NYT*, February 15, 1972, and "Tenant Association in Newark Faces Contempt Charges," *NYT*, February 24, 1972, Folder: 1972, January–March Clipping Files: Tenants' Rights; Joseph P. Fried, "'Tenant Power' Is a Spreading Slogan," *NYT*, March 19, 1973, Folder: 1973, March–April Clipping Files: Tenants' Rights, all in Box 58, Series 75, RG 48, BCA.

66. NTO Biography—Anthony Henry, NTO Biography—Jesse Gray, and NTO

Biography—Rose Wylie, all in Folder 6: NTO, 1972, Box 30, GWP, WHS; Peter Marcuse, "The Rise of Tenant Organizations," *Nation*, July 19, 1971, Folder 7: NTO, 1972 (cont.), Box 30, GWP, WHS.

67. "Rent Escrow Faces Rough House Action," *BAA*, March 22, 1969; Paul D. Samuel, "Low-Income Groups More Active," *BES*, December 27, 1972.

68. "National Tenants Organization—National Officers," Folder 7: NTO, 1972 (cont.), Box 30, GWP, WHS.

69. Embry interviews.

70. Minutes of Election Committee, November 18, 1968, Folder: 1968–69—RAB, Box 13, Series 13, RG 48, BCA.

71. RAB Meeting Minutes, December 5, 1968, Folder: 1968–69—RAB, Box 13, Series 13, RG 48, BCA.

72. Embry interviews. Also see RAB Meeting Minutes, December 5, 1968.

73. Letter from R. C. Embry to Katherine [*sic*] Monroe, August 14, 1969, Folder: 1969—RAB, Box 13, Series 13, RG 48, BCA.

74. Wise interviews. Also see Paul D. Samuel, "Low-Income Groups More Active," *BES*, December 27, 1972; RAB Minutes, Eighth Meeting of RAB, May 1, 1969, Folder: 1970—RAB, Box 33, Series 13, RG 48, BCA.

75. Paul D. Samuel, "Project Resident Named to Housing Authority," *BES*, July 20, 1970, Folder 49: 1970, July–August, Public Housing—Local, Box 49, RG 48, BCA.

76. Untitled, unsigned statement appearing in RAB Minutes folder between March and May 1970 memos. Folder: 1970—RAB, Box 33, Series 13, RG 48, BCA.

77. Baker interviews.

78. Letter to Victorine Adams from Gordine Blount, October 31, 1969, Folder: Resident Aides, Box 13, Series 13, RG 48, BCA.

79. Letter to WomanPower from Gordine Blount, February 9, 1970; letters to WomanPower and League of Women Voters from Robert C. Embry, all in Folder: 1970—RAB, Box 33, Series 13, RG 48, BCA.

80. Wise interviews.

81. NTO National Conference Agenda, October 29–November 2, 1971, Folder: 1971—RAB, Box 33, Series 13, RG 48, BCA.

82. Wise interviews.

83. Ibid.

84. Paul D. Samuel, "Low-Income Groups More Active," *BES*, December 27, 1972.

85. Wise interviews.

86. "Supreme Court Decides to Rule on Eviction Case," *BAA*, April 18, 1967; "Court Halts Eviction of Tenants' Spokesman," *JOH* 24, no. 7 (1967): 401; "Court Suits Contest Public Housing Evictions," *JOH* 24, no. 5 (1967): 259; "Tenants' Rights Boosted in Michigan," *JOH* 25, no. 8 (1968): 423.

87. Minutes of Eighth RAB Meeting, May 1, 1969, Folder: 1970—RAB, Box 33, Series 13, RG 48, BCA.

88. John Herbers, "Government Expected to Make Big Concessions to Public Housing Tenants," *NYT*, November 16, 1970, Folder: 1970, November–December

Clipping Files: Tenants' Rights; quote appears in "Tenant Protection Policy," *Sun*, March 14, 1971, Folder: 1971, January–April Clipping Files: Tenants' Rights, both in Box 58, Series 75, RG 48, BCA; George R. Genung, Jr., "HUD's New Public Housing Lease and Grievance Procedures Cause of Controversy," *JOH* 28, no. 3 (1971): 119–121; John Herbers, "Model Lease Set in Public Housing," *NYT*, February 24, 1971, Folder 7: NTO, 1972 (cont.), Box 30, GWP, WHS.

89. Wise and Wright interviews.

90. Neil Gilbert describes the War on Poverty's goal as the "democraticization [*sic*] of social welfare" through "transforming clients into constituents." Gilbert, *Clients or Constituents*, x, 9, 29–32.

91. Baker interviews.

92. Thornton interview.

93. Anna Warren interviews.

94. Ibid.

95. Wright interview; "Residents Get Familiar with Community Action," *BAA*, August 2, 1969; Memo to Van Story Branch from Jacob Fisher, October 30, 1968, Folder: O'Donnell Heights—CASC, 1966, Box 37, Series 14, RG 48, BCA.

96. "Mrs. Turner Cited by Murphy Council," *BAA*, January 25, 1969.

97. Spell interviews.

98. "United Front Charges Continued Harassment," *BAA*, January 18, 1969; Elizabeth M. Oliver, "Claims Cops Planted Dope on Client," *BAA*, January 25, 1960; "Black Front Protests 'Skull Cap Incident,'" *BAA*, September 23, 1969.

99. Spell interviews.

100. Ibid.

101. Ibid.

102. Schofield interview.

103. Jewell Chambers, "Community Leaders Explore Forming Black Unity Front," *BAA*, March 16, 1968.

104. "Deficit of Action Agency Squeezes Out 10 Centers," *BNA*, March 19, 1971, Folder 12, Box 9, Series I, BCP, UBA.

105. "Opening Statement by Governor Spiro T. Agnew," April 11, 1968, Folder: Civil Rights—Part I, Box 14, Governors' Records, MDSA. Also see Parren J. Mitchell, interview (1973) by Nick Kotz, Series III: Equality Series, Nick Kotz Papers (unprocessed), WHS.

106. "Angry Leaders Walk Out on Agnew," *BAA*, April 20, 1968; "Walter Lively, Rights Advocate, Dies at 34," *Sun*, September 11, 1976, Folder: Lively, Walter H., MDVF, EPFL.

107. Lively resigned in November 1968 to protest the city council's refusal to appoint Walter P. Carter as CAC chair. Parren Mitchell resigned in 1968 and eventually ran for Congress. "Lively, Mitchell, Favor Get Urban Coalition Posts," *BAA*, January 20, 1968.

108. "Angry Leaders Walk Out on Agnew," *BAA*, April 20, 1968.

109. Baker interviews.

110. Stephenson interview.

111. Quoted in Jewell Chambers, "Community Leaders Explore Forming Black Unity Front," *BAA*, March 16, 1968.

112. Farber uses "customized wars" in *The Age of Great Dreams*, 107.

Chapter 6

1. "Welfare Clients to Get Hearing," *BAA*, September 20, 1966; Statement of Daisy Snipes, September 22, 1966, Folder: WEL, Box 85, 1965–66 Public Welfare, General Files, Governors' Records, MDSA.

2. "Mother Rescuers Fight for More Welfare Help," *BAA*, July 2, 1966.

3. Ibid.

4. Department of Housing and Community Development, *Types of Families Living in Baltimore's Low-Rent Projects, 1968* (1969).

5. Most of the 1,000 delegates at the NTO convention were black, but there was a sizable number of Chicanos/Chicanas, Native Americans, and whites. "Tenants Prepare a National Drive," *NYT*, November 7, 1971; Wise interviews.

6. Grant, *Ella Baker*; Harley, "'Chronicle of a Death Foretold'"; Lee, *For Freedom's Sake*; Ransby, *Ella Baker & the Black Freedom Movement*; Robnett, *How Long? How Long?*; Crawford, Rouse, and Woods, eds., *Women in the Civil Rights Movement*.

7. "Cooperatives: A Weapon in the War on Slums," *VISTA Volunteer* 3 (April 1967), courtesy of Eugenia Davis; Christopher Caul, "Families on Welfare Pool Funds in Co-op Food Buying Plan," *BES*, November 22, 1966.

8. Hine, "Housewives' League of Detroit," 223–241; Kornbluh, "To Fulfill Their 'Rightly Needs,'" 80–83; Orleck, "We Are That Mythical Thing," 381–389; Skotnes, "'Buy Where You Can Work,'" 735–761.

9. Chateauvert, *Marching Together*, 140.

10. Chateauvert, *Marching Together*, 138–162, quote on 142.

11. Caul, "Families on Welfare Pool Funds in Co-op Food Buying Plan," *BES*, November 22, 1966.

12. "Food-Buying Club," *Lafayette-Douglass Newsletter* 1, no. 1 (June 1969), courtesy of Clyde Hatcher; Caul, "Families on Welfare Pool Funds in Co-op Food Buying Plan," *BES*, November 22, 1966; handwritten notes of Clyde Hatcher, c. 1969, courtesy of Hatcher.

13. Surveys in Folder: 1968–1969, HS1–530, Civil Disturbance Areas, Box 3, Series 8, RG 48, BCA; Callcott, *Maryland & America*, 165.

14. Schofield interview.

15. Grant interview.

16. Stephenson interview.

17. "Ghetto Leaders Think Nonwhites Setting Policy," *BAA*, February 10, 1968.

18. "Angry Leaders Walk Out on Agnew," *BAA*, April 20, 1968.

19. Hatcher interview; personal notes and *Lexington-Poe Newsworthy Notes*,

courtesy of Hatcher; "Cooperatives: A Weapon in the War on Slums," *VISTA Volunteer* 3 (April 1967).

20. Letter to Van Story Branch from Lafayette-Douglass Food Store Board of Directors, January 6, 1970, Folder: Lafayette Courts—CASC, Box 21, Series 14, RG 48, BCA.

21. Memo to Van Story Branch from Joel Newton, December 24, 1970, Folder: Perkins Homes—CASC, 1954–1970, Box 41; Memo regarding Westport Homes' Attempt to Start a Food Store, Folder: Westport Homes—CASC, 1949–72, Box 16; Memo to Van Story Branch from Bruce Fales, February 4, 1975, Folder: Flag House—CASC, 1955–76, Box 15, all in Series 14, RG 48, BCA. In Baltimore, the Black Panthers and black clergy also attempted to establish community groceries; see "Panthers Here Chart Resistance," *BAA*, February 8, 1969; "Community Grocery Opening Tomorrow," *BAA*, March 29, 1969.

22. Hatcher interview.

23. Liberators for Black Consumers, flyer (n.d.), courtesy of Hatcher.

24. "Consumer Education," *Lafayette-Douglass Newsletter* 1, no. 3 (September 1969), courtesy of Hatcher.

25. "Credit Union," *Lafayette-Douglass Newsletter* 1, no. 1 (June 1969); "Credit Union Announcement," *Lafayette-Douglass Newsletter* 1, no. 3 (September 1969), both courtesy of Hatcher.

26. "Controversial U-JOIN," *BAA*, January 10, 1966; "Rent Strike Unit Plans New Attack," *BAA*, April 22, 1966.

27. "Relief Mothers Start Fighting for Checks, Respect," *BAA*, June 14, 1966.

28. Pamphlet, *What Is U-JOIN?* (1965), found in Envelope: Lively, Walter H., MDVF, EPFL.

29. "Mother Rescuers Fight for More Welfare Help," *BAA*, July 2, 1966.

30. Joan Berezin, "The Welfare Jungle," *JOBS Now* newsletter, Folder 12: Baltimore, Newsletters and Leaflets, 1964, Box 22, Series 2B, SDS Papers, WHS.

31. "Mothers on Welfare Tell of Their Troubles," *BAA*, September 6, 1966; McCarty interview.

32. "U-JOIN Pickets Stun Landlord's Home Area," *BAA*, June 28, 1966; Bailis, *Bread or Justice*, 8; Green, "Battling the Plantation Mentality," 366; Kotz and Kotz, *Passion for Equality*, 189–190; Sobel, ed., *Welfare & the Poor*, 23–24; Guida West, *National Welfare Rights Movement*.

33. Rudell Martin, Ellen Douglass, and Cynthia Morgan, all public housing tenants, served on the National Coordinating Committee; see Folder 4: Membership and Chapter Reports 1967–1972, Box 8, GWP, WHS; "Welfare Mothers to Form National Body," *BAA*, August 9, 1966.

34. National Welfare Rights Organization, "Bill of Welfare Rights," 1966, Folder 5: Membership Miscellany, 1967–1972, Box 8, GWP, WHS.

35. "Mothers on Welfare Tell of Their Troubles," *BAA*, September 6, 1966.

36. "Poverty Rescuers Write Candidates," *BAA*, October 25, 1966.

37. "Protest Set on Welfare Cuts," *BAA*, March 21, 1967.

38. "Welfare Recipient to Be Named to DPW Committee," *BAA*, June 10, 1967; State Board of Public Welfare, Minutes of Meeting, July 21, 1967, MDSA.

39. "Mother Rescuers Fight for More Welfare Help," *BAA*, July 2, 1966; McCarty interview.

40. *Public Welfare—Myth vs. Fact*, Folder: MC-MZ, Box 72, General Files, Governors' Records, MDSA.

41. State Board of Public Welfare, Meeting Minutes, July 15, 1966, MDSA.

42. The former director of public welfare in Richmond, Virginia, Hobson succeeded Judge Thomas J. Waxter, who retired in 1963; see *Richmond Times-Dispatch*, July 10, 1963, Folder: Welfare Department, Director, 1963, Box 72, General Files, Governors' Records, MDSA; "Welfare Head Ends First Year, Sees Improvements Coming," *BAA*, August 22, 1964; Elizabeth M. Oliver, "New Welfare Director Concerned 'Mind and Soul' with the Poor," *BAA*, August 23, 1969; Krefetz, "Urban Politics and Public Welfare."

43. State Board of Public Welfare, Meeting Minutes, July 15, 1966, MDSA; "Protest Set on Welfare Cuts," *BAA*, March 21, 1967; Kotz and Kotz, *Passion for Equality*, 218.

44. State Board of Public Welfare, Meeting Minutes, July 15, 1966; "Mothers on Welfare Tell of Their Troubles," *BAA*, September 6, 1966.

45. Statement of June Booth, September 1966, Folder: WEL, Box 85, 1965–66 Public Welfare, General Files, Governors' Records, MDSA.

46. State Board of Public Welfare, Meeting Minutes, July 15, 1966, MDSA.

47. Martin interviews.

48. Statement of Alease Coleman, September 1966, Folder: WEL, Box 85, 1965–66 Public Welfare, General Files, Governors' Records, MDSA.

49. State Board of Public Welfare, Meeting Minutes, October 7, 1966.

50. "Mother Rescuers Fight for More Welfare Help," *BAA*, July 2, 1966.

51. National Welfare Rights Organization, "Bill of Welfare Rights," Folder 5: Membership, Miscellany, 1967–72, Box 8, GWP, WHS.

52. "Mother Rescuers Fight for More Welfare Help," *BAA*, July 2, 1966.

53. State Board of Public Welfare, Meeting Minutes, August 19, 1966, MDSA; "Welfare Recipients May Get Work Break," *BAA*, August 23, 1966; David Filker, "Employing Young Mothers to Assist the Elderly," *JOH* 23, no. 11 (1966): 650–653. Also see Walkowitz, *Working with Class*, especially part 3 on the rules and standards governing private and public social work.

54. In the 1964 campaign, Furman Templeton and Howard H. Murphy helped lead this fight. Raleigh Hobson made the recommendation to terminate night visits to the Department of Public Welfare board. "DPW Board Rules Out Night Visits," *BAA*, January 21, 1964.

55. "Mothers on Welfare Tell of Their Troubles," *BAA*, September 6, 1966; Statement of Daisy Snipes, September 22, 1966, Folder: WEL, Box 85, 1965–66 Public Welfare, General Files, Governors' Records, MDSA.

56. "Now 'Man in the House' Won't Stop Welfare," *BAA*, April 21, 1970.

57. Flug, "Organized Labor and the Civil Rights Movement of the 1960s," 329–332.

58. J. Linn Allen, "Freedom Union Wins Raises in Pay, Benefits," *BAA*, June 14, 1966; Flug, "Organized Labor and the Civil Rights Movement," 322–346.

59. "Fines, Suspended Terms for Welfare Recipients," *BAA*, January 7, 1967; Roger J. Nissly, "Welfare Fraud Defendants Start Asking for Lawyers," *BAA*, January 28, 1967; "Collapse, Dismissal as 'Fraud' Trials Continue," *BAA*, February 4, 1967; "Legal Aid Being Planned for Welfare Recipients," *BAA*, February 25, 1967.

60. Agnew set aside $300 million in a supplemental budget, but McCarty called this a "drop in the bucket." See "Rescuers from Poverty Take Fight to Agnew," *BAA*, February 21, 1967; "Protests Set on Welfare Cuts," *BAA*, March 21, 1967.

61. "Protests Set on Welfare Cuts," *BAA*, March 21, 1967.

62. Carol Honsa, "Welfare Bill Called 'Betrayal of Poor,'" *Washington Post*, August 29, 1967; Betty James, "Welfare Rally Threatens Riots," *Evening Star*, August 29, 1967, Folder 7: Founding Meetings, Box 7, GWP, WHS.

63. "Power for Poor People: Should Be Our Slogan," *BAA*, June 20, 1967.

64. "75 Welfare Workers Protest Pay, Cases," *BAA*, February 18, 1967; "Welfare Strike Appears Certain for Next Week," *BAA*, April 29, 1967; Sterling A. Paige, "Bernard Miller: Man behind Welfare Union," *BAA*, May 13, 1967.

65. Letter from Maryland Conference of Social Welfare to the Senate Finance Committee, Folder: Budget—Fiscal 1969 (SDSS Budget), Box 8, Cole File, MDSA.

66. The MCSW organized a letter-writing campaign. See Folder: Budget Fiscal Year 1969, Box 8; letter from Dandridge to Agnew, December 12, 1968, and Cole response letter, December 17, 1968, both in Folder: AFDC Program, SDSS, Box 9, Cole File, MDSA.

67. "Opening Statement by Governor Spiro T. Agnew," April 11, 1968.

68. King, "Where Do We Go from Here?" in Washington, *Testament of Hope*, 246.

69. Sobel, ed., *Welfare & the Poor*, 28–29.

70. "Goals for a National Welfare Rights Movement," the Report of Workshop Z, National Welfare Rights Meeting, Chicago, Illinois, August 6–7, 1966, Folder 7: Founding Meetings, Box 7, GWP, WHS.

71. Green, "Battling the Plantation Mentality," 377; Kotz and Kotz, *Passion for Equality*, 219; Orleck, "'If It Wasn't for You, I'd Have Shoes for My Children,'" 112–118.

72. Thornton interview.

73. Quotes appear, respectively, in State Board of Public Welfare, Meeting Minutes, November 15, 1968; Meeting Minutes, February 21, 1969. Also see memos to Van Story Branch from Jacob Fisher, March 3, 1969, April 3, 1969, May 2, 1969, September 4, 1969, all in Folder: O'Donnell Heights—Monthly Reports, 1965–70, Box 39; resolution dated April 15, 1969; letter to Rosaline Lundsford from John Meehan, May 2, 1969, both in Folder: O'Donnell Heights—General, 1968–69, Box 37, all in Series 14, RG 48, BCA.

74. Letter to Charlotte Minton from R. C. Embry, Jr., August 26, 1969, Folder: O'Donnell Heights—General, 1968–69, Box 37; Memos to Van Story Branch from Jacob Fisher, March 3, 1969, April 3, 1969, both in Folder: O'Donnell Heights—Monthly Reports, 1965–70, Box 39, all in Series 14, RG 48, BCA.

75. State Board of Public Welfare, Minutes of Meeting, November 21, 1969, January 16, 1970, February 20, 1970, MDSA.

76. "Action Demanded on Unemployment," *BAA*, September 3, 1949.

77. Baker interviews.

78. Baker and Marriott interviews.

79. Martin interviews.

80. Quoted in Kotz and Kotz, *Passion for Equality*, 199. For a similar experience by a white woman, Terry Szpak, who became a welfare rights organizer in Boston, see Kotz and Kotz, *Passion for Equality*, 223.

81. Anna Warren interviews.

82. Eugenia Davis interviews.

83. Martin interviews; Welford L. McLellan, "Getting Her Rights as Welfare Client," *BES*, August 8, 1971.

84. Fred Barbash, "Welfare Group Sees Progress," *BMS*, September 15, 1971; "PRAC/ National Welfare Rights Meeting," Chicago, August 1966, Folder 7: Founding Meetings, Box 7, GWP, WHS.

85. Randall and Keaton interviews.

86. King, Riverside speech, April 4, 1967, in Washington, *Testament of Hope*, 232.

87. "Cherry Hill Welfare Rights Hits Viet War," *BAA*, October 14, 1969. For King's words, see King, Riverside speech and "Where Do We Go from Here?"; Green, "Battling the Plantation Mentality," 367–368.

88. State Board of Public Welfare, Meeting Minutes, April 18, 1969, MDSA.

89. "Welfare Sit-in Protests Delays," *BMS*, May 13, 1969. Also see, regarding the involvement of O'Donnell Heights' IMPACT, Memos to Van Story Branch from Jacob Fisher, April 3, 1969, June 13, 1969, both in Folder: O'Donnell Heights—Monthly Reports, 1965–70, Box 39, Series 14, RG 48, BCA.

90. Mueller resigned in 1971; see State Board of Public Welfare, Meeting Minutes, March 19, 1971, MDSA.

91. "Welfare Board Chairman under Fire for Statements," *BAA*, July 26, 1969; "Welfare 'Harassment,'" *BAA*, July 26, 1969.

92. "Welfare Sit-in Protests Delays," *BMS*, May 13, 1969.

93. Piven and Cloward, *Poor People's Movements*, 274.

94. Marriott, Martin, and Baker interviews. On the Fulton Improvement Association, see Kenneth Durr, *Behind the Backlash*, 85–87.

95. Baker and Martin interviews; "Welfare Rights Group Opens Office," *BMS*, December 15, 1971; "Stricken by Fiscal Paralysis," *BMS*, September 1, 1974.

96. The Catholic Campaign for Human Development also funded other Baltimore organizations in the late 1970s, including Baltimoreans United in Leadership Development (BUILD) and Project PLASE (Persons Lacking Ample Shelter

and Employment). Campaign for Human Development Records (unprocessed), ACUA.

97. Memo to Van Story Branch, June 23, 1971, and attached flyer, "Demonstration on 1st National Bank," May 4, 1971, both in Folder: Perkins Homes—CASC, 1971–79, Box 41, Series 14, RG 48, BCA.

98. "Work of Welfare Organization Is Described," *Brooklyn News*, January 30, 1975, in Folder: Brooklyn Homes: Monthly Progress Reports, 1971–76, Box 5, Series 14, RG 48, BCA. Also see Randall and Keaton interviews.

99. "Trustee at Provident," *BMS*, August 8, 1976; "Board Elects Mrs. Martin," *BES*, August 9, 1976.

100. "Housing Chief Wants Reduction in Rents," *BAA*, July 28, 1970; Sandra Grant, "Lower Rents Eyed for Aid Recipients in Public Housing," *BES*, October 30, 1970. Also see, for instance, Rhode Island Fair Welfare, *How to Organize a Brooke Amendment Campaign and WIN Lower Rents in Public Housing*, NWRO in cooperation with NTO, 1972, Box 2069, NWRO Papers, MSRC.

101. NWRO Fact Sheet, February 9, 1971, Folder 5: Guaranteed Adequate Income, General Materials, 1971–73, Box 22, GWP, WHS; Kotz and Kotz, *Passion for Equality*, 266. On Mills, see Julian E. Zelizer, *Taxing America: Wilbur D. Mills, Congress, and the State, 1945–1975* (Cambridge: Cambridge University Press, 1998), 315–317.

102. George Wiley resigned from the NWRO in 1973, apparently because members did not want to dilute their strength by engaging in coalition politics and forming a massive economic justice organization. He died that same year in a boating accident. The NWRO office closed in 1975. Kotz and Kotz, *Passion for Equality*, 290.

103. Martin interviews.

104. "Stricken by Fiscal Paralysis," *BMS*, September 1, 1974; Martin interviews.

105. Baker interviews.

106. Ibid.

107. Martin interviews; "Cheeks to Poor: You Can Fight City Hall," *Baltimore Sun Magazine*, September 13, 1981; Milton Kent, "Bobby Cheeks, Welfare Rights Advocate, Voice of the Poor," *BES*, September 16, 1988, AAVF, EPFL.

108. Annie Rogers Chambers has dropped the use of "Rogers." For historical accuracy, however, I refer to her as Annie Rogers because she went by that name when she was involved with the WRO.

109. Chambers interviews.

110. Letter to Charlotte Minton from R. C. Embry, Jr., May 2, 1969; letter to Delores Westerfield from R. C. Embry, Jr., May 2, 1969; letter to Helen Ford from John Meehan, May 2, 1969, all in Folder: O'Donnell Heights—General—1968–69, Box 37, Series 14, RG 48, BCA; Memos to Van Story Branch from Margaret Keen, October 10, 1977, December 6, 1977, both in Folder: O'Donnell Heights—Monthly Reports, 1976–79, all in Box 39, Series 14, RG 48, BCA.

111. Protest letter to Robert C. Embry, Jr., from O'Donnell Heights Community Council, May 27, 1969, Folder: O'Donnell Heights—General, 1968–69, Box 37, Series 14, RG 48, BCA.

112. Lundsford interview.

113. Memo to Van Story Branch from Margaret Keen, March 3, 1978, Folder: O'Donnell Heights—Monthly Reports, 1976–79, Box 39, Series 14, RG 48, BCA.

114. Memos to Van Story Branch from Margaret Keen, March 8, 1978, April 10, 1978, May 8, 1978, August 7, 1978, all in Folder: O'Donnell Heights—Monthly Reports, 1976–79, Box 39, Series 14, RG 48, BCA; "Ouster of City Welfare-Rights Agency Opposed," *Sun*, August 1, 1978, found in Envelope: Housing—Baltimore—O'Donnell Heights, MDVF, EPFL.

115. "Ouster of City Welfare-Rights Agency Opposed," *Sun*, August 1, 1978. For Ivey's credentials, see "Poverty War in 2nd Year," *BAA*, June 18, 1966; "CAA's Ivey Elected to UF [United Fund of Maryland] Board," *BAA*, June 19, 1971; Lenwood Ivey, interview (1973) by Nick Kotz, Series III: Equality Series, Kotz Papers (unprocessed), WHS.

116. Chambers interviews.

117. Ibid.

118. Chambers and Wise interviews; Tracie Rozhon, "City Aides Get Tenant Complaints," *Sun*, November 5, 1978; "O'Donnell Tenant Leads Rent Strike Testimony," *Sun*, January 19, 1979.

119. Quoted in Tracie Rozhon, "O'Donnell Heights: The City's Forgotten Edge," *Sun*, October 1, 1978.

120. "Schaefer Pledges to Help O'Donnell Tenants," *Sun*, October 10, 1978.

121. "Schaefer Pledges to Help O'Donnell Heights Tenants," *Sun*, October 10, 1978; "City Construction Teams to Check O'Donnell," *Sun*, October 16, 1978; "City Aides Get Tenant Complaints," *Sun*, November 5, 1978.

122. "Poor People's Advocate Taking Fight to the Streets," *BNA*, December 17, 1978.

123. Memo to M. J. Brodie from Van Story Branch, September 13, 1979, Folder: O'Donnell Heights—Monthly Reports, 1976–79, Box 39, Series 14, RG 48, BCA.

124. Chambers interviews.

125. Ibid. On Pope case, see "O'Donnell Tenant Leads Rent Strike Testimony," *Sun*, January 19, 1979.

126. "Bobby Cheeks' Welfare Righters Win Important Court Decision," *BAA*, February 10, 1979.

127. Memo to M. J. Brodie from Van Story Branch, September 13, 1979, Folder: O'Donnell Heights—Monthly Reports, 1976–79, Box 39, Series 14, RG 48, BCA; "Poor People's Advocate Taking Fight to the Streets," *BNA*, December 17, 1978; "O'Donnell Heights Project to Get an $18 Million New Look," *BNA*, November 21, 1981, found in Envelope: Housing—Baltimore—O'Donnell Heights, MDVF, EPFL. On Newark, see "Newark Tenant Will Defy Court," *NYT*, February 15, 1972; "Tenant Association in Newark Faces Contempt Charges," *NYT*, February 24, 1972.

128. "Bobby Cheeks' Welfare Righters Win Important Court Decision," *BAA*, February 10, 1979.

129. "Poor People's Advocate Taking Fight to the Streets," *BNA*, December 17, 1978.

Epilogue

1. Melody Simmons, "Tenants Angered by Move from High-Rise to High-Rise," *Sun*, January 15, 1993; Michael A. Fletcher, "Work Crews Follow on the Heels of Mayor's Visit to Public Housing," *Sun*, January 31, 1993.

2. Melody Simmons and Michael A. Fletcher, "Schmoke Promises to Improve High-Rise Conditions," *Sun*, January 30, 1993.

3. Helen Glover Cook, "Residents Stop Begging, Demand 'Safe, Clean, Place to Live,'" *Baltimore Times*, February 1–7, 1993.

4. Simmons, "Tenants Angered by Move from High-Rise to High-Rise," *Sun*, January 15, 1993; Melody Simmons, "Tenants to Withhold Rent at 2 High-Rises," *BES*, January 22, 1993; Melody Simmons and Michael A. Fletcher, "Schmoke Promises to Improve High-Rise Conditions," *Sun*, January 30, 1993. Also see Barbara McKinney interview.

5. See chapter 2.

6. Melody Simmons, "At Lexington Terrace Cisneros Orders Immediate Help for Blighted High-Rises," *Sun*, February 4, 1993.

7. Ibid. Also, "HUD Is Urged to Help Fund War on Drugs," *BES*, July 26, 1988; Bob Cohn, "Looking Beyond the HUD Scandal," *Newsweek*, August 21, 1989; Ann Mariano, "New Chief Finds HUD $11 Billion to Spend," *Washington Post*, February 6, 1993.

8. William F. Zorzi, Jr., and Melody Simmons, "Henson Is Viewed as 'the Enforcer,'" *Sun*, March 6, 1993.

9. John Rivera, "Mayor Schmoke Offers Apology to Project Residents," *Sun*, January 24, 1993; Melody Simmons and John Rivera, "Clarke Spends the Night at Lexington Terrace," *BES*, January 25, 1993.

10. Melody Simmons, "Lexington Terrace Spruced Up before Mayor's Visit," *BES*, January 28, 1993.

11. Simmons, "At Lexington Terrace, Cisneros Orders Immediate Help for Blighted High-Rises," *Sun*, February 4, 1993.

12. Anna Warren interviews; author's taped proceedings, February 18, 1997, Board of Commissioners meeting.

13. Author's taped proceedings, February 18, 1997, Board of Commissioners meeting.

14. Marable, 113–124.

15. "The American Ghetto: What's the Future?" *JOH* 25, no. 11 (1968): 563.

16. Smith, *We Have No Leaders*, 25.

17. Cathy Cohen, *Boundaries of Blackness*.

18. Wise interviews.

19. George Rodrigue and Craig Flournoy, *Dallas Morning News*, February 10–18, 1985; Hirsch, *Making the Second Ghetto*.

20. *Carmen Thompson et al. v. U.S. Department of HUD et al.*, class-action complaint MJ 95–309, filed January 31, 1995, in the U.S. District Court for the District of Maryland.

21. "ACLU Wins Appeal in Public Housing Desegregation Suit," July 14, 2000. Online. Available: http://www.aclu.org; e-mail exchange with Barbara Samuels, October 10, 2003.

22. E-mail exchange with Barbara Samuels, January 8, 2004, and March 8, 2004. If the judge issues a ruling finding liability, the ACLU will enter the "remedy phase" of its case.

23. Michael Anft, "Facing the End at Flag House Courts, the City's Last High-Rise Project," *Baltimore City Paper*, December 22–December 28, 1999.

24. Letter to Mayor William Donald Schaefer from Bob Cheeks, April 13, 1983, in *The Housing Authority of Baltimore City's Four Family High-Rise Developments*, December 1, 1989 (updated February 1990), Appendix C; HABC, "Answers to CPHA Questionnaire regarding Severely Distressed Properties," 1992, both in author's possession.

25. "HABC Overview," in Lafayette Courts Implosion Media Kit, August 19, 1995.

26. Schofield interview.

27. Acel Moore, "Knocking Down the Towers Is Just the Beginning," *PI*, May 2, 1995; "Towers of Despair: It Makes More Sense to Raze Rather than Repair High-rises That Have Torn Tenants' Hopes Down," *PI*, January 19, 1995; "Bridgeport Housing Project to Close, a Victim of Crime," *NYT*, July 9, 1994; "Symbols of Policy Ills, High-Rises Fall," *NYT*, April 3, 1995.

28. See statements of U.S. representatives Barbara Cubin (R-Wyo.) and John L. Mica (R-Fla.), *CR*, March 24, 1995, 3766, 3772.

29. Baker interviews.

30. Richard A. Cloward and Frances Fox Piven use this phrase in the foreword to West, *National Welfare Rights Movement*, vii; Piven and Cloward, *Poor People's Movements*.

31. Frances Fox Piven uses this phrase in the foreword to Bailis, *Bread or Justice*, xv.

32. Randall and Martin interviews.

33. Anna Warren interviews. Also see Childers, "A Spontaneous Welfare Rights Protest," 90–101.

34. Boris, "When Work Is Slavery," 37. Also see Piven and Cloward, *Poor People's Movements*, 273.

35. Quoted in Lassiter, "Welfare: Reform or Revolt. Part V: Income, Dignity, Democracy," *BNA*, May 1, 1969, Folder 16: Welfare—DSS, Box 22, Series 24, BCP, UBA.

36. On systems of racial, gender, and class oppression, see Orleck, "Introduction: Tradition Unbound," in *Politics of Motherhood*, 12.

37. Quadagno, *Color of Welfare*, 117.

38. Mink, *Welfare's End*, 2, 4.

Bibliography

Manuscript Collections

African-American Vertical Files, EPFL
Baltimore City Department of Planning Collection, UBA
Baltimore Urban Renewal and Housing Association Collection, UBA
Ernest J. Bohn Collection, KSL
Campaign for Human Development Records (unprocessed), ACUA
Citizens Planning and Housing Association Collection, UBA
Melvin Cole File, MDSA
Commission on Government Efficiency and Economy Collection, UBA
Committee on Fair Employment Practices Records, RG 228, NARA
Community Services Administration Records, RG 381, NA
Congress of Racial Equality Papers, WHS
Department of Housing and Community Development (1937–Present), RG 48, BCA
Governors' Records, MDSA
Nick Kotz Papers (unprocessed), WHS
Edward S. Lewis Papers, SCRBC
Maryland Vertical Files, EPFL
Mayors' Administrative Files, RG 9, BCA
National Association for the Advancement of Colored People Branch Files, LC

National Welfare Rights Organization Papers, MSRC
Office of Price Administration Records, RG 188, NA
State Board of Public Welfare, Minute Books, Department of Human Resources—
    Social Services, MDSA
State Publications, Human Relations Commission, MDSA
State Publications, Housing, MDSA
Students for a Democratic Society Papers, WHS
Carmen Thompson et al. (1995) Case Documents, ACLU
U.S. Department of Housing and Urban Development Records, RG 207, NA
U.S. Public Housing Administration Records, RG 196, NA
George Wiley Papers, WHS

Oral History Collections

Baltimore Neighborhood Heritage Project, UBA
McKeldin-Jackson Project, MHS

Interviews Conducted by Rhonda Y. Williams

All the interviewees live in Baltimore, and most interviews were conducted in person. Some interviews and follow-up conversations were conducted by telephone from the author's office or home in Cleveland.

"Samantha Allen"	2 March 1996, 6 March 1996
Goldie Baker	29 January 1997, 15 July 2000,
	24 September 2001, 13 October 2001
Marion C. Bascom	20 February 1997
Martha R. Benton	14 February 1996
Sue Birdsong	16 October 1995
Jean Booker	6 May 1997
Annie Rogers Chambers	10 January 1997, 14 February 1997
William H. Craig	26 October 1995
Clarence "Tiger" Davis	9 October 2002
Eugenia "Bonnie" Ellis Johnson Davis	27 February 1996, 24 September 1996
Steve and Mary Doss	21 November 1995
Jonathan Edges	10 April 1996
Robert C. Embry	24 April 1996, 1 May 1996
Clara P. Gordon	15 January 1996, 16 February 2002,
	10 February 2003
Coleman D. and Rose Grant	15 April 1996
Joyce Gray	30 January 1996
Esther M. Harvin	26 October 1995
Clyde Hatcher	26 May 1998
Mary F. Holmes	1 November 1996
William F. and Mary L. Hynes	15 September 1995

Betty Keaton   26 February 1997
Elmer Klavens   24 January 1996
Malachi Lewis   9 May 1996
Rosaline Lundsford   18 October 1996
Margaret "Peggy" McCarty   21 June 2003
Barbara "Bobbie" McKinney   9 October 1995
Salima Marriott   4 November 2002, 8 November 2002
Rudell Martin   25 February 1997, 30 September 2003
Julia Matthews   19 December 1996
Parren J. Mitchell   26 February 1997
Geraldine Randall   26 February 1997
Frances Reives   16 September 1995, 7 March 1996
Lillie Ida Robinson   9 October 1995
Margaret Ruffin   26 January 1996
Rosetta Schofield   5 November 1993
Jean Sherrod   10 April 1996
Evelena and Joann Simon   20 November 1995
Gladys Spell   22 October 1993, 4 November 1993
Maxine Stephenson   4 November 1993
Loretta Thompson   18 November 1995
Ann Thornton   28 May 1996
Horace and Loubertha Ward   25 September 1995
Anna Warren   26 November 1996, 17 February 1997,
    29 July 2000
Dwight S. Warren   10 April 1996
Warren W. Weaver   15 May 1996, 18 November 1996
Sedonia Williamson   6 February 1996
Shirley M. Wise   22 January 1996, 7 February 1996,
    23 April 1996, 1 November 1997,
    21 June 2002
Elizabeth Wright   30 April 1996

Newspapers and Periodicals

Baltimore Afro-American
Baltimore Evening Sun
Baltimore News American (formerly *Baltimore News-Post*)
Baltimore Sun
Christian Science Monitor
Congressional Record
Dallas Morning News
Journal of Housing
Los Angeles Times
New York Times

Bibliography

Philadelphia Inquirer

Washington Post

Books, Dissertations, and Articles

Abramovitz, Mimi. "Fighting Back: From the Legislature to the Academy to the Streets." In *A New Introduction to Poverty: The Role of Race, Power, and Politics,* ed. Louis Kushnick and James Jennings, 217–240. New York: New York University Press, 1999.

Anderson, Karen Tucker. "Last Hired, First Fired: Black Women Workers during World War II." *Journal of American History* 69 (June 1982): 82–97.

Argersinger, Jo Ann E. *Toward a New Deal in Baltimore.* Chapel Hill: University of North Carolina Press, 1988.

Arnold, Joseph L. "Baltimore: Southern Culture and a Northern Economy." In *Snowbelt Cities: Metropolitan Politics in the Northeast and Midwest since World War II,* ed. Richard M. Bernard, 25–39. Bloomington: Indiana University Press, 1990.

Auletta, Ken. *The Underclass.* New York: Random House, 1982.

Bailis, Lawrence Neil. *Bread or Justice: Grassroots Organizing in the Welfare Rights Movement.* Lexington, Mass: Lexington Books, 1974.

Bartelt, David W. "Housing the 'Underclass.'" In *The "Underclass" Debate: Views from History,* ed. Michael B. Katz, 118–157. Princeton, N.J.: Princeton University Press, 1993.

Bauman, John F. *Public Housing, Race, and Renewal: Urban Planning in Philadelphia, 1920–1974.* Philadelphia, Pa.: Temple University Press, 1987.

Bauman, John, Norman P. Hummon, and Edward K. Muller. "Public Housing, Isolation, and the Urban Underclass: Philadelphia's Richard Allen Homes, 1941–1965." *Journal of Urban History* 17 (May 1991): 264–292.

Bayor, Ronald H. *Race & the Shaping of Twentieth-Century Atlanta.* Chapel Hill: University of North Carolina Press, 1996.

Bell, Winifred. *Aid to Dependent Children.* New York: Columbia University Press, 1965.

Berry, Mary Frances. *The Politics of Parenthood: Child Care, Women's Rights and the Myth of the Good Mother.* New York: Viking Penguin, 1993.

Biles, Roger. *The South and the New Deal.* Lexington: University Press of Kentucky, 1994.

Biondi, Martha. *To Stand and Fight: The Struggle for Civil Rights in Postwar New York City.* Cambridge, Mass.: Harvard University Press, 2003.

Borchert, James. *Alley Life in Washington: Family, Community, Religion, and Folklife in the City, 1850–1970.* Urbana: University of Illinois Press, 1980.

Boris, Eileen. "'The Right to Work Is the Right to Live!' Fair Employment and the Quest for Social Citizenship." In *Two Cultures of Rights: The Quest for Inclusion and Participation in Modern America and Germany,* eds. Manfred Berg and Martin H. Geyer, 121–141. Cambridge: Cambridge University Press, 2002.

————. "When Work Is Slavery." In *Whose Welfare?* ed. Gwendolyn Mink, 36–55. Ithaca, N.Y.: Cornell University Press, 1999.

Bullard, Robert D., ed. *Unequal Protection: Environmental Justice and Communities of Color.* San Francisco, Calif.: Sierra Club Books, 1994.

Bullard, Robert D., ed. *Confronting Environmental Racism: Voices from the Grassroots.* Boston: South End Press, 1993.

Burghardt, Stephen, ed. *Tenants and the Urban Housing Crisis.* Dexter, Mich.: New Press, 1972.

Buss, Fran Leeper, ed. *Dignity: Lower Income Women Tell of Their Lives and Struggles.* Ann Arbor: University of Michigan Press, 1985.

Callcott, George H. *Maryland & America, 1940–1980.* Baltimore, Md.: Johns Hopkins University Press, 1985.

Camacho, David E., ed. *Environmental Injustices, Political Struggles: Race, Class, and the Environment.* Durham, N.C.: Duke University Press, 1998.

Capeci, Dominic J., Jr. *Race Relations in Wartime Detroit: The Sojourner Truth Housing Controversy of 1942.* Philadelphia, Pa.: Temple University Press, 1984.

Capek, Stella M., and John I. Gilderbloom. *Community versus Commodity: Tenants and the American City.* Albany: State University Press of New York, 1992.

Carby, Hazel V. "Policing the Black Woman's Body in an Urban Context." *Critical Inquiry* 18 (Summer 1992): 738–755.

Carson, Clayborne. *In Struggle: SNCC and the Black Awakening of the 1960s.* Cambridge, Mass.: Harvard University Press, 1981.

Chateauvert, Melinda. *Marching Together: Women of the Brotherhood of Sleeping Car Porters.* Urbana: University of Illinois Press, 1998.

Childers, Mary M. "A Spontaneous Welfare Rights Protest by Politically Inactive Mothers: A Daughter's Reflections." In *The Politics of Motherhood: Activist Voices from Left to Right,* ed. Alexis Jetter, Annelise Orleck, and Diana Taylor, 90–101. Hanover, N.H.: University Press of New England for Dartmouth College, 1997.

Clark, Kenneth B. *Dark Ghetto: Dilemmas of Social Power.* New York: Harper & Row, 1965.

Clark-Lewis, Elizabeth. *Living In, Living Out: African American Domestics in Washington, D.C., 1910–1940.* Washington, D.C.: Smithsonian Institution Press, 1994.

Cohen, Cathy J. *The Boundaries of Blackness: AIDS and the Breakdown of Black Politics.* Chicago, Ill.: University of Chicago Press, 1999.

Cohen, Lizabeth. *A Consumer's Republic: The Politics of Mass Consumption in Postwar America.* New York: Knopf, 2003.

Collier-Thomas, Bettye, and V. P. Franklin, eds. *Sisters in the Struggle: African American Women in the Civil Rights–Black Power Movement.* New York: New York University Press, 2001.

Collins, Patricia Hill. *Black Feminist Thought: Knowledge, Consciousness, and the Politics of Empowerment.* New York: Routledge, 1991.

Coontz, Stephanie. *The Way We Never Were: American Families and the Nostalgia Trap.* New York: Basic, 1992.

Crawford, Margaret. "Daily Life on the Home Front: Women, Blacks, and the Struggle for Public Housing." In *World War II and the American Dream,* ed. Donald Albrecht, 90–143. Cambridge, Mass.: MIT Press, 1995.

Crawford, Vicki L., Jacqueline Anne Rouse, and Barbara Woods, eds. *Women in the Civil Rights Movement: Trailblazers and Torchbearers, 1941–1965.* Bloomington: Indiana University Press, 1993.

Crook, William H., and Ross Thomas. *Warriors for the Poor: The Story of VISTA, Volunteers in Service to America.* New York: Morrow, 1969.

Davis, Martha F. "Welfare Rights and Women's Rights in the 1960s." In *Integrating the Sixties,* ed. Brian Balogh, 144–165. University Park: Pennsylvania State University Press, 1996.

Dittmer, John. *Local People: The Struggle for Civil Rights in Mississippi.* Urbana: University of Illinois Press, 1994.

Drake, St. Clair, and Horace R. Cayton. *Black Metropolis: A Study of Negro Life in a Northern City.* New York: Harcourt, Brace, 1945.

Du Bois, W. E. B. *The Philadelphia Negro: A Social Study.* 1899. Philadelphia: University of Pennsylvania Press, 1996.

Durr, Kenneth D. *Behind the Backlash: White Working-Class Politics in Baltimore, 1940–1980.* Chapel Hill: University of North Carolina Press, 2003.

———. "When Southern Politics Came North: The Roots of White Working-Class Conservatism in Baltimore, 1940–1964." *Labor History* 37 (Summer 1996): 309–333.

Durr, William Theodore. "The Conscience of a City: A History of the Citizens Planning and Housing Association and Efforts to Improve Housing for the Poor in Baltimore, Maryland, 1937–1954." Ph.D. diss., Johns Hopkins University, 1972.

Edin, Kathryn, and Laura Lein. *Making Ends Meet: How Single Mothers Survive Welfare and Low-wage Work.* New York: Russell Sage Foundation, 1997.

Etter-Lewis, Gwendolyn. *My Soul Is My Own: Oral Narratives of African American Women in the Professions.* New York: Routledge, 1993.

Etter-Lewis, Gwendolyn, and Michéle Foster, eds. *Unrelated Kin: Race and Gender in Women's Personal Narratives.* New York: Routledge, 1996.

Fairbanks, Robert B. *Making Better Citizens: Housing Reform and the Community Development Strategy in Cincinnati, 1890–1960.* Urbana: University of Illinois Press, 1988.

Fairclough, Adam. *Better Day Coming: Blacks and Equality, 1890–2000.* New York: Viking, 2001.

Farber, David. *The Age of Great Dreams: America in the 1960s.* New York: Hill and Wang, 1994.

Fee, Elizabeth, Linda Shopes, and Linda Zeidman, eds. *The Baltimore Book: New Views of Local History.* Philadelphia, Pa.: Temple University Press, 1991.

Feldman, Roberta M., Susan Stall, and Patricia A. Wright. "'The Community Needs to Be Built by Us': Women Organizing in Chicago Public Housing." In *Community Activism and Feminist Politics: Organizing across Race, Class, and Gender*, ed. Nancy A. Naples, 257–274. New York: Routledge, 1998.

Feldstein, Ruth. *Motherhood in Black and White: Race and Sex in American Liberalism, 1930–1965*. Ithaca, N.Y.: Cornell University Press, 2000.

Fisher, Robert Moore. *20 Years of Public Housing: Economic Aspects of the Federal Program*. New York: Harper, 1959.

Flug, Michael. "Organized Labor and the Civil Rights Movement in the 1960s: The Case of the Maryland Freedom Union." *Labor History* 31 (Summer 1990): 322–346.

Frazier, E. Franklin. *The Negro Family in the United States*. 1939. Chicago, Ill.: University of Chicago Press, 1966.

Freeman, Roland L. *The Arabbers of Baltimore*. Centreville, Md.: Tidewater, 1989.

Friedman, Lawrence M. *Government and Slum Housing: A Century of Frustration*. Chicago, Ill.: Rand McNally, 1968.

Frost, Jennifer. *"An Interracial Movement of the Poor": Community Organizing and the New Left in the 1960s*. New York: New York University Press, 2001.

Gaines, Kevin K. *Uplifting the Race: Black Leadership, Politics, and Culture in the Twentieth Century*. Chapel Hill: University of North Carolina Press, 1996.

Gardner, Bettye, and Cynthia Neverdon-Morton. "Blacks in Baltimore, 1950–1980: An Overview." In *Baltimore: A Living Renaissance*, ed. Lenora Heilig Nast, Laurence N. Krause, and R. C. Monk. Baltimore, Md.: Historic Baltimore Society, 1982.

Genevro, Rosalie. "Site Selection and the New York City Housing Authority, 1934–1939." *Journal of Urban History* 12 (August 1986): 334–352.

Giddings, Paula. *When and Where I Enter: The Impact of Black Women on Race and Sex in America*. New York: Morrow, 1984.

Gilbert, Neil. *Clients or Constituents*. San Francisco, Calif.: Jossey-Bass, 1970.

Gilmore, Glenda Elizabeth. *Gender & Jim Crow: Women and the Politics of White Supremacy in North Carolina, 1896–1920*. Chapel Hill: University of North Carolina Press, 1996.

Gluck, Sherna Berger, and Daphne Patai, eds. *Women's Words: The Feminist Practice of Oral History*. New York: Routledge, 1991.

Goings, Kenneth W., and Raymond A. Mohl. "Toward a New African-American Urban History." *Journal of Urban History* 21 (March 1995): 283–295.

Gordon, Linda. "Black and White Visions of Welfare: Women's Welfare Activism, 1890–1945." *Journal of American History* 78 (September 1991): 559–590.

———. *Pitied but Not Entitled: Single Mothers and the History of Welfare, 1890–1935*. Cambridge, Mass.: Harvard University Press, 1994.

Gordon, Linda, ed. *Women, the State, and Welfare*. Madison: University of Wisconsin Press, 1990.

Grant, Joanne. *Ella Baker: Freedom Bound*. New York: Wiley, 1998.

Green, Laurie Beth. "Battling the Plantation Mentality: Consciousness, Culture, and the Politics of Race, Class and Gender in Memphis, 1940–1968." Ph.D. diss., University of Chicago, 1999.

Greenberg, Cheryl Lynn. "*Or Does It Explode?*": *Black Harlem in the Great Depression*. New York: Oxford University Press, 1991.

Greene, Christina. "'Our Separate Ways': Women and the Black Freedom Movement in Durham, North Carolina, 1940s–1970s." Ph.D. diss., Duke University, 1996.

Greenstone, J. David, and Paul E. Peterson. *Race and Authority in Urban Politics: Community Participation and the War on Poverty*. New York: Russell Sage Foundation, 1973.

Gregory, Steven. *Black Corona: Race and the Politics of Place in an Urban Community*. Princeton, N.J.: Princeton University Press, 1998.

Halpern, Robert. *Rebuilding the Inner City: A History of Neighborhood Initiatives to Address Poverty in the United States*. New York: Columbia University Press, 1995.

Harley, Sharon. "'Chronicle of a Death Foretold': Gloria Richardson, the Cambridge Movement, and the Radical Black Activist Tradition." In *Sisters in the Struggle: African American Women in the Civil Rights–Black Power Movement*, ed. Bettye Collier-Thomas and V. P. Franklin, 174–196. New York: New York University Press, 2001.

———. "For the Good of the Family and the Race: Gender, Work, and Domestic Roles in the Black Community, 1880–1930." *Signs* 15 (Winter 1990): 336–349.

Harris, William H. *The Harder We Run: Black Workers since the Civil War*. New York: Oxford University Press, 1982.

Henderson, A. Scott. "'Tarred with the Exceptional Image': Public Housing and Popular Discourse, 1950–1990." *American Studies* 36 (Spring 1995): 31–52.

Henderson, Peter H. "Local Deals and the New Deal State: Implementing Federal Public Housing in Baltimore, 1933–68." Ph.D. diss., Johns Hopkins University, 1994.

———. "Suburban Visions and the Landscape of Power: Public Housing, Suburban Diversity, and Participation in Metropolitan Baltimore, 1930s–1950s." In *Contested Terrain: Power, Politics, and Participation in Suburbia*, ed. Marc L. Silver and Martin Melkonian, 195–210. Westport, Conn.: Greenwood, 1995.

Higginbotham, Evelyn Brooks. *Righteous Discontent: The Women's Movement in the Black Baptist Church, 1880–1920*. Cambridge, Mass.: Harvard University Press, 1993.

Hine, Darlene Clark, "The Housewives' League of Detroit: Black Women and Economic Nationalism." In *Visible Women: New Essays on American Activism*, ed. Nancy A. Hewitt and Suzanne Lebsock, 223–241. Urbana: University of Illinois Press, 1993.

Hirsch, Arnold R. "'Containment' on the Home Front: Race and Federal Housing Policy from the New Deal to the Cold War." *Journal of Urban History* 26 (January 2000): 158–189.

————. *Making the Second Ghetto: Race and Housing in Chicago, 1940–1960.* Cambridge: Cambridge University Press, 1983.

————. "Massive Resistance in the Urban North: Trumbull Park, Chicago, 1953–1966." *Journal of American History* 82 (September 1995): 522–550.

Hodgson, Godfrey. *America in Our Time: From World War II to Nixon, What Happened and Why.* New York: Vintage, 1976.

Hunter, Tera W. "The 'Brotherly Love' for Which This City Is Proverbial Should Extend to All: The Everyday Lives of Working-Class Women in Philadelphia and Atlanta in the 1890s." In *W. E. B. Du Bois, Race, and the City: The Philadelphia Negro and Its Legacy,* ed. Michael B. Katz and Thomas J. Sugrue, 127–151. Philadelphia: University of Pennsylvania Press, 1998.

————. "Domination and Resistance: The Politics of Wage Household Labor in New South Atlanta." *Labor History* 34 (Spring–Summer 1993): 205–220.

————. *To 'Joy My Freedom: Southern Black Women's Lives and Labors after the Civil War.* Cambridge, Mass.: Harvard University Press, 1997.

Jacobs, Meg. "'How about Some Meat?': The Office of Price Administration, Consumption Politics, and State Building from the Bottom Up, 1941–1946." *Journal of American History* 84 (December 1997): 911–941.

Jackson, Kenneth T. *Crabgrass Frontier.* New York: Oxford University Press, 1985.

Jackson, Thomas F. "The State, the Movement, and the Urban Poor: The War on Poverty and Political Mobilization in the 1960s." In *The "Underclass" Debate: Views from History,* ed. Michael B. Katz, 403–439. Princeton, N.J.: Princeton University Press, 1993.

James, Joy. *Transcending the Talented Tenth: Black Leaders and American Intellectuals.* New York: Routledge, 1997.

Jennings, James, ed. *The Politics of Black Empowerment: The Transformation of Black Activism in Urban America.* Detroit, Mich.: Wayne State University Press, 1992.

————. *Race and Politics: New Challenges and Responses for Black Activism.* New York: Verso, 1997.

————. *Race, Politics, and Economic Development: Community Perspectives.* New York: Verso, 1992.

Jetter, Alexis, Annelise Orleck, and Diana Taylor, eds. *The Politics of Motherhood: Activist Voices from Left to Right.* Hanover, N.H.: University Press of New England, 1997.

Jewell, K. Sue. *From Mammy to Miss America and Beyond: Cultural Images & the Shaping of U.S. Social Policy.* New York: Routledge, 1993.

Jones, Jacqueline. *The Dispossessed: America's Underclasses from the Civil War to the Present.* New York: Basic, 1992.

————. *Labor of Love, Labor of Sorrow: Black Women, Work, and Family from Slavery to the Present.* New York: Basic, 1985.

Jonnes, Jill. *Hep-Cats, Narcs, and Pipe Dreams: A History of America's Romance with Illegal Drugs.* New York: Scribner's, 1996.

Katz, Michael B. *Improving Poor People: The Welfare State, the "Underclass," and Urban Schools as History.* Princeton, N.J.: Princeton University Press, 1995.

———. *The Undeserving Poor: From the War on Poverty to the War on Welfare.* New York: Pantheon, 1989.

Katz, Michael B., ed. *The "Underclass" Debate: Views from History.* Princeton, N.J.: Princeton University Press, 1993.

Katznelson, Ira. *City Trenches: Urban Politics and the Patterning of Class in the United States.* Chicago, Ill.: University of Chicago Press, 1981.

Kelley, Robin D. G. "The Black Poor and the Politics of Opposition in a New South City, 1929–1970." In *The "Underclass" Debate*, ed. Michael B. Katz, 293–330. Princeton, N.J.: Princeton University Press, 1993.

———. *Race Rebels: Culture, Politics, and the Black Working Class.* New York: Free Press, 1994.

———. *Yo' Mama's Disfunktional! Fighting the Culture Wars in Urban America.* Boston: Beacon, 1997.

Kivisto, Peter. "A Historical Review of the Changes in Public Housing Policies and Their Impacts on Minorities." In *Race, Ethnicity and Minority Housing in the United States*, ed. Jamshid A. Momeni, 1–18. New York and Westport, Conn.: Greenwood, 1996.

Kluger, Richard. *Simple Justice: The History of Brown v. Board of Education and Black America's Struggle for Equality.* New York: Vintage, 1975.

Kornbluh, Felicia. "To Fulfill Their 'Rightly Needs': Consumerism and the National Welfare Rights Movement." *Radical History Review* 69 (Fall 1997): 76–113.

Kotz, Nick, and Mary Lynn Kotz. *A Passion for Equality: George A. Wiley and the Movement.* New York: Norton, 1977.

Krefetz, Sharon Perlman. "Urban Politics and Public Welfare: On the Treatment of Welfare Recipients in Baltimore and San Francisco." Ph.D. diss., Brandeis University, 1975.

Kunzel, Regina G. *Fallen Women, Problem Girls: Unmarried Mothers and the Professionalization of Social Work, 1890–1945.* New Haven, Conn.: Yale University Press, 1993.

Lawson, Ronald, with Mark Naison, eds. *The Tenant Movement in New York City, 1904–1984.* New Brunswick, N.J.: Rutgers University Press, 1986.

Lee, Chana Kai. *For Freedom's Sake: The Life of Fannie Lou Hamer.* Urbana: University of Illinois Press, 1999.

Lewis, Earl. *In Their Own Interests: Race, Class, and Power in Twentieth-Century Norfolk.* Berkeley: University of California Press, 1991.

Lieberman, Robert C. "Race and the Organization of Welfare Policy." *In Classifying by Race*, ed. Paul E. Peterson, 156–187. Princeton, N.J.: Princeton University Press, 1995.

Lipsitz, George. *A Life in the Struggle: Ivory Perry and the Culture of Opposition.* Philadelphia, Pa.: Temple University Press, 1988.

————. *Rainbow at Midnight: Labor and Culture in the 1940s*. Urbana: University of Illinois Press, 1994.

Lubiano, Wahneema. "Black Ladies, Welfare Queens, and State Minstrels: Ideological War by Narrative Means." In *Race-ing Justice, En-gendering Power*, ed. Toni Morrison, 323–363. New York: Pantheon, 1992.

Lusane, Clarence. *African Americans at the Crossroads: The Restructuring of Black Leadership and the 1992 Elections*. Boston: South End Press, 1994.

————. *Race in the Global Era: African Americans at the Millennium*. Boston: South End Press, 1997.

McDougall, Harold A. *Black Baltimore: A New Theory of Community*. Philadelphia, Pa.: Temple University Press, 1993.

Mahoney, Martha. "Law and Racial Geography: Public Housing and the Economy of New Orleans." *Stanford Law Review* 42 (May 1990): 1251–1290.

Marable, Manning. *Race, Reform, and Rebellion: The Second Reconstruction in Black America, 1945–1990*. 2nd edition. Jackson: University Press of Mississippi, 1991.

Marcuse, Peter. "The Beginnings of Public Housing in New York." *Journal of Urban History* 12 (August 1986): 353–390.

Martin, Waldo E., Jr. *Brown v. Board of Education: A Brief History with Documents*. Boston: Bedford, 1998.

Massey, Douglas S., and Nancy A. Denton. *American Apartheid: Segregation and the Making of the Underclass*. Cambridge, Mass.: Harvard University Press, 1993.

Medoff, Peter, and Holly Sklar. *Streets of Hope: The Fall and Rise of an Urban Neighborhood*. Boston: South End Press, 1994.

Meyer, Stephen Grant. *As Long as They Don't Move Next Door: Segregation and Racial Conflict in American Neighborhoods*. Lanham, Md.: Rowman & Littlefield, 2000.

Milkman, Ruth. *Gender at Work: The Dynamics of Job Segregation by Sex during World War II*. Urbana: University of Illinois Press, 1987.

Mink, Gwendolyn. "The Lady and the Tramp: Gender, Race, and the Origins of the American Welfare State." In *Women, the State, and Welfare*, ed. Linda Gordon, 92–122. Madison: University of Wisconsin Press, 1990.

————. *The Wages of Motherhood: Inequality in the Welfare State, 1917–1942*. Ithaca, N.Y.: Cornell University Press, 1995.

————. *Welfare's End*. Ithaca, N.Y.: Cornell University Press, 1998.

Mink, Gwendolyn, ed. *Whose Welfare?* Ithaca, N.Y.: Cornell University Press, 1999.

Mollenkopf, John H. *The Contested City*. Princeton, N.J.: Princeton University Press, 1983.

Momeni, Jamshid, ed. *Race, Ethnicity and Minority Housing in the United States*. New York and Westport, Conn.: Greenwood, 1996.

Moore, William, Jr. *The Vertical Ghetto: Everyday Life in an Urban Project*. New York: Random House, 1969.

Morris, Aldon D. *The Origins of the Civil Rights Movement: Black Communities Organizing for Change*. New York: Free Press, 1984.

Morton, Patricia. *Disfigured Images: The Historical Assault on Afro-American Women*. New York: Greenwood, 1991.

Muncy, Robyn. *Creating a Female Dominion in American Reform, 1890–1935*. New York: Oxford University Press, 1991.

Nadasen, Premilla. "Expanding the Boundaries of the Women's Movement: Black Feminism and the Struggle for Welfare Rights." *Feminist Studies* 28 (Summer 2002): 271–301.

Naples, Nancy A. *Grassroots Warriors: Activist Mothering, Community Work, and the War on Poverty*. New York: Routledge, 1998.

Naples, Nancy A., ed. *Community Activism and Feminist Politics: Organizing across Race, Class, and Gender*. New York: Routledge, 1998.

Neverdon-Morton, Cynthia. "Black Housing Patterns in Baltimore City, 1885–1953." *Maryland Historian* 16 (Spring–Summer 1985): 25–39.

Olson, Karen. "Old West Baltimore: Segregation, African-American Culture, and the Struggle for Equality." In *The Baltimore Book: New Views of Local History*, ed. Elizabeth Fee, Linda Shopes, and Linda Zeidman, 57–78. Philadelphia, Pa.: Temple University Press, 1991.

Olson, Lynne. *Freedom's Daughters: The Unsung Heroines of the Civil Rights Movement from 1830 to 1970*. New York: Simon and Schuster, 2001.

Olson, Sherry H. *Baltimore: The Building of an American City*. 1980. Baltimore, Md.: Johns Hopkins University Press, 1997.

Orleck, Annelise. *Common Sense & a Little Fire: Women and Working-class Politics in the United States, 1900–1965*. Chapel Hill: University of North Carolina Press, 1995.

———. "'If It Wasn't for You, I'd Have Shoes for My Children': The Political Education of Las Vegas Welfare Mothers." In *The Politics of Motherhood: Activist Voices from Left to Right*, ed. Alexis Jetter, Annelise Orleck, and Diana Taylor, 102–118. Hanover, N.H.: University Press of New England, 1997.

———. "Introduction: Tradition Unbound." In *The Politics of Motherhood*, 3–20.

———. "'We Are That Mythical Thing Called the Public': Militant Housewives during the Great Depression." In *Unequal Sisters: A Multicultural Reader in U.S. Women's History*, 3^d ed., ed. Vicki L. Ruiz and Ellen Carol DuBois, 376–392. New York: Routledge, 2000.

Orser, W. Edward. *Blockbusting in Baltimore: The Edmondson Village Story*. Lexington: University Press of Kentucky, 1994.

———. "Flight to the Suburbs: Suburbanization and Racial Change on Baltimore's West Side." In *The Baltimore Book: New Views of Local History*, ed. Elizabeth Fee, Linda Shopes, and Linda Zeidman, 203–225. Philadelphia, Pa.: Temple University Press, 1991.

———. "Secondhand Suburbs: Black Pioneers in Baltimore's Edmondson Village, 1955–1980." *Journal of Urban History* 16 (May 1990): 227–262.

Payne, Charles M. *I've Got the Light of Freedom: The Organizing Tradition and the Mississippi Freedom Struggle.* Berkeley: University of California Press, 1995.

Pedersen, Vernon L. *The Communist Party in Maryland, 1919–1957.* Urbana: University of Illinois Press, 2001.

Phillips, Kimberley L. *AlabamaNorth: African-American Migrants, Community, and Working-Class Activism in Cleveland, 1915–45.* Urbana: University of Illinois Press, 1999.

Piven, Frances Fox, and Richard A. Cloward. *Poor People's Movements: Why They Succeed, How They Fail.* New York: Vintage, 1977.

Platt, Anthony M., ed. *The Politics of Riot Commissions, 1917-1970: A Collection of Official Reports and Critical Essays.* New York: Macmillan, 1971.

Pope, Jacqueline. *Biting the Hand That Feeds Them: Organizing Women on Welfare at the Grassroots Level.* New York: Praeger, 1989.

Portelli, Alessandro. *The Death of Luigi Trastulli and Other Stories: Form and Meaning in Oral History.* Albany: State University of New York Press, 1991.

Power, Garrett. "Apartheid Baltimore Style: The Residential Segregation Ordinances of 1910–1913." *Maryland Law Review* 42 (1983): 289–328.

Pritchett, Wendell E. *Brownsville, Brooklyn: Blacks, Jews, and the Changing Face of the Ghetto.* Chicago, Ill.: University of Chicago Press, 2002.

———. "Race and Community in Postwar Brooklyn: The Brownsville Neighborhood Council and the Politics of Urban Renewal." *Journal of Urban History* 27 (May 2001): 445–470.

Quadagno, Jill S. *The Color of Welfare: How Racism Undermined the War on Poverty.* New York: Oxford University Press, 1994.

Radford, Gail. *Modern Housing for America: Policy Struggles in the New Deal Era.* Chicago, Ill.: University of Chicago Press, 1996.

Rainwater, Lee. *Behind Ghetto Walls: Black Families in a Federal Slum.* Chicago, Ill.: Aldine, 1970.

Rainwater, Lee, and William L. Yancey, eds. *The Moynihan Report and the Politics of Controversy.* Cambridge, Mass.: MIT Press, 1967.

Ransby, Barbara. *Ella Baker & the Black Freedom Movement: A Radical Democratic Vision.* Chapel Hill: University of North Carolina Press, 2003.

Reid, Ira De A. *The Negro Community of Baltimore: A Summary Report of a Social Study Conducted for the Baltimore Urban League.* Baltimore, Md.: Urban League, 1935.

Robinson, Jo Ann Gibson. *The Montgomery Bus Boycott and the Women Who Started It: The Memoir of Jo Ann Gibson Robinson,* ed. David J. Garrow. Knoxville: University of Tennessee Press, 1987.

Robnett, Belinda. *How Long? How Long? African-American Women in the Struggle for Civil Rights.* New York: Oxford University Press, 1997.

Ryon, Roderick. "An Ambiguous Legacy, Baltimore Blacks and the CIO, 1936–1941." *Journal of Negro History* 65 (Winter 1980): 18–33.

Schwartz, Joel. "Tenant Power in the Liberal City, 1943–1971." In *The Tenant Move-*

ment in New York City, 1904–1984, ed. Ronald Lawson with Mark Naison, 134–208. New Brunswick, N.J.: Rutgers University Press, 1986.

———. "Tenant Unions in New York City's Low-Rent Housing, 1933–1949." *Journal of Urban History* 12 (August 1986): 414–443.

Self, Robert. "'To Plan Our Liberation': Black Power and the Politics of Place in Oakland, California, 1965–1977." *Journal of Urban History* 26 (September 2000): 759–792.

Shopes, Linda. "Fells Point: Community and Conflict in a Working-Class Neighborhood." In *The Baltimore Book: New Views of Local History*, ed. Elizabeth Fee, Linda Shopes, and Linda Zeidman, 121–153. Philadelphia, Pa.: Temple University Press, 1991.

Silver, Christopher. *Twentieth-Century Richmond: Planning, Politics, and Race.* Knoxville: University of Tennessee Press, 1984.

Silver, Marc L., and Martin Melkonian. *Contested Terrain: Power, Politics, and Participation in Suburbia.* Westport, Conn.: Greenwood, 1995.

Sitkoff, Harvard. *A New Deal for Blacks: The Emergence of Civil Rights as a National Issue: The Depression Decade.* New York: Oxford University Press, 1978.

Skocpol, Theda. "African Americans in U.S. Social Policy." In *Classifying by Race*, ed. Paul E. Peterson, 129–155. Princeton, N.J.: Princeton University Press, 1995.

Skotnes, Andor D. "The Black Freedom Movement and the Workers' Movement in Baltimore, 1930–1939." Ph.D. diss., Rutgers University, 1991.

———. "'Buy Where You Can Work': Boycotting for Jobs in African-American Baltimore, 1933–1934." *Journal of Social History* 27 (Summer 1994): 735–761.

Smith, Robert C. *We Have No Leaders: African Americans in the Post–Civil Rights Era.* Albany: State University of New York Press, 1996.

Sobel, Lester A., ed. *Welfare & the Poor.* New York: Facts on File, 1977.

Solinger, Rickie. *Wake Up Little Susie: Single Pregnancy and Race before Roe v. Wade.* 1992. 2nd Edition. New York: Routledge, 2000.

Spillers, Hortense. "Mama's Baby, Papa's Maybe: An American Grammar Book." *diacritics* 17 (Summer 1987): 65–81.

Sugrue, Thomas J. "Crabgrass-Roots Politics: Race, Rights, and the Reaction against Liberalism in the Urban North, 1940–1964." *Journal of American History* 82 (September 1995): 551–578.

———. *The Origins of the Urban Crisis: Race and Inequality in Postwar Detroit.* Princeton, N.J.: Princeton University Press, 1996.

Sullivan, Patricia. *Days of Hope: Race and Democracy in the New Deal Era.* Chapel Hill: University of North Carolina Press, 1996.

Takaki, Ronald. *Double Victory: A Multicultural History of America in World War II.* Boston: Little, Brown, 2000.

Trotter, William Joe, Jr. *The Great Migration in Historical Perspective: New Dimensions of Race, Class, & Gender.* Bloomington: Indiana University Press, 1991.

Vale, Lawrence J. *From the Puritans to the Projects: Public Housing and Public Neighbors.* Cambridge, Mass.: Harvard University Press, 2000.

Venkatesh, Sudhir Alladi. *American Project: The Rise and Fall of a Modern Ghetto.* Cambridge, Mass.: Harvard University Press, 2000.

Walkowitz, Daniel J. *Working with Class: Social Workers and the Politics of Middle-Class Identity.* Chapel Hill: University of North Carolina Press, 1999.

Washington, James M. *A Testament of Hope: The Essential Writings and Speeches of Martin Luther King, Jr.* San Francisco, Calif.: HarperCollins, 1986.

Weiss, Nancy J. *Farewell to the Party of Lincoln: Black Politics in the Age of FDR.* Princeton, N.J.: Princeton University Press, 1983.

Welfield, Irving H. *Where We Live: A Social History of American Housing.* New York: Simon and Schuster, 1988.

West, Guida. *The National Welfare Rights Movement: The Social Protest of Poor Women.* New York: Praeger, 1981.

West, Guida, and Rhoda Lois Blumberg, eds. *Women and Social Protest.* New York: Oxford University Press, 1990.

West, Herbert Lee, Jr. "Urban Life and Spatial Distribution of Blacks in Baltimore, Maryland." Ph.D. diss., University of Minnesota, 1973.

White, Deborah Gray. "The Cost of Club Work, the Price of Black Feminism." In *Visible Women: New Essays on American Activism,* ed. Nancy A. Hewitt and Suzanne Lebsock, 247–269. Urbana: University of Illinois Press, 1993.

———. *Too Heavy a Load: Black Women in Defense of Themselves, 1894–1994.* New York: Norton, 1999.

Wilson, William Julius. *The Truly Disadvantaged: The Inner City, the Underclass, and Public Policy.* Chicago, Ill.: University of Chicago Press, 1987.

Wolcott, Victoria W. *Remaking Respectability: African American Women in Interwar Detroit.* Chapel Hill: University of North Carolina, 2001.

Woodard, Komozi. *A Nation within a Nation: Amiri Baraka (LeRoi Jones) and Black Power Politics.* Chapel Hill: University of North Carolina Press, 1999.

Wright, Gwendolyn. *Building the Dream: A Social History of Housing in America.* New York: Pantheon, 1981.

Index

DPW (Department of Public Welfare), 27, 95, 104, 204–5, 207–9, 220, 224, 274n54. *See also* DSS
drug policy, 232
drug traffic, 131, 134, 140, 148, 229–30
DSS (Department of Social Services), 213, 218, 222–23. *See also* DPW
Du Bois, W. E. B., 39

East Baltimore Citizens Center and Legal Services, 186
economic rights, 192–228
    activist mothers' demands for, 205–10
    broadening activist assault on poverty, 210–12
    BWRO and rent strikes, 222–28
    citizenship and, 203–5
    cooperative economics and, 195–96
    empowering consumers and, 198–200
    public housing as organizational base for, 212–22
    urban rebellion and, 196–98
    welfare rights activism and, 200–212
Edges, Mary, 90, 132
Edgewood Arsenal, 40, 56, 74
educational activities, 46–47, 52
Edward Meade v. Mary Estelle Dennistone et al., 249n35
elderly companion program, 143, 208
elderly people, 106, 139, 147–48, 166
Ellis, Bonnie, 164–65, 168–70, 173, 177, 182, 195, 198, 215. *See also* Davis, Eugenia
Embry, Robert C., Jr., 149–50, 172–73, 177, 179, 181, 223, 226
environmental issues, 146–47
environmental racism, 147, 265n54
eviction, 74–76, 80, 102, 133, 232
    retaliatory, 170, 182
Ewing, Edgar, 109, 139, 144
extremism, 121–23

Fairfield Homes, 57, 111, 176–78, 184, 225, 238
FAP (Family Assistance Plan), 220
Farmer, James, 121
Fathers Association of Baltimore, 52
federal housing agencies. *See* FHA; HHFA; HUD; NHA; USHA
Felder, Lois, 76, 82
female-headed households. *See* single-mother families
feminization of poverty, 94–96

Fenn, Don Frank, 75, 79, 83–84, 91, 98
Ferguson, Dale, Mrs., 64
Fernandis, Sarah, 30, 32–33
FHA (Federal Housing Administration), 6, 37, 75, 93
financial eligibility, 37–38
Finks, Albert and Estelle, 42, 44
Fischer, Ethel, 64
Flag House Courts, 101, 108, 113, 116, 126, 159, 173, 199, 235, 237–38
food-buying clubs, 195–96, 198–99, 217
Forman, James, 180
Foy, Mary Savilla Blackwell, 39–40, 94–95
freedom-of-choice policies, 108, 111, 260n55
FWA (Family Welfare Association), 27

Gates, Robert and Estella, 76
GI Bill of Rights, 96, 110, 258n19
Gilmor Homes
    as defense housing, 54, 57–58, 67–69, 255n46
    disrepute of public housing and, 137, 140–41, 147, 149, 151
    in postwar era, 92, 230
    rent strike at, 225
    struggle for public housing and, 40, 42
    tenant activism at, 178
    tenant advocacy at, 73, 76–77, 80
    tenant organizations and, 50
girls' clubs, 49, 52, 232
Gordon, Clara, 21–22, 27–28, 28
    on disrepute of public housing, 140
    as tenant of Poe Homes, 9, 36–37, 41–42, 44–45, 89
    tenant organizations and, 47–48, 50–52
Gordon, Linda, 7
Gore, Al, 238
Gorsuch, Walden K., 145, 188
Gosnell, Faith, 130
Gould, Mae, 80
Graham, Edith A., 62
Graham, Hattie, 180
Grant, Coleman D., 130–31, 139–40, 176–77, 180, 197
Grant, Rose, 130, 139
Gray, Jesse, 175, 194
Gray, Joyce, 176, 180
Great Depression, 26–29
Great Society, 4, 162, 165, 240, 242
grievance procedures, 53–54, 170, 180, 182–83
Gutman, Marion, 82